# The Didache

# The Didache
## A Commentary

Shawn J. Wilhite

Foreword by
Clayton N. Jefford

James Clarke & Co

JAMES CLARKE & CO
P.O. Box 60
Cambridge
CB1 2NT
United Kingdom

www.jamesclarke.co
publishing@jamesclarke.co

Paperback ISBN: 978 0 227 17723 5
PDF ISBN: 978 0 227 90724 5

*British Library Cataloguing in Publication Data*
A record is available from the British Library

First published by James Clarke & Co, 2020

Copyright © Shawn J. Wilhite and Michael A. G. Haykin, 2019

Published by arrangement
with Cascade Books

All rights reserved. No part of this edition may be reproduced, stored electronically or in any retrieval system, or transmitted in any form or by any means, electronic, mechanical, photocopying, recording, or otherwise, without prior written permission from the Publisher (permissions@jamesclarke.co).

To

Michael A. G. Haykin
*both mentor and friend*

# Contents

*Series Preface* | ix
*Foreword by Clayton N. Jefford* | xvii
*Preface* | xxi
*List of Abbreviations* | xxv
*List of Tables* | xxxi
*Translation of the Didache* | xxxiii

## Part I: Introductory Articles

1. An Introduction to the Didache | 3
   MS Tradition of the Didache | 6
   Use of Didache in Antiquity: Canon Lists and Possible Quotations | 10
   Date and Provenance of the Didache | 18
   Structural Overview of the Didache | 22

2. The Reception of Sacred Scripture in the Didache | 30
   Reception History, Intertextuality, and Literary Identity | 33
   Reception History of Biblical Tradition in the Didache | 36
   Concluding Remarks: The Reception of Sacred Scripture in the Didache | 57

3. The Theology of the Didache | 60
   Theology and Trinitarianism | 61
   Communal Liturgies: Baptismal, Fasting, Prayer, and Eucharist Liturgies | 66
   Communal Preservation and Soteriology | 70
   Corporate Gathering and Ecclesial Structures | 78
   The "Last Days" and the Didache's Eschatological Orientation | 86

## Part II: Commentary on the Didache

| | | |
|---|---|---|
| Didache 1.1—6.2: | Ethical Instruction of the Two-Ways Ethic | 99 |
| Didache 6.3—10.7: | Liturgical Rituals | 163 |
| | Additional Commentary: [Coptic Addition] Concerning the Ointment (Didache 10.8) | 192 |
| Didache 11.1—15.4: | Ecclesial and Communal Order | 196 |
| Didache 16.1–8: | Eschatological Ethics and Teaching | 217 |
| | Additional Commentary: Lost Ending (Didache 16.9-12) | 232 |

*Bibliography* | 237

*Commentary Index* | 259

# Series Preface

"Introduction to the Apostolic Fathers Commentary Series"

## Who Are the Apostolic Fathers?

THE LABEL "APOSTOLIC FATHERS" reflects a narrow collection of early Christian texts that generally date from the first and second centuries CE.[1] The works of the Apostolic Fathers offer a remarkable window into early (especially second-century) Christianity, as communities forged their religious and social identities within the broader Graeco-Roman culture.[2] As these early authors defined themselves and their readers in relationship to pagan culture, Jewish religiosity, and internal rivals, they ultimately influenced Christian movements for generations to come. Each book within the collection sheds unique light on the diversity of theology, worship, and life within nascent Christian communities.

The collection of "Apostolic Fathers" is an "artificial corpus" and a "modern construct."[3] Authors in antiquity did not use the label to describe such a collection.[4] Some of the Apostolic Fathers appear in the fourth-

---

1. Clayton N. Jefford, *Reading the Apostolic Fathers: A Student's Introduction*, 2nd ed. (Grand Rapids: Baker Academic, 2012), xvii. Some scholars have dated the Letter to Diognetus or the Martyrdom of Polycarp into the third century. See Candida R. Moss, "On the Dating of Polycarp: Rethinking the Place of the *Martyrdom of Polycarp* in the History of Christianity," *EC* 1 (2010) 539–74.

2. Clayton N. Jefford, *The Apostolic Fathers: An Essential Guide* (Nashville: Abingdon, 2005).

3. Paul Foster, "Preface," in Paul Foster (ed.), *The Writings of the Apostolic Fathers*, T. & T. Clark Biblical Studies (London: T. & T. Clark, 2007), vii.

4. According to Robert Grant, the term "Apostolic Fathers" was employed by the Monophysite Severus of Antioch in the sixth century, but not of a collection of writings as now recognized. See Robert M. Grant, "The Apostolic Fathers' First Thousand Years,"

century Codex Sinaiticus (Barnabas and Hermas) and the fifth-century Codex Alexandrinus (1 Clement and 2 Clement).[5] Some were read in public worship, were cited as "scripture," or were mentioned in the context of early canonical discussions.[6] Codex Hierosolymitanus (1056 CE), which was discovered in 1873, contains the Didache, Barnabas, 1 Clement, 2 Clement, and a long recension of the Ignatian epistles.

Jean-Baptiste Cotelier produced the first printed edition of a collection akin to the Apostolic Fathers in 1672.[7] Cotelier's Latin collection was titled *SS. patrum qui temporibus apostolicis floruerunt; Barnabae, Clementis, Hermae, Ignatii, Polycarpi.*[8] Inclusion within the collection was thus associated with an assumed historical connection to the times of the apostles (*temporibus apostolicis*). Within the text of his work, Cotelier spoke of an *Apostolicorum Patrum Collectio.*[9] In 1693, William Wake put forth an English edition of the Apostolic Fathers: *The Genuine Epistles of the Apostolical Fathers: S. Barnabas, S. Ignatius, S. Clement, S. Polycarp, the Shepherd of Hermas, and the Martyrdoms of St. Ignatius and St. Polycarp.*[10] In 1699, Thomas Ittig abbreviated Cotelier's Latin title to *Bibliotheca patrum apostolicorum Graeco-Latina.*[11] Early commentators continued to insist that at least some of the Apostolic Fathers had contact with the original apostles.[12]

Andreas Gallandi added the Letter to Diognetus, extant material from the Apology of Quadratus, and the Papias fragments to the corpus of

---

*CH* 31, no. 4 (1962) 21, 28.

5. Dan Batovici, "The Apostolic Fathers in Codex Sinaiticus and Codex Alexandrinus," *Bib* 97 (2016) 581–605.

6. See D. Jeffrey Bingham, "Senses of Scripture in the Second Century: Irenaeus, Scripture, and Noncanonical Christian Texts," *JR* 97 (2017) 26–55; M. C. Steenberg, "Irenaeus on Scripture, *Graphe*, and the Status of *Hermas*," *SVTQ* 53 (2009) 29–66.

7. David Lincicum, "The Paratextual Invention of the Term 'Apostolic Fathers,'" *JTS* 66 (2015) 139–48.

8. J. B. Cotelier, *SS. Patrum qui temporibus apostolicis floruerunt; Barnabae, Clementis, Hermae, Ignatii, Polycarpi: opera edita et inedita, vera et supposititia* . . . (Paris: Petri Le Petit, 1672).

9. For this and related history, see J. A. Fischer, *Die ältesten Ausgaben der Patres Apostolici: ein Beitrag zu Begriff und Begrenzung der Apostolischen Väter* (Munich: Alber, 1974).

10. William Wake, *The Genuine Epistles of the Apostolical Fathers: S. Barnabas, S. Ignatius, S. Clement, S. Polycarp, the Shepherd of Hermas, and the Martyrdoms of Ignatius and St. Polycarp* (London: Ric. Sare, 1693).

11. Clare K. Rothschild, *New Essays on the Apostolic Fathers*, WUNT 375 (Tübingen: Mohr Siebeck, 2017), 9. See Thomas Ittig, *Bibliotheca Patrum Apostolicorum Graeco-Latina* (Leipzig: J. H. Richter, 1699).

12. Jefford, *Reading the Apostolic Fathers*, xvii.

the Apostolic Fathers in 1765.[13] The Didache, since its rediscovery in the nineteenth century, has regularly accompanied the collection as well.[14] The scholarly work of J. B. Lightfoot, Theodore Zahn, and others elevated the "middle recension" of Ignatius's epistles as the preferred form of the Ignatian correspondence.[15]

In the Anglophone world, the "most readily available" and "widely used" editions of the Apostolic Fathers are Bart Ehrman's entry in the Loeb Classical Library (2003) and Michael Holmes's thorough revision of Lightfoot and Harmer's work, now in its third edition (2007).[16] Both Ehrman and Holmes include the Didache, 1 Clement, the fragment of Quadratus, the seven letters of the middle recension of the Ignatian correspondence, Polycarp's *Epistle to the Philippians*, the fragments of Papias, the Epistle of Barnabas, 2 Clement, the Shepherd of Hermas, the Martyrdom of Polycarp, and the Epistle to Diognetus. This list of eleven has attained somewhat of a quasi-canonical status within Apostolic Fathers studies, though a few works float in and out of the boundaries of investigations within the field.[17] Although early modern scholars tended to insist upon the direct contact of the Apostolic Fathers with the apostles, contemporary scholars recognize the phenomenon of pseudepigraphal attribution within the corpus, and they acknowledge a diverse notion of "apostolicity" within the primary source texts themselves.[18]

---

13. Andreas Gallandi, *Bibliotheca veterum partum antiquorumque scriptorium ecclesiasticorum* (Venice: Joannis Baptistae Albritii Hieron Fil., 1765).

14. Jefford, *Reading the Apostolic Fathers*, xix.

15. J. B. Lightfoot, *The Apostolic Fathers* (London: Macmillan, 1890); Theodore Zahn, *Ignatius von Antiochien* (Gotha: Friedrich Andreas Perthes, 1873). For a history of this debate, see Paul A. Hartog, "A Multifaceted Jewel: English Episcopacy, Ignatian Authenticity, and the Rise of Critical Patristic Scholarship," in Angela Ranson, André A. Gazal, and Sarah Bastow, *Defending the Faith: John Jewel and the Elizabethan Church*, Early Modern Studies Series (University Park, PA: Pennsylvania State University Press, 2018), 263–83.

16. Jefford, *Reading the Apostolic Fathers*, xiii. See Bart D. Ehrman, *The Apostolic Fathers*, 2 vols., LCL (Cambridge: Harvard University Press, 2003); Michael W. Holmes, *The Apostolic Fathers: Greek Texts and English Translations*, 3rd ed. (Grand Rapids: Baker Academic, 2007).

17. See Wilhelm Pratscher, "The Corpus of the Apostolic Fathers," in Wilhelm Pratscher (ed.), *The Apostolic Fathers: An Introduction* (Waco, TX: Baylor University Press, 2010), 1–6.

18. Taras Khomych, "Diversity of the Notion of Apostolicity in the Apostolic Fathers," in Theresia Hainthaler, Franz Mali, and Gregor Emmenegger (eds.), *Heiligkeit und Apostolizität der Kirche* (Innsbruck: Tyrolia, 2010), 63–81.

## Why Are the Apostolic Fathers Important?

The works of the "Apostolic Fathers" represent a spectrum of literary genres, including a church manual (Didache), occasional letters (1 Clement, the Ignatian correspondence, Polycarp's *Epistle to the Philippians*), a theological tractate in epistolary form (Barnabas), apocalyptic and visionary materials (Hermas), a martyr narrative in epistolary form (Martyrdom of Polycarp), a homily (2 Clement), an apology with appended homiletic material (Diognetus), and fragments of both expositional and apologetic works (Papias and Quadratus).[19] The Apostolic Fathers also represent a wide range of geographical provenance and intended audience, pointing interpreters to early Christian communities in locations scattered throughout the Roman Empire, such as Corinth, Philippi, Rome, Asia Minor, Egypt, and Syria.[20]

The Apostolic Fathers reflect variegated facets of early church life and organization, theological and liturgical development, spirituality and prayer, moral instruction and identity formation.[21] The Apostolic Fathers are important witnesses to the transmission and consolidation of earlier traditions, including the reception of the scriptures (both the Hebrew Scriptures and works now found in the New Testament).[22] A number of the Apostolic Fathers draw from Jesus traditions and especially the Pauline letters.[23] For example, Papias hands on traditions concerning the origins

---

19. Simon Tugwell, *The Apostolic Fathers*, Outstanding Christian Thinkers (London: Continuum 2002); Jefford, *Reading the Apostolic Fathers*.

20. See Christine Trevett, *Christian Women and the Time of the Apostolic Fathers (AD c 80-160): Corinth, Rome and Asia Minor* (Cardiff: University of Wales Press, 2006).

21. Helmut Koester, "The Apostolic Fathers and the Struggle for Christian Identity," in Foster (ed.), *Writings of the Apostolic Fathers*, 1–12; Kenneth Berding, "'Gifts' and Ministries in the Apostolic Fathers," *WTJ* 78 (2016) 135–58; Clayton N. Jefford, "Prophecy and Prophetism in the Apostolic Fathers," in Joseph Verheyden, Korinna Zamfir, and Tobias Nicklas (eds.), *Prophets and Prophecy in Jewish and Early Christian Literature*, WUNT 2/286 (Tübingen: Mohr Siebeck, 2010), 295–316; C. F. A. Borchardt, "The Spirituality of the Apostolic Fathers," *Studia historiae ecclesiasticae* 25 (1999) 132–52.

22. Wilhelm Pratscher, "Die Rezeption des Neuen Testament bei den Apostolischen Vätern," *TLZ* 137 (2012) 139–52; Clayton N. Jefford, *The Apostolic Fathers and the New Testament* (Peabody, MA: Hendrickson, 2006); Andrew F. Gregory and Christopher M. Tuckett, *The Reception of the New Testament in the Apostolic Fathers* (Oxford: Oxford University Press, 2005); Richard A. Norris, "The Apostolic and Sub-Apostolic Writings: The New Testament and the Apostolic Fathers," in Frances M. Young, Lewis Ayres, and Andrew Louth (eds.), *The Cambridge History of Early Christian Literature* (Cambridge: Cambridge University Press, 2004), 11–14; Oxford Society of Historical Theology, *The New Testament in the Apostolic Fathers* (Oxford: Clarendon, 1905).

23. Stephen E. Young, *Jesus Tradition in the Apostolic Fathers: Their Explicit Appeals to the Words of Jesus in Light of Orality Studies*, WUNT 311 (Tübingen: Mohr Siebeck,

of the Gospels, and Polycarp seemingly provides evidence of the reception of 1 Timothy, 1 Peter, and 1 John.[24] The Apostolic Fathers provide insights into biblical interpretation, as well as valuable assistance with linguistic and philological investigations.[25]

The Apostolic Fathers do not delve deeply into philosophical theology but rather address specific pastoral concerns in particular contexts.[26] They reflect a diversity of theological perspectives and emphases, although sharing a common yet malleable core kerygma. The works assume the role of the one God as Creator and Ruler, and they proclaim Jesus Christ as the crucified, risen, and exalted Lord.[27] Relatively fewer texts discuss the Holy Spirit's continuing work in the *ekklesia*, while some warn of the continuing threats of satanic opposition.[28] The Apostolic Fathers underscore future resurrection and judgment. They center salvation in the person and work of Christ, although differing in their explanations of grace and human response.[29]

---

2011); Andreas Lindemann, "The Apostolic Fathers and the Synoptic Problem," in Paul Foster, Andrew F. Gregory, John S. Kloppenborg, and Joseph Verheyden (eds.), *New Studies in the Synoptic Problem* (Leuven: Peeters, 2011), 689–719; Todd D. Still and David E. Wilhite (eds.), *The Apostolic Fathers and Paul*, Pauline and Patristic Scholars in Debate 2 (London: T. & T. Clark, 2017).

24. Jonathon Lookadoo, "Polycarp, Paul, and the Letters to Timothy," *NovT* 59 (2017) 366–83; Paul A. Hartog, "The Opponents in Polycarp, *Philippians*, and 1 John," in Andrew F. Gregory and Christopher M. Tuckett (eds.), *Trajectories through the New Testament and the Apostolic Fathers* (Oxford: Oxford University Press, 2005), 375–91.

25. Joseph W. Trigg, "The Apostolic Fathers and Apologists," in J. Alan Hauser and Duane Frederick Watson (eds.), *A History of Biblical Interpretation*, vol. 1 (Grand Rapids: Eerdmans, 2003), 304–33. A valuable linguistic tool is Daniel B. Wallace, *A Reader's Lexicon of the Apostolic Fathers* (Grand Rapids: Kregel Academic, 2013).

26. J. Lawson, *A Theological and Historical Introduction to the Apostolic Fathers* (New York: Macmillan, 1961).

27. A. R. Stark, *The Christology in the Apostolic Fathers* (Chicago: University of Chicago Press, 1912); John A. McGuckin, "Christ: The Apostolic Fathers to the Third Century," in D. Jeffrey Bingham (ed.), *The Routledge Companion to Early Christian Thought* (New York: Routledge, 2010), 256–70.

28. I. Howard Marshall, "The Holy Spirit in the Apostolic Fathers," in Graham N. Stanton, Bruce W. Longenecker, and Stephen C. Barton (eds.), *The Holy Spirit and Christian Origins* (Grand Rapids: Eerdmans, 2004), 257–69; Jonathan Burke, "Satan and Demons in the Apostolic Fathers: A Minority Report, *SEÅ* 81 (2016): 127–68; Thomas J. Farrar, "Satanology and Demonology in the Apostolic Fathers: A Response to Jonathan Burke," *SEÅ* 83 (2018) 156–91.

29. Christopher Todd Bounds, "The Understanding of Grace in Selected Apostolic Fathers," StPatr 48 (2013) 351–59; Michael R. Whitenton, "After ΠΙΣΤΙΣ ΧΡΙΣΤΟΥ: Neglected Evidence from the Apostolic Fathers," *JTS* 61 (2010) 82–109; Christopher Todd Bounds, "The Doctrine of Christian Perfection in the Apostolic Fathers," *WesTJ* 42 (2007) 7–27. See also the influential but now dated Thomas F. Torrance, *The Doctrine of Grace in the Apostolic Fathers* (Edinburgh: Oliver and Boyd, 1948).

The Apostolic Fathers serve as a window into theological trajectories and themes that emerged in early Christianity. Specific developments include the incorporation of the "Two Ways" literary tradition (Didache, Barnabas), apostolic succession (1 Clement), the Eucharist as sacrifice and medicine (Didache, Ignatius), a three-fold ministry resembling monoepiscopacy (Ignatius), emphatic Sunday observance (Didache, Ignatius, Barnabas), baptism as a seal (2 Clement), stipulations concerning post-baptismal sin and repentance (Hermas), the metaphor of the church as the "soul" within the world (Diognetus), references to the "catholic church" (Ignatius, Martyrdom of Polycarp), and an incipient veneration of martyrs (Martyrdom of Polycarp). The Apostolic Fathers confronted so-called "docetic" and "judaizing" opponents (Ignatius, Polycarp), as well as pagan critics (Quadratus, Diognetus). The Apostolic Fathers illuminate differing courses of the "parting of the ways" between Judaism and Christianity.[30]

## What is the Apostolic Fathers Commentary Series?

The Apostolic Fathers Commentary Series (AFCS) proposes to offer a literary and theological reading of individual works among the Apostolic Fathers corpus. Although the compositional development and textual history of some of the texts are quite complex, the series offers a literary and theological reading of the final form text in an intelligible fashion for a broad audience.

Each volume in the series will offer a similar, two-part structure. Part one will include introductory essays, and part two will consist of exegetical, theological, and historical commentary on the final-form text in a section-by-section format. In the first part, each volume will include an essay on preliminary matters, such as historical placement, provenance, and social setting; an essay on the use of scripture; and an essay on themes and theology. All volumes will offer a fresh and readable translation of the text, along with brief textual notes.

The AFCS is designed to engage historical-critical scholarship and to synthesize such material for a wide range of readers. The series will make use of international scholarship, ancient languages (with English co-translations), and primary research, aiming to elucidate the literary form of the

---

30. Thomas A. Robinson, *Ignatius of Antioch and the Parting of the Ways: Early Jewish-Christian Relations* (Peabody, MA: Hendrickson, 2009); Pierluigi Lanfranchi, "Attitudes to the Sabbath in Three Apostolic Fathers: *Didache*, Ignatius, and *Barnabas*," in Rieuwerd Buitenwerf, Harm W. Hollander, and Johannes Tromp (eds.), *Jesus, Paul, and Early Christianity*, NovTSup 130 (Leiden: Brill, 2008), 243–59.

text for students and scholars of earliest Christianity. The exegesis of AFCS will engage grammatical, rhetorical, and discourse features within the given work. In particular, the series will expansively discuss the elements relevant to theological interpretation of the texts. The AFCS thus seeks to fill a niche by offering a theological and literary reading of the Apostolic Fathers in both an economical and accessible form for a wide readership.

Paul A. Hartog
Shawn J. Wilhite
AFCS Series Editors

# Foreword

ANYONE WHO SEEKS TO know the wisdom and experience of ancient literature soon becomes entangled in at least three basic problems. The initial focus must be to gain an accurate rendering and, thereafter, translation of the text(s) in question. In this effort there is a secondary concern to evaluate the manuscripts from which that rendering is derived as well as the reliability of those sources. Finally, careful readers must recreate a milieu within which oral and/or literary foundations for the manuscripts arose, both with respect to the origin of the textual tradition itself and in relation to its usage by later readers and editors. In practice, such dilemmas of translation, text, and context tend to ring true for virtually all ancient writings.

Similar conditions exist in the case of early Christian literature, though this is complicated by the fact that ecclesiastical custom has ascribed "canonical" (= biblical) status to one set of writings in distinction from all other works. In truth, sophisticated researchers who engage canonical writings have hopefully done so with an alert, educated eye toward the very issues related to all ancient texts as outlined above. But more typically, readers operate with some tacit notion that the authors, manuscript traditions, and translations of scripture are as a rule broadly accepted by all users of the literature, and thus they leave the basic issues of text and history to those who engage such problems professionally. Thus it is that we now have a diverse variety of translations available in unlimited modern languages and copious commentaries at hand for the many individual writings within scripture.

Naturally, when one encounters early Christian literature outside the canon, the situation becomes even more problematic, providing circumstances with which most readers (no longer wearing the restrictive blinders of any particular faith tradition) might readily agree. This typically holds true for most works within Christendom, even among the so-called Apostolic Fathers, which patristic authors and later pre-modern scholars considered to derive from traditions related to the original apostles and subsequent disciples of Christ. But the situation is not determined so easily. Indeed, supposed apostolic roots notwithstanding, the contexts of this collection of works have never been clearly defined, nor (in most cases) have the authors of their composition been readily identified without some amount of debate. For example, names such as Clement, Ignatius, Barnabas, and Polycarp tend to dominate the collection, but the reliability of many specific figures now associated with the texts that bear their names is largely dubious. Added to this is the limited number of manuscripts that preserve these writings, many of which are fragmentary in nature and few of which date to within a century of the composition of their "autographs." Truly, for non-canonical Christian writings the problems that plague today's researchers of ancient literature are often greatly enhanced. In the case of the Apostolic Fathers, one finds this to be especially evident.

All this having been observed as distinctive of literary sources in general, perhaps no other work within the collection of the Apostolic Fathers exemplifies the complexity of authorship, context, and manuscript evolution than the Didache. For any reader who is new to this unique work, parallels to well-known scriptural traditions within its account seem especially obvious. Indeed, the longer title of the tradition's primary manuscript of "teaching ... by the twelve apostles" should offer some reassurance in this respect. Yet other elements, such as references to ancient prayers and baptismal rituals, community customs and regulation of prophetic activity, Trinitarian language intermingled with an apparently "low" Christology throughout may come across as rather new and strange to contemporary Christians and to the practices of our own individual faith experiences. Here then lies the mystery of the text, as well as its special role within the evolutionary history of Christian tradition.

In the pages that follow the reader will find a solid and intriguing introduction to the writing known as the Didache from the hand of one of the discipline's newest scholars in the field, Shawn Wilhite. In this, his inaugural volume on the topic, Wilhite offers a worthy review of issues that face users of the text from various angles of translation, manuscripts, and context, themes that typically plague both new readers and tested scholars alike. He provides sound historical background and interpretation of materials to help those who seek to uncover the various details of the early Christian experience preserved by the tradition. Within this process he moves carefully in a way that does not leave those who are novices to the Church's oldest literature behind, offering a consistent analysis of the most important elements within a framework easily understood and quickly appreciated.

Wilhite begins his introduction with a clean and clear translation of the Didache, providing the reader with welcomed opportunity to read the text before considering its origins and meaning. After that he offers a succinct discussion of the manuscripts that lie behind the writing, including review of those that have preserved the tradition for later ecclesiastical usage. From this he offers a "window" of opportunity during which the tractate may have come into its basic form around the end of the first century and suggests an Antiochean or north Palestinian setting worthy of consideration for insight into the broader background of the tradition's origins. As he is careful to observe, his conclusions are drawn from the various options currently popular in scholarship as they relate to the work.

Next, Wilhite offers a helpful excursus on the relationship of the Didache to what may be known of scripture and its role within the tradition. His analysis of the "reception history" of biblical traditions, together with considerations of intertextuality and literary character, helps to frame the writing for the reader in its role between the production of canonical literature generally and later ecclesiastical works that incorporate scripture together with Didache traditions and rituals within their evolving frameworks. He identifies five "source traditions" behind the writing and identifies hermeneutical patterns typical of the author/editor(s). These variables—employing the Gospel of Matthew as their primary point of contact within scripture—help to set the basic tone of the writing by which the reader may best understand the text.

On the heels of this discussion of sources and scripture, Wilhite engages the crucial issue of the Didache's theology within context. The problems are manifold, yet they are prudently reviewed as a forward to what may be said about the meaning of the tractate itself. Topics covered here are oriented around the focus of theology, including the author's own implicit expressions, especially related to baptismal liturgy and Eucharist. After a quick review of Trinitarian imagery itself, Wilhite explores how such allusions arise within the context of salvation and soteriological consciousness. This is expressed in ethical parameters, including concern for Jewish Torah, focus on giving of self, virtues and vices, various strictures of the Decalogue, and most especially, elements related to the communal life of the faithful. Thereafter appears some consideration of the concept of "teacher" within the text, both as it applies to the life of wisdom and to the author directly. This element becomes a springboard for consideration of ecclesiastical offices and, finally, eschatological orientation (both individual and corporate)—a focus previously featured as an essential component of Wilhite's 2017 doctoral dissertation on the Didache.

Part II of the volume is a presentation of the Didache text in its essence, offered as a verse by verse commentary on the various materials within the work. Wilhite offers vigilant appraisal of the manuscript evidence available for his discussions, beginning with the various "titular" options for early identifications of the text. In his subsequent consideration of the Didache's "two ways" materials (1.1–6.2), he gives extensive comparison with Matthew's Sermon on the Mount as a reflection of these same teachings in large part. Reflecting the structural design of the Didache itself, the commentary gives weighty coverage to these "two ways" instructions as a major aspect of what the tractate contains. Thereafter, Wilhite covers the liturgical materials in 6.3–10.7, ecclesial and communal considerations in 11.1–15.4, and closing eschatological teachings of 16.1–8, including an analysis of possible lost endings for the original form of the tradition.

In a word, the reader will find this volume to offer a delightful translation of the Didache text based on the available manuscripts, a precise analysis of the materials that came to form that tradition, and the contexts within which those sources rose to existence. Wilhite clearly recognizes that what is preserved in this material is a reflection of lengthy considerations of the early Christian experience, now preserved in literary form for a living community of faith. He is sensitive to that truth in his presentation; he is careful for how that is reconstructed in his comments. Here one will find an earnest introduction to what the Didache preserves for contemporary considerations of an important piece of ancient literature from the Church's origins. It should be read carefully so that each observation may be fully considered and analyzed by the reader. To do so will surely bring light in one's research of the Didache itself—whether encountered for the first time or as a time-honored focus of investigation.

Clayton N. Jefford
St. Meinrad, Indiana
4 June 2019

# Preface

ALTHOUGH MY NAME APPEARS on the front cover, I am immensely privileged to benefit from all the many hands and minds that helped me shape this material. Over the course of about six years, many individuals gave of their time, resources, and occasionally, finances to help me compose this book.

During the final stages of the book, I re-watched the series *Lost*. In season six episode seventeen, "The End," Christian Shephard tells his son Jack: "The most important part of your life was the time that you spent with these people on that island. That's why all of you are here. Nobody does it alone, Jack. You needed all of them, and they needed you." Although much of this book was written in isolation, one learns the art of deeply appreciating the many voices and the presence of friends during the whole process. I would like to acknowledge formally some of these individuals who helped me become a better person, which in turn made this contribution possible. Any good that this project provides can serve as a testimony to their influence on me, while any deficiency still remains mine.

First and foremost, my deep thanks are reserved for Michael A. G. Haykin. He has become a mentor, served on my dissertation committee, and, as Augustine recalls, reordered my loves for the field of early Christianity and patristics in particular. I have been considerably grateful for his model and his generous disposition as a scholar. His voice—either in written form, public discourse, or private discussion—shapes much of who I have become as a thinker, a junior scholar, and a professor. It is to him that I dedicate this book.

I, additionally, reserve extended amounts of thanks for Paul Hartog, my co-editor. Over the course of this project, we have co-labored well together during these projects and he has patiently guided my own vision for publishing. He displays great patience in working with others and models well *how* to read texts closely. During the final stages of this book, his expertise in the field and keen editorial eye is one to be emulated.

The journey to this book began during my PhD residency. It received meager attention during my dissertation writing, but afterward the book finally surfaced to the top of my writing schedule. Many features in this commentary were written, re-written, and re-written once more. I mention this because my doctoral residency at Southern Seminary shaped the way I perceive commentary writing. Mark Seifrid, Thomas Schreiner, and Brian Vickers would open up about their own commentary writing in private and public settings. Jonathan Pennington sent me on a quest to hunt down different commentary writing strategies—something I now do for some of my own students. Dear friends, including Coleman Ford, Trey Moss, and Kevin Hall, would listen to me ceaselessly tease out ideas early in my thought process. Brian Davidson, not only my neighbor but also a dear friend, would withstand hour-long conversations in our driveway and created room to stumble towards clearer ideas. His first-hand knowledge of Jewish texts, Dead Sea Scrolls, language abilities, and his incessant concern for balanced and informed arguments have only made this project better and me a better thinker.

Clayton Jefford in particular shaped many of the chapters in this commentary. During my PhD residency, I had the honor and privilege of living an hour away from him. Since then, we have shared a number of meals and walks around Louisville, Tell City, or Chicago. The core of this commentary took shape during a directed study that I took with Jefford. He has since turned into a friend and a mentor in many ways. A visit with Nancy Pardee early in this process at the University of Chicago deeply influenced the way I perceive the Didache text and our time has also continued to blossom into a collegial relationship. Jonathan Draper, Jonathan Schwiebert, Alan Garrow, and William Varner have likewise helped at various stages in the process and, as a result, informed my thinking.

Study groups at the Society of Biblical Literature, the North American Patristics Society, and the Evangelical Theological Society, in their respective ways, permitted space to "air out" ideas that shape many of these pages. John Meade and Brian Arnold have become good and close friends over the years. Madison Pierce, Eric Vanden Eykel, Ryan Clevenger, Charles Meeks, and many others have periodically discussed elements of early Christianity that shaped my language.

My institution permitted the necessary space to finish this book. California Baptist University, which served as my baccalaureate education, now serves as my first post as a professor. Chris Morgan, Tony Chute, Jeff Mooney, Jeff Cate, John Gill, and Joe Slunaker have been wonderful colleagues in the School of Christian Ministries. Our school president, Dr. Ron Ellis, Dirk Davis, Riste Simnjanovski, and Yvette Hale have provided phenomenal institutional support to ensure my success. Jeff Biddle, a CBU therapist patiently helps me navigate my depression and anxiety—much of which peaked its head during many stages of this book. Many CBU students patiently listened to me explain ideas about the Didache and early Christianity.

While at Southern Seminary, many librarians helped find books and many became friends themselves, including Whitney Motley, Ben Ruppert, Christi Osterday, Ryan Vasut, and Barry Driver. Jason Fowler provided my first outlet to lead a Greek reading group and teach on minor portions of the Didache. At CBU, Keri Murcray went well above and beyond in helping me find books, acting with patience as I returned my ILL books late, and she would help point out ways to locate sources. She is a tremendous asset to the research at CBU.

Redeemer Baptist Church has become home for me and my family. The liturgy, friendships, and instruction have shaped many portions of these pages. Many who will never open the pages of this book, though, have served as a respite for my soul. Renee Flannery has become a spiritual sister to me and has worked tirelessly to help me rewrite and edit many portions of this commentary. Many in the elders fellowship group (Helen, Luther, Rosemary, Kay, and Sydney) have ministered deeply to me. Emmanuel Siordia, an intern at the time, read many portions of the work because of his growing interest in patristics, and he commented on the readability of particular sections.

Writing this commentary, while writing and completing my dissertation on the Didache, has been a very tiring and taxing season on my body, my mind, and relationships. During the mid-point of writing, my family experienced bouts with cancer, brain tumors, fears of death, and invasive surgeries—moments and experiences that will forever shape me. It should come as no surprise that even writers and scholars and teachers experience the frailty of life. I am deeply grateful for the support and encouragement of my family, including Joe and Sandra (my Papa and Maga), Walter and Janet, and my mother, Kelli.

I reserve the final comment to name and to speak about my dream, Allyson, and my beloved children. When I first took an academic interest in the Didache, my sweet daughter was merely three months old—now six. Along this journey, I saw her say her first words and take her first steps. As she would color in her books, I, too, attempted to craft my own. My son warmed my soul merely by "interrupting daddy to play baseball in the front yard," which happily prolonged me completing this book. Allyson's support speaks to her patience, her interests, and her love. She endured my writing frustrations, accentuated my joys, and continues to extend nothing but love and support and deep affection. She motivated me to write one word at a time—just a little each day. My home study policy is to "never have a closed door" and I have *never once* regretted having my wife and kids come to interrupt me—they make me more human and only increase my joys as a person, which affect me as a writer. To complete this book points to their patient co-laboring efforts!

Shawn J. Wilhite<br>
Riverside, California<br>
Advent 2018

# Abbreviations

## 1. Ancient

| | |
|---|---|
| Acts Paul | Acts of Paul |
| *Ant. rom* | Dionysius of Halicarnassus, *Antiquitates romanae* |
| Apoc. Pet. | Apocalypse of Peter |
| Apos. Can. | Apostolic Canons |
| Apos. Con. | Apostolic Constitutions |
| *Bapt.* | Tertullian, *De baptismo* |
| Barn. | Barnabas |
| *Comm. Eccl.* | Didymus the Blind, *Commentary on Ecclesiastes* |
| *Comm. Isa.* | Cyril of Alexandria, *Commentary on Isaiah* |
| *Comm. Ps.* | Didymus the Blind, *Commentary on the Psalms* |
| Did. | Didache |
| *Didasc.* | *Didascalia* |
| *Doctr.* | *De Doctrina Apostolorum* |
| DSS | Dead Sea Scrolls |
| *Enarrat. Ps.* | Augustine, *Enarrationes in Psalmos* |
| *Ep.* | Seneca, *Epistulae morales* |
| *Ep. fest.* | Athanasius, *Epistulae festales* |
| *Exp. Pss.* | John Chrysostom, *Expositions of the Psalms* |
| H54 | Codex Hierosolymitanus (Jerusalem Manuscript) |
| *Hist.* | Rufinus, *Eusebii Historia ecclesiastica a Rufino translata et continuata* |
| *Hist. eccl.* | Eusebius, *Historia ecclesiastica* |
| *m. Meg.* | *Mishnah Megillah* |

| | |
|---|---|
| *m. Ta'an.* | *Mishnah Taanit* |
| *Mut.* | Philo, *De mutatione nominum* |
| POX 1782 | Oxyrhynchus Papyrus 1782 (fourth century; containing Did. 1.3c–1.4a; 2.7b—3.2a) |
| *Prax.* | Tertullian, *Adversus Praxean* |
| *Princ.* | Origen, *De principiis* |
| *Protr.* | Clement of Alexandria, *Protrepticus* |
| *Ps.-Phocyl.* | *Pseudo-Phocylides* |
| *Quis div.* | Clement of Alexandria, *Quis dives salvetur* |
| *Serm.* | Augustine, *Sermones* |
| Sib. Or. | *Sibylline Oracles* |
| Sir | Sirach |
| *Spec.* 1, 2, 3, 4 | Philo, *De specialibus legibus* I, II, III, IV |
| *Suppl.* | Euripides, *Supplices* |
| *Symb.* | Rufinus, *Commentarius in symbolum apostolorum* |
| T. Ash. | Testament of Asher |
| T. Benj. | Testament of Benjamin |
| T. Iss. | Testament of Issachar |
| T. Reu. | Testament of Reuben |
| T. Sim. | Testament of Simeon |
| *Trad. ap.* | Hippolytus, *Traditio apostolica* |

## 2. Modern

| | |
|---|---|
| Abib | Academia Biblica |
| AB | Anchor Bible |
| ACC | Alcuin Club Collections |
| ACH | Ancient Society and History |
| AF | The Apostolic Fathers |
| AGJU | Arbeiten zur Geschichte des antiken Judentums und des Urchristentums |
| AJEC | Ancient Judaism and Early Christianity |
| *Andover Rev* | *Andover Review* |
| *AugStud* | *Augustinian Studies* |
| AV | Die Apostolischen Väter |

| | |
|---|---|
| BDAG | Danker, Frederick W., Walter Bauer, William F. Arndt, and F. Wilbur Gingrich. *Greek-English Lexicon of the New Testament and Other Early Christian Literature*. 3rd ed. Chicago: University of Chicago Press, 2000 |
| BDF | Blass, Friedrich, Albert Debrunner, and Robert W. Funk. *A Greek Grammar of the New Testament and Other Early Christian Literature*. Chicago: University of Chicago Press, 1961 |
| BECNT | Baker Exegetical Commentary of the New Testament |
| BETL | Bibliotheca Ephemeridum Theologicarum Lovaniensium |
| BibAC | Bible in Ancient Christianity |
| BibInt | Biblical Interpretation Series |
| *Bib* | *Biblica* |
| *BN* | *Biblische Notizen* |
| *BSac* | *Bibliotheca Sacra* |
| BTB | *Biblical Theology Bulletin* |
| BVB | Beiträge zum Verstehen der Bible |
| BZAW | Beihefte zur Zeitschrift für die alttestamentliche Wissenschaft |
| BZNW | Beihefte zur Zeitschrift für die neutestamentliche Wissenschaft |
| *CBQ* | *Catholic Biblical Quarterly* |
| CCSL | Corpus Christianorum: Series Latina |
| *CH* | *Church History* |
| ConBNT | Coniectanea Biblica: New Testament Series |
| ConcC | Concordia Commentary |
| CRINT | Compendia Rerum Iudaicarum ad Novum Testamentum |
| CSEL | Corpus Scriptorium Ecclesiasticorum Latinorum |
| EBC | The Expositor's Bible Commentary |
| *EBib* | *Études Bibliques* |
| *EC* | *Early Christianity* |
| ECA | Early Christian Apocrypha |
| ECHC | Early Christianity in Its Hellenistic Context |
| ECL | Early Christianity and Its Literature |
| ECNT | Exegetical Commentary on the New Testament |
| ECS | Early Christian Studies |

| | |
|---|---|
| *EuroJS* | *European Journal of Sociology* |
| *ExpTim* | *Expository Times* |
| *FRARL* | *The Fourth R: An Advocate for Religious Literacy* |
| GCS | Die griechischen christlichen Schriftsteller der ersten Jahrhunderte |
| GE | Montanari, Franco. *GE – The Brill Dictionary of Ancient Greek*. Leiden: Brill, 2015 |
| GP | Gospel Perspectives |
| GPP | Gorgias Précis Portfolios |
| HS | Homage Series |
| HTR | Harvard Theological Review |
| HTS TheoStud | HTS Theologiese Studies |
| IBC | Interpretation: A Bible Commentary for Teaching and Preaching |
| ICC | International Critical Commentary |
| *Irén* | *Irénikon* |
| ISBL | Indiana Series in Biblical Literature |
| *JAC* | *Jahrbuch für Antike und Christentum* |
| *JBL* | *Journal of Biblical Literature* |
| JECS | Journal of Early Christian Studies |
| JR | Journal of Religion |
| *JSJ* | *Journal for the Study of Judaism* |
| JSJSup | Supplements to the Journal for the Study of Judaism |
| *JSNT* | *Journal for the Study of the New Testament* |
| JSNTSup | Journal for the Study of the New Testament Supplement Series |
| *JTS* | *Journal of Theological Studies* |
| KAV | Kommentar zu den Apostolischen Vätern |
| Lampe | Lampe, G. W. H. *A Patristic Greek Lexicon*. Oxford: Clarendon, 1961 |
| LCL | Loeb Classical Library |
| LEC | Library of Early Christianity |
| *List* | *Listening: Journal of Religion and Culture* |
| LLL | Longman Linguistics Library |
| LNTS | Library of New Testament Studies |

| | |
|---|---|
| LSJ | Liddell, Henry George, Robert Scott, Henry Stuart Jones. *A Greek-English Lexicon*. 9th ed. with revised supplement. Oxford: Clarendon, 1996 |
| *MSJ* | *The Master's Seminary Journal* |
| NAC | The New American Commentary |
| *Neot* | *Neotestamentica: Journal of the New Testament Society of South Africa* |
| NGS | New Gospel Studies |
| *NIB* | *The New Interpreter's Bible* |
| NICNT | The New International Commentary on the New Testament |
| *NovT* | *Novum Testamentum* |
| NovTSup | Supplements to Novum Testamentum |
| NTAF | The New Testament and the Apostolic Fathers |
| *NTS* | *New Testament Studies* |
| PCNT | Paideia Commentaries on the New Testament |
| *PEGLMBS* | *Proceedings: Eastern Great Lakes and Midwest Biblical Studies* |
| PNTC | The Pillar New Testament Commentary |
| PPS | Popular Patristics Series |
| *ProEccl* | *Pro Ecclesia* |
| *PRSt* | *Perspectives in Religious Studies* |
| PS | Pauline Studies |
| PTA | Papyrologische Texte und Abhandlungen |
| PTMS | Princeton Theological Monograph Series |
| PVTG | Pseudepigrapha Veteris Testamenti Graece |
| *RB* | *Revue Biblique* |
| RJFTC | The Reception of Jesus in the First Three Centuries |
| RRTS | Reading Religious Texts Series |
| SBLSS | Society of Biblical Literature: Symposium Series |
| SC | Sources chrétiennes |
| *SecCent* | *The Second Century: A Journal of Early Christian Studies* |
| SHBC | Smyth & Helwys Bible Commentary |
| *SL* | *Studia Liturgica* |

| | |
|---|---|
| Smyth | Smyth, Herbert Weir. *Greek Grammar*. Cambridge: Harvard University Press, 1956 |
| SNTSMS | Society for New Testament Studies Monograph Series |
| *ST* | *Studia Theologica* |
| STCPRIB | Scriptural Traces: Critical Perspectives on the Reception and Influence of the Bible |
| STI | Studies in Theological Interpretation |
| StPatr | Studia Patristica |
| STR | Studies in Theology and Religion |
| STTEEMT | Studia Traditionis Theologiae: Explorations in Early and Medieval Theology |
| SU | Schriften des Urchristentums |
| *SEÅ* | *Svensk Exegetisk Årsbok* |
| SVTP | Studia in Veteris Testamenti Pseudepigrapha |
| *SVTQ* | *St. Vladimir's Theological Quarterly* |
| TANZ | Texte und Arbeiten zum neutestamentlichen Zeitalter |
| TDNT | *Theological Dictionary of the New Testament*. Edited by Gerhard Kittel and Gerhard Friedrich. Translated by Geoffrey W. Bromiley. 10 vols. Grand Rapids: Eerdmans, 1946–76 |
| *TLZ* | *Theologische Literaturzeitung* |
| TUGAL | Texte und Untersuchungen zur Geschichte der alterchristlichen Literatur |
| *TS* | *Theological Studies* |
| *VC* | *Vigiliae Christianae* |
| VCSup | Supplements to Vigiliae Christianae |
| VTGAASG | Vetus Testamentum Graecum. Auctoritate Academiae Scientiarum Gottingensis Editum |
| WBC | Word Biblical Commentary |
| *WesTJ* | *Wesleyan Theological Journal* |
| *WTJ* | *Westminster Theological Journal* |
| WUNT | Wissenschaftliche Untersuchungen zum Neuen Testament |
| *WS* | *Wiener Studien* |
| ZNW | *Zeitschrift für die neutestamentliche Wissenschaft* |

# Tables

Table 1. Thematic Symmetry between Matt 6 and Didache | 38

Table 2. Occurrences of οὐρανός in the NT by singular and plural forms | 40

Table 3. Occurrences of οὐρανός in the Apostolic Fathers corpus by singular and plural forms | 40

Table 4. Shorter and Longer Liturgical Doxologies | 43

Table 5. Didache 2 and the Decalogue | 75

Table 6. Didache 15.1 and Comparable Lists of Ethics | 84

Table 7. Titles of the Didache in Other Patristic Authors | 93

Table 8. Didache 1 and the Sermon on the Mount | 106

Table 9. Didache 1.6 and "Giving Alms" | 117

Table 10. Decalogue and Did. 2 | 119

Table 11. Text Comparison of Did. 2.1–7, Barn. 19.1–12, *Doctr.* 2.2–7, and *Ps.-Phocyl.* | 121

Table 12. δέ + prepositional phrase (περί δέ or μετά + inf.) literary structure for Did. 6.3—10.7 | 163

Table 13. Did. 6.2–3 and the Jerusalem Council | 166

Table 14. Shorter and Longer Liturgical Doxologies | 176

Table 15. Similarities between Did. 16.1–8 and Matt 24–25 | 221

Table 16. Differences between Did. 16.1–8 and Matt 24–25 | 222

Table 17. A Lost Ending to the Didache Reconstructed in Apos. Con., Georgian Version, and St. Boniface | 233

# Translation of Didache

## Title:

"The Teaching of the Twelve Apostles:
The Teaching of the Lord to the Gentiles by the Twelve Apostles"

## Chapter 1

1. There are two ways, one of life and one of death, and there is a great difference between the two ways.

2. This is the way of life. First, love God, the one who made you; second, your neighbor as yourself. And whatever you do not desire to happen, do not do to another.

3. This is the teaching of these words: Bless those cursing you and pray for your enemies and fast on behalf of those persecuting you. For what credit is it if you love those loving you? Do not the gentiles do the same? Love those hating you and you will have no enemy.

4. Abstain from fleshly and bodily passions. If someone gives you a blow to your right cheek, turn to them also the other. And then you will be perfect. If someone compels you to go one mile, go with them two miles. If someone takes your coat, give to them also your tunic. If someone takes your belongings from you, do not ask for it back, for you are not able to do so.

5. Give to each one who asks you and do not request it back. For the Father desires *things* from his own gifts to be given to each one. Blessed is the one who gives according to the commandment, for this one is without guilt. Woe to the one who receives. For if someone having need receives, then this one is innocent. Yet, the one who does not have any need *will give* an account for why they received and for what

purpose. While being confined to prison, they will be questioned concerning the things that were done, and they will not be released from there until they repay the last cent.

6. But it has also been said concerning this, "Let your alms sweat in your hands until you know to whom you will give."

## Chapter 2

1. The second commandment of the teaching:
2. Do not murder, do not commit adultery, do not [sexually] corrupt a child, do not commit fornication, do not steal, do not practice magic, do not engage in sorcery, do not kill a child in the womb nor kill [a child] having been born, do not covet the things of your neighbor,
3. do not swear falsely, do not give false testimony, do not speak evil, do not remember evil.
4. Do not be double-minded, nor double-tongued, for the double-tongue is a trap of death.
5. Let your word not be false nor empty, but be fulfilled by action.
6. Do not be greedy nor rapacious nor a hypocrite nor malicious nor haughty. Do not conceive an evil plan against your neighbor.
7. Do not hate any person, instead reprimand some, pray from some, and love some beyond your own soul.

## Chapter 3

1. My child, flee from all forms of evil and from everything resembling it.
2. Do not become angry, for anger leads to murder. Neither become jealous nor quarrelsome nor hot-tempered, for from all of these things murders are begotten.
3. My child, do not become lustful, for lust leads to adultery. Neither become vulgar nor one who lifts up their eyes, for from all of these things adulteries are begotten.
4. My child, do not become an auger, since it leads to idolatry. Neither become an enchanter nor an astrologer nor a magician nor desire to see such things, for from all these things idolatry is begotten.

5. My child, do not become a liar, since the act of lying leads to theft. Do not become a lover of money nor conceited, for from all of these things thefts are begotten.
6. My child, do not become a grumbler, since it leads to blasphemy. Neither become arrogant nor evil-minded, for from all of these things blasphemies are begotten.
7. Instead, be humble, since the humble will inherit the earth.
8. Become patient and merciful and innocent and quiet and good, and revering the words that you have heard continually.
9. Do no exalt yourself nor permit your soul to become arrogant. Let not your soul be united with the haughty, but dwell with the righteous and the humble.
10. Receive the things that happen to you as good, knowing that nothing happens apart from God.

## Chapter 4

1. My child, remember night and day the one speaking to you the word of God, and honor that one as the Lord. For wherever the Lord's nature is spoken, there the Lord is.
2. Seek out each day the presence of the saints that you might find rest in their words.
3. Do not create division but live in peace with those who quarrel. Judge righteously. Do not demonstrate favoritism when you judge [lit. receive a face to expose] between offenses.
4. Do not waver [lit. do not be double-souled], whether it is or not.
5. Do not become like those stretching out their hand to receive, yet withdrawing it so as not to give.
6. If you have *resources* through your hands, then give a ransom for your sins.
7. Do not hesitate to give nor grumble while giving. For you know who is the good paymaster of the reward.
8. Do not turn away someone who is in need, but share all things with your <sisters and brothers> and do not claim anything to be one's own. For if you are sharers in what is immortal, how much more in the perishable things.

9. Do not withhold your hand from your son or your daughter, but from their youth teach them the fear of God.

10. Do not give orders to your male or female slaves—to those who hope in the same God—in your anger, lest they no longer fear God who is over both of you. For he does not come to call according to partiality, but upon whom the Spirit has prepared.

11. And you servants, be obedient to your masters as a type of God with modesty and reverence.

12. Hate all hypocrisy and everything that does not please the Lord.

13. Do not abandon the commandments of the Lord, but guard what you have received, neither adding nor subtracting.

14. Confess your transgressions in the church and do not approach your prayer with an evil conscience. This is the way of life.

## Chapter 5

1. This is the way of death: above all, it is evil and full of curses, including murders, adulteries, lusts, fornications, thefts, idolatries, magic, sorcery, robberies, false testimonies, hypocrisies, duplicities, deceit, pride, wickedness, stubbornness, covetousness, obscene speech, jealousy, arrogance, haughtiness, and pretension.

2. [It also includes] persecutors of good, those who hate truth, love a lie, do not know the reward of righteousness, do not bind closely to good nor judge righteously, do not watch for what is good, but what is evil, of which meekness and endurance are far away, love worthless things, pursue reward, not being merciful to the poor, not working for the cause of the oppressed, not knowing the one who made them, murder children, corrupt God's creation, turn away those in need, oppress the afflicted, intercessors for the wealthy, lawless judges of the poor, [and] altogether sinful. Children, be delivered from all these things.

## Chapter 6

1. See to it that no one leads you astray from this way of teaching, since that one teaches without concern for God.

2. For if you are able to bear the whole yoke of the Lord, you will be perfect. But if you are unable, do what you are able.

3. Concerning food, bear what you are able. Beware of what is offered to idols, for it is worship of dead gods.

## Chapter 7

1. Concerning baptism, baptize in this way: after you have reviewed all these things, baptize into the name of the Father and of the Son and of the Holy Spirit in running water.
2. If you do not have running water, baptize in some other water. If you are not able [to baptize] in cold water, then in warm water.
3. If you have neither, pour water upon the head three times in the name of the Father and Son and Holy Spirit.
4. Prior to baptism, let the one who baptizes and the baptizand fast, and others if they are able. Instruct the baptizand to fast one or two days beforehand.

## Chapter 8

1. Let not your fast be with the hypocrites. For they fast on the second (Monday) and fifth (Thursday) days after the sabbath. But you fast on the fourth [day] (Wednesday) and day of preparation (Friday).
2. Nor pray like the hypocrites but, as the Lord has commanded in his Gospel, pray in like manner:

    Our Father who is in heaven,

    hallowed be your name;

    let your kingdom come;

    let your will be done as in heaven and upon earth.

    Give to us this day our daily bread

    and forgive us our debt as we also forgive our debtors.

    And do not lead us into temptation,

    but deliver us from the evil one.

    For yours is the power and the glory forever.

3. Pray like this three times a day.

## Chapter 9

1. Concerning the Eucharist, give thanks in this way:
2. First, concerning the cup:

    We give thanks to you, our Father,

    on behalf of the holy vine, David your servant,

    whom you have made known to us

    through Jesus, your servant.

    To you be glory forever.

3. Concerning the broken bread:

    We give thanks to you, our Father,

    on behalf of life and knowledge,

    which you have made known to us

    through Jesus, your servant.

    To you be glory forever.

4. Just as this broken bread was scattered upon the hills and having been gathered together it became one,

    thusly, let your church be gathered from the corners of the earth into your kingdom.

    For yours is the glory and power through Jesus Christ forever.

5. But let no one eat or drink from the your Eucharist except those who are baptized into the name of the Lord. For the Lord has also spoken concerning this: "Do not give the holy things to the dogs."

## Chapter 10

1. After being satisfied, give thanks in this way:
2. We give thanks to you, O Holy Father,

    On behalf of your holy name, which you caused to dwell in our hearts

    and on behalf of knowledge and faith and immortality,

    which you have made known to us through Jesus, your servant.

    To you be glory forever.

3. You, almighty Master, have created all things for your name's sake.

   You have given food and drink to all humanity to enjoy

   so that they might give thanks.

   But you have graced us with spiritual food and drink

   And eternal life through your servant.

4. Above all, we give thanks to you because you are mighty.

   To you be glory forever.

5. Remember, O Lord, your church

   to deliver her from all evil

   and to perfect her in your love

   and gather her from the four winds, whom you have sanctified,

   into your kingdom,

   which you have prepared for her.

   For yours is the power and the glory forever.

6. Let grace come and

7. let this earth pass away.

   Hosanna to the God of David.

   If some are holy, let them come.

   If some are not, let them repent.

   Maranatha. Amen.

8. But permit the prophets to give thanks as they wish.

9. **[Coptic Addition]** Concerning the saying for the ointment, give thanks just as you say: "We give thanks to you, Father, concerning the ointment which you showed us, through Jesus your Son. Yours is the glory forever! Amen."[31]

## Chapter 11

1. Therefore, if one comes and teaches you all these previous things, welcome them.

---

31. This translation assumes the following work: Jones and Mirecki, "Considerations of the Coptic Papyrus," 53.

2. If the one who teaches turns and teaches another teaching so as to annul [the previous teachings], do not listen to them. But so as to contribute to righteousness and knowledge, welcome them as the Lord.

3. Concerning the apostles and the prophets, proceed as follows according to the rule of the gospel.

4. Let every apostle who comes to you be welcomed as the Lord.

5. They should not stay except one day. If they have need, then [they are permitted to stay] another [day]. But if they stay three [days], they are a false prophet.

6. As the apostles are leaving, let them take nothing except bread until they find lodging. But if they ask for money, they are a false prophet.

7. Also neither test or judge any prophet who speaks in the spirit. For every sin will be forgiven, but this sin will not be forgiven.

8. Not everyone who speaks in the spirit is a prophet, but if [only] they have the ways of the Lord.

9. And any prophet who arranges for food in the spirit must not eat from it. If they do not do otherwise, they are a false prophet.

10. Any prophet who teaches the truth, if they do not practice what they teach, is a false prophet.

11. Any prophet who has been proven true, who performs for the earthly mystery of the church, not teaching [others] to do what they do, their judgment is not with you. For their judgment is with God. For the ancient prophets acted in like manner.

12. If someone might say in the spirit, "Give me money," or another thing, do not listen to them. If they tell [you] to give on behalf of another who has need, let no one judge them.

## Chapter 12

1. Let any who comes in the name of the Lord be welcomed. Afterward, by examining them, for you will have discernment, you will know what is true and what is false.

2. If one who comes is a traveler along the way, help them in whatever way possible. They are not to stay with you except two or three days if they need.

3. If they desire to settle with you, being a craftsperson, let them work and eat.
4. If they do not have a trade, decide according to your conscience how they might live among you as a Christian not being idle.
5. If they do not wish to do thusly, they are a Christmonger. Beware of such people.

## Chapter 13

1. Every true prophet desiring to stay with you is worthy of their food.
2. Likewise, a true teacher is also worthy and this, like the worker, of their food.
3. Thus, taking all the firstfruits that is produced from the winepress and the threshing floor, and of the cows and also the sheep, give the firstfruits to the prophets, for they are your high priests.
4. If you do not have a prophet, give [the firstfruits] to the poor.
5. If you make bread, take the firstfruits and give according to the commandment.
6. Likewise when you open the jar of wine or oil, take the firstfruits and give to the prophets.
7. And of money, clothes, and all possessions, take the firstfruits, as it seems right to you, give according to the commandment.

## Chapter 14

1. Gathering together each Lord's day, break bread and give thanks, first having confessed your sins so that your sacrifice may be pure.
2. Let no one who has a quarrel with their companion join you until they have been reconciled so that your sacrifice may not be defiled.
3. For these are the words having been given, "In every place and season offer to me a pure sacrifice because 'I am a great king,' says the Lord, 'and my name is marvelous among the nations.'"

## Chapter 15

1. Therefore, appoint for yourselves bishops and deacons worthy of the Lord, men who are humble and not lovers of money and are true and have been approved, for they render service to you, the ministry of the prophets and the teachers.

2. Do not disregard them, for they are honored among you along with the prophets and the teachers.

3. Do not reprove one another in anger but in peace, as you have in the Gospel. And to any who has a wrong against another, let no one speak [to them] nor hear from them until they have repented.

4. Your prayers and almsgiving and all your deeds, thusly do them as you have it in the Gospel of our Lord.

## Chapter 16

1. Watch over your life. Let not your lamps be extinguished, do not be unprepared [lit. let not your loins become weary], but become ready. For you do not the know the hour in which our Lord is coming.

2. Gather together frequently seeking the beneficial things for your soul. For the time of your faith will be of no value for you unless you are perfected in the last time.

3. For in the final days false prophets and corrupters will increase, and sheep will be turned into wolves, and love will be turned into hatred.

4. For as lawlessness increases, they will hate and persecute and betray one another. And then the world deceiver will appear as a son of God. He will perform signs and wonders and the earth will be delivered over into his hands and he commit abominations that have never happened from [the beginning of] existence.

5. Then all created humanity will undergo the fire of testing and many will be caused to sin and perish. Those who endure in their faith will be saved from the accursed one himself.

6. And then the signs of truth will appear: first the sign of the opening in heaven; then the sign of the sound of a trumpet; and third, the resurrection of the dead.

7. But not all, as it has been said, "The Lord will come, and all his saints with him."

8. Then the world will see the Lord coming upon the clouds of heaven.

9. **[Lost Ending]**[32] with the angels of his power, in the throne of his kingdom to condemn the devil, the deceiver of the world, and to render to every one according to his deeds.

10. Then shall the wicked go away into everlasting punishment, but the righteous shall enter eternal life,

11. to inherit those things which eye hath not seen, nor ear heard, nor have entered into the heart of man, such things as God hath prepared for them that love him.

12. And they shall rejoice in the kingdom of God, which is in Christ Jesus.

---

32. This translation assumes the following work: Aldridge, "Lost Ending of the Didache," 233–64.

# Part I

# Introductory Articles

# 1

# Introduction to the Didache

WHEN PHILOTHEOS BRYENNIOS DISCOVERED the Teaching of the Twelve Apostles (Didache) in 1873, it sparked an immediate and lasting interest among early church historians.[1] Joan Walker captures the sentiment quite well:

> The discovery of the Didache in 1873 has been acclaimed in many a eulogy, in many a language and by many a scholar. And rightly so. For this work has cast a spell over even the most cautious who, finding its magic irresistible, seek time and again to prise its secrets.[2]

This ancient text (early second century CE) caught the attention of many early Christian scholars shortly thereafter: Adolf Hilgenfeld (1884),[3] Adolf von Harnack (1884),[4] Paul Sabatier (1885),[5] Roswell D. Hitchcock and Francis Brown (1885),[6] Philip Schaff (1885),[7] and Charles Taylor (1886).[8] This ancient writing has generally created problems among Didache scholars—Giet deeming it an "enigma" (1970)[9] and Vokes calling the work a "riddle" (1938).[10]

Bryennios discovered the Didache in 1873 within an eleventh-century codex (Codex Hierosolymitanus [H54]). The Didache was not released to

---

1. Jefford, *Teaching of the Twelve Apostles*, 1.
2. Walker, "New Edition of the Didache," 35.
3. Hilgenfeld, *Evangeliorum secundum Hebraeos*.
4. von Harnack, *Lehre der zwölf Apostel*.
5. Sabatier, *La Didache ou l'Enseignement des douze apôtres*.
6. Hitchcock and Brown, *Teaching of the Twelve Apostles*.
7. Schaff, *Oldest Church Manual*.
8. Taylor, *Teaching of the Twelve Apostles*.
9. Giet, *L'énigme de La Didache*.
10. Vokes, *Riddle of the Didache*.

the public until 1883, with the first facsimiles appearing in 1887, because it was overlooked during Bryennios's initial assessment of H54.[11] Upon noticing this neglect, Bryennios exclaimed:

> This! This! This! This! This must be the Διδαχη, the book that so many ancient fathers quote, the book that was lost, that the church mourns over to this day, the foundation of part of the Apostolic Constitutions. Εὕρηκα εὕρηκα εὕρηκα.[12]

In addition to the Didache, the codex contained other works from the Apostolic literature and early Christianity, namely, the Epistle of Barnabas,[13] 1 and 2 Clement, the longer recension of the Ignatian corpus (13 letters), a *Synopsis Veteris et Novi Testamenti* of Chrysostom, and a list of Hebrew/Aramaic Hebrew Bible titles with their Greek correspondent titles entitled ὀνόματα τῶν βιβλίων παρ' Ἑβραίοις[14]—more on this codex below.

The Didache serves as a window into the life of earliest Christianity, the community's self-identity, and related problems surrounding a nascent (post-) apostolic period.[15] Most Didache and early Christian scholars date the Didache to the latter half of the first or the early half of the second century. According to Nancy Pardee, this relatively early date makes the Didache an important witness to the composition and development of the New Testament literature.

> Such an early date and stature by themselves would make the *Didache* an important witness alongside the New Testament of the development of the early Church, but the additional fact that the text is of a more utilitarian nature means that it does not merely supplement the biblical texts, but complements them.[16]

According to Clayton Jefford, the current landscape of Didache scholarship is reaping the rewards from the labors of previous generations. With

---

11. Harris, *Pages of the Bryennios Manuscript*; Harris, *Teaching of the Apostles*.

12. Grosvenor, "An Interview with Bishop Bryennios," 516.

13. See some of the following sources that reflect upon more recent Barn./Did. scholarship. Draper, "Riddle of the Didache Revisited," 89–113; Rhodes, *Barnabas and the Deuteronomic Tradition*; Rhodes, "Two Ways Tradition," 797–816; Tomson, "Didache, Matthew, and Barnabas," 348–82; Smith, "Two Ways of Teaching Authority," 465–97.

14. Harris, *Pages of the Bryennios Manuscript*.

15. Pardee, *Genre and Development of the Didache*, 1. According to Eusebius, Did. is situated among the disputed books in early Christian canon formation. Eusebius includes Did. and the following books as νόθος: the Acts of Paul, Herm., Apoc. Pet., Barn., and the τῶν ἀποστόλων αἱ λεγόμεναι Διδαχαί. Eusebius, *Hist. eccl.* 3.25.4.

16. Pardee, *Genre and Development of the Didache*, 1.

the efforts of the initial scholars, several schools of thought emerged in an attempt to reconstruct the context and traditions behind the Didache.[17] In the past twenty-or-so years, Didache research has seen a resurgence of both collaborative efforts and specialized monographs. Particularly notable in this regard was an exploratory series of paper presentations, "Didache Consultation Unit," at the Society of Biblical Literature (SBL) from 2003–2005 and "Didache in Context" from 2005–2011 under the direction of Aaron Milavec, Jonathan Draper, Nancy Pardee, Clayton Jefford, Huub van de Sandt, and Alan Garrow. This nearly decade focus eventually produced the recent 2015 collection of articles.[18] Given this continued attention, Didache scholars produced two additional commentaries,[19] monographs on the composite text and genre,[20] focused studies on the liturgical traditions,[21] and examinations of the Didache's relationship to Matthew, Q, and James.[22]

Yet as we near 150 years of devoted scholarship, debate still surrounds some of the basic components of the text. Issues such as dating the final form, the editorial and composite nature of the document, the function and genre of the Didache, its relationship to New Testament literature, and the provenance remain largely unresolved. In this introduction, I do not pretend to offer new answers or new insights to these highly difficult questions. Rather, I will provide some basic arguments and data to orient how the Didache is placed within antiquity, its date and provenance, and the essential structure of the book—essentially providing my critical observations to orient the present commentary.[23]

---

17. The best of these studies appear in three different twentieth-century commentaries. In 1958, Jean-Paul Audet considered the implications of the DSS for the study of the Did.; at the time of Audet's publication, the DSS had only been recently discovered. Willy Rordorf and André Tuilier assessed the broad literary traditions in relation to ancient ecclesiastical settings. Finally, Kurt Niederwimmer, whose contribution may represent a pinnacle of Did. research, gave considerable attention to the source critical and editorial composition of the Did. Jefford, "Dynamics, Methodologies, and Progress," 2. Audet, *La Didachè*; Rordorf and Tuilier, *Didachè*; Niederwimmer, *Die Didache*; Niederwimmer, *Didache*.

18. Draper and Jefford, *Missing Piece of the Puzzle*.

19. Milavec, *Didache: Faith, Hope, & Life*; Milavec, *Didache: Commentary*.

20. Pardee, *Genre and Development of the Didache*.

21. Schwiebert, *Knowledge and the Coming Kingdom*.

22. Garrow, *Matthew's Dependence on the Didache*; van de Sandt, *Matthew and the Didache*; van de Sandt and Zangenberg, *Matthew, James, and Didache*.

23. Although many of the following ideas and arguments may not be new, much of the data and structure assumes the research from Niederwimmer, *Didache*, 1–57.

## MS Tradition of the Didache

The textual history of the Didache remains quite complicated. As the Didache often reflects a late first- or early second-century social setting, the manuscript tradition does not model such a date, and is, in fact, quite varied in terms of MS dates. Some direct MS witnesses survive, but the only surviving and generally complete MS dates to the mid-eleventh century (Codex Hierosolymitanus [H54]). Additionally, two early fragments exist, one being a fourth-century Greek fragment and the other being a fifth-century Coptic fragment: Papyrus Oxyrhynchus 1782, containing Did. 1.3c–4a and 2.7–3.2;[24] Br. Mus. Or. 9271, including Did. 10.3b—12.2.[25] Also, early in the twentieth century a Georgian version of the Didache appeared but was subsequently lost.[26] David Palmer, helpfully, has collated many reading variants, versions, and copies of the Didache that point to a collective witness of the Didache.[27] The following discussion will remain rather brief as I only point out the MS traditions for the Didache and offer cursory remarks about the uniqueness of each witness.[28]

### Direct MS Witnesses

#### Codex Hierosolymitanus (H54)

The most complete Didache MS appears in Codex Hierosolymitanus (H54), also known as the Bryennios or Jerusalem Manuscript. Bryennios discovered this MS in 1873 in the library of the Monastery of the Holy Sepulchre

---

24. Hunt, *Oxyrhynchus Papyri*, 15:12–15.

25. Horner, "New Papyrus Fragment of the *Didache*," 225–31; Jones and Mirecki, "Considerations of the Coptic Papyrus," 37–46.

26. I will gloss over the Georgian version because it is somewhat debated whether or not this MS consists of a copy of the Did. based upon an older version of the Did. or if it functions as a modern translation. This latter idea signifies the Georgian not as an independent witness to the Did. Peradse, prior to the destruction of the Georgian version, was able to see Pheikrishvili's copy of the Georgian text, copied it, and collated it with von Harnack's Greek text of the Did. However, it is only the collation that remains of this Georgian version. Peradse, "Der Georgischen Überlieferung," 111–16; Ehrman, *Apostolic Fathers I*, 412–13.

27. Palmer, "Teaching of the Twelve Apostles: Greek Edition."

28. For the sake of this commentary, I will refrain from explaining how the Did. corresponds to a variety of independent witnesses. Regrettably, I still feel I am of many minds when attempting to navigate this problem. So, I will merely point to suggested sources that assess the indirect relationship of the Did. with *Doctr.*, Barn., Apos. Con., Epitome, Canons, and others. Niederwimmer, *Didache*, 28–52; Kloppenborg, "Transformation of Moral Exhortation," 88–109; Kloppenborg, "*Didache*, James, Matthew, and Torah," 193–221; Stewart-Sykes, *On the Two Ways*.

in Constantinople, and the Didache was not made public until 1883.[29] The MS itself identifies the scribe and offers a completion date in a colophon folio (120a): "Leon, notary and sinner," 11 June 1056.[30]

The MS contains 120 leaves including nine different works. The Didache appears in folio 76a–80b. This MS contains the following volumes,[31]

1. Ps.-Chrysostom *Synopsis Veteris et Novi Testamenti*: fol. 1a–38b
2. Epistle of Barnabas: fol. 39a–51b
3. 1 Clement: fol. 51b–70a
4. 2 Clement: fol. 70a–76a
5. ὀνόματα τῶν βιβλίων παρ' ἑβραίοις ("Names of the Books by the Hebrews"): fol. 76a
6. Didache: fol 76a–80b
7. Letter of Maria of Cassoboloi to Ignatius of Antioch: fol. 81a–82a
8. Longer Recension of the Ignatian corpus (12 Letters), followed by the colophon: fol. 82a–120a
9. Discussion of the genealogy of Jesus: fol. 120a–120b

The immediate value of H54 clearly rests in its witness to the Didache. It is the most whole and complete version, to date, that we currently have of the Didache. The ending of the Didache, however, seems highly problematic as it contains an unfinished conclusion—see section in commentary.[32]

## *Papyrus Oxyrhynchus 1782*

This witness to the Didache consists of two, small, fragmentary, parchment leaves. According to Grenfell and Hunt, this fragment dates to the end of the fourth century.[33] The size of the fragment is quite small (fol. 1: 5.5 cm. by 4.5 cm; fol. 2: 5.7 cm. by 4.8 cm.).[34] On folio 1, it contains seven lines of the Greek text, namely Did. 1.3c–1.4a. On folio 2, the eight lines of the Greek

---

29. See the photocopies of the Did. in Harris, *Teaching of the Apostles*; Niederwimmer, *Didache*, 19.

30. See a photograph in Schaff, *Church Manual*, 6. The full subscription, as Schaff provides, reads, "Finished in the month of June, upon the 11th (of the month), day 3d (of the week, *i.e.*, Tuesday), Indiction 9, of the year 6564. By the hand of Leon, notary and sinner."

31. Niederwimmer, *Didache*, 19.

32. Niederwimmer, *Didache*, 20; Aldridge, "Lost Ending of the Didache," 1–15.

33. Hunt, *Oxyrhynchus Papyri*, 15:12–13.

34. Niederwimmer, *Didache*, 21.

text record Did. 2.7b–3.2a.³⁵ Lincoln Blummell and Thomas Wayment comment on the importance of the tiny MS: "P.Oxy. XV 1782 is important not only because of its early date but also because it demonstrates a significantly different text than that of H. The leaves include entirely new readings (ll. 8–12) and a variety of variant wordings."³⁶ These differences do point to the historical problem of relying solely upon H54 for our understanding of the Didache and for assessing the Didache's community. The following records the additional reading and variant wordings:

| H54 1.3c–4 | POxy 1782 Folio 1 | Key: |
|---|---|---|
| | (Fol. 1r) | Plain: 100% agreement |
| (1.3c) οὐκὶ καὶ τὰ ἔθνη | ουχι και τα ε | **Bold:** similar material with different spelling |
| τὸ αὐτὸ | θνη τουτο | |
| (3d) ποιοῦσιν; ὑμεῖς | ποιουσιν υμ | <u>Underline</u>: Unique material in H54 or POxy 1782 |
| δὲ ἀγαπᾶτε | εις δε φιλειτ | |
| τοὺς μισοῦντας | (5) ε τους μισου | |
| ὑμᾶς καὶ | τας υμας και | |
| οὐχ ἕξετε | ουχ εξετε εχ | |
| | (Fol. 1v) | Trans POxy 1782: ll. 8–15 |
| ἐχθρόν· | θρον <u>ακου</u> | Hear |
| | <u>ε τι σε δει ποι</u> | what is necessary for you |
| | (10) <u>ουντα σωσαι</u> | to do in order for |
| | <u>σου το πνα π[ρ]ω</u> | the Spirit to rescue you: |
| | <u>τον παντω</u> | first of all |
| (1.4) ἀπέχου τῶν | αποσχου των | abstain from |
| σαρκικῶν <u>καὶ σωματικῶν</u> | σαρκε[ι]κων ε | fleshly |
| ἐπιθυμιῶν | (15) πιθυμειων | passions |

---

35. See Varner, as a more recent author, who engages this MS. Varner, "Christian Enchiridion," 651–61; Varner, "How Did the 'Teaching' Teach?" 184–87.

36. Blumell and Wayment, *Christian Oxyrhynchus*, 284.

## Versions

### Coptic Fragment: Br. Mus. Or. 9271

This Coptic MS generally dates to the fifth century.[37] Carl Schmidt supplies a photograph of the MS and then provides an inscription.[38] The MS fragment is rather large (44 cm. long and 28.5 cm. high) and contains writing on both sides.[39]

In this Coptic fragment, we can observe a portion of the Didache text: Did. 10.3b–12.2a.[40] The brief section includes the liturgical instruction and the traveling teachers. Additionally, and of a more notable inclusion, the Coptic fragment includes the *Myron* prayer.[41] The Coptic MS includes instruction on the ointment liturgy, which also appears in Apos. Con. VII, 27, 1–2—see section in commentary.

### Ethiopic Version

Regrettably, the Ethiopic translation cannot be dated with any certainty, and the whole translation no longer remains extant.[42] Audet presents a hypothesis regarding the Ethiopic version and how the Didache became part of this tradition.[43]

The Ethiopic version contains a portion of the Didache, including Did. 8.1–2 and 11.3–7. According to Niederwimmer, the Ethiopic version is helpful in three ways: "it secures εἰ μή in 11.5 and πρὸς ὑμᾶς in 12.1 (together with the Coptic and *Apostolic Constitutions*), and it shows that the gloss in 13.4 must be old (although the Ethiopic presupposes τῷ πτωχῷ)."[44]

---

37. Horner, "New Papyrus Fragment of the *Didache*," 225; Rordorf and Tuilier, *Didachè*, 112.

38. Schmidt, "Das koptische Didache-Fragment," 81–99.

39. Niederwimmer, *Didache*, 24.

40. For the Coptic text and a readable translation, consult: Jones and Mirecki, "Considerations of the Coptic Papyrus," 37–46.

41. For more on the Coptic MS, consider: Jefford and Patterson, "Note on *Didache* 12.2a," 65–75.

42. Niederwimmer, *Didache*, 26.

43. Audet, *La Didachè*, 34–45.

44. Niederwimmer, *Didache*, 27.

# Uses of the Didache in Antiquity: Canon Lists and Quotations

In early Christianity, the Didache appears in canon lists, functions as Scripture, and is used in catechisms.[45] Karl Bihlmeyer, at one point, suggests that the Didache was counted by some in antiquity to be part of the New Testament canon.[46] The following brief sample suggests possible quotations by ancient writers and how it appears in early canon lists—whereby a possible distinction between canon and scripture emerges. By doing so, the Didache assumed many different roles in antiquity and most likely was perceived in diverse ways by various communities. This list, also, is not meant to imply that the Didache was universally known in antiquity, contained a monolithic perception, or received equal attention throughout early Christianity. Rather, the opposite may be the case as the Didache eventually fell out of use (cf. Apos. Con.; Did. Apos.; Epitome; Canons).[47] Many of the following examples remain quite disputed, but nonetheless they remain worthy to be mentioned.

## Clement of Alexandria

Two examples from Clement of Alexandria's literature shed light upon Didache sayings that suggest traditions similar to the Didache may at least be familiar to other early Christian writers.[48] Of the two instances, the first mentions Scripture in reference to the Didache. To strengthen the possibility of Clement's use of the Didache as a whole, one will need to find material from Did. 7–16 in Clement's material. Otherwise, it could be argued that Clement makes use of a Two Ways tractate similar to the Didache and not the Didache as we currently have it.

---

45. The following section is a selected summary of Niederwimmer, *Didache*, 4–18.

46. Bihlmeyer, *Die apostolischen Väter*, xvi.

47. See the research by Alistair Stewart-Sykes. Stewart-Sykes, *Apostolic Church Order*; Stewart-Sykes, *On the Two Ways*.

48. Niederwimmer suggests a third possible reference in Clement. He considers Did. 9.2 as a possible reference in *Quis div.* 29.4. Because the "vine of David" is the only lexical connection and because Clement mentions "blood," I am far less inclined to see less awareness of the Did. here. Niederwimmer, *Didache*, 8.

## Example 1: Clement of Alexandria, *Strom.* 1.20[49] and Did. 3.5.

| Clement of Alexandria<br>*Strom.* 1.20, 100.4 | Did. 3.5 |
|---|---|
| ἔμπαλιν οὖν ἀδικεῖ ὁ σφετερισάμενος τὰ βαρβάρων καὶ ὡς ἴδια αὐχῶν, τὴν ἑαυτοῦ δόξαν αὔξων καὶ ψευδόμενος τὴν ἀλήθειαν. οὗτος "κλέπτης" ὑπὸ τῆς γραφῆς εἴρηται. φησὶ γοῦν· "υἱέ, μὴ γίνου ψεύστης· ὁδηγεῖ γὰρ τὸ ψεῦσμα πρὸς τὴν κλοπήν" | τέκνον μου, μὴ γίνου ψεύστης, ἐπειδὴ ὁδηγεῖ τὸ ψεῦσμα εἰς τὴν κλοπήν |
| On the other hand, therefore, whoever appropriates what belongs to the barbarians, and boasts it as his own, does wrong by increasing his own glory and falsifying the truth. It is this kind of person scripture calls a "thief." Therefore it is said, "Son, be not a liar, for falsehood leads to theft." | My child, do not become a liar, since the act of lying leads to theft |

This example (example 1) slightly varies but remains close enough to consider the Didache as a source for Clement. Clement of Alexandria appears to use Did. 3.5 or at least utilizes a Two Ways tractate similar to Did. 3.5.[50] Clement quotes this material in a rather peculiar way. He frames the argument (i.e., not to become a thief) as a quotation rooted in scripture (ὑπὸ τῆς γραφῆς). Thus, in this way, Clement correlates the saying to γραφή, and if the quotation is from Did. 3.5, then a Two Ways tractate (and possibly the Didache) is being used as Scripture.

It is highly possible that Clement of Alexandria simply reflects upon the Decalogue. However, all three Clement texts utilize the expression οὐ παιδοφθορήσεις, a phrase that is strikingly absent from the Decalogue, yet it appears in the Didache. So, the Decalogue material along with παιδοφθορήσεις suggest that Clement possesses a closer relationship with the Didache material than with the Decalogue.

---

49. GCS 23.64.
50. So, Niederwimmer, *Didache*, 7.

*Example 2: Clement of Alexandria, Protr. 10.108,*[51] *Paed. 2.10, 89.1,*[52] *Strom. 3.4, 36.5,*[53] *and Did. 2.2–3.*

| Clement of Alexandria, Protr. 10.108.5 | Clement of Alexandria, Paed. 2.10, 89.1 | Clement of Alexandria, Strom. 3.4, 36.5 | Did. 2.2–3 |
|---|---|---|---|
| οὐ πορνεύσεις, οὐ μοιχεύσεις, οὐ παιδοφθορήσεις | οὐ μοιχεύσεις, οὐκ εἰδωλολατρήσεις, οὐ παιδοφθορήσεις, οὐ κλέψεις, οὐ ψευδομαρτυρήσεις | τὸ μὲν οὐ μοιχεύσεις καὶ οὐ παιδοφθορήσεις καὶ ὅσα εἰς ἐγκράτειαν συμβάλλεται | Οὐ φονεύσεις, οὐ μοιχεύσεις, οὐ παιδοφθορήσεις, οὐ πορνεύσεις, οὐ κλέψεις, οὐ μαγεύσεις, οὐ φαρμακεύσεις, οὐ φονεύσεις τέκνον ἐν φθορᾷ οὐδὲ γεννηθὲν7 ἀποκτενεῖς. οὐκ ἐπιθυμήσεις τὰ τοῦ πλησίον· (3) οὐκ ἐπιορκήσεις, οὐ ψευδομαρτυρήσεις |
| You shall not commit sexual immorality, you shall not commit adultery, you shall not corrupt boys. | You shall not commit adultery, you shall not worship idols, you shall not corrupt boys, you shall not steal, you shall not bear false witness. | The *commands* "you shall not commit adultery" and "you shall not corrupt boys" and "all the others come together for self-control." | (2) Do not murder, do not commit adultery, do not [sexually] corrupt a child, do not commit fornication, do not steal, do not practice magic, do not engage in sorcery, do not kill a child in the womb nor kill [a child] having been born, do not covet the things of your neighbor, (3) do not swear falsely, do not give false testimony, do not speak evil, do not remember evil. |

51. GCS 13.77.
52. GCS 13.211.
53. GCS 23.212.

## Origen of Alexandria

Another example similar to Clement also appears in the Alexandrian tradition. Origen of Alexandria (*De Princ.* 3.2.7[54]) utilizes an expression similar to Did. 3.10. A problem arises as to the probability of Origen actually using the Didache. Because this expression appears in the Two Ways section, Origen may mention this expression with or without awareness of a Two Ways tractate (cf. Barn. 19.6).

| Origen of Alexandria, *De Princ.* 3.2.7 | Barn. 19.6 | Did. 3.10 |
| --- | --- | --- |
| *Propterea docet nos scriptura divinia Omnia quae accidunt nobis tamquam a deo illata suscipere, scientes quod sine deo nihil fit* | τὰ συμβαίνοντά σοι ἐνεργήματα ὡς ἀγαθὰ προσδέξῃ, εἰδὼς ὅτι ἄνευ θεοῦ οὐδὲν γίνεται | τὰ συμβαίνοντά σοι ἐνεργήματα ὡς ἀγαθὰ προσδέξῃ, εἰδὼς ὅτι ἄτερ θεοῦ οὐδὲν γίνεται |
| That is why divine Scripture teaches us to receive everything that happens to us as coming from God, knowing that without God nothing comes to be. | Receive the things that happen to you as good, knowing that nothing happens without God. | Receive the things that happen to you as good, knowing that nothing happens apart from God. |

## Eusebius, *Hist. eccl.* 3.25

Eusebius, *Hist. eccl.* 3.25.4: "Among the books which are not genuine must be reckoned the Acts of Paul, the work entitled the Shepherd, The Apocalypse of Peter, and in addition to them the letter called of Barnabas and the so-called Teachings of the Apostles. And in addition, as I said, the Revelation of John, if this view prevail. For as I said, some reject it, but others count it among the Recognized Books."[55]

Eusebius of Caesarea's canonical list helpfully reflects upon the works accepted by the Church as canon and delimits other texts that do not meet canonical status. Eusebius provides a four-tiered structure whereby three of

---

54. GCS 5.255.

55. A translation of Eusebius and critical texts are listed by Gallagher and Meade, *Canon Lists from Early Christianity*, 102.

the four categories are received and helpful literature whereas one category consists of rejected literature.

In Eusebius's four-fold rubric, the Didache (τῶν ἀποστόλων αἱ λεγόμεναι Διδαχαί) appears in category three, νόθος (illegitimate).[56] Eusebius's four categories for canonical Christian literature are: (1) Recognized Books (ὁμολογούμενα), (2) Disputed Books (ἀντιλεγόμενα), (3) Rejected Books (νόθος), and, (4) Heretical Books.[57] Eusebius distinguishes between groups two and three, and then group four. By doing so, category three (including the Didache) qualifies as recognized and useful material for the Christian communities. Eusebius attributes orthodoxy to categories 1–3.[58] Canonical Category three, though orthodox, was not regarded as canon but was still regarded by a variety of Church Fathers as useful and beneficial.[59]

I am more willing to affirm the presence of the Didache in Eusebius's canon list than a broad reference to a Two Ways tractate. Eusebius mentions both the "so-called" Didache (αἱ λεγόμεναι Διδαχαί) and the "one being called" the Epistle of Barnabas (ἡ φερομένη Βαρναβᾶ ἐπιστολή) in immediate relation to one another. In addition to Barnabas, the Didache appears alongside of the Shepherd of Hermas. The following consists of the books listed within category three (νόθος):

1. Acts of Paul
2. Shepherd of Hermas
3. Apocalypse of Peter
4. Epistle of Barnabas
5. Didache
6. Apocalypse of John (also listed in category 1)
7. Gospel according to the Hebrews

---

56. On νόθος, consult Nienhuis, *Not By Paul Alone*, 65–68. Although νόθος is pejoratively used in other places in Eusebius, Nienhuis argues that no reason exists to see this negatively and argues that this term is part of the canonization process. Simply, as Nienhuis suggests, the term signifies that the work is not legitimate as a canonical work. LSJ s.v. νόθος; Lampe s.v. νόθος.

57. Gallagher and Meade offer an explanation of the Eusebian categories found in Eusebius, *Hist. eccl.* 3.25.1–7. Gallagher and Meade, *Canon Lists from Early Christianity*, 108–9.

58. Gallagher and Meade, *Canon Lists from Early Christianity*, 106; Nienhuis, *Not By Paul Alone*, 66.

59. Kruger, *Canon Revisited*, 268.

## Athanasius, *Festal Letter* 39

Athanasius, *Ep. fest.* 39.20: "But for the sake of greater accuracy, I add this, writing from necessity. There are other books, outside of the preceding, which have not been canonized, but have been prescribed by the ancestors to be read to those who newly join us and want to be instructed in the word of piety: the Wisdom of Solomon, the Wisdom of Sirach, Esther, Judith, Tobit, the book called Teaching of the Apostles, and the Shepherd."[60]

Athanasius's *Festal Letter* 39 serves as another document that points to the formation of the canon in early Christianity. This letter lists books in the canonical Old and New Testaments. Strictly for our purposes, Athanasius mentions the Didache as useful for catechumen instruction.[61]

A number of books, although not necessarily canon, function as texts for early piety and theological formation for the early Christian communities. Athanasius lists a number of works beyond the Christian canon that contribute to catechizing new persons joining the community. These books include Jewish and Christian literature, as seen in the following list:

1. Wisdom of Solomon
2. Wisdom of Sirach
3. Esther
4. Judith
5. Tobit
6. Didache (Διδαχή καλουμένη τῶν ἀποστόλων)
7. Shepherd of Hermas

## Rufinus, *Expositio symboli* 36[62]

Rufinus presents a canon list quite similar to Athanasius's list of books. He mentions texts that are recognized as canon and followed by a list of books for the benefit of the Church. Rufinus mentions,

---

60. A translation of Athanasius and critical texts are listed by Gallagher and Meade, *Canon Lists from Early Christianity*, 124–25.

61. Within Ps.-Athanasius *Synops. script. sacr.* 76, the Did. appears in a canonical list as Διδαχή ἀποστόλων.

62. CCSL 20.171.

> *alii libri . . . qui non canonici, sed ecclesiasitici a maioribus appelati sunt*

> Trans: "other books . . . which by most are called non-canonical but ecclesiastical"

Then, Rufinus lists a number of books that fit within these non-canonical but ecclesiastical books, including the Two Ways. He describes how the Church should desire to read these additional books and, as a result, be strengthened in their faith.

> *quae omnia legi quidem in ecclesiis voluerunt, non tamen proferri ad auctoritatem ex his fidei confirmandam. Ceteras vero scripturas apochryphas nominarunt, quas in ecclesia legi noluerunt.*

> Trans: "All of which they desired to be read in the churches, not, however, in order to thereby support the faith. But they mention other apocryphal writings which they did not want read in the church."

Rufinus lists three books that fit into this additional category.

1. The Shepherd of Hermas (*libellus qui dicitur Pastoris sive Hermae*; "a little book called 'The Pastor' or 'of Hermas'")
2. The Two Ways (*et his qui appelatur Duae viae*; "and the one that is called the 'Two Ways'")
3. Sentence according to Peter (*vel Iudicium secundum Petrum*; "or 'Sentences according to Peter'")

As it pertains to our study of the Didache, this list is problematic on many counts.[63] First, to what does *Duae viae* refer? It is possible that the *Duae viae* refers to a general Two Ways tractate or the Didache. Second, the conjunctions *et* and *vel* for books two and three present an interpretive problem. It could be that the "Sentences" is another rendition of the Two Ways and Rufinus only mentions two books. Or Rufinus mentions the "Sentences" as a distinct third book.

---

63. See Robert Aldrige's article that explores more of the relationship between Peter's sentences and the Two Ways. Aldridge, "Peter and the 'Two Ways,'" 233–64.

# Ps.-Cyprian.

## Example 1: Ps.-Cyprian De aleat. 4[64] and Did. 14.2; 15.3b

The following Latin tradition offers an intriguing witness. A single section in *De aleatoribus* combines Did. 14.2 and 15.3b.

| Ps.-Cyprian *De aleat.* 4 | Did. 14.2 | Did. 15.3b |
|---|---|---|
| *Et in doctrinis apostolorum: si quis frater delinguit in ecclesia et non paret [v.l. apparet] legi, hic nec colligatur [v.l. colligitur], donec paenitentia agat, et non recipiatur, ne inquinetur et inpediatur oratio vestra* | πᾶς δὲ ἔχων τὴν ἀμφιβολίαν μετὰ τοῦ ἑταίρου αὐτοῦ μὴ συνελθέτω ὑμῖν, ἕως οὗ διαλλαγῶσιν, ἵνα μὴ κοινωθῇ ἡ θυσία ὑμῶν. | καὶ παντὶ ἀστοχοῦντι κατὰ τοῦ ἑτέρου, μηδεὶς λαλείτω μηδὲ παρ' ὑμῶν ἀκουέτω, ἕως οὗ μετανοήσῃ. |
| And in the Teachings of the Apostles: if a brother offends in the church and disobeys the law, let him not be considered until he does penance, nor received, lest he defile and obstruct your prayer. | Let no one who has a quarrel with their companion join you until they have been reconciled so that your sacrifice may not be defiled. | And to any who has a wrong against another, let no one speak [to them] nor hear from them until they have repented. |

This passage from Ps.-Cyprian contains a rather loose quotation of and freely mixes Did. 14.2 and 15.3b. In addition, the introduction to the possible quote models itself after the title of the Didache, "The Teachings of the Apostles." According to Niederwimmer, "This quotation is a welcome proof of the existence of a Latin translation of the Didache (and not merely of the tractate on the 'ways') around 300 (in Africa?), as well as of the title it bore: '*doctrinae apostolorum*.'"[65]

## Example 2: Ps.-Cyprian De centesima, sexagesima, tricesima 14[66] and Did. 6.2

A second example from Ps.-Cyprian contains a possible reference to Did. 6.2.

---

64. CSEL 3.3.96.
65. Niederwimmer, *Didache*, 9.
66. Reitzenstein, "Ps.-Cyprian," 60–90.

| Ps.-Cyprian *De centesima, sexagesima, tricesima* 14 | Did. 6.2 |
|---|---|
| *et alio in loco scriptura haec testatur et admonet dicens: 'Si potes quidem, fili, omnia praecepta domini facere, eris consummatus; sin autem, vel duo praecepta, amare dominum ex totis praecordiis et similem tibi quasi (te ipsum)* | εἰ μὲν γὰρ δύνασαι βαστάσαι ὅλον τὸν ζυγὸν τοῦ κυρίου, τέλειος ἔσῃ· εἰ δ' οὐ δύνασαι, ὃ δύνῃ, τοῦτο ποίει. |
| And at another place this scripture bears witness and admonishes, with words, "If you are able, son, to do all the commandments of the Lord, you will be perfect; but if only one or two commandments, love the Lord with all your heart and those like you as [yourself]." | For if you are able to bear the whole yoke of the Lord, you will be perfect. But if you are unable, do what you are able. |

Ps.-Cyprian's tradition labels this material as Scripture. It could be possible that Ps.-Cyprian's use of *scriptura* references the "double love" command, but it is not totally impossible that *scriptura* refers to a modified form of Did. 6.2.

## Date and Provenance of the Didache

As I attempt to provide a dating schema for the Didache, it will immediately reveal a domino effect of problems, assumptions about provenance, presuppositions about the text and source influences of the Didache, and much more. With these critical questions, the most that can be present are probable guesses—and, hopefully, educated guesses at best.[67] Huub van de Sandt and David Flusser lucidly identify this problem when they express, "In making a statement about the date and place of origin of the Didache, no answer can

---

67. I do not share the exact skepticism of Andrew Gregory, here, but I am quite open to how he expresses these concerns. He notes, "There is widespread recognition that there continued to be Jewish followers of Jesus throughout the second century CE and beyond who continued to follow Jewish law and whose practices and beliefs may have been quite different from those of other followers of Jesus. Thus it matters less precisely when or where the Didache was located, because there should be little difficulty in positing a Jewish-Christian community made up of the ideal readers that its text would appear to imply *at some location* in the eastern Mediterranean world (whether it be Egypt, Asia Minor, Palestine, or Syria) *at some point* between the middle of the first and the end of the second or even the beginning of the third century CE." Gregory, "Reflections on the Didache," 124.

pretend to be better than a reasonable guess. The many differing opinions show how meager and puzzling are the clues given by the Didache."[68]

## Available Options in Didache Scholarship

The dates and provenance of the Didache vary in scholarship. Furthermore, some suggest the Didache is a coherent whole and reflects a static moment.[69] However, others are more willing to observe the composite additions to the Didache and thereby see development in the composition process.[70] Both of these text presuppositions affect the given date about the Didache. Among Didache Scholars, a gap of 100 years roughly comprises the divergent opinions. Aaron Milavec has documented some of these dates for the Didache that range between 70–165 CE.[71] Audet suggested a dating window of 50 and 70 CE.[72] Alan Garrow has creatively suggested a pre-Matthean date for the Didache, which compares to other first-century pieces of literature.[73] Some have argued for dates that range throughout the second century.[74] According to Draper, a window to date the general formation of the Didache coalesces as a pre-Matthean source up through the mid-second century: 50–150 CE.[75]

Clayton Jefford has assumed a different line of inquiry that compares the composition of the Didache in concert with Matthew. He presents a three-fold dating taxonomy as follows. First, the Didache was composed

---

68. van de Sandt and Flusser, *Didache*, 48.

69. Varner, *Way of the Didache*; Milavec, *Didache: Faith, Hope & Life*; Milavec, "Pastoral Genius of the Didache," 89–125.

70. Garrow, *Matthew's Dependence on the Didache*; Pardee, *Genre and Development of the Didache*.

71. Consider Milavec for a brief history of scholarship on the dating of the Did. Milavec, *Didache: Faith, Hope, & Life*, 695–98.

72. Audet, *La Didachè*, 199; Varner, *Way of the Didache*, 4. Varner offers five specific reasons to affirm a group of Jewish-Christians in the generation following 70 CE: (1) the primitive simplicity of the Didache's teaching about the person and work of Jesus; (2) the absence of any warning about specific doctrinal aberrations; (3) the continued existence of itinerant apostles and prophets; (4) a simple pattern for the church's leadership (overseers and deacons); (5) its silence about any persecution experienced by its readers or writers.

73. Consider Garrow's conclusion for concise ways to observe the early composite features of the Did. and potential ways to place the Did. in a first-century setting, even among the "first Christians" as Garrow suggests. Garrow, *Matthew's Dependence on the Didache*, 244–52.

74. van de Sandt and Flusser, *Didache*, 48.

75. Draper, "Puzzle or Wild Goose Chase?" 530.

after Matthew so that the Didache is able to utilize a literary form of Matthew or Matthean traditions.[76] Second, the Didache predates Matthew's composition. So, if dependency exists, Matthew takes literary cues from the Didache.[77] Third, the two texts were composed, more or less, during the same time. It is possible, then, that both writers are aware of each other or they draw from a similar oral tradition—even extending to the redactional process of both Didache and Matthew.[78]

To provide a date for the Didache and to determine a given provenance still remains rather difficult, and it is nearly impossible to please all parties. So, I want to suggest a few methodological factors for consideration, and then list my presuppositions about date and provenance. Methodologically, one must distinguish the difference between the source traditions of the Didache and the composite redactions when trying to date the Didache. In other words, some material in the Didache might pre-date the actual Didache (cf. *Duae viae*). So, even if Didache material pre-dates the Didache, to use Arius's expression, "there was a time when the Didache was not," even though material later found in the Didache previously existed. Additionally, constellations of geographical and theological cues likewise appear.[79] For example, what geographical region exists to encompass the moving water for baptisms (Did. 7.1–4)? Does the Didache community use "hypocrite" in the same way that first-century Christians used the term (Did. 8.1–2)? When the Didache mentions "Gospel," is the *kerygma* or a codex in mind, or something else?[80]

## My Presuppositions about Date and Provenance

In addition to these methodological considerations, I offer the following presuppositions. (1) First, I see a general correspondence between the Didache and the Gospel of Matthew—which, by no means, serves as a novel feature.[81] This correspondence affects both dating and provenance. Contra Garrow's unique thesis, I do not see the Didache being composed

---

76. Jefford, "Social Locators," 245.

77. So Garrow, *Matthew's Dependence on the Didache*; Jefford, "Social Locators," 245–46.

78. So Draper, "The Didache in Modern Research," 18–19; Jefford, "Social Locators," 246.

79. van de Sandt and Flusser helpfully document some of these theological and literary cues. van de Sandt and Flusser, *Didache*, 49–52.

80. Kelhoffer, "ΕΥΑΓΓΕΛΙΟΝ as a Reference to 'Gospel,'" 1–34.

81. Jefford, "Glue of the Matthew-Didache Tradition," 8–23.

prior to Matthew but the Didache written concurrently with or after the composition of Matthew. Thus, the date of Matthew's Gospel will inform the date of the Didache.

(2) Along with the majority of Didache scholarship, I affirm that the Didache is generally a composite text. At this point in my thinking (still somewhat nascent on this present issue), I really have no systemic disagreements with Nancy Pardee's reconstruction.[82] My particularly agnostic tendency emerges when these arguments are pressed to encompass microliterary expressions and *where* these composite features occur.

Therefore, related to the previous presupposition, (3) I see no reason for the Didache to be written in a single setting. This premise affects the dating of the text. The question, "at what point does the Didache *become* Didache?" really matters. To further complicate this problem, the Didache may not overnight become the "Didache" but will most likely "become Didache" over time. So, a dating "window" seems like a more viable option.

As it relates to the textual stability of the Didache, H54 is a rather late MS and is really the only document that we have to assess a second-century setting. Thus, (4) given the divergent years between the eleventh-century H54 and the possible second-century social setting of the Didache, I hold loosely any date given to the Didache. Until more Didache MS(S) are found, we have to make historical judgments about a second-century setting with a text nearly 900 years later.

Therefore, (5) to provide a specific date for the Didache may not be the most helpful approach. Rather, to speak of a "window" for the Didache seems far more palatable for me. I assume the majority of Didache scholarship and essentially affirm the mean of diverging opinions on the date. For the sake of the commentary and my surrounding arguments, I assume a window of 80–110 CE when the Didache *becomes Didache*—even if composite additions and redactions from the community may appear in subsequent generations. That is, the core of the Didache appears in this window, although I remain open to allowing composite additions to the text in subsequent years. And, I assign Antioch or the northern regions of Palestine as the given provenance.[83] Bart Ehrman simply and concisely sums up the date of the Didache to sometime around the year 100 CE:

---

82. Pardee, *Genre and Development of the Didache*.

83. To affirm a Palestinian provenance has fallen out of vogue among recent scholarship. Palestine location was associated with early British scholarship. According to Jefford and Pardee, and I would generally affirm these presuppositions, the Did., Matt, and Antioch providence share the following points of contact: (1) prominence given to the double commandment to love God and neighbor; (2) a baptismal trinitarian formula; (3) shared wording of the Lord's Prayer; (4) similar "M" material in Matt 7:6a and

The teaching of the two paths may have been taken over from a Jewish (or Jewish-Christian) source written as early as the mid-first century; the church order seems to presuppose a situation prior to the second century, before internal church structures were widely in place; the apocalyptic discourse could have been composed almost any time during the first two centuries. As to the date of the Didachist himself, opinions again vary, but most would put the time of his composition sometime around the year 100, possibly a decade or so later.[84]

## Structural Overview of the Didache

The structure of the Didache is also more complex than I would want it to be. Even among the more recent works on the Didache, available options lack unanimity on the structure of the Didache. This problem can be the result of complex composite layers or the difficulty in tracing how smaller sections relate to one another.

Rather than providing a single outline, I have highlighted the outlines of Clare Rothschild, Klaus Wengst, and Nancy Pardee prior to offering my own outline of the Didache, which I will use for the remainder of the commentary. This overview seeks to refrain from creating an internal debate about the structure of the Didache but to demonstrate how even those invested in the study of early Christianity still cannot agree on the essential structures and divisions of the Didache.

My outline will serve as the base of the commentary, but it will be helpful to list and briefly comment upon other outlines first. As seen rather quickly, clear agreements and disagreements surface among the various structures. A helpful literary structure reveals interpretive and exegetical decisions based upon topical, linguistic, and argumentative developments. According to Niederwimmer, the Didache consists of "four clearly separate sections."[85] Although my literary divisions cohere with a four-fold division, it remains clearly observable that none of the subsequent structures cohere with this

---

Did. 9.5b; (5) the signs of the end and partial resurrection cohere with the Matthean Olivet Discourse; (6) "hypocrites" occurring in settings on prayer and alms; (7) reproving community members in Matt 18:16–17 and Did. 15.3; (8) the instruction on alms, prayers, fasting, and hypocrites. Jefford, "Milieu of Matthew, Didache, and Ignatius," 37; Jefford, "Didache," in *Eerdmans Dictionary*, 345; Jefford, "Reflections on the Role of Jewish Christianity," 147–67; Jefford, "Locating the *Didache*," 39–68; Pardee, "Visualizing the Christian Community," 69–90; Wengst, *Didache*, 61–63.

84. Ehrman, *Apostolic Fathers I*, 411.
85. Niederwimmer, *Didache*, 1.

four-fold structure. Few scholars agree on how to structure or where to place the material in Did. 6, how Did. 11.1–2 functions as a transition between two major sections, and how to frame the material in Did. 14 and 15.

## Clare K. Rothschild

The primary value to Clare Rothschild's structure of the Didache is its simplicity.[86] She clearly identifies the Two Ways morality section and the Sacraments. However, I wonder why Leadership (section V) functions as an independent section that is neither connected to Did. 14 or Did. 15.3–4? Furthermore, I also want to push against the final section, entitled Punishment (section VI), that begins in Did. 15.3 and includes the coming of the Lord, the eschatological figures, and apocalyptic features in Did. 16.

    I. Morality (Did. 1–6)

        I.1. Way of Life: Prescriptions (Did. 1–4)

        I.2. Way of Death: Descriptions + 1 Prescription (Did. 5)

        I.3. Two Ways Summation (Did. 6)

    II. Sacraments (Did. 7–10)

        II.1. Baptism: Fasting Stipulation (Did. 7–8)

        II.2. Eucharist: Baptism Stipulation (Did. 9–10)

    III. Hospitality (Did. 11–13)

        III.1. Teachers (Did. 11.1–2)

        III.2. Apostles (Did. 11.3–6)

        III.3. Prophets (Did. 11.7–12; 13.1–7)

        III.4. Travelers (Did. 12.1–5)

    IV. Weekly Worship: Eucharist (Did. 14)

    V. Leadership: Elect Resident Prophets and Teachers (Did. 15.1–2)

    VI. Punishment (Did. 15.3–16.8)

## Klaus Wengst

For the most part, I nearly agree with Klaus Wengst's structure in every way.[87] The value to Wengst's structure is the inclusion of the Coptic oint-

---

86. Rothschild, *Essays on the Apostolic Fathers*, 178–79.

87. Wengst, *Didache*, 15–16.

ment section (Did. 10.8). However, he does not postulate on the lost ending of the Didache (Did. 16.9ff.).

- I. Ethical Instruction: The Two Ways (Did. 1.1–6.3)
    - I.1. Introduction to the Two Ways (Did. 1.1)
    - I.2. The Way of Life (Did. 1.2–4.14)
    - I.3. The Way of Death (Did. 5.1f.)
    - I.4. Closing Remarks to the Two Ways (Did. 6.1–3)
- II. Liturgical Instruction (Did. 7.1–10.8)
    - II.1. Arrangement for Baptism (Did. 7.1–4)
    - II.2. Arrangement for Fasting (Did. 8.1)
    - II.3. Arrangement for Praying (Did. 8.2f.)
    - II.4. Arrangement for the Eucharist (Did. 9.1–10.7)
    - II.5. Arrangement for the Anointing (Did. 10.8)
- III. Instruction in Dealing with Teachers and Ordinary Christians, who want to travel or settle (Did. 11.1–13.7)
    - III.1. Regarding the Reception of Wandering Teachers (Did. 11.1f.)
    - III.2. Regarding the Dealings with Wandering Apostles and Prophets (Did. 11.3–12)
        - III.2.a. Apostles (Did. 11.4–6)
        - III.2.b. Prophets (Did. 11.7–12)
    - III.3 Regarding the Dealings with Foreign Christians (Did. 12.1–5)
        - III.3.a. Those Passing Through (Did. 12.2)
        - III.3.b. Those Willing to Settle (Did. 12.3–5)
    - III.4. Concerning the Service of the Community towards Those Willing to Settle and the Resident Prophets and Teachers and the Process thereby to maintain (Did. 13.1–7)
- IV. Instruction on Community Life (Did. 14.1–15.4)
    - IV.1. Arrangement for the Sunday meeting (Did. 14.1–3)
    - IV.2. Arrangement for the Election of Bishops and Deacons and How to Deal with Them (Did. 15.1f.)
    - IV.3. Arrangement for Community Discipline (Did. 15.3f.)
- V. Eschatological Instruction: Admonition for Vigilance in view of the Coming of the Lord (Did. 16.1–8)

## Nancy Pardee

Nancy Pardee's structure is by far the most complex and by far the most methodologically thorough.[88] She assumes the broad field of text linguistics and applies this methodology to H54.[89] Any thorough consideration of the Didache's structure will need to consider Pardee's argument. More specifically, she assumes the methodology of delimitation to assess the text as a whole. She defines delimitation markers as "signs within a text that serve to set off its component parts from one another while yet connecting these parts in an overarching structure."[90] She modifies the delimitation markers to contain a three-level hierarchy: pragmatic, semantic, and syntactic markers.[91] For our purposes here, her structure is too complex for non-specialists and generally accessible only to those in the guild. So, I will assume many of her arguments with an attempt to make her research more accessible to a novice.

> I. A Compilation of Instruction on Christian Life and Practice, on Church Rites and on Certain Practical Aspects of Community Life (Did. 1.1–15.4)
>> I.1. Instructions on Christian Life/Practice and on Liturgy (Did. 1.1–11.2)
>>> I.1.a. Instruction on Christian life/Practice, recited prior to Baptism (Did. 1.1–6.3)

---

88. Pardee, *Genre and Development of the Didache*, 96.
89. Pardee, *Genre and Development of the Didache*, 65.
90. Pardee, *Genre and Development of the Didache*, 69.
91. Pardee, *Genre and Development of the Didache*, 74. She offers the following delimitation structure,

I. Pragmatic markers
  a. meta-communicative sentences
  b. substitutions on the meta-leval
II. Semantic markers
  a. episode markers (temporal, local)
  b. change in *dramatis personae*
  c. change in topic via word association
III. Syntactic markers
  a. renominalization
  b. exact repetition of phraseology
  c. change in syntactical style
  d. sentence and text connectors

- I.1.a.α. The Intermediate Stage of the Two Ways (Did. 1.1–6.2)
  - I.1.a.α.1. The Body of the Two Ways (Did. 1.1–5.2)
    - I.1.a.α.1.a. Way of Life (Did. 1.2–4.14)
    - I.1.a.α.1.b. Way of Death (Did. 5.1–2)
  - I.1.a.α.2. The Conclusion of the Recitation/Warning (Did. 6.1–2)
- I.1.a.β. Addition to the Two Ways Teaching (Did. 6.3)
- I.1.b. Instruction on Various Church Rites and Activities (Did. 7.1–11.2)
  - I.1.b.α. Instructions Regarding Baptism and Other Christian Obligations (Did. 7.1–8.3)
    - I.1.b.α.1. Instructions on Performing Baptism (Did. 7.1–4)
    - I.1.b.α.2. Instructions on Fasting (Did. 8.1)
    - I.1.b.α.3. Instructions on Prayer (Did. 8.2–3)
  - I.1.b.β. Instructions on Celebrating the Eucharist (Did. 9.1–10.7)
    - I.1.b.β.1. Instructions for the Meal (Did. 9.2–4)
    - I.1.b.β.2. Prohibition of Meal to Unbaptized (Did. 9.5)
    - I.1.b.β.3. Prayers Following the Meal (Did. 10.1–7)
  - I.1.b.γ. Conclusion (Did. 11.1–2)
- I.2. Instruction Regarding Hospitality to Itinerant Ministers and Travelers, New Settlers in the Community, Obligations to Resident Ministers, Worship, and Selection of Ministers Within the Community (Did. 11.3–15.3)
  - I.2.a. Instructions Regarding Hospitality to Itinerant Ministers, Travelers, and New Settlers, and Obligations to Resident Ministers (Did. 11.3–13.7)
    - I.2.a.α. General Teaching to Act in Accordance with the Gospel (Did. 11.3)
    - I.2.a.β. Specific Instructions Regarding Hospitality to Itinerant Ministers, Prophets, Travelers; Stipulations Regarding Those Who Wish to Settle in the Community (Did. 11.4–13.7)

I.2.b. Miscellaneous Instructions Concerning Worship and Selection of Ministers within the Community (Did. 14.1–15.3)

I.2.b.α. The Command to Meet for Worship and the Necessity of Community Harmony for Worship to be Considered Correctly Performed (Did. 14.1–3)

I.2.b.β. Selection of Overseers/Bishops and Deacons (Did. 15.1–2)

I.2.b.γ. Instruction on Relations with Errant Members (Did. 15.3)

I.3. Conclusion: Always Act According to the Gospel (Did. 15.4)

II. Conclusion in the Form of an Eschatologically Oriented Warning to Maintain Faithful Living (Did. 16.1–8)

## Structure of the Didache

The following is my structure of the Didache and the base by which I read the Didache. I generally see four primary divisions, whereas section three, "Ecclesial and Communal Order," could be divided into two different sections. I do assume Pardee's argument about Did. 6.3 as not part of the Didache's Two Ways, but I place it within the customs section (II). For the sake of additional study, I do include the Coptic section (Did. 10.8) and the lost ending of the apocalypse section (Did. 16.9–12)—I point readers to the section in the commentary where I discuss these features in greater length.

I. Ethical Instruction of the Two-Ways Ethic (Did. 1.1–6.2)

I.1. Introduction to the Two Ways (Did. 1.1)

I.2. The Way of Life (Did. 1.2–4.14)

I.2.a. First Commandment of the Way of Life (Did. 1.2–6)

I.2.b. Second Commandment of the Way of Life (Did. 2.1–7)

I.2.c. *Teknon Sayings:* Flee Every Form of Evil (Did. 3.1–6)

I.2.d. Be Humble and Virtuous to Inherit the World (Did. 3.7–10)

I.2.e. Communal Ecclesial Ethics (Did. 4.1–4)

I.2.f. Giving to Those in Need (Did. 4.5–8)

  I.2.g. Household Code (Did. 4.9–11)
  I.2.h. Covenant Renewal (Did. 4.12–14)
 I.3. The Way of Death (Did. 5.1–2)
 I.4. Conclusion to the Two Ways (Did. 6.1–2)
II. Liturgical Rituals (Did. 6.3–10.7)
 II.1. Concerning Food (Did. 6.3)
 II.2. Concerning Baptism, Fasts, and Prayer (Did. 7.1–8.3)
  II.2.a. Baptismal Instructions (Did. 7.1–4)
  II.2.b. Fasting Instructions (Did. 8.1)
  II.2.c. Prayer Instructions (Did. 8.2–3)
 II.3. Concerning the Eucharist (Did. 9.1–10.7)
  II.3.a. Initial Eucharist Prayer and Stipulations (Did. 9.1–5)
  II.3.b. Final Eucharist Prayer and Stipulations (Did. 10.1–7)
 II.4. [Coptic Addition]: Concerning the Ointment (Did. 10.8)
III. Ecclesial and Communal Order (Did. 11.1–15.4)
 III.1. Conduct for Reception of Outsiders: Teachers, Apostles, and Prophets (Did. 11.1–13.7)
  III.1.a. Concerning Teachers (Did. 11.1–2)
  III.1.b. Concerning Genuine and False Itinerate Apostles and Prophets, and Traveling Christians (Did. 11.3–13.7)
   III.1.b.α. Concerning Apostles and Prophets (Did. 11.3–12)
   III.1.b.β. Examining Traveling Christians (Did. 12.1–5)
   III.1.b.γ. Settling of Genuine Prophets and Provisions for High Priests (Did. 13.1–7)
 III.2. Conduct for Communal Order (Did. 14.1–15.4)
  III.2.a. Additional Instructions for the "Lord's Day": Communal Confession and Eucharist Sacrifice (Did. 14.1–3)
  III.2.b. On the Appointment of Bishops and Deacons (Did. 15.1–2)
  III.2.c. Ethical Orientation in Accordance with the Gospel (Did. 15.3–4)
IV. Eschatological Ethics and Teaching (Did. 16.1–8)

IV.1. Eschatological Moral Conduct (Did. 16.1-2)

IV.2. Motivation: Eschatological Descriptions and Apocalyptic Return of the Lord (Did. 16.3-8)

    IV.2.a. Introduction to the False Prophets and Corrupters (Did. 16.3-4a)

    IV.2.b. Introduction to the World Deceiver (Did. 16.4b)

    IV.2.c. The Fiery Test, Persecution, and Salvation (Did. 16.5)

    IV.2.d. The Signs of Truth and a Partial Resurrection (Did. 16.6-7)

    IV.2.e. The Revelation of the Coming Lord (Did. 16.8)

IV.3. [Lost Ending] (Did. 16.9-12)[92]

---

92. It is very possible to label this "Lost Ending" as IV.2.f. To do so would require a more stable conclusion and ways to assess its discourse structure. I label it IV.3 not exclusively because it is a new subsection but because it is not completely stable to ascertain its exact placement.

# 2

## The Reception of Sacred Scripture in the Didache

### Considering the Canonical Sources and Hermeneutics of the Didachist

SCHOLARS AND STUDENTS OF the New Testament and of early Christianity continue to remain intrigued by early reception of the biblical traditions. For example, the typological reading of Scripture in Melito's *Peri Pascha*, Origen of Alexandria's tri-partite reading in *De Principiis* 4.2.1–4, Irenaeus's ambivalence towards allegorical exegesis in lieu of eschatological readings in *Haer.* 5.35.5, and pro-Nicene theological exegesis. Early Christianity is rife with different hermeneutical and reception patterns.

Our interest here concerns the use of Scripture in H54, the final form of the Didache. As early Christian scholars often begin in Origen's literature or late second-century material and move into the heart of the patristic era,[1] I want to inquire about the salient canonical traditions and their hermeneutical reception among the earliest communities, especially the Didache's reception of canonical traditions.[2]

As the Didache and much of the canonical tradition develop in a similar setting and era, a number of methodological and historical problems arise—many of which I do not seek to answer in this chapter. What material is available to the Didachist and his community during the Didache's composition? What authoritative or sacred status is granted to canonical material in the first-century communities that would cause the Didachist to

---

1. Blowers, "Patristic Interpretation," 81–89; O'Keefe and Reno, *Sanctified Vision*; Boersma, *Scripture as Real Presence*.

2. Paget, "Interpretation of the Bible," 549–83; Bokedal, "Scripture in the Second Century," 43–61; Farkasfalvy, *Inspiration & Interpretation*, 88–119.

use such material? Does the Didachist use available written canonical material, oral traditions, communal memory, or other conventions?

*Wirkungsgeschichte* or the reception history of the Bible observes the *after life* of a given text in a variety of communication media—any act of interpretation whether written, visual, or oral.[3] As texts assume a life of their own, they may transcend an authorial and contextual meaning, and as a result, broaden the variable meanings of a text.[4]

As one considers the influence of sacred literature and other sources upon the composition of the Didache, a number of potential sources emerge. For example, Clayton Jefford suggests that Sirach could be the "glue" that links the Didache-Matthew traditions.[5] John Welch has masterfully demonstrated how the Sermon on the Mount influences and appears within the Didache's material.[6] Joseph Verheyden, Vicki Balabanski, John Kloppenborg, and Jonathan Draper have creatively accentuated how the Olivet Discourse underscores the mini-apocalypse in Did. 16.[7] Furthermore, smaller occurrences of source influences also emerge. Consider the following examples and phrases: "fiery trial" (1 Pet 4:12//Did. 16.5), the Decalogue (Did. 2), "bless the ones persecuting you" (Rom 12:14//Did. 1.3), and the trinitarian formulae in Did. 7.1-4 (Matt 28:18). These examples do not solely imply any detectable literary dependency but they demonstrate some parallel biblical traditions and how the Didachist appropriates source traditions.[8]

Thus, I ask my primary question: what is the reception history of biblical tradition in the Didache? I ask this question, not as a means to uncover the meanings of biblical traditions but to observe the effect of biblical

---

3. For the complexity of such discipline, consult: Evans, *Tradition and Biblical Interpretation*, 1–25. I reflect a similar idea portrayed by Clark, minus the adjective "ascetic." She says, "So different are ancient and modern (i.e., historical-critical) exegetical modes that only occasionally will I contrast interpretations devised by early Christian ascetic writers with those of our contemporaries, who are often keen to locate the 'original' settings of Biblical texts and the 'intentions' of their authors. I am interested rather in the history of the *effects* that Biblical texts produced in late ancient Christian communities, that is, in an asceticized *Wirkungsgeschichte*." Clark, *Reading Renunciation*, 4; Lieb, Mason, and Roberts, "Introduction," 1–10.

4. Parris, *Reception Theory*, xv.

5. Jefford, "Glue of the Matthew-Didache Tradition."

6. Welch, "Sermon on the Mount," 335–61.

7. Verheyden, "Eschatology in the Didache," 193–215; Balabanski, *Eschatology in the Making*; Kloppenborg, "Special Matthaean Tradition," 54–67; Draper, "Eschatology in the Didache," 567–82.

8. For more on possible biblical traditions in the Did., consult: Tuckett, "Didache and the Writings," 83–127.

traditions upon the literary structure and interpretation of the Didache. Do canonical traditions cohere with their original contextual meaning, has their meaning expanded, or has there been a complete change of referent or meaning?[9] As I attempt to answer this primary question and related auxiliary questions, I want to suggest as well that *Wirkungsgeschichte* functions as a better methodology to assess the function of received traditions in the Didache. In this way, interpreters will shift from source influences and "original" settings of the source material to assess the effects of the biblical traditions upon the Didache.

Therefore, the following argument suggests that the Didachist's reception of quoted biblical traditions depicts social, hermeneutical, and ethical readings of the canonical source material. In other words, this biblical material affected the shape of the Didachist's argument in terms of social categories, ethical outcomes, and hermeneutical patterns. Given the examples above about other possible embedded biblical traditions, I will only limit my analysis to those traditions that are more clearly identifiable. The exclusive traditions that I will consider all meet the following criteria:

1. they include an introductory formula (e.g., "as it has been said")

2. they are a canonical tradition

3. they are used in the Didache as a proof-text for an already-existent, internal argument for the Didachist

4. their use reflects an intention by the Didachist to quote a canonical source tradition

Given these criteria, I will only assess the function of four canonical traditions and their effect on the literary argument of the Didache.[10] The only biblical traditions that I consider are Matt 6:9–13, Matt 7:6, Zech 14:5, and Mal 1:11, 14.[11]

---

9. Lanfer offers helpful ideas, although I do not affirm all of his introduction, and the praxis and benefit of reception history. The final form of a text may or may not offer a singular meaning or identify authorial intent, when received by other traditions, but they may contain opportunity for the interpreter to identify "symbolic capital." Lanfer, *Remembering Eden*, 5–7.

10. My argument depends upon a prior methodology to adjudicate canonical traditions. This suggestion, however, does not imply the contrary in that there are other "less clear" traditions. Rather, the traditions excluded (1) are typically embedded within the Didachist's argument, (2) literarily and thematically allude to a particular text, and (3) appear without a quotation formula (e.g., "as it has been said").

11. I do not consider the source tradition in Did. 1.6. It remains quite debated what source might serve as the foundation of such a quote. Even though the Didachist uses a quotation formula, scholars remain a bit perplexed as to its actual source. Giambrone,

## Reception History, Intertextuality, and Literary Identity

Christopher Edwards classifies the language for reception history in biblical studies.[12] He moves away from standard categories of quotation, allusion, and echo for two reasons.[13] First, such language tends to assume textual sources as opposed to oral influence. Second, these categories may presume to judge what the author intends.

Thus, for the present study, I will use reception history that seeks to build upon Edwards's research.[14] First, reception history permits both a literary and a non-literary relationship to previous canonical material. One is not compelled to choose between literary and non-literary means. According to Roberts and Rowland, "*Wirkungsgeschichte* is an attempt to be truly diachronic and to appreciate the history of texts through time as a key to their interpretation. It contests the idea that *exegesis should be confined to written explication of texts* or to the views of a few academic exegetes."[15] Especially for Didache studies, this approach permits oral, aural, and memory as valid categories of reception.[16] For example, by solely focusing on the literary source, we may overlook the social and liturgical effect of the Lord's Prayer (Did. 8.2–3). Second, reception history focuses on the diachronic effect of biblical tradition; and in this present case, reception history focuses upon the influence of the biblical traditions throughout the composite phases of the Didache. This particular focus permits both hermeneutical and non-hermeneutical patterns to emerge.[17] Both of these ideas will help shift a

---

"According to the Commandment," 448–65.

12. Edwards, *Ransom Logion*, 16–17.

13. For more on the language of "intertextuality" and how this method is used in biblical studies, consider the following sources. Hays, *Echoes of Scripture in the Letters of Paul*; Hays, *Echoes of Scripture in the Gospels*; Moyise, "Intertextuality and the Study of the Old Testament," 14–41; Allen, "Introduction," 3–16; Huizenga, "Intertextuality and Allegory," 17–35; Foster, "Echoes without Resonance," 96–111.

14. The field of *reception theory* is quite difficult to navigate. Here is a sampling of texts that inform and are still informing my journey in this discipline. Breed, *Nomadic Text*; most notably the introduction by Jonathan Roberts and "Memory, Imagination" by Carruthers in *Oxford Handbook of the Reception History of the Bible*; Bockmuehl, *Seeing the Word*; also, volume 33 of the *Journal for the Study of the New Testament* devotes an entire issue (no. 2) to the concept of reception history. Roberts and Rowland, "Introduction," 131–36; Knight, "Reception History, Reception Theory," 137–46; Elliot, "Effective-History," 161–73.

15. Roberts and Rowland, "Introduction," 132.

16. Memory was a crucial tool in ancient Christianity. Consider the function of memory in Jerome, *Letter* 60.10. For a meaningful article on the topic of memory, even extending up to the Middle Ages, consult Carruthers, "Memory, Imagination," 214–34.

17. Varner's essay on the use of the OT and NT in the Did. resembles much of what

focus from source criticism to the effect of the sources in the structure and ideology of the Didache's community.

Some Didache scholars agree with the interests of intertextuality. First, a broad consensus emerges at the macro level regarding what specific traditions influence the Didache (i.e., use of Jewish tradition, Jesus tradition).[18] Second, some agree about how to regard the composite form of the Didache and the process by which we may assess the biblical traditions.[19]

However, I too observe a stalemate in the reception and intertextual attempts in Didache scholarship. First, some predominantly discuss the literary dependency[20]—with some exceptions.[21] Andrew Gregory and Christopher Tuckett comment on literary dependency.

> Any discussion of the possible dependence of one writing on another implies some degree of confidence that we have at least sufficient access to the form in which those texts were originally written to make meaningful judgments about possible literary relationships between them.[22]

---

I am asking as well. Up to this point in Did. scholarship, questions of hermeneutics are not necessarily the focal point of discussion. Rather, source and tradition identification consumes much of the energies. Varner, "Didache's Use of the Old and New," 127–51.

18. For example, consider the pattern set forth in Draper, "Attitude of the Didache to the Gentiles," 242–58; Zangenberg, "Social and Religious Milieu of the Didache," 50–54.

19. The following works will prove helpful: Pardee, *Genre and Development of the Didache*; Garrow, *Matthew's Dependence on the Didache*.

20. Tuckett, "Synoptic Tradition in the Didache," 92–128; These concerns are not solely limited to Did. scholarship but also extend to broader Patristic scholarship. Gregory provides two different possibilities when identifying previous traditions. He labels them "writer-centred" and "reader-centred." By writer-centred, of which Gregory models, "I mean one in which consideration is given as to whether an author is referring to an early text." Thus, by reader-centred, "I mean an approach which addresses the question of whether the reader or the hearer of a text is aware that the author of that text is drawing on an earlier text." Gregory, *Reception of Luke and Acts*, 5–7; Also note how Petersen makes "normative" versus "non-normative" comments dependent upon literary text traditions. "Instead of retrojecting the text of a modern critical edition of the New Testament into the second century, and then measuring Patristic parallels against it, a 'non-normative' approach acknowledges our ignorance of the form of the text (and, indeed, even the name of the document[s]) used by early writers." Thus, Petersen's larger argument depends upon literary symmetry. Petersen, "Patristic Biblical Quotations," 411–19.

21. Varner, "Didache's Use of the Old and New"; Draper, "Resurrection and Zechariah 14.5," 155–79.

22. Gregory and Tuckett, "Reflections on Method," 62.

However, I want to suggest that social memory, communal liturgical practices, and oral tradition may also provide additional reasons why the Didache coheres with canonical traditions.[23]

Second, few Didache scholars interpret the received tradition because of the overt attention to source dependency.[24] Didache scholarship often seeks to ascertain the source of such a tradition and minimally comments on *how* such traditions affect the argument and structure of the Didache. This lacuna exists because the signs of literary dependency and temporal antecedent traditions need to appear prior to interpreting the text. Additionally, the evolutionary development and composite nature of the Didache often abate opportunity to consider these elements, too.[25] Asked rhetorically, if the Didachist desires—and I do not claim to know the authorial intent—to use a textual tradition but needs to adapt wording, word length, or any expression of a source tradition, are they able to do so? Is the Didachist able to modify a previous text in order to cohere with an internal argument?[26] To these rhetorical inquiries, I suggest that *Wirkungsgeschichte* and reception history are ways to make advances within Didache scholarship.[27] Yes, adjudicating the source traditions is

---

23. Gregory is not dismissive of possible oral traditions, but to identify oral traces lack a stable methodology to identify traditions. Gregory and Tuckett, "Reflections on Method," 15.

24. For example, consider Jefford's comments, "From the outset it is assumed that if the sayings which appear in the Didache can be placed in the wider tradition of first-century sayings materials, both with respect to the Sayings Gospel Q and in relationship to the broader biblical canon, then the sayings will serve as a valid source for a description of the community that maintained the sayings tradition itself" (Jefford, *Sayings of Jesus*, 21). A few exceptions exist for this claim. Take for example the following articles: Draper, "Resurrection and Zechariah 14.5"; Varner, "Didache's Use of the Old and New."

25. For more discussion on the composite nature of the Did., consult Jefford, *Sayings of Jesus*, 20. Also, Garrow presents a fine example of such a point. Because Did. 9.5b appears to be an addendum to a previous edition of the Did., the addendum may prohibit the reader from reading 9.5b as part of the literary argument. Garrow, *Matthew's Dependence on the Didache*, 26; Niederwimmer, *Didache*, 42–54; Draper, "Jesus Tradition in the Didache," 76.

26. Garrow argues that Did. 9.5 is part of later redactional additions and therefore part of a later composite development of the Did. text. This position influences, moreover, how Garrow observes the function of the Matthean tradition. Garrow, *Matthew's Dependence on the Didache*, 125–26.

27. We too could add to these reasons. One reason would be the multiplicity of possible traditions that a subsequent tradition utilizes. In this case, the most primitive saying sets the trajectory of meanings. For example, the prohibition of eating the Eucharist (Did. 9.5) may correspond to previous traditions in Lev, Qumran traditions, and, subsequently, Matthew's Gospel. For Draper, it remains unclear whether or not Matthew is being used because of the previous similar traditions. Thus, the more

helpful, but at some point, we need to assess *how* these reframed and re-oriented traditions are *received* within the Didache.

Therefore, reception history offers more fluidity and flexibility than other means of locating biblical tradition. Reception history will observe both hermeneutical and non-hermeneutical patterns of received source traditions. Also, it will permit textual and non-textual influences upon the Didache when scholars identify previous source traditions.

## Reception History of Biblical Tradition in the Didache

The following examples will examine the effect of quoted biblical traditions. The following will comment on the Didachist's use of Matt 6:9–13, Matt 7:6, Mal 1:11, 14, and Zech 14:5. My remarks will point to some literary symmetry between the Didache and canonical traditions, but I will dedicate my analysis to the result of the canonical traditions within the literary and contextual argument of the Didachist.

### Didache 8.2 and Matthew 6:9–13

| Did. 8.2 | Matt 6.9–13 |
|---|---|
| μηδὲ προσεύχεσθε ὡς οἱ ὑποκριταί, ἀλλ' ὡς ἐκέλευσεν ὁ κύριος ἐν τῷ εὐαγγελίῳ αὐτοῦ | |
| οὕτως προσεύχεσθε | Οὕτως οὖν προσεύχεσθε ὑμεῖς |
| Πάτερ ἡμῶν ὁ ἐν τῷ οὐρανῷ | Πάτερ ἡμῶν ὁ ἐν τοῖς οὐρανοῖς |
| ἁγιασθήτω τὸ ὄνομά σου | ἁγιασθήτω τὸ ὄνομά σου |
| ἐλθέτω ἡ βασιλεία σου | ἐλθέτω ἡ βασιλεία σου |
| γενηθήτω τὸ θέλμά σου | γενηθήτω τὸ θέλημά σου |
| ὡς ἐν οὐρανῷ καὶ ἐπὶ γῆς | ὡς ἐν οὐρανῷ καὶ ἐπὶ γῆς |
| τὸν ἄρτον ἡμῶν τὸν ἐπιούσιον δὸς ἡμῖν σήμερον | τὸν ἄρτον ἡμῶν τὸν ἐπιούσιον δὸς ἡμιν σήμερον |

---

primitive tradition, according to Draper, maintains the trajectory of the tradition. Draper, "Attitude of the Didache to the Gentiles," We could add to these reasons too. One such reason would be the multiplicity of possible traditions a subsequent tradition is utilizing. In this case, the most primitive saying sets the trajectory of meanings. For example, the prohibition of eating the Eucharist (Did 9:5).

| Did. 8.2 | Matt 6.9–13 |
|---|---|
| καὶ ἄφες ἡμῖν τὴν ὀφειλὴν ἡμῶν | καὶ ἄφες ἡμῖν τὰ ὀφειλήματα ἡμῶν |
| ὡς καὶ ἡμεῖς ἀφίεμεν τοῖς ὀφειλέταις ἡμῶν | ὡς καὶ ἡμεῖς ἀφήκαμεν τοῖς ὀφειλέταις ἡμῶν |
| καὶ μὴ εἰσενέγκῃς ἡμᾶς εἰς πειρασμόν | καὶ μὴ εἰσενέγκῃς ἡμᾶς εἰς πειρασμόν |
| ἀλλὰ ῥῦσαι ἡμᾶς ἀπὸ τοῦ πονηροῦ | ἀλλὰ ῥῦσαι ἡμᾶς ἀπὸ τοῦ πονηροῦ |
| ὅτι σοῦ ἐστιν ἡ δύναμις καὶ ἡ δόξα εἰς τοὺς αἰῶνας | |
| (2) Nor pray like the hypocrites but, as the Lord has commanded in his gospel, pray in like manner: "Our Father who is in heaven, hallowed be your name, let your kingdom come, let your will be done as in heaven and upon earth. Give to us this day our daily bread and forgive us our debt as we also forgive our debtors and do not lead us into temptation. But deliver us from the evil one. For yours is the power and the glory forever." | Therefore, pray thusly, "Our Father who is in heaven, hallowed be your name, let your kingdom come, let your will be done as in heaven and upon earth. Give to us daily our sustaining bread, forgive us our debts as we have forgiven our debtors. And do not lead us into temptation, but deliver us from the Evil One." |

The reception of the Lord's Prayer proves more difficult than what a *prima facie* glance may provide.[28] The thematic topics and symmetrical phrases in Did. 8.1–2 insinuate that the Didachist may be generally aware of the Matthean traditions (literary or oral). Yet the liturgy of the prayer (Did. 8.3) indicates a communal memory of the Matthean traditions. Thus, any reception of the Matthean tradition includes a social function as the primary use, and any hermeneutical patterns will be foreground to the Didachist's argument.

The Lord's Prayer occurs in both the Matthean and Lukan tradition (Matt 6:9b–13; Luke 11:2b–4).[29] Didache 8.2b parallels the Matthean tradition with more continuity than the Lukan version of the Lord's Prayer. The Didache matches Matt 6:9b–13 (NA28) nearly 100%. Of the four textual differences, three consist only of spelling discrepancies.

---

28. According to Jefford, determining the source of such prayer proves difficult due to later additions by a redactor and the lack of evidence for dating such an addition. Yet, the added material, according to Jefford, "reflects that of the Matthean Gospel to such an extent that one probably need go no further than the composition of the Matthean text for the source of the Didache's reading." I, however, am not making judgments as to its potential composite form but am making observations of the Didachist's literary argument to opt also for the potential of liturgical use. Jefford, *Sayings of Jesus*, 137–38.

29. See Nijay Gupta's work on the Lord's Prayer: Gupta, *Lord's Prayer*.

Additionally, Did. 7–8 coheres with much of the material in Matt 6. The thematic and textual symmetry hint towards the Didachist being cognizant of the Matthean tradition. The contextual topics of prayer and hypocrites (Did. 8.1–2)[30] mirror the Matthean Sermon on the Mount.[31] Matthew 6:5–18 highlights topics such as the prayer patterns of the hypocrites (vv. 5–7), habits of ethical distinction—pray differently (v. 8), the Lord's Prayer (vv. 9–13), forgiveness (vv. 14–15), and fasting (vv. 16–18). Didache 8 provides a similar list of topics. Enough thematic and textual symmetry exists to suggest that the Didachist is aware of a burgeoning Matthean Gospel or they share a similar compositional setting.

Table 1. Thematic Symmetry between Matt 6 and Didache

| | |
|---|---|
| Secretive Almsgiving (left hand and right hand): Matt 6:3 | Almsgiving: do not withhold your hand: Did. 1.5–6; 4.9 |
| Prayers of the hypocrites: Matt 6:5–7 | Prayers of the hypocrites: Did. 8.1 |
| Do not pray like the hypocrites: Matt 6:8 | Do not pray like the hypocrites: Did. 8.2 |
| Instruction on Prayer: Matt 6:9–13 | Instruction on Prayer: Did. 8.2–3 |
| Instruction on Forgiveness: Matt 6:14–15 | |
| Instruction on Fasting: Matt 6:16–18 | Communal Instruction on Fasting: Did. 7.4 |

Also, the Didachist attributes the prayer to a command of κύριος as found ἐν τῷ εὐαγγελίῳ (Did. 8.2). Because of the already contextual association with the Sermon on the Mount, κύριος refers to Jesus (cf. Did. 9.5; 11.2, 4, 8; 12.1; 14.1; 16.8) and ἐν τῷ εὐαγγελίῳ refers to an emerging authority of the Matthean tradition (cf. Apos. Con. VII, 24).[32]

---

30. Did. 8.1 prohibits fasts on Monday and Thursday so as to refrain sharing the same religious identity as the "hypocrites." To prohibit a fast on these days demarcates a new religious and social identity as compared to these hypocrites. Moreover, Jewish traditions correspond to these two days and are public fasts (cf. *m. Ta'an.* 2.9).

31. See the following for a competing idea: Draper, "Christian Self-Definition," 223–43.

32. Kelhoffer, "ΕΥΑΓΓΕΛΙΟΝ as a Reference to 'Gospel,'" 16–29. Hengel, upon whom I depend, asserts, "Sometimes it is also not easy to decide whether the reference is to a writing or to the living voice of the preaching of Christ" (Hengel, *Four Gospels and the One Gospel*, 64). Pennington, much like Hengel, argues for a both/and solution to the idea of Gospel as both oral and written in early Christianity (Pennington, *Reading the Gospels Wisely*, 5). By the middle of the second century, Justin Martyr recalls the memoirs composed by the apostles (Justin, *1 Apol.* 66).

But what might this imply about how Matthew and the Didache relate to one another? Do these slight differences reflect a purposeful departure from the Matthean tradition? Is it possible to attribute the textual differences to interpretative differences?

## The Heavens

A different spelling of οὐρανός consists of the first difference, namely a change in number: τῷ οὐρανῷ in Did. 8.2 and τοῖς οὐρανοῖς in Matt 6:9b. Jonathan Pennington, in *Heaven and Earth in the Gospel of Matthew*,[33] argues that Matthew displays an "idiolectic pattern," uninherited from Semitic morphology or a multiple heavens cosmology.[34] In this case, the singular and plural disparity speaks more to the unique use of οὐρανός in Matthew than it does to a purposeful detour by the Didachist. The second use of οὐρανός in the Prayer paired with ἐπὶ γῆς shows no spelling or literary discrepancy (ὡς ἐν οὐρανῷ καὶ ἐπὶ γῆς Matt 6:10//Did. 8.2).

Οὐρανός occurs four times in the Didache, and each use is singular. The Matthean singular and plural forms of οὐρανός reflect Matthew's nuanced terminology rather than the Didachist's idiolectic patterns.[35] The Didache possibly does not adopt the unique "heaven and earth" cosmological structures of Matthew 6,[36] let alone the broad cosmology in Jesus tradition.[37] Matthew 6 affects the liturgy of the Didache's community (Did. 8.3) and the primary reception retains the Jesus tradition. While the "heaven and earth" vocabulary is rather disproportionate in the Gospel of Matthew, the use of οὐρανός does not mimic this uneven use in the Apostolic Fathers corpus in general and the Didache in particular (see Table 3).

---

33. Pennington, *Heaven and Earth*.

34. Pennington, *Heaven and Earth*, 149. Pennington further concludes how the singular term forms one semantic pole, whereas the plural forms the other. The singular term identifies the visible, earthly realm, whereas the plural the invisible, divine realm.

35. Consult Pennington's "Table 6.1 Occurrences of Οὐρανός in the NT by Singular and Plural Forms" (also listed as Table 2) in Pennington, *Heaven and Earth*, 125.

36 For more on the pairing of "heaven and earth," consult, Pennington, *Heaven and Earth*, 99–216.

37. Pennington and McDonough, *Cosmology and New Testament*.

Table 2. Occurrences of οὐρανός in the NT by singular and plural forms

|  | Singular | Plural | Total |
|---|---|---|---|
| Matthew | 27 | 55 | 82 |
| Mark | 13 | 5 | 18 |
| Luke | 31 | 4 | 35 |
| John | 18 | 0 | 18 |
| Acts | 24 | 2 | 26 |
| Pauline Epistles | 11 | 10 | 21 |
| Hebrews | 33 | 7 | 40 |
| Catholic Epistles | 5 | 6 | 11 |
| Revelation | 51 | 1 | 52 |
| Total | 183 | 90 | 273 |

Table 3. Occurrences of οὐρανός in the Apostolic Fathers corpus by singular and plural forms

|  | Singular | Plural | Total |
|---|---|---|---|
| 1–2 Clement | 6 | 4 | 10 |
| Letters of Ignatius | 2 | 1 | 3 |
| Polycarp, *To the Philippians* | 0 | 0 | 0 |
| Martyrdom of Polycarp | 3 | 0 | 3 |
| Didache | 8 | 1 | 9 |
| Barnabas | 6 | 1 | 7 |
| Shepherd of Hermas | 11 | 4 | 15 |
| Diognetus | 5 | 7 | 12 |
| Fragment of Quadratus | 0 | 0 | 0 |
| Fragments of Papias | 0 | 1 | 1 |
| Total | 45 | 19 | 64 |

## Debts, Debt, and Sin

A different lexeme consists of the second difference: ὀφειλή in Did. 8.2 and ὀφείλημα in Matt 6:12. Matthean scholars recognize the Jewish influence of τὰ ὀφειλήματα.[38] A different lexeme appears altogether in the Lukan parallel (ἁμαρτίας; Luke 11:4). Additionally, 1 Macc 15:8, as the only LXX reference, joins ἀφίημι and ὀφειλήν together to convey a release of royal debt. "Debt," as a religious term, assumes the meaning of "sin" (cf. Deut 24:10; 1 Macc 15:8; Rom 4:4).[39] Yet for our purposes, does the Didache continue to refer to the singular "debt" (τὴν ὀφειλήν) as sin even though a minor change from the Matthean term (τὰ ὀφειλήματα) emerges?[40] Raymond Brown argues that the plural and singular form essentially carry the same meaning.[41] Aaron Milavec disagrees and suggests that to change from plural to singular also entails a change in meaning. He tentatively argues that "debt" refers to "the final judgment wherein the Lord will examine one's entire life."[42]

I would like to provide a *via media*. I side with those that desire to differentiate between the two slightly different lexemes of "debt," but I will distance myself from those arguing for purely eschatological forgiveness. I suggest that the term, as used by the Didachist, implies both a forgiveness from "the Debt" that has accrued on the way of life journey by not bearing underneath the "yoke of the Lord" (Did. 6.1–2) and "the eschatological Debt" to secure perfection (Did. 16.1–2).

First, the Didachist describes the Two Ways under the singular use of ἡ ὁδός (1.1, 2; 5.1; 6.1)—which happens also to match the feminine use of "debt" (ἡ ὀφειλή) and is distinct from the plural "debts" (τὰ ὀφειλήματα). The Didachist again warns those straying from "the way of this teaching" (Did. 6.1). Although both "way" and "teaching" are in the singular form, they both refer to the variety of ethical practices and essential dogmas. To abide by "the way of life" also means the community member bears under the "yoke of the Lord" (Did. 6.2).

Next, the metaphors of "way" (Did. 1.1, 2; 5.1; 6.1) and "yoke" (Did. 6.2) allow for the possibility of failure, moral deterrent, and correction. Especially notable is the "yoke" image, because the Didachist adds "but if you are not able [to bear the whole yoke], then do what you are able" (Did. 6.2).

---

38. Davies and Allison, *Matthew 1–7*, 611.

39. Davies and Allison, *Matthew 1–7*, 611.

40. N. T. Wright observes this as a sign of the year of Jubilee in Matt. Although mentioning the Did. text, it is difficult to discern if Wright applies the same Jubilean referent to the Didachist's meaning. Wright, "Lord's Prayer as a Paradigm," 143.

41. Brown, "Pater Noster," 200n101.

42. Milavec, *Didache: Faith, Hope & Life*, 331.

Last, because synonyms of "sin" appear elsewhere in the Didache, there could have been a conscious choice to use "debt" rather than "sin" (cf. Luke 11:4). Two different terms for sin appear, ἁμαρτία (Did. 4.6; 11.7) and παράπτωμα (Did. 4.3, 14; 14.1). All but two uses (4.6; 11.7) give an ecclesial referent; that is, members confess sin to one another prior to taking the Eucharist, members confess sin while they corporately gather, and they administer no partiality when reproving others. Additionally, the literary placement of Did. 8.2 logically procedes baptism and a catechumen's entrance into the new community (7.1–4), and it precedes the eschatological Eucharist liturgies (chs. 9–10)—I especially see eschatological and repentance language in 9.4–5 and 10.5–6. So, the daily ritual of prayer would require the members to appeal for God to forgive them from "the Debt" that they may have accumulated as some veer on the way of life.

Therefore, if the lexeme change is purposeful, if the term has some internal consistency, and if to partake of the liturgical Lord's Prayer presumes entrance into the new community, then "debt" cannot exclusively refer to eschatological debt. Those in the community already petition for forgiveness, and "debt" could refer both to the ethical and moral lapses of the convert as she/he journeys along the *way of life*.

## The Doxology

The doxology consists of the final difference that I will mention.[43] It is not my intent to detail the text-critical readings or engage with how Matthean scholarship has commented on the variants for the Matthean Lord's Prayer. The earliest forms of this prayer did not appear with any doxological conclusion in the Matthean MS. A similar doxology occurs in the Hebrew Bible that is often amended to the Matthean version: "for yours is the kingdom

---

43. I don't necessarily feel compelled to discuss at great length the nature of the verbal forms. Matthew's tradition has ἀφήκαμεν (aorist verbal form), whereas the Did. has ἀφίεμεν (present verbal form). A few too many conjectures affect why a change appears in the first place. First, the change could be due to discourse and literary needs of both sources. Second, there are other MSS that have a present verb in the Matthean tradition—either αφιομεν (D L W) or αφιεμεν (אc2). Because the Did. predates these MS traditions, it is possibile for the Did. to serve as the origin of such traditions. Third, the Didachist could be aiming for the aspectual affect of continuance. If Matthew was originally composed in a Semitic form (cf. Papias 3.16), then it could be possible that Matthew uses an aorist form as a mechanical translation (see Metzger, *A Textual Commentary on the Greek New Testament*, 13). It would be too much to read into a given verbal form to speak of the community and current practices and customs in this case—or, even, the potential Semitic tradition behind the Greek Matthew text. For more on a Semitic background, see Edwards, *Hebrew Gospel*.

and the power and the glory unto the ages, Amen" (cf. 1 Chr 29:11–13). Even if the doxological ending is or is not part of the Matthean tradition, why does the Didache stand alone as a unique variant among the earliest MS traditions (Did. 8.2)?

My hypothesis is that the Didache's longer doxological form concludes or serves as a final stop to the liturgical recitations.[44] The Didachist maintains internal consistency within the Didache to necessitate such an ending to the Lord's Prayer. Two types of doxological endings emerge within the other liturgical portions of the Didache: (1) ἡ δόξα εἰς τοὺς αἰῶνας (Did. 9.2, 3; 10.2, 4) and (2) ὅτι σοῦ ἐστιν ἡ δύναμις καὶ ἡ δόξα εἰς τοὺς αἰῶνας (Did. 8.2; 9.4; 10.5).

Table 4. Shorter and Longer Liturgical Doxologies

| | |
|---|---|
| Longer Doxology: Conclusion to Prayer Liturgies (Did. 8.2) | ὅτι σοῦ ἐστιν ἡ δύναμις καὶ ἡ δόξα εἰς τοὺς αἰῶνας |
| Shorter Doxology: After Cup and Bread in First Meal Liturgy (Did. 9.2, 3) | σοὶ ἡ δόξα εἰς τοὺς αἰῶνας |
| Longer Doxology: Conclusion to First Meal Liturgy (Did. 9.4) | ὅτι σοῦ ἐστιν ἡ δόξα καὶ ἡ δύναμις διὰ Ἰησοῦ Χριστοῦ εἰς τοὺς αἰῶνας |
| Shorter Doxology: After Cup and Bread in Second Meal Liturgy (Did. 10.2, 4) | σοὶ ἡ δόξα εἰς τοὺς αἰῶνας |
| Longer Doxology: Conclusion to Second Meal Liturgy (Did. 10.5) | ὅτι σοῦ ἐστιν ἡ δύναμις καὶ ἡ δόξα εἰς τοὺς αἰῶνας |

Patterns begin to emerge as the shorter and longer doxologies appear in the Didachist's liturgies. The shorter doxology exclusively appears at the end of a topical liturgy in Eucharist settings—after the cup and again after the bread. The longer doxology exclusively appears at the end of longer liturgical recitations. So, internal consistency for a shorter or longer doxology coheres with the liturgical patterns of the Didachist.

One feature I have not mentioned thus far is the role of liturgy and repetition, and its effect upon the form of the tradition. According to Did. 8.3, this prayer was repeated three times a day (cf. Dan 6:9–12 LXX). The prayer becomes a part of the fabric of the individual and the community at large through continual performance. As Hvalvik and Sandnes argue for early nascent Christian communities and prayer,

44. Contra Hans Kvalbein who argues that Jewish Prayers influence the doxological conclusion. Albeit, 1 Chr 29:11–13 does have this longer doxological conclusion, it does not necessitate direct or indirect influence upon the Did. Kvalbein, "Lord's Prayer," 245.

> The prayer life of nascent Christianity is a phenomenon at the crossroads between idiosyncrasy and common ground with other people, between verbal and non-verbal aspects, between texts and rituals, between rhetoric and reality, between construction and fact, between texts shaping Christian belief and actual social practices, between what is found in the sources and what is observable in real life, between male and female, between slaves and people of status and means.[45]

Not only does prayer influence the identity of an individual but a repetitious liturgy is bound to shape others by the mere habitual nature of the performance.[46]

The liturgy of the prayer not only influences personal formation but its repeated use also distinguishes the participants from others in the larger religious society. Didache 8.2 expresses how the new community members refrain from being identified as οἱ ὑποκριταί by praying on different days.

## *Summary*

Therefore, I suggest that the hermeneutical and theological elements serve as secondary features, whereas a social and personal formation occupy the foreground ideas for the reception of Matt 6:9–13 in Did. 8.2. The prayer helps form the Didache's community and their social identity. Also, if the lexeme and liturgical function purposely change the Matthean tradition, then these changes convey hermeneutical and theological decisions. "Debt" now refers to the failure of keeping "the way of life" and the extended liturgy conforms to other liturgical patterns of the community.

The social identity serves as the most prominent feature of the Matthean tradition. The prayer helps define the community. "Our Father" is the necessary theological language to convey familial and sonship language. Also, this prayer (content and form) distinguishes the Didache community from οἱ ὑποκριταί.[47] The prayer operates as a liturgy for the Christian community

---

45. Hvalvik and Sandnes, "Early Christian Prayer and Identity Formation," 5.

46. This is especially true given the early Christian traditions of the Lord's Prayer. Tertullian and Cyprian both note how the Lord's Prayer reflects rich doctrine and essentially sums up the entire Gospel. Tertullian, *Or.* 1: ". . . in the Prayer is comprised an epitome of the whole Gospel." Cyprian, *Dom. or.*, 9.9: "But what matters of deep moment are contained in the Lord's prayer! How many and how great, briefly collected in the words, but spiritually abundant in virtue so that there is absolutely nothing passed over that is not comprehended in these our prayers and petitions, as in a compendium of heavenly doctrine."

47. Draper, "Christian Self-Definition."

that repeats it three times a day (Did. 8.3). This liturgical knack may give a reason for all the changes: differences that occur because of repeated use. The prayer functions as a social separator that distinguishes the Christian community from other religious groups (Did. 8.1-2a). Finally and more peripherally, the prayer hermeneutically and theologically portrays signs of internal consistency—e.g., "debt," doxology.

## Didache 9.5 and Matthew 7:6

| Did. 9.5 | Matt 7:6 |
| --- | --- |
| μηδεὶς δὲ φαγέτω μηδὲ πιέτω ἀπὸ τῆς εὐχαριστίας ὑμῶν, ἀλλ' οἱ βαπτισθέντες εἰς ὄνομα κυρίου, καὶ γὰρ περὶ τούτου εἴρηκεν ὁ κύριος· Μὴ δῶτε τὸ ἅγιον τοῖς κυσί. | Μὴ δῶτε τὸ ἅγιον τοῖς κυσὶν μηδὲ βάλητε τοὺς μαργαρίτας ὑμῶν ἔμπροσθεν τῶν χοίρων, μήποτε καταπατήσουσιν αὐτοὺς ἐν τοῖς ποσὶν αὐτῶν καὶ στραφέντες ῥήξωσιν ὑμᾶς. |
| But let no one eat or drink from the your Eucharist except those who are baptized into the name of the Lord. For the Lord has also spoken concerning this: "Do not give the holy things to the dogs." | Do not give the holy things to dogs; do not cast your pearls before swine, lest they trample them under their feet and turning around they might tear you in pieces. |

The contextual setting of Matt 7:6 in the Sermon on the Mount sits between a warning against hypocritical judgments (Matt 7:1–5) and brief instruction about prayer (Matt 7:7–11). Matthean scholarship highlights the difficulty to determine the literary and contextual setting of Matt 7:6. Does this verse conclude Matt 7:1–5 or does it inform the section about prayer in Matt 7:7–11? The modern, interpretative quagmire is nearly certain of one thing: Matt 7:6 proves nearly impossible to decipher. A cursory summary reveals at least seven different interpretative options: (1) limit time and energy towards those neglecting the gospel message;[48] (2) discern how to share "the holy things" of the gospel with outsiders;[49] (3) refrain from sharing esoteric teachings and practices with those outside the Christian

---

48. Davies and Allison, *Matthew 1–7*, 676; Morris, *Matthew*, 168; Osborne, *Matthew*, 263–64.

49. France, *Gospel of Matthew*, 277; Blomberg, *Matthew*, 128; Hagner, *Matthew 1–13*, 170–72; Carson, "Matthew," 185; Turner, *Matthew*, 206–7; Talbert, *Matthew*, 93; Hare, *Matthew*, 77.

community;⁵⁰ (4) regard God as an exclusive priority;⁵¹ (5) prohibit any extension of the Kingdom message to those responding with contempt;⁵² (6) do not hypocritically judge a brother or place limits on "brotherliness";⁵³ and (7) refrain from offering an interpretative option.⁵⁴ I dare to propose an eighth option that suggests Matt 7:6 functions as a *Janus* verse; that is, it functions to conclude Matt 7:1–5 and to introduce Matt 7:6–11.

As the list of vague meanings for Matt 7:6 only increases, the Didachist renders a portion of Matt 7:6 rather clearly.⁵⁵ Didache 9.5 restricts or prohibits the non-baptized from partaking the Eucharist and uses Matt 7:6a as an authoritative base.⁵⁶ Jesus tradition, as suggested by the Didachist, restricts the Eucharist, and Matt 7 functions as a proof-text to support these ideas. Similarly, the Apostolic Constitutions likewise prohibits the unbaptized from partaking the Eucharist, but it offers no Gospel tradition as support.⁵⁷ As people are prohibited from eating or drinking the Eucharist

---

50. Davies and Allison, *Matthew 1–7*, 676; Betz interprets "dogs" as heretics, or "perhaps the Samaritans or Gentile Christianity under Paul's leadership." Betz, *Sermon on the Mount*, 499–500; Luz, *Matthew 1–7*, 355–56.

51. Nolland, *Gospel of Matthew*, 323.

52. Quarles, *Sermon on the Mount*, 294; Albright and Mann, *Matthew*, 84.

53. Luz, *Matthew 1–7*, 356. Luz subsequently follows this option by saying, "I am going to permit myself not to interpret the logion in its Matthean context. Matthew was a conservative author; out of faithfulness to his tradition he included the saying simply because it appeared in his copy of Q." Also see: Gibbs, *Matthew 1:1–11:1*, 373–74.

54. Boring, "Gospel of Matthew," 212.

55. The reception of Matt 7:6 in early Christian literature is marked with multivalent renderings. Did. 9.5 is the first reception of Matt 7:6. Other Eucharistic readings are also found in Tertullian (*Bapt.* 18), Athanasius (*Apol. sec.* 1.11), Apos. Con. (Apos. Con. VII, 25), Cyril of Jerusalem (*Lecture* XX–XXIII ), Ambrose (*Paen.* 2.9.87), Jerome, John Cassian (*Conference* 7.29, 30), and John of Damascus (*Exp.Orth.Faith* 4.13). Other early interpretative traditions of Matt 7:6 extend well beyond the Eucharist and a baptismal referent. For example, Origen identified the "pearls" with mystical teachings and the "swine" who roll around in impiety (Origen, *Comm. Matt.* 2.8; also Origen, *Comm. Matt.* 10.8). The Apos. Con. reflects modern interpretations to discern when conversing with unbelievers (Apos. Con. III, 5). Augustine prohibits those who clamor against divine elements and enjoy carnal pleasures under the name of religion from "the pearls of the Church" (*Letters of Augustine* 29.3). Augustine, again, prohibits the constant and repetitious extension of divine things (i.e., gospel) to those ceaselessly refusing (*Serm.* 27.9). Gregory of Nyssa vaguely refers to a virtuous life of virginity (*On Virginity* 17).

56. Varner is more apt to assign continuity with the Matthean context than what I will argue. The context of Matt 7, Varner observes, maintains the Didachist's "discerning to deny the eucharist." Thus, discernment and judgment link the two texts together. I concede the possibility of such a position. Yet the Didachist offers too many allegorical reappropriations to maintain such a tight connection. Varner, "Didache's Use of the Old and New," 135.

57. Apos. Con. VII, 35. "Let no one eat of these things that is not initiated; but only

(ἀπὸ τῆς εὐχαριστίας), except those having been baptized (cf. Did. 7.1–4), the Didachist creates two people groups within their community—the non-baptized, who are prohibited from the liturgy and the Eucharist, and the baptized, who may partake of the divine meal.[58]

The Didachist assumes a partial rendering of Matt 7:6 as the basis of such an ethical and ecclesial position.[59] A divine backing governs this Jesus tradition in the Didache, "the Lord (ὁ κύριος) has spoken concerning this." Κύριος (Lord) appears twice in Did. 9.5. First, the term replaces the baptismal trinitarian formula, as found in Did. 7.1, 3. Next, the term refers to Jesus because of the conjoined Matthean tradition.[60]

The Didachist leaves a number of questions unanswered. First, how is holiness conferred to the Eucharist?[61] Nothing in the Didache explains *why* the Eucharist is deemed as holy. Second, how is the anthropological property of the baptized changed? The baptized community, now recognized as a holy community, may partake of holy things. So, if the Christian community confesses their sins corporately (Did. 4.14) and individually (Did. 14.1), why is baptism required to partake of the Eucharist? According to the Didachist, baptism may be part of the sanctifying process through which,

---

those who have been baptized into the death of the Lord."

58. According to Pliny's account in *Letters and Panegyricus*, II.6.1–6, meals were a time to show a social cast system. That is, chinaware, food, flasks for wine, and others were divided into three categories. These three categories began with the most extravagant and choicest foods all the way to scraps of food. This comparison may influence common meal social dimensions. The Eucharist becomes a Christianized social system. According to the Did., a two-tiered social system of "insiders" and "outsiders" emerges. The "non-holy" become social "outsiders" and are excluded as "non-holy" members. Yet it is the "insiders"—baptized members—who are able to partake of the entire meal.

59. The final two clauses are governed by two important connectives. Γάρ halts the progression of the argument and provides support to the previous claim. It is not considered part of the larger argument, but is used to provide substance to the preceding claim or idea. According to Levinsohn, "The presence of γάρ constrains the material that it introduces to be interpreted as *strengthening* some aspect of the previous assertion, rather than as distinctive information" (Levinsohn, *Discourse Features*, 91.). Also, an additive καί is used to confirm or strengthen an earlier idea (Levinsohn, *Discourse Features*, 99). Another "function of additives is to confirm some previous proposition or assumption" (Runge, *Discourse Grammar*, 340). Therefore, the final two clauses serve to strengthen the idea of prohibiting the non-baptized from partaking the Eucharist. These connectives (i.e., γάρ and καί) govern how to interpret περὶ τούτου. On near and far demonstratives, consult: Runge, *Discourse Grammar*, 365–84.

60. According to Draper, "the Lord" may be a conscious connection to Jesus's teaching via Matt, but it could equally be argued that it refers to YHWH and Torah instruction (Draper, "Attitude of the Didache to the Gentiles," 247). Also consult: Draper, "Ritual Process and Ritual Symbol in Didache," 134n12.

61. Riggs observes how there is a transition from table-sharing towards divine food when compared to other biblical traditions. Riggs, "Sacred Food of Didache 9–10," 265.

"if anyone is holy, let them come" to partake of the Eucharist (Did. 10.6).[62] Rather than "holy" signifying moral purity, Draper suggests that baptism demarcates a ritual separation from one community and being joined into another community.[63] Although no mention of forgiveness and repentance language appears during the baptism ritual (cf. Did. 7.1–4), baptism changes both the social and moral status of the new community.[64]

Therefore, the Didachist's use of Matthew's tradition redefines and forms an ecclesial social class.[65] In another place in Matthew's Gospel, "dogs" is used as a derogatory term to refer to a gentile woman (cf. Matt 15:21–28). Irrespective of the meaning of Matt 7:6 in Matthew's Sermon on the Mount, a Eucharistic context was most likely not in the purview of this Jesus tradition. Moreover, the words "holy things" and "dogs" have now been allegorically attributed to the Eucharist items and the non-baptized, respectively.[66] Thus, the baptismal ceremony (Did. 7.1–4) confers a status of holiness upon the baptizand, according to the Didachist, so that the baptized and the community members partake of the "holy things."[67] By doing so, the Didachist creates an "us" and "them" reference point to distinguish who may partake of the Eucharist.

---

62. Rordorf, "Τὰ ἅγια τοῖς ἁγίος," 364.

63. Draper, "Ritual Process and Ritual Symbol in Didache," 133–34.

64. So, Draper, "Attitude of the Didache to the Gentiles," 244.

65. It is debated whether or not this tradition stems back to Matthew's Gospel. For those favoring a Matthean tradition: Jefford, *Sayings of Jesus*, 140. For a non-Matthean tradition: Tuckett, "Didache and the Writings," 106.

66. The exclusion of the non-baptized plays an important role in cultic traditions. According to Draper, mentioning "running water" is purposeful (cf. Did. 7.1) and Draper connects baptism to ritual purity as found in Lev 15:13. Furthermore, 1QS has a similar ritual of exclusion. 1QS V, 13 prohibits participants to be cleansed by water, ultimately prohibiting them from sharing a communal meal. 1QS V, 13–14 says, "They shall not enter the water to partake of the pure Meal of the saints, for they shall not be cleansed unless they turn from their wickedness." The Did.'s version is different in that it doesn't prohibit people from baptism. Rather, it prohibits people from participating in the Eucharist prior to water cleansing. Nothing is mentioned in Did. 7 regarding the purity brought about by the cleansing. Τὸ ἅγιον, according to Draper, is the reason why the non-baptized are excluded from the meal. Τὸ ἅγιον is referenced in the LXX as the food permitted to priests (cf. Lev 21:1–16). Therefore, this food, as given in the Eucharist meal, is cultic and sacred for the new community. "The result is that the purity of food and drink become the boundary marker and guarantor between insiders and outsiders for both Qumran and the community of the Did. Those outside are in a state of impurity which prohibits them from sharing in the pure meal of the community." Draper, "Attitude of the Didache to the Gentiles," 245, 247.

67. It may be helpful to observe early traditions of baptism and their relationship to the efficacious nature. Thus, conferring a state of holiness upon individuals in baptism is not totally foreign among ancient Christian writers. Cf. Justin, *1 Apol.* 61. Tert. *Bapt.* 12.

## Didache 14.3 and Malachi 1:11, 14

| Did. 14.3 | Mal 1:11 (LXX)[68] | Mal 1:14b (LXX) |
|---|---|---|
| αὕτη γάρ ἐστιν ἡ ῥηθεῖσα ὑπὸ κυρίου· Ἐν παντὶ τόπῳ καὶ χρόνῳ προσφέρειν μοι θυσίαν καθαράν· ὅτι βασιλεὺς μέγας εἰμί, λέγει κύριος, καὶ τὸ ὄνομά μου θαυμαστὸν ἐν τοῖς ἔθνεσι. | διότι ἀπὸ ἀνατολῶν ἡλίου ἕως δυσμῶν τὸ ὄνομά μου δεδόξασται ἐν τοῖς ἔξνεσι, καὶ ἐν παντὶ τόπῳ θυμίαμα προσάγεται τῷ ὀνόματί μου καὶ θυσία καθαρά, διότι μέγα τὸ ὄνομά μου ἐν τοῖς ἔθνεσι, λέγει κύριος παντοκράτωρ. | διότι βασιλεὺς μέγας ἐγώ εἰμι, λέγει κύριος παντοκράτωρ, καὶ τὸ ὄνομά μου ἐπιφανὲς ἐν τοῖς ἔθνεσιν. |
| For these are the words having been given, "In every place and season offer to me a pure sacrifice because 'I am a great king,' says the Lord, 'and my name is marvelous among the nations.'" | For from the rising of the sun until the sunset, my name is glorified among the nations. And in every place incense is brought forward in my name and a pure sacrifice. For, great is my name among the nations, says the Lord Almighty. | "For I am a great king," says the Lord Almighty, "and my name is manifest among the nations." |

The reception of Malachi (Mal 1:11, 14) in Did. 14.3 gives numerous indicators that this is not literarily dependent. Rather, the Didachist more freely recites Mal 1:11, 14, and gives a *fuller sense*, omits phrases, and exchanges words. These changes, however, do not necessarily imply that the Didachist is changing a textual tradition. Rather, these changes permit the author to use an existing tradition and to modify more freely for contextual reasons.

The textual changes extend to the following examples, and they demonstrate how the Didachist expresses a necessary freedom to amend sources in order to make the internal argument coherent. First, "in every place and time" (Did. 14.3) renders "from the rising of the sun to its setting" (Mal 1:11 LXX) as a *fuller sense* of the expression. Next, the Didachist neglects to use a major portion of Mal 1:11, especially the use of θυμίαμα ("incense"), and adds προσφέρειν ("offer") to link with θυσίαν καθαράν ("pure sacrifice") as a textual connection. The Didachist jumps from the middle of Mal 1:11 to the second διότι in Mal 1:14 explained by parablepsis, homeoteleuton in particular if a textual source is present, but I remain unpersuaded that the Didachist uses a Malachi text to compose Did. 14. I suggest the use of

---

68. All LXX texts from the 12 Prophets are based on Ziegler, *Duodecim Prophetae*.

memory instead. Last, the Didachist modifies the Malachi tradition by (1) dropping out παντοκράτωρ in Mal 1:14 and (2) exchanging θαυμαστόν (Did. 14.3c) for ἐπιφανές (Mal 1:14). It would be beyond our ability to ascertain what the Didachist *intends* and that is not necessarily a goal of reception history. Yet these differences tilt against literary influence and hint towards memory as the Didachist utilizes Mal 1:11, 14.

The reception of Malachi's tradition in Did. 14.3 reveals how the Didachist figurally reads Mal 1:11.[69] A "pure sacrifice" primarily connects Did. 14.1–3 with Mal 1:11. When reconciled members gather to partake of the Eucharist (cf. Matt 5:23–25), the community participates in a cultic ritual and offers a "pure sacrifice."[70] Didache 14.2 couches this idea negatively. That is, unreconciled community members ought not to partake of the Eucharist liturgies, and they must be expelled from communal gatherings if any harbored sin remains so that "the sacrifice may not be defiled." The basis of this ethical instruction appeals to the Lord (κύριος), who has previously spoken about this "pure sacrifice" in Mal 1:11: "for this is the sacrifice which was spoken by the Lord" (Did. 14.3). Although the Eucharist is not in the purview of Malachi, the Didachist offers a figural reading of Mal 1:11 in order to apply the language of "pure sacrifice" to the reconciled community who partakes of the Eucharist.[71]

Furthermore, if the "pure sacrifice" lexically joins Mal 1:11 together with Did. 14.1, why does the Didachist continue with the expression, "for I am a great king says the Lord and my name *is* marvelous among the nations" (cf. Mal 1:14)?[72] There really is no need for this final expression about God in order to connect "pure sacrifice" with Did. 14.1.

---

69. Within early Christian and New Testament scholarship, figural reading consists of a complex set of hermeneutical assumptions. I am influenced by the following few sources and would point readers to them to inquire more about a figural reading of the Christian scriptures: Seitz, *Figured Out*; Dawson, *Christian Figural Reading*; Hays, *Echoes of Scripture in the Gospels*; Radner, *Time and the Word*; Young, "Typology," 29–48; Young, *Formation of Christian Culture*.

70. So Niederwimmer, *Didache*, 199. Claussen, likewise, asks a similar question about what the "pure sacrifice" signifies? He posits that the pure sacrifice is not the elements of the Eucharist but the prayers of thanksgiving. I, however, desire to connect the ethical elements in Did. 14.1–2 as part of the pure sacrifice. Because without the communal reconciliation, the Eucharist fails to be a "pure sacrifice." Thus, the ethical components are intricately tied to the liturgies, cup, and bread. Claussen, "Eucharist in the Gospel of John," 156.

71. McGowan argues the Did. is the first explicit text to connect sacrifice and Eucharist together. But to connect to the sacrifice with the Eucharist underscores the concern for purity and identity. McGowan, "Eucharist and Sacrifice," 197–98.

72. A similar question is also asked by Varner ("Didache's Use of the Old and New," 139).

There are multiple planes of contact and intratextual[73] connections with the use of Malachi in Did. 14 and the rest of the Didache. These subsidiary clauses from Malachi join to other portions of the Didache. The royal themes maintained in Did. 14.3 intratextually correspond to the royal themes in the liturgical prayers. "Kingdom" motifs appear in the daily prayers of the community (Did. 8.2-3). Twice, "David" refers to Jesus (Did. 9.2) and is placed in relationship to God (Did. 10.6). Additionally, the Lord will gather the church and bring her into the "kingdom" (Did. 9.4; 10.5). These royal themes help strengthen the intratextual allusions with the Malachi tradition as found in the Eucharist liturgy.

Second, while the incipit of the Didache designates τοῖς ἔθνεσιν as the broad recipient, the conclusion of Mal 1:14 may vie for an evangelistic hortatory appeal to the outside Gentiles and the inner Christian community. The primary function of Mal 1:11 connects the "pure sacrifice" to the communal ethics, and, as a result, the name of God will be "marvelous among the nations." Thus, this conclusion serves as paraenetic hortatory for the community to exemplify the "pure sacrifice" (cf. Did. 14.1-2). As a result, the reception of Mal 1:14 may also have a protreptic effect. A hortatory function of the Malachi tradition calls Gentiles to a new and different way of life (cf. Did. 9.5; 10.6), and this new life may be accomplished through the outside community watching the inward community.[74]

Therefore, the reception of Mal 1:11 and 14 includes multiple planes of contact with the Didache.[75] The primary point of contact presents a figural

---

73. I was first introduced to intratextual readings from Dale Allison, and thus I attempt to model what he does in Allison, *Studies in Matthew*, 84-88.

74. According to Stowers, protreptic works "urge the reader to convert to a way of life, join a school, or accept a set of teachings as normative for the reader's life." I want to be mindful of the potential overstatement. I am not suggesting the Did. is a protreptic work, as a whole; rather, I am suggesting the use of biblical tradition, especially in this case, contains protreptic elements (Stowers, *Letter Writing*, 92, 113). For more on the debated elements and relationship with paraenesis and protrepsis in letter writing, consult the following: Whang, "Paul's Letter Paraenesis," 255-58; Pitts, "Pauline Paraenesis," 270-74.

75. The history of interpretation of Mal 1:11, 14 offers a host of readings in ancient Christianity. With the following selection of patristic texts, three readings are more prominent: (1) A Eucharist reading; (2) identifying elements of Christian worship; and (3) noting Gentile salvation. Pertinent to our current study, a Eucharist reading is rather common. For example, Justin Martyr uses Mal 1:10-12 and states, "by making reference to the sacrifices which we Gentiles offer to Him everywhere, the Eucharistic Bread and the Eucharistic Chalice" (Justin, *Dial.* 41). Or Mal 1:10-12 is a foreshadowing prophecy of a sacrifice being offered in the name of Jesus "in the Eucharist of the Bread and of the Chalice" (Justin, *Dial.* 117). Likewise, Irenaeus, using Mal 1:10-11, contends God had said beforehand that the former people [i.e., Jews] shall cease making offerings to God, but everywhere Gentiles shall offer a pure one in the Eucharist (Irenaeus,

reading of "pure sacrifice" in Mal 1:11 and corresponds with a reconciled community that partakes of the Eucharist.[76] Furthermore, and albeit subsidiary to the primary function, Mal 1:14 may also present a few intratextual connections of royal themes to the daily prayers (Did. 8.2) and to the Eucharist liturgy (Did. 9–10). Also, by including the final expressions of Mal 1:14, a paraenetic and protreptic effect may influence the existing Christian community and the excluded community respectively.

## Didache 16.7 and Zechariah 14:5

| Did. 16.7 | Zech 14:5 (LXX) |
|---|---|
| οὐ πάντων δέ, ἀλλ' ὡς ἐρρέθη· "Ἥξει ὁ κύριος, καὶ πάντες οἱ ἅγιοι μετ' αὐτοῦ. | ἥξει κύριος ὁ θεός μου καὶ πάντες οἱ ἅγιοι μετ' αὐτοῦ |
| But not all, but as it has been said, "The Lord will come and all the holy ones with him." | The Lord God will come and all the holy ones with him. |

---

Haer. 4.17.5–6). Albeit not a direct Eucharist reading, Tertullian uses Mal 1:10 to depict Gentile salvation and mentions nearby "the sacraments of the churches, and the pureness of the sacrifices" (Tertullian, *Marc.* 3.22). Others, however, do not offer a Eucharist reading. For example, Justin Martyr observes how a man may be Scythian or Persian and know God, most likely activating the expression of "My name is honored among the Gentiles" (Justin, *Dial.* 28). Or applying Jewish language to the converted Gentiles who are now the "true priestly family of God" (Justin, *Dial.* 116). Or Tertullian notes the prophetic voice of Mal 1:10–11 noting the shift of physical to spiritual sacrifices offered (Tertullian, *Adv. Jud.* 5.4, 7). Or again he uses Mal 1:10–11 in order to connect pure sacrifices with "simple prayer out of a pure conscience" (Tertullian, *Marc.* 4.1). Lactantius observes numerous texts making a similar observation of gentile salvation (Lactantius, *Inst.* 4.11). Or consider Didymus the Blind opting for prayers and oratories from people in every place as the pure sacrifice (Didymus, *Comm. Zach.* 8). Or a sacrifice of praise according to the new covenant (Eusebius, *Dem. ev.* 1.10). Consider other early Church Fathers using Mal 1:10–14: Clement of Alexandria, *Strom.* 5.14, 136.2–3; Origen, *Hom. Gen.* 13.3; Eusebius, *Dem. ev.* 3.2.74; Cyril of Alexandria, *Catechesis ad Illuminados* A 18.25; Cyrpian, *Test.* 1.16; John Chyrsostom, *Adv. Jud.* 5; *Exp. Ps.* 8, 113; *Hom. Act.* 4. Basil of Caesarea, *Bapt.* 2.8; *Dem. ev.* 1.6, 10; 3.2; *Generalis Elementaria Introductio* 3.29; Cyril of Jerusalem *Catecheses ad illuminandos* 18.

76. According to Varner, the Didachist sees these future sacrifices spiritually fulfilled in the Eucharist observances celebrating the great sacrifice of Jesus. My main contention is the lack of cross-theology in Eucharist prayers (Did. 9–10). The death and resurrection of Jesus is not clearly articulated in the Eucharist liturgies. Rather, the "pure sacrifice," in this case, also ties itself to the purity of the community as they partake of the Eucharist (see Varner, "Didache's Use of the Old and New," 139). For another reading of Did. 14, consider Draper's article. He argues the Did. text is a form of *aggadah* within a Christian Jewish community that details reconciliation motifs from offences against God and one's neighbor. Draper, "Pure Sacrifice in Didache 14," 223–52.

The source tradition for Did. 16.7 remains among the easier sources to identify. Many scholars recognize Zech 14:5 as the source tradition, and for good reason.[77] Because other canonical texts similarly express this idea (cf. Matt 25:31; 1 Thess 3:13), the Didachist could utilize a different source tradition or at least maintain a theological tradition similar to Zech 14:5.[78] Didache 16.7 agrees with Zech 14:5 with a high amount of literary agreement. Scholars maintain Zech 14:5 as the possible tradition because Zechariah serves as the basis for the subsequent, New Testament traditions.[79] In what follows, I want to know *how* and *why* the Didachist uses Zech 14:5. I suggest that Zechariah 14 functions as the proof-text to affirm a partial resurrection of the dead, and additionally to serve as a paraenesis for martyr theology.[80]

Didache 16 begins with a paraenetic exhortation of personal and communal vigilance (Did. 16.1–2; cf. Matt 25:1–13; Luke 21:34; 1 Thess 5:6). A brief apocalyptic excursus follows the exhortation to motivate ethical vigilance (Did. 16.3–8). Four groups of people emerge in this final apocalypse. Group one is false prophets (Did. 16.3), and eventually, one that appears as "a son of God" (Did. 16.4). The second group receives chastisement from those in group one (Did. 16.4), yet they endure in their faith (Did. 16.5). The third and fourth groups are saints and non-saints that perish during the fiery trial (Did. 16.5)—implied by the partial resurrection of the dead in Did. 16.6.

Zechariah 14:5 serves as a proof text to affirm a partial resurrection of the dead—only the dead saints. According to the Didachist, there will be three signs of truth: (1) the opening of heaven; (2) the sound of a trumpet; and (3) the resurrection from the dead (Did. 16.6). The expression "but not all" limits those who are resurrected (Did. 16.7a). Because Did. 16.3–8 only mentions the outcome of those who endure "in their faith" (Did. 16.5), the partial resurrection is limited to the saints who have previously died. Otherwise, why would the author focus on the partial resurrection of the wicked?

---

77. So, Draper, "Resurrection and Zechariah 14.5"; Niederwimmer, *Didache*, 224–25.

78. Although attributing the Did. tradition to a possible Matthean background, Kloppenborg vies that "the quotation from Sachariah, though considerably modified, is nevertheless still recognizable." Kloppenborg, "Special Matthaean Tradition," 58; Jefford, *Sayings of Jesus*, 89; Butler, "Literary Relations," 277.

79. Niederwimmer, *Didache*, 225; Draper, "Resurrection and Zechariah 14.5," 164.

80. Draper argues that the backdrop of Did. 16.7 is a theology of martyrdom emerging from the Maccabean crisis. I, likewise, affirm a martyr theology but refrain from making any connection to Maccabean traditions. This refrain is not due to disagreement with Draper, but I am attempting to identify a different line of argumentation. Draper, "Resurrection and Zechariah 14.5," 156.

The events in Did. 16 culminate with the coming of the Lord "with all his saints"[81]—even though a lacuna is quite probable in 16:8.[82] This return of the Lord implies two items for the righteous and non-righteous: (1) salvation and vindication, and (2) judgment and destruction.

Some difficulty remains in determining the identity of the "saints" who return with the Lord. Are they angels? Are they persons? Ancient Jewish and Christian traditions will, at times, specify that angels return with God (1 En. 100.5; Dan 7:13–14;[83] Matt 25:31; Mark 8:38; Luke 9:26; 2 Thess 1:7; Ascen. Isa. 4.14–16a).[84] In the Apocalypse of Elijah, sixty-four thousand angels will accompany God in vengeance (Apoc. El. 5.2, 20–21). Other traditions remain vague about who returns with God (1 En. 1.9; Sib. Or. 8.221; T. Job. 43.14–15; Zech 14:5; 1 Thess 3:13)—1 En. 1.9 and Sib. Or. 8.221 connect the return of God with vindictive judgment, which is different than the apocalyptic scene in Did. 16.

Some Jewish and Christian traditions begin to merge resurrected humanity with an angelic identity. For example, Enoch looks at himself and declares, "I had become like one of his glorious ones, and there is no observable difference" (2 En. 22.10). In Qumran literature, the King of Glory dwells together with "the Holy Ones," which are both the angelic beings and elect people of God (1QM XII, 1–7). "Holy Ones" may also be a title given to resurrected saints in Sib. Or. 8.227–28.[85] Within Jesus tradition, the resurrection may convey a change in substance so that resurrected humans will be ὡς ἄγγελοι (Matt 22:20; Mark 12:25; cf. 1 Cor 15:40, 42, 44),[86] or οἱ ἅγιοι refers solely to saints distinct from angels (1 Cor 6:2–3). Moreover, Cyril of Alexandria and Didymus the Blind interpret the "holy ones" in Zechariah

---

81. Apos. Con. VII, comparable to the Did., ends in the following way: ". . . with the angels of his power, in the throne of His kingdom, to condemn the devil, the deceiver of the world, and to render to every one according to his deeds. Then shall the wicked go away into everlasting punishment, but the righteous shall enter eternal life, to inherit those things which eye hath not seen, nor ear heard, nor have entered into the heart of man, such things as God hath prepared for them that love Him; and they shall rejoice in the kingdom of God, which is in Christ Jesus." If a lacuna in Did. 16 does exist and this tradition is similar to such lacuna, then the return of Jesus would include vindictive judgment on the evil and restoration of the righteous.

82. For more on this problem, consult Aldridge, "Lost Ending of the Didache."

83. Murray Smith has an extended discussion on the relationship between Dan 7 and Did. 16. Smith, "Lord Jesus and His Coming," 395–406.

84. For example, the textual variants for Matt 25:31 read αγιοι instead of αγγελοι (A K W Γ Δ). I'm not suggesting αγιοι or αγγελοι is a better reading. Rather, I'm noting how the variant may point towards a conflating tradition to make αγγελοι less explicit.

85. Sib. Or. 8:227–28: "Then all the flesh of the dead, of the holy ones, will come to the free light."

86. Also, Draper, "Resurrection and Zechariah 14.5," 165.

14:5 as both humans and angels.[87] Even the language of the Constitutions highlights the angelic presence (Apos. Con. VII, 32): τότε ἥξει ὁ κύριος καὶ πάντες οἱ ἅγιοι μετ'αὐτοῦ ἐν συσσεισμῷ ἐπάνω τῶν ωεφελῶν μετ'ἀγγέλων δυνάμεως αὐτοῦ ἐπὶ θρόνου βασιλείας.

In some traditions, the martyrdom of saints and the return of the Lord join together to provide support for those being persecuted. For example, Ignatius notes how the return of Christ will bring a reward to those having been martyred (Ign. *Magn.* 8.2–9.2).[88] Often, martyrs will accompany God so as to vindicate other persecuted persons (cf. Rev 19:11–16). These martyrs are an army arrayed in white and pure linen (Rev 19:14). The souls recieve a white robe, are slain on behalf of the word of God, and cry out to God in order to avenge their blood (Rev 6:9–11). The Apocalypse of Abraham details the "chosen one" returning to summon those "humiliated by the heathen" (Apoc. Ab. 31.1). The persecution of the saints in the Apocalypse of Elijah offers an assurance of a resurrection (Apoc. El. 4.25–27). Finally, the Epistle of the Apostles details how the return of God will "come with those who were killed for my sake" (Ep. Apos. 15).

If biblical and Jewish traditions allow for an indistinguishable group to accompany the Lord in His return, who are the one's referred to in Did. 16.7? Their identity also depends upon whom the Didachist depicts as those resurrected in Did. 16.6. The Didachist portrays κύριος in Did. 16 as a redeemer instead of a judge (cf. gathering motifs in Did. 9.4; 10.5). The "accursed one"—Jesus (Gal 3:13; cf. Barn. 7.6–12)—rescues those who endure the "fiery trial" (Did. 16.5).[89] Also, κύριος is depicted as one returning to resurrect the dead—this does not imply that κύριος does not judge the wicked or other such condemning acts, the Didachist does not frame the account in such a manner.[90] The false prophet and corruptors—whom I previously labeled "group 1"—increase in lawlessness, hatred, persecution, and betrayal

---

87. Cf. Cyril of Alexandria, *Zach.* 14. Also, note the reading from Didymus the Blind: "He comes also with great 'power,' however, because holy ones accompany him, not men only but also angels. It is logical, in fact, that 'those who have been eyewitnesses and servants' and 'ministering spirits assigned to his service' by him should with him be resplendent, so that he should be acknowledged as their king, and they as his powers, that is, his forces." Didymus, *Zach.* 14.

88. Draper also notes this Ignatius reference. Draper, "Resurrection and Zechariah 14.5," 174.

89. van de Sandt and Flusser, *Didache*, 36; Pardee, "Curse that Saves," 175–76.

90. I am in agreement with Draper, who says, "the coming of the Lord is no doubt for judgment, but it is not judgment of the resurrected departed." Moreover, I would contend, the literary argument makes no mention of judgment upon the wicked, although that is certainly implied. Draper, "Resurrection and Zechariah 14.5," 178.

(Did. 16.3–4).[91] Thus, the "fiery trial" may not be vindictive wrath from God (cf. Rev 15–16), but the persecution and such actions from the false prophets and one like the Son of God (cf. Did. 16.3).[92] The ones resurrected from the dead may be the martyrs who fall prey during the "fiery trial."[93] According to van de Sandt and Flusser, those resurrected are probably "those who have suffered and endured the above [Did. 16.3–5] hardship."[94]

If this is so, then the Lord's return aims to encourage potential martyrs. The "saints," who return with the Lord, could have been martyred in previous generations. This Didache tradition similarly corresponds to Rev 19 when an army returns with the Lord (Rev 19:14). This army is clothed in white and pure linen. According to Rev 7:13–14, the martyrs from the tribulation are clothed in white robes. Similar martyr traditions may influence the apocalypse of the Didache. Subsequently, those who return with the Lord (Did. 16.7; cf. Rev 19:14) vindicate those who have died by the hands of persecutors (Did. 16.3, 5; cf. Rev 6:9–11).

Zechariah's tradition in Did. 16.7 is difficult to unravel and has multiple layers of interconnected ideas. Its use, most likely, serves as a paraenetic martyr tradition providing hope to those slain by potential persecutors in the last days.[95] Both texts maintain the same image of the Lord returning with a host of resurrected persons/angels. However, Did. 16.7 uses Zechariah's tradition to give hope for future saints who may fall prey to the "fiery trial"—partial resurrection—whereas Zech 14:5 conveys judgment upon the world. The tradition of the Lord's return with saints occurs enough in Jewish and Christian teaching to note that the Didachist has modified the tone and paraenetic message of such tradition (cf. Matt 25:31–40).

---

91. So Verheyden, "Eschatology in the Didache," 202–4.

92. Contra Milavec, who argues that the "fire" is a metaphor for the "terrible, eschatological judgment of God." Milavec, "Saving Efficacy," 138.

93. So Draper, "Eschatology in the Didache," 580. I also affirm a broader meaning of the text to also include those who have died in previous generations. This would include such themes as found in 1 Thess 4:13–17. Paul encourages (cf. 1 Thess 4:18) the Thessalonians that when the Lord returns with his saints (1 Thess 3:13), he will gather together all those who have passed in previous generations (1 Thess 4:14). In Did. 16, the focal point does not appear to be saints of all generations, but those who have suffered at the hands of lawless persecutors.

94. van de Sandt and Flusser, *Didache*, 36.

95. Balabanski and Verheyden, likewise, observe a paraenetic effect of such tradition. Balabanski, *Eschatology in the Making*, 205; Verheyden, "Eschatology in the Didache," 213.

## Concluding Remarks: The Reception of Sacred Scripture in the Didache

Because of the complexity of such a topic, this chapter briefly inquires about the more clear biblical traditions in the Didache. Again, this does not imply that the traditions of the Sermon on the Mount (cf. Did. 1), or Decalogue (cf. Did. 2), or the Olivet Discourse (cf. Did. 16) are less prominent. Rather, they merely lack the criteria set out in the introduction to determine a quote in the Didache. Each tradition assessed:

1. includes an introductory formula (e.g., "as it has been said")
2. uses canonical tradition as a source
3. uses quoted canonical tradition as a proof-text for an already existent, internal argument for the Didachist
4. reflects an intention to quote a canonical source tradition

Given these four criteria, the Didache contains five different source traditions. One of these traditions (cf. Did. 1.6) was not included because it does not reflect canonical material. Therefore, I exclusively reserved my focus upon the four canonical sources quoted (Matt 6:9–13; Matt 7:6; Mal 1:11, 14; and Zech 14:5).

After evaluating these four traditions, we may now offer cursory comments. I attempted to focus on the reception of such a tradition in order to adjudicate the *why's* and *how's* of the source within the Didachist's argument, rather than to center upon source critical concerns. As was argued, these four proof-texts in the Didache focus upon social formation, and ethical paraenesis, and they hermeneutically reframe canonical material.

The following presents a few thematic and concluding comments about the reception of canonical material in the Didache. First, Scripture helps formulate and identify social practices. For example, the mere presence of the Lord's Prayer in the community distinguishes members from other religious groups in Did. 8.2–3. The rituals of prayer and fasting help distinguish their religious identity from the "hypocrites" (Did. 8.1–2). And the prayer forms part of the daily liturgy for the community (Did. 8.3).

Additionally, to use Matt 7:6 in Did. 9.5 helps distinguish between two distinct communities: (1) those that are holy, have been baptized, and are permitted to partake the Eucharist; and (2) those that are dogs, remain unbaptized, and are prohibited from partaking the Eucharist. The Didachist, through prohibiting the Eucharist to some, creates "us" and "them" categories (cf. Did. 10.3). Thus, this use of Scripture helps to create a community that is distinct from others and offers social identity barriers.

Second, the use of quoted Scripture reveals the hermeneutical patterns of the Didachist. What are the interpretative practices of the Didachist and how do they interpret Scripture? The "meaning" of the biblical quotations seem rather fluid and quite different than an original setting of the canonical material. Even in the places that we can identify a quoted source, I do not presume to suggest that the Didachist retains an "original meaning" of the biblical tradition.[96] The Didachist, as a later author, does not preserve the "original meaning" of the quoted material. Additionally, the editors of the Didache have reshaped and given new referents to the biblical traditions, thus expanding their "meaning" and allowing them to function as prooftexts for issues of direct relevance to the community.

Thus, the Didachist will detour from any kind of contextual readings or any readings produced by historical standards in order to provide allegorical and figural readings.[97] I even want to suggest that the Didachist, if we can adjudicate H54 instead of a second-century composite text, could have inadvertently or intentionally created intratextual readings of the canonical tradition in relation to other sections of the Didache. The Didachist allegorically reads Matt 7:6 and thereby modifies the referent of "dogs" and "holy things" (Did. 9.5). By reframing the referents of Matt 7:6, the Didachist uses Jesus tradition to block some participants from partaking the Eucharist. The Matthean phrases now mean something different (i.e., "dogs"=non-baptized and "holy things"=Eucharist).

Intratextual readings of canonical material surface in Did. 14. As I have suggested earlier, the use of Malachi's tradition might reflect both figural and intratextual readings. Figural is distinguished from allegorical in that traditions connect via word associations and with little regard to historical readings of the canonical material.[98] The phrase "a pure sacrifice"

---

96. Candida Moss makes a similar, yet more determinative, observation happening in the Martyrdom of Polycarp. She observes, "Yet even in those rare cases where texts are accurately and directly quoted, only the identification of the intertext—not its meaning—can be confidently asserted. We cannot assume, in those cases where texts are directly replicated in the form of quotation, that the 'original meaning' of a text is being preserved by a later author." Moss, "Nailing Down and Tying Up," 136.

97. Contra Varner, "Didache's Use of the Old and New," 141.

98. Reno and O'Keefe refer to "associative strategies" within intensive reading patterns. The choice of "figural" is to offer a hermeneutical category and to distinguish from Reno and O'Keefe's use of typology. Figural, here, is being used in a similar way Reno and O'Keefe are using "associative strategies." Word associations connect the texts together, not contextual associations (O'Keefe and Reno, *Sanctified Vision*, 63–68, 69–84). Overlap emerges with my definition of typology and allegory in Knapp's hermeneutical comments on Melito. Typology "explores the intentional divine links which God providentially provides throughout the course of redemptive history." Knapp, "Melito's Use of Scripture," 350.

holds together the argument between the Didachist and Mal 1:11. Despite any contextual reading of Mal 1, the Didachist links the argument with Malachi's tradition so as to reorient how the community partakes of the Eucharist (Did. 14.1).

Also, and secondary to my argument, the Didachist's reception of Mal 1 forms an opportunity for intratextual readings. There really is little need for the Didachist to use Mal 1:14 within the argument of Did. 14. However, by using this additional tradition, the kingdom motifs (i.e., "I am a great King") correspond to the royal motifs in Eucharist liturgies—especially if "pure sacrifice" references the Eucharist practices.

Third, and last, the Didachist's use of canonical traditions helps to convey ethical paraenesis.[99] More specifically, the Didachist presents paraenetic and protreptic readings of Scripture. Both Mal 1:11, 14, and Zech 14:5 emerge within exhortations. In Did. 14, the Didachist exhorts the community to maintain ecclesial purity as they partake the Eucharist. The figural reading of Mal 1:11 aids this already existent, paraenetic rhetoric. Furthermore, Did. 16.3–8 underscores the ethical vigilance in the apocalyptic conclusion (Did. 16.1–2). The ethical care will secure their perfection for the return of the Lord (Did. 16.2). Zechariah 14:5 undergirds such vigilance by offering hope to those who might fall prey to persecution during the final days. Moreover, the Didachist offers a protreptic reading of Mal 1:14. If the community maintains ecclesial purity as they partake of the Eucharist, it will result in the name of the Lord being "marvelous among the nations" (Did. 14.3). Therefore, the internal actions of a community call outsiders to consider a new way of life (cf. Matt 5:16; John 13:35).

---

99. Paget offers similar observations. The mere presence and use of scripture in some contexts is paraenetic. It is, in a way, how "Christians could be understood as living out scripture's contents." Moreover, the "popularity in the second century of Matthew's Gospel with its strongly ethical content fits into this general concern with Jesus as a teacher, or, as Clement of Alexandria, admittedly in a somewhat more complex setting, would call him, a *paidagogos*." Paget, "Bible in the Second Century," 566–67.

# 3

## The Theology of the Didache

EARLY CHRISTIAN THEOLOGY REMAINS an open arena for theological inquiry. Lewis Ayres offers a list of methodological and theological considerations to assess second-century theology.[1] For example, how do we assess the proto-orthodoxy and development of Christian theology? How does the Didache compare and contrast to canonical theology, to contemporary works in the second century, or to various forms of Jewish theology?[2] As I raise these brief questions, I do not aim to solve them fully and hope for continued integration of the Didache into early Christian theological descriptions.

With a variety of problems at the helm, my task in the present chapter will be quite simple. Even though a variety of complications emerge when we consider the stability of the Didache's text tradition, the following will only assess the theology of the Didache and assume a whole and unified document. This methodological decision is not designed to ignore the possible composite features of the Didache or to miscalculate the theological ideals in the second century. Rather, I will attempt to offer a theological vision of the Didache with minimal help from other second-century texts and canonical material. This orientation aims to hear the voice of H54 (Codex Hierosolymitanus), to ascertain a theological vision within the unified text, and to permit the internal features of the Didache to interact within a theological constellation of ideas.[3]

---

1. Ayres, "Continuity and Change," 106–7.

2. For example, consider Michel Barnes's article that details some of the pneumatological contours of Jewish and early Christian theology. Barnes, "Beginning and End of Early Christian Pneumatology," 169–86.

3. As is quickly observable, I will limit my interaction with secondary Did. research when offering a theological vision of the Did. This reason is two-fold: (1) I want my assessment of the theology of the Did. to be driven by the reading of the Greek text and less by raising questions and answering problems in Did. scholarship. For those already attuned to the contours of Did. secondary literature, it should be relatively simple to

## Theology and Trinitarianism

As we consider the theology of the Didache, it is rather striking to consider how the Didachist frames its trinitarian theology. The Didache contributes to the early ideas of second-century Christian theology. The Didachist presents ideas that reflect both trinitarian and binitarian ideas.[4] Even as binitarian comments emerge in the Didache, this does not rule out the presence of a trinitarian theology within the Didache.[5] Θέος appears 13x and often contains a modifier or descriptor: "the word of God" (Did. 4.1), "a type of God" (Did. 4.11), "corrupters of God's creation" (Did. 5.2). Additionally, the name of Jesus appears exclusively in the Eucharist prayers (Did. 9.2, 3, 4; 10.2), although his identity appears elsewhere in the Didache. The Eucharist prayers are exclusively binitarian, whereas the presence of the Spirit throughout the Didache remains relatively slim. Even explicit references to "Father" remain rather sparse outside of the baptismal and Eucharistic liturgies.

---

assess some of the following theological reflections. (2) I do not want to frame the theology of the Did. around quotations of Did. scholars so as to agree or disagree with their claims. This decision is to avoid theological controversy while identifying the positions of others and permitting the voice of the Didachist to emerge more naturally. I will limit my use of secondary scholarship to demonstrate where selected sources will be helpful to pursue, or where quotes or references uphold my argument. And I will scantly quote sources with disagreement.

4. Christian theological language, in the second century, often consisted of both trinitarian and binitarian language (Hildebrand, "Trinity in the Ante-Nicene Fathers," 95–96). Richard Bauckham briefly notes how binitarian confessions relate to understanding the Spirit and Christology in early theological formation (Bauckham, *Jesus and the God of Israel*, 132n20, 160).

5. Michael Bird comments on the familiarity of trinitarian and binitarian ideals in earliest Christianity. Of binitarian theology, Bird offers the following argument with canonical material, "Early Christian worship was largely binitarian in content as it was focused on God the Father and his Son, and their worship was charismatic in character as it was animated by the Holy Spirit. Veneration of Jesus beside the Father can be seen in the prayers offered to Jesus (Acts 7:59), thanksgiving offered to God through Jesus (Rom 1:8; Eph 5:20; Col 1:3; 3:17), baptism in his name (Acts 2:38; 8:16; 10:48; 19:5), benedictions involving Father/Son/Spirit (2 Cor 13:14; 1 Thess 5:23), confession of Jesus as 'Lord' (Acts 2:31; Rom 10:9; 1 Cor 16:22; Phil 2:11), hymns or confessions about Jesus (John 1:1–18; Phil 2:5–11; Col 1:15–20), doxologies to Jesus in the New Testament Letters (Rom 16:27; Eph 3:21; 2 Pet 3:18; Jude 25) and celebration of his death and exaltation at the Lord's Supper (1 Cor 11:23–25). Thus, the worship of the first Christians, within a few years of Jesus' death, was already edging in a Trinitarian direction." Bird, *Evangelical Theology*, 105.

## Trinitarian Expressions and the Baptismal Liturgy (Did. 7.1–4)

A trinitarian formula appears in the baptismal section of the Didache. The trinitarian phrase, "in the name of the Father, and of the Son, and of the Holy Spirit," occurs twice and in relationship to the mode of baptism. After the baptizand "reviews these things" (cf. Did. 7.1), they will be baptized into the trinitarian name with rushing water, stagnant or still water, or with water poured over their head. The liturgical tri-fold expression solely relates to the community's baptismal liturgy. Although no tri-fold name emerges with the stagnant water ritual, the community may pour water over the head three times in accordance with the tri-fold name of God (Did. 7.4).

"Lord" (κύριος) does not explicitly refer to trinitarianism in the Didache (Did. 8.2; 12.1; 14.3), except for one specific occurrence (Did. 9.5). In this single referent (cf. Did. 9.5), "Lord" (κύριος) is the name by which people are baptized and, as a result, they may partake of the Eucharist. Only those baptized in the "name of the Lord" (οἱ βαπτισθέντες εἰς ὄνομα κυρίου; Did. 9.5) participate in the Eucharist ritual. Due to the baptismal connection, "Lord" is trinitarian in orientation.[6]

## Binitarian Theology and the Eucharist (Did. 9.2–4; 10)

Similar to the close association between trinitarian theology and the baptism rituals, binitarian theology singularly corresponds to the Eucharist liturgies. The Father is perceived as a benevolent Father who gives to the community the benefits of the Son. The Father makes Jesus known to the community and he grants to them life and knowledge (Did. 9.2).

The activity of the Father more prominently appears in Did. 10. He makes Jesus known to the community, and he also grants the community to possess knowledge, faith, and immortality (Did. 10.2). Because the Father receives the direct address of the community throughout the Eucharist liturgies (9.2, 3; 10.2), the Father is also given the name Almighty Master (δέσποτα παντοκράτορ; 10.3). Additionally, the Father serves as the creator of all things and provides for all humanity (10.3). The Father provides physical food to all people but has especially given spiritual food to the community (10.3). The "Lord" (κύριος) in Did. 10.5 probably does not refer to the Father but to God in general as the one who protects the church.

As the Son's identity materializes in the Eucharist liturgies, the Didachist does not necessarily utilize clearly defined, canonical material when describing the Eucharist events. Jonathan Schwiebert has suggested that

---

6. Baptism occurs in the name of Jesus in Acts (2:38; 8:12; 8:16; 12:48; 19:5).

the absence of material reflects multiple, concurrent, and early Eucharist liturgies.[7] Regarding the Son, he is given the name of a servant (παῖς; 9.2, 3; 10.2, 3). As the Father functions as the primary agent in the liturgies, the Son serves as the means by which a few items are accomplished. Through the Son, the "holy vine of David" is made known to the community (9.2); through the Son, life, knowledge, faith, and immortality are made known (9.3; 10.2); through the Son, glory and power belong to the Father (9.4; 10.2); and through the Son, people may experience the Eucharist elements and partake of eternal life (10.3).

In Did. 10.2, the "holy name" dwells within the hearts of those who partake of the Eucharist prayers (10.2). As previously argued, the name of the "Lord" may refer to the trinitarian name (9.5). However, in 10.2, the "name" can be either the Father or the trinitarian being. The closest antecedent to "name" is the Holy Father. Either way, the being of God dwells within the hearts of those present to partake of the Eucharist (cf. John 14:20; 1 Jn 4:12–13). The close connection of "knowledge, faith, and immortality" may result in this divine indwelling (10.2).

## A Theology of Trinitarian Persons

### God and Father

The Didache's theology proper does not necessarily convey a fully-fledged development of the doctrine of God; it is more a subtle disposition towards and description of God. One prominent motif presents God as creator. The way of life ethic begins with an ethical orientation to love God (Did. 1.2). An additional descriptor modifies God by saying "the one who made you" (ἀγαπήσεις τὸν θεὸν τὸν ποιήσαντά σε). In the way of death instruction, adherents to this way "corrupt what God has made" (φθορεῖς πλάσματος θεοῦ; Did. 5.2). Furthermore, the Almighty Master has "created all things" for the sake of his own name (Did. 10.3).

Ownership and dominion develop as a related motif to God as creator. God also receives the name Almighty Master (δέσποτα παντοκράτορ; Did. 10.3). His complete reign even extends over the events of humanity. The way of life wayfarers must welcome anything that befalls them because "nothing happens apart from God" (ἄτερ θεοῦ οὐδὲν γίνεται; Did. 3.10). Within the household codes, harsh orders must not be given to household servants because they fear the same God, who reigns over both (Did. 4.10). Judgments belong to this master, who will judge false teachers

---

7. Schwiebert, *Knowledge and the Coming Kingdom*, 3–4.

(Did. 11.11). In the *sectio evangelica*, the Father desires of his gifts to be given to others (Did. 1.5). This generous disposition of the Father relates to how the community gives to their oppressors.

God, likewise, is deemed holy and is given the relational title of "Father" (Did. 8.2; 9.2; 10.2). By doing so, qualitative attributes describe God and theological language subsequently assumes a relational dynamic with either the Son or the people of God. Particularly, however, the "holy" language and Fatherhood titles exclusively materialize in the liturgical recitations.

## *Jesus, Son, and Servant*

The Didache's theology of the Son predominately coalesces in the liturgical rituals and then appears scattered in vague appearances throughout the rest of the book. The trinitarian formula positions the Son as the second trinitarian person in the baptismal expressions (Did. 7.1–4). According to J. Andrew Overman, "The Christology of the Didache is somewhere between low and non-existent, so there is little here to help us place the text on maps of early Christianities or Judeo-Christianities."[8] I agree with the premise that the Didache helps point to the diversity of early Christian theology, but the Christology of the Didache would cohere more with a theology beyond the "low-Christology" of early Christianity. As will be seen, Jesus operates as a servant and agent of the Father, he plays a role in the trinitarian formula, he returns as the figure in the end who provides rescue to the people of God, and when teachers instruct the community, the sacramental presence of Jesus emerges. Albeit this is not a "high-Christology," but these brief ideas would cohere with a Christology higher than Overman might suggest.[9]

In addition to the baptismal rituals, the Eucharist liturgies provide much reflection on the Son. Jesus is called the servant (παῖς) of the Father (9.2). Because παῖς appears in the previous phrase ("on behalf of the holy vine of David, your servant"), the identity language closely joins the Son to David, the chalice, and the holy vine. It is quite possible that the Son's "servant" identity parallels or typologically compares to the holy vine and David.[10] Furthermore, the Son, as παῖς, acts as the agent through which life, knowledge, faith, and immortality are made known (9.3; 10.2). The Son's agency serves as the means by which glory and power are ascribed to the Father (9.4).

---

8. Overman, "Pluralism in Second Temple Judaism," 265.
9. Smith, "Lord Jesus and His Coming."
10. Young, "Typology," 29–48.

The use of "Lord" (κύριος) has multiple referents in the Didache. I, at least, perceive of three possible identities for the use of κύριος in the Didache: (1) a generic term for God (4.12, 13; 10.5; 14.3; 15.1); (2) a human master (4.11); and (3) a term applicable to Jesus (8.2-3). One could create a neologism of *kuri-ology* for the study of κύριος in the Didache. If κύριος manifestly refers to Jesus in some occurrences, then it builds a cumulative case to see other uses of κύριος as possible referents to Jesus. For example, material found in Matt 6:9-13 follows the expression "as the Lord commanded in his gospel" in Did. 8.2-3. Because the tradition corresponds to a saying of Jesus in Matthew's Gospel and κύριος joins together with ἐν τῷ εὐαγγελίῳ, κύριος most likely refers to Jesus in Did. 8.2.

Additionally, another Jesus logion from Matthew's tradition (Matt 7:6) appears alongside κύριος in Did. 9.5. Two uses of κύριος occur in Did. 9.5. The first use of κύριος refers to the trinitarian name (cf. Did. 7.1-4), and the second use of κύριος relates to the Matthean Logion (Matt 7:6): "Do not give what is holy to the dogs." Even though locating a precise source tradition proves quite difficult,[11] this expression can assume the material in Matt 7:6. Thus, the use of κύριος corresponds to Jesus as a probable referent.

Next, the phrase "welcome him as the Lord" appears with some regularity (Did. 11.2, 4; 12.1; cf. 11.1). A logical inference of κύριος as Jesus, especially in these cases, portrays a traveling prophet or teacher that is to be welcomed as one would welcome the incarnate Jesus. Thus, for a prophet to be welcomed as κύριος is for him or her to welcome as Jesus would be welcomed.

If the Didache evidences the use of κύριος as a referent to Jesus, then it helps build a cumulative case for other vague references of κύριος. In Did. 12.1, κύριος refers to the authority by which a prophet enters the community. Although nothing inherently Christological emerges from this verse, Did. 12.5 permits a Christological referent and thus informs a particular reading of Did. 12.1. If this person does not come to the community accompanied with a particular ethic, then they are Christ-mongers (χριστέμπορός).[12]

Furthermore, Did. 4.1 and 14.1 may join together to refer to the Son. In both Did. 4.1 and 14.1, additional κυρ-roots associate themselves with κύριος. For example, the presence of the Lord appears in the community when the teachers speak of the Lord's nature (ὅθεν γὰρ ἡ κυριότης λαλεῖται, ἐκεῖ κύριός ἐστιν; 4.1). If this refers to the Son, then the public preaching of Jesus accords with a sacramental presence of Jesus.[13] The phrase "on the

---

11. Draper, "Attitude of the Didache to the Gentiles."

12. Rothschild, *Essays on the Apostolic Fathers*, 175-89. See chap. 12 entitled, "Travelers and Christ-Mongers in Didache 12:1-5."

13. See Hans Boersma's work on sacramental exegesis in the early Church. Sacramentalism, according to Boersma, is the Scriptures bringing to bear the presence of

Lord's day," expressed by κατὰ κυριακὴν κυρίου (Did. 14.1; cf. Ign. *Mag.* 9.1), precedes a description of weekly gathering, public confession of sins, and partaking of the Eucharist (Did. 14.2–3). So, this Lord's day actualizes the items that belong to the Lord and the day most likely reflects early expressions of Christian worship on the day of Resurrection (Rev 1:10; Pliny *Letters* 10.96–97).

Finally, κύριος appears as an exclusive title for the divine figure in the eschatological section. Here, the κύριος will return at an unknown time (Did. 16.1), the κύριος will return with his holy ones (16.7) and the κύριος will appear in the sky (16.8). In the canonical traditions, Jesus himself appears in the final days (cf. Matt 24:29–31).

### Spirit as a Preparer (Did. 4.10)

Explicit references to the Spirit of God are rather rare throughout the Didache. Two uses of the Spirit occur in the trinitarian baptismal formula (Did. 7.1–4). Additionally, prophets must speak "in the spirit" (11.7, 8, 9, 12), but it remains unclear if this use functions as an explicit reference to the third person of the Trinity.

The soteriological calling of God builds from the actions of the Spirit (Did. 4.10). God shows no social status favoritism and will call those from a lower social class, including male and female slaves (Did. 4.10). The duty of the Spirit "prepares" those whom God has called (ἐφ' οὓς τὸ πνεῦμα ἡτοίμασεν; Did. 4.10; cf. Barn. 19.7).

## Communal Liturgies: Baptismal, Fasting, Prayer, and Eucharist Liturgies

It remains rather difficult to consider the Didache and not reflect upon both the liturgical sections and the ethical paradigms. The liturgical section encompasses at least four different liturgical and ritual practices. The following analysis will look exclusively at the four liturgies and then inquire if the practices manifest themselves in other portions of the Didache.

### Baptismal Liturgies (Did. 7.1–4)

The baptismal liturgies include ethical formation, a trinitarian confession, communal participation, and an ecclesiological acceptance to partake of the

---

Jesus. Boersma, *Scripture as Real Presence*.

Eucharist. If the final form of the Didache can be assumed, then the expression ταῦτα πάντα προειπόντες includes an ethical recitation of the Two Ways. It is not clear whether or not the preceding material (Did. 1.1–6.2) functions as catechesis, material to memorize, communal recitation, or merely a review of the contents. The Two Ways prepares the baptizand to enter into the community.[14]

The baptismal formula includes the trinitarian names: Father, Son, and Holy Spirit. With all the Jewish features in the Didache, to include the trinitarian name categorizes the Didache and the Didache community as a Christian community. When commenting on the mode of baptism (cf. Did. 7.1, 3), the Didachist, twice, makes use of the trinitarian name, reminiscent of the formula in Matt 28:19. The baptizand may be placed within a river or pool of water and then be baptized into the trinitarian name, or they may have water poured over their head three times in accordance with the trinitarian name. The Didachist concedes and offers an ordered mode of baptism depending upon geographical considerations: preference is given to running water, then consideration is partial to stagnant water, and finally allowance is extended to water poured over one's head.

The community may participate, although not necessarily, in the ceremonial process. The one baptizing and the baptizand fast for one to two days prior to the baptism (Did. 7.4). If the community chooses to participate in this event, they fast along with the participants. This communal fast during the baptism process reframes the communal identity.

Because the baptism event affects the communal formation, the communal presence along with the baptismal fast transfers a new identity to the one being baptized. In addition, the trinitarian baptismal event transforms their inner identity so that they can partake of the Holy Eucharist (Did. 9.5). Only "holy people" may partake of "holy things"; thus, the baptismal event causes the new members to become holy so that they can partake of the Eucharist.[15]

## Fasting Liturgies (Did. 8.1)

The weekly fasting liturgy in the Didache reflects more upon a societal identity and less upon the spiritual contours of the liturgy (Did. 8.1). In other words, the Didachist seems to present more of how to perform this liturgy than what the spiritual effect of this liturgy might be for the community.

14. Audet, *La Didachè*, 358–59.

15. Draper helpfully documents the Jewish practices of washing and ritual cleansing. Draper, "Attitude of the Didache to the Gentiles," 243–52.

The fasting ritual, for the community, is to be performed on given days so as to avoid any religious confusion with hypocrites (Did. 8.1). Other religious "hypocrites" participate on Monday and Thursday, but the Didache's community performs their fasts on Wednesday and Friday. By changing days, the Didache community distinguishes themselves by their religious practices.

As previously mentioned, communal fasts are likewise performed during the baptismal liturgies (Did. 7.4). Additionally, the initial instruction of the way of life includes a fasting ethic (Did. 1.3). It remains vague whether or not the instruction to fast in Did. 1.3 corresponds to the weekly fasts in Did. 8.1—most likely not. The fasting practices correspond to the peaceful disposition of the community and their care for persecutors (Did. 1.3). They are to "bless," "pray," and "fast" on behalf of their enemies. Thus, by participating in a fast, the community sought the good of their societal enemies.

## Prayer Liturgies (Did. 8.2–3)

The liturgical prayers, likewise, are to be performed counter to a shared religious and societal identity with the "hypocrites" (Did. 8.2). While being discussed differently than the previous instruction on fasting, the Didachist introduces the content of the prayers and a daily office for prayers. The community's prayers do not imitate or sound like the "hypocrites." They distinguish themselves by praying what "the Lord commanded in his gospel." This material, with the exception of some spelling differences and the liturgical ending of the prayer, resembles the material found in Matt 6:9–13 (see commentary). The contents of the prayer are likewise Christianized as the community recites Matthean Jesus tradition.

This prayer is performed or recited three times a day. Thrice-daily prayers are not totally unique to the Didache's community or early Christianity in general, for they appear in the Hebrew Bible (cf. Ps 55:17; Dan 6:10) and in other early Christian traditions (cf. Tertullian, *On Prayer*, 25). As prayers are offered three times a day, the ritual becomes part of the theological fabric and communal formation of the people.

While possibly unrelated to the prayer liturgies (Did. 8.2–3), the Didache also includes other communal and corporate commands to pray. They are to pray for their enemies (Did. 1.3) and pray for others (Did. 2.7). Communal prayers must be performed with a pure conscience (Did. 4.14). This instruction hints of the possibility to prohibit others from participating in the communal prayers. The community's prayers, expressions of charity, and communal living reflect an ethic they have "in the gospel of our Lord" (Did. 15.4).

## Eucharist Liturgies (Did. 9–10; 14.1–3)

The Didache's Eucharist liturgies may be considered the most theologically saturated section of the entire work (Did. 9–10). The range of theological concepts consists of the broadest topics, including theology proper, Christology, eschatology, soteriology, and other related theological categories.

The first noticeable item in the Eucharist liturgies is the binitarian imagery of the Godhead. It can be assumed that some trinitarian relations emerge here because of the language of "Father" and Jesus as παῖς. The Didachist neglects to mention how these two persons relate to one another, but their theological categories portray some binitarian relations. The Father is portrayed as the one who gives the "holy vine of David" (Did. 9.2); functions as the base of epistemological revelation (Did. 9.2); gives life, knowledge, faith, and immortality (Did. 9.3; 10.2); and will gather his church (Did. 9.4). Jesus, being the Son, serves as the agent of the Father's revelations and assists in making known the Didache's soteriological categories (Did. 9.2–3; 10.2).

Related to the binitarian persons, soteriological and epistemological categories emerge as community members partake of the Eucharist elements. For example, the Father gives the "holy vine of David" and makes this vine known through Jesus, the Son (Did. 9.2). Furthermore, as participants partake of the bread, the Father makes known to them life, knowledge, faith, and immortality (Did. 9.3; 10.2). As persons partake of the Eucharist elements, they experience the salvation and immortality given to them by the binitarian persons.

In both sets of Eucharist liturgies (Did. 9 and 10), eschatological overtones emerge as a concluding motif. First, the making of the bread is like the current expression of the church being gathered in the final days (Did. 9.4). The bread fragments are scattered upon the hill only to be gathered together to make bread. In like manner, the church will be gathered from the ends of the earth into the Kingdom of God. Second, the liturgy petitions the Lord to remember the church, to protect the church from evils, to make the church whole in love, and to gather her from the four winds of the earth (Did. 10.5). Both sayings are eschatological in orientation as God gathers the church from the deep recesses of the world.

Although not part of the liturgical section (Did. 9–10), per se, Did. 14 also presents additional insight into the Eucharistic theology for the Didache's community. When the community gathers together, they will partake of the

Eucharist and publicly confess sins. By doing so, the community will partake of a "pure sacrifice." The gathering together, confession of sin, and the Eucharist cumulatively offer a pure sacrifice (cf. Heb 13:15).

Considering the overt awareness of the Last Supper canonical Traditions, one naturally notices some glaringly absent features. The Didache's Eucharist liturgies seem to give credibility to multiple *kinds* of liturgical expressions present in antiquity.[16] One of the more obvious absences in the Didache's Eucharistic theology is any form of blood or cross-theology (Matt 26:28; Mark 14:24; Luke 22:20–22). Additionally, no allusion to the covenant or forgiveness appears (Matt 26:28; Luke 22:20; 1 Cor 11:24). No Christological expression to drink again in the Kingdom appears (Matt 26:29; Mark 14:25; Luke 22:16). Finally, no material recitates "Do this in remembrance" (1 Cor 11:24) or contains interpretive comments that correspond to "this is my body" and "this is my blood" (Matt 26:26; Mark 14:22; Luke 22:19, 20; 1 Cor 11:24–25).

## Communal Preservation and Soteriology

The soteriological vision of the Didache is not fully exhaustive or even elaborate in its descriptions. Hints remain of *how* to experience salvation, but the Didachist does not necessarily communicate with explicit theological categories. The Didachist uses what I want to call "soteriological metaphors" because no explicit soteriological formulas appear nor do clear soteriological categories emerge.

### Salvation Metaphors

With every soteriological metaphor displayed in the Didache, other instructions or motifs are closely linked. For example, the Didachist will often discuss a particular topic and then subtly link a soteriological metaphor to the topic of instruction. A metaphor of salvation is the ransom motif (Did. 4.6). However, generosity and almsgiving reorder the ransom language as merely a subtopic (Did. 4.5–8). As someone receives according to their needs, they likewise give generously and "give as a ransom for their sins" (Did. 4.6).

Another metaphor that corresponds to human effort is the Didachist's use of the Matthean phrase, "bear the yoke of the Lord" (Did. 6.2).[17] By bearing the "yoke of the Lord," the way of life wayfarers will be made

---

16. Schwiebert, *Knowledge and the Coming Kingdom*, 3–4.
17. Deutsch, *Hidden Wisdom and the Easy Yoke*.

whole (τέλειος ἔσῃ). The Didachist creates a reward paradigm whereby those who bear this Two Ways "yoke of Lord" will be made τέλειος—see commentary on Did. 6.2.

Two additional soteriological metaphors appear in the Eucharist liturgies. First, if people have not been made holy, then they may not partake of the Eucharist (Did. 10.6). If they are holy, then they may partake of the Eucharist. However, if they are not holy, then they must repent. Second, the Father, through means of the Son, offers life, faith, and immortality to the Eucharist participants (Did. 9.3; 10.2). These soteriological expressions are connected to the Bread (Did. 9.3) and to the concluding liturgical prayer (10.2). So, it remains unclear if these soteriological categories merely symbolize soteriological imagery in and through the Bread, or if the Bread becomes more sacramental in nature.

A final metaphor to consider is the role of the Spirit. The Didache, as a whole, is predominantly binitarian in nature. However, the one clear reference to the Spirit relates to salvation within the household code (Did. 4.9–11). Masters must not abuse their servants, lest the servants no longer fear God (Did. 4.10); God does not call a given social caste but calls those whom the "Spirit has prepared" (Did. 4.10).

## Baptism and a Change of Nature?

A soteriological connection corresponds to a relationship between personal holiness and baptism. Although the Didache's language remains vague, these two items merely imply an ability to change the nature of a person when they partake of the Eucharist liturgies and the baptismal rituals. For example, Did. 9.5 prohibits certain persons from joining the community and partaking the Eucharist. The fencing of the Eucharist limits those who can partake of the Eucharist to only those who have been baptized. A Jesus logion offers a reason for such an argument (cf. Matt 7:6).

However, Did. 10.6 might present a different way to participate in the Eucharist liturgies. If anyone is holy, they are permitted to come and to partake of the meal. However, if they are not holy, they must repent prior to participating in the Eucharist.

I place these two texts in comparison because they link together the concept of "holy" natures. Consider the two texts:

| Did. 9.5 | Did. 10.6 |
|---|---|
| μηδεὶς δὲ φαγέτω μηδὲ πιέτω ἀπὸ τῆς εὐχαριστίας ὑμῶν, ἀλλ' οἱ βαπτισθέντες εἰς ὄνομα κυρίου, καὶ γὰρ περὶ τούτου εἴρηκεν ὁ κύριος· Μὴ δῶτε τὸ ἅγιον τοῖς κυσί. | Εἴ τις ἅγιός ἐστιν, ἐρχέσθω· εἴ τις οὐκ ἐστί, μετανοείτω. |
| But let no one eat or drink from the your Eucharist except those who are baptized into the name of the Lord. For the Lord has also spoken concerning this: "Do not give the holy things to the dogs." | If some are holy, let them come. If some are not, let them repent |

By placing these two Eucharist instructions together, the ideas of holiness, baptism, and repentance appear all together. Although an inferential feature, the act of baptism might be the physical process to make someone holy. If so, repentance and baptism join together to change the nature of a community member and to enable their participation in the Eucharist rituals.

## An Unforgivable Sin

Additionally, one may commit an unforgivable sin (Did. 11.7), even though this motif briefly appears in relation to the Didachist's soteriological vision. If a community member tests a prophet, then they will not be forgiven. Any prophet coming to the community, who speaks in the spirit, must not be tested (πειράζω) or judged (διακρίνω). The community immediately accepts a prophet speaking in the spirit. However, every sin will be forgiven except the sin of testing or judging a prophet.

The Didachist's instruction remains rather vague as it pertains to the communal or eschatological outcome of such an individual who judges a prophet. This person probably already resides in the community. So, what does the unforgivable sin entail, especially for a community member? To commit this sin may mean merely excommunication from the community or full rejection from God—the Didachist refrains from explaining.

## Ethics and Use of Torah

It is near impossible to discuss the theology of the Didache without also discussing the ethical vision of the Didache. Moreover, and especially given that the Didache provides extensive focus on the ethics of the community, we will need to discuss the ethics without commenting on the whole of the Didache. Without averting into "commentary" in the following section, I will attempt to identify some repeatable, ethical themes throughout the entire Didache.

## Pacifism and Persecution

One prominent theme that appears in multiple sections of the Didache is the mutual relationship between persecution and pacifism. For example, the initial instruction of the way of life is to "bless," "pray," and "fast" on behalf of their enemies and persecutors (Did. 1.3). When an oppressive community or persons come upon the Didache's community, they must turn the other cheek in order to be perfect (ἔσῃ τέλειος; Did. 1.4). In response, the persecuted community gives the gifts that the Father has already bestowed upon them (Did. 1.5).

As the instruction proceeds to highlight the way of death, persecution and communal oppression mark the community's identity (Did. 5.2). Those walking along the way of death persecute goodness (διῶκται ἀγαθῶν) and demonstrate no mercy to the poor (οὐκ ἐλεοῦντες πτωχόν). To be called out of this way of being is to begin walking in the way of life ("may you be delivered from all these things"; Did. 5.2b). These forms of oppression and persecution will no longer define the Didache's community.

Moreover, in the final days, persecution will increase as lawlessness increases (Did. 16.4). Love, hatred, and betrayal will appear with much confusion. In this closing chapters, persecution refers to the exclusive actions of an oppressor from the Didachist's vantage point. Furthermore, these oppressors will even persecute and betray one another (Did. 16.4).

## Almsgiving, Generosity, and Giving "according to the Commandment"

Almsgiving and generosity intersect with a variety of other themes. For example, the community's almsgiving informs some persecutional and soteriological notions. If someone takes a cloak, they should be given a shirt as well (Did. 1.4). Additionally, the community gives generously to all who ask, without expectation or making a request for anything in return (Did. 1.5). The Didache's Patrology informs such demeanor: "for the Father desires to give to anyone from his own gifts" (Did. 1.5). Additionally, a macarism further qualifies those who give according to "the commandment." So, to give generously, even when persecuted, is to give in accordance with the commandment; to give will result in divine blessing (μακάριος ὁ διδούς); and to give culminates with the Father's gifts being shared with humanity (Did. 1.5). The community's generosity extends the generosity of the Father.

An ethic of generosity also corresponds to one's acceptance into the community and thereby gives a ransom for sin (Did. 4.5–8). The correct ethic, according to the Didachist, receives, if in need, while generously giving to others. For, to give provides a "ransom for your sins" (Did. 4.6). If a community member happens to be in need, the community must not withhold from this person but must provide for their needs (Did. 4.8).

The community generously cares for the poor and provides for their residential prophets (Did. 13.3–4). If a prophet resides in the community, then the offered first-fruits serve as a means of provision. However, if no prophet resides in the community, the community still collects the first-fruits and provides for the poor. This art of giving accords with "the commandment" (Did. 13.7).

Among the final sets of ethical instructions, quick staccato expressions correspond to prayers and to the giving of alms (Did. 15.4). The last expression communicates that almsgiving and generosity cohere with the gospel. So, this ethic relates to a commandment that is already known to the community but remains unquoted in the Didache; or, this ethic corresponds with the general tenor of a particular gospel text.[18]

## List of Virtues and Vices

The ways of life and of death are contrastibly extensive lists of virtues and vices that mark the ethical moorings of the community. These ethics reflect a reorganized Christian Torah, Gospel traditions, possibly material from Gal 5, and broad ethical interests for the purity of the community.

In Did. 2, the ethical material uniquely corresponds with the material in the second half of the Decalogue. The Didachist most likely reflects upon the Decalogue to provide a positive reception of the Torah for the community. For example, consider the following comparisons:

---

18. Giambrone, "According to the Commandment."

Table 5. Didache 2 and the Decalogue

|  | Exod 20//Deut 5 | Did. 2 |
| --- | --- | --- |
| Decalogue Commandment # 6 | Do not murder | Do not: murder (2.2), murder newly born children or fetuses (2.2), entertain a wicked plot (2.6), hate anyone (2.7). |
| Decalogue Commandment # 7 | Do not commit adultery | Do not commit: adultery (2.2), pederasty (2.2), sexual immorality (2.2). |
| Decalogue Commandment # 8 | Do not steal | Do not: steal (2.2). |
| Decalogue Commandment # 9 | Do not bear false witness | Do not: commit perjury (2.3), bear false witness (2.3), speak evil (2.3), be double minded or double tongued (2.4), use empty or false speech (2.5). |
| Decalogue Commandment # 10 | Do not covet | Do not: desire your neighbor's belongings (2.3), be greedy (2.6), receive an evil will against your neighbor (2.6). |

Didache 3 presents an list of vices, which lead to death, and virtues, which lead to life. All forms of evil will lead to particular expressions of vices (Did. 3.1). For example, anger will lead to murder and other vices (Did. 3.2). Passions will lead to sexual immorality and other vices (Did. 3.3). The contrary is likewise presented. Rather than abiding by this list of vices, the community must become meek and a subsequent list of virtues will follow (Did. 3.7–8). According to Jonathan Draper, considerable overlap surfaces between the virtues and vices in both Gal 5 and Did. 1–5.[19] Furthermore, I want to suggest that considerable overlap exclusively appears in the list of virtues and vices in Gal 5 and Did. 3.[20]

Of the ten virtues listed in Gal 5:22–23, four of these virtues appear in the Didache's Two Ways.

---

19. Draper, "Two Ways and Eschatological Hope," 229–30.
20. See Wilhite, *"One of Life and One of Death."*

| | |
|---|---|
| γάπη (Gal 5:22) | γαπάω (Did. 2.7) |
| μακροθυμία (Gal 5:22) | μακρόθυμος (Did. 3.8) |
| γαθωσύνη (Gal 5:22) | γαθός (Did. 3.8) |
| πραΰτης (Gal 5:23) | πραΰς (Did. 3.8); πραΰτης (Did. 5.2) |

Of the fourteen vices listed in Gal 5:19-21, eight of these vices appear in the Didache's Two Ways.

| | |
|---|---|
| πορνεία (Gal 5:19) | πορνεία (Did. 3.3; 5.1) |
| εἰδωλολατρία (Gal 5:20) | εἰδωλολατρία (Did. 3.4; 5.1) |
| φαρμακεία (Gal 5:20) | φαρμακεύω (Did. 2.2); φαρμακεία (Did. 5.1) |
| ἔρις (Gal 5:20) | ἐριστικός (Did. 3.2) |
| ζῆλος (Gal 5:20) | ζηλωτής (Did. 3.2) |
| θυμοί (Gal 5:20) | θυμικός (Did. 3.2) |
| διχοστασίαι (Gal 5:20) | διπλοκαρδία (Did. 5.1); διστάζω (Did. 4.7); διψυχέω (Did. 4.4) |
| καὶ τὰ ὅμαια τούτοις (Gal 5:21) | καὶ ἀπὸ παντὸς ὁμοίου αὐτοῦ (Did. 3.1) |

In addition to the virtues and vices throughout the Didache's way of life, a list of vices compose the material in the way of death (Did. 5). The list of vices consists of two parts, divided between Did. 5.1 and 5.2.[21] Part one lists 22 vices that generally cohere with the second half of the Decalogue (cf. Exod 20:13-16; Deut 5:17-20). Additionally, these vices similarly appear as part of the prohibitions in Did. 2.1-7; and this comparison may offer a reason why Did. 5 completely deviates from the way of darkness vice list in Barn. 20.1.

The second part of the way of death presents the participants as social pariahs upon an oppressed identity group. Part two changes from a vice list to a particular list of deeds and actions. The way of death voyagers are social oppressors. They do not judge rightly, they have no mercy on the poor, they fail to "toil for the oppressed,"[22] they "murder children,"

---

21. Didache scholars already note this bipartite division or distinction in Did. 5. Niederwimmer, *Didache*, 114-15; van de Sandt and Flusser, *Didache*, 29.

22. Greek reads: οὐ πονοῦντες ἐπὶ καταπονουμένῳ.

they "torment the afflicted,"[23] they refuse to help the needy, and they have a corrupt legal system—they advocate for the wealthy and they act unlawfully against the poor.

## Communal Separation and Disassociation

As the Didachist presents a vision for ethical formation and ethical identity, it should come as no surprise to encounter an ethical separation or a communal disassociation from those who do not adhere to a particular ethic. For example, the way of death instruction does not purely portray an ethical framework in description only. Rather, it directs the way of life wayfarers or soon-to-be way of life wayfarers: "May you be delivered from all these things" (Did. 5.2). This call beckons for people to dissociate with the way of death ethical identity.

The Didachist employs social language to convey an "us" and "them" referent point. The fasts and prayers of the Didache community distinguish themselves from the "hypocrite" (Did. 8.1, 2). Within the Eucharist liturgies, the soteriological identity permits or disassociates one's ability to participate in the communal affairs. Only those who are holy can partake of holy things, a condition brought about through baptism and repentance (Did. 9.5; cf. 7.1–4). If anyone is holy, they may come forward and partake, but if they are not holy, then they must repent (Did. 10.6). Even the Eucharist prayers reflect an "us" and "them" framework. The Almighty Master has created food and drink for all people, but "has graciously given to us spiritual food and drink" (Did. 10.3).

False teachers and false prophets are likewise to be avoided and rejected by the community. If teachers lead people astray from the Two Ways, then they teach without regard for God (Did. 6.1). If a teacher displays an ethic contrary to proper teaching, then they must be ignored (Did. 11.2). A prophet who behaves improperly is a Christ-monger and must be avoided (Did. 12.5).

## Τέλειος as Wholeness

Although this chapter focuses upon the theology of the Didache, and more specifically on the ethical theology of the Didache in this section, it remains difficult not to mention how the Didachist uses τέλειος and its related derivatives. Τέλειος corresponds to Greek and Roman virtue formation and

---

23. Greek reads: καταπονοῦντες τὸν θλιβόμενον.

Jewish concepts of *shalom*. Within the Didache, the τελ-root appears in four different settings and exclusively applies to persons (Did. 1.4; 6.2; 10.5; 16.2). As this term joins with ancient forms of virtue and personal wholeness, the Didache likewise utilizes this term to refer exclusively to the spiritual wholeness of a person. This wholeness can be achieved in the present life and is a necessary quality to join the community.

The first use of τέλειος occurs in Did. 1.4 and corresponds to a non-retaliation ethic. If anyone slaps your cheek, turn to them the other, and then ἔση τέλειος. For those familiar with the Matthean Jesus non-retaliation tradition, this material in Did. 1.4 is rearranged Matthean Sermon on the Mount tradition. The Didachist inserts the τέλειος expression after the non-retaliation ethic, whereas Matthew utilizes this τέλειος motif in relation to loving one's enemies (Matt 5:48).

Next, the Didachist mentions the τέλειος motif as a conditional outcome of bearing the whole yoke of the Lord (Did. 6.2). It remains relatively debated what the yoke might be; for our purposes here, I will assume it vaguely corresponds to the whole Two Ways—see section in commentary. Thus, if persons bear under the whole ethical paradigm of the Two Ways, then they will be given τέλειος as a result. A concession is offered to those who cannot bear all the elements in the Two Ways. They are still encouraged to perform as much as they can.

The other two uses are verbal forms of τέλειος (Did. 10.5; 16.2). In the Eucharist liturgies, the Lord will perfect (τελειόω) the church in love (Did. 10.5). Additionally, a command calls for a continual corporate gathering so that the community will be spiritually whole (τελειόω) in the last moment (Did. 16.2). Both of these two uses correspond to apocalyptic or eschatological ethics, and they relate to the spiritual condition of the community prior to the final events. Τέλειος is the needed spiritual condition prior to entering into the kingdom.

## Corporate Gathering and Ecclesial Structures

Instruction for the community's gathering practices and ecclesial structures appear quite scattered all throughout the Didache. These scattered appearances offer enough of a vision of the community's practices to discern some practices and hierarchical structures.

## Lord's Day Gathering and Communal Rituals

### Sacramental Teaching (Did. 4.1)

The community of the Didache must remember "night and day" the one who teaches them the word of God (Did. 4.1; cf. Heb 13:7). The reason is two-fold. First, the community welcomes the teacher as one who mediates the presence of the Lord himself.[24] This gives an inherent authority to the teaching figure. Moreover, when the teacher instructs about lordship, the presence of the Lord appears in the community's midst.

When the Lordship (κυριότης) is spoken, the presence of the Lord emerges. Κυριότης likewise signifies the power of the Lord (Herm. Sim. 5.6.1 [59.1]) and corresponds to the Lord's authority (Jude 8; 2 Pet 2:10). Thus, in Did. 4.1, κυριότης most likely refers to a discussion of the nature of Jesus as Lord, accompanied by his dominion. While discussing this lordship, the presence of Jesus emerges in the midst of the community (ἐκεῖ κύριός ἐστιν).[25] Therefore, to remember the teachers provides the means for the sacramental presence of Jesus to remain within the covenant community.

### Communal and Baptismal Fasts (Did. 7.4)

Beyond the theology of fasts given above, I want to mention that the community will fast during the baptismal liturgies. The Didachist does not mention within the baptismal liturgy the spiritual effect on the community or *why* the community members ought to fast. Because Did. 7–8 concerns itself about the religious identity of the community—fast and pray on different days than the hypocrites—the baptismal communal fast helps secure the community's corporate identity. Given that the baptizand is baptized into the trinitarian name, the communal fasting joins together with the fasts of the one baptizing and the baptizand.

Corporate gathering and Eucharist as a pure sacrifice (Did. 14). The weekly gathering of the Didache's religious community provides an

---

24. For works that have influenced my understanding of sacramental theology, consider the following volumes by Hans Boersma and Matthew Levering. Boersma, *Nouvelle Théologie*; Boersma, *Heavenly Participation*; Boersma and Levering, *Oxord Handbook of Sacramental Theology*.

25. A remaining question about Did. 4 relates to a collection of motifs in Matt. If, as the consensus of Did. scholarship affirms, Did. and Matt. share a social setting and a mutual composite relationship, then how does this "lordship" motif in Did. 4 correlate to themes in Matt? I want tentatively to propose that the "presence of the Lord" in Did. 4 may correspond with the "God with us"/"Immanuel" motif in Matt. Obviously, this idea is nascent in form and will require more thematic and textual support.

opportunity to express ritual liturgies. On each Lord's Day (κατὰ κυριακὴν δὲ κυρίου), the communal members gather together, partake of the Eucharist meal, and confess sins corporately (14.1). By collectively participating in these three rituals, the community will offer a "pure sacrifice." As the community participates in these rituals, communal schisms will be purged and they will freely participate in the Eucharist rituals. However, if members quarrel and perpetuate unconfessed sin, then the community's Lord's Day ritual practices will not be a "pure sacrifice."

### *Communal Ethics (Did. 15.3–4)*

Immediately following the election of bishops and deacons, the Didachist offers a brief staccato list of communal ethics. This close proximity between the ecclesial offices would suggest that these ethics influence the corporate gathering. If so, then the community demands a kind of ethic that coheres with the "gospel of the Lord" (ὡς ἔχετε ἐν τῷ εὐαγγελίῳ τοῦ κυρίου ἡμῶν; Did. 15.3–4). Two prominent communal ethics correspond to the "gospel of the Lord." The community must not speak against one another in anger and they must participate in almsgiving. The communal activities of the gospel, for the Didache's community, require reproof that is given in peace and almsgiving with generosity.

## Intrapersonal Relationships and Communal Practices

### *Communal Gatherings to Maintain Piety*

The Didache community regularly gathers to maintain personal and communal piety. As the way-of-life wayfarer received instruction, they must remember daily the teacher and seek out the company of the saints (τὰ πρόσωπα τῶν ἁγίων; Did. 4.1–2). The words of the teacher provide a sacramental presence of the Lord in the midst of the community (Did. 4.1). The company of the saints provides rest (ἐπαναπαύομαι) for the individual.

Additionally, the community gathers together frequently to seek out the "the things relating to your soul" (τὰ ἀνήκοντα ταῖς ψυχαῖς ὑμῶν; Did. 16.2). As Ignatius argues, the frequent meetings create opportunities to give God glory and to mete out the satanic forces of the community through the unanimity of faith (Ign. *Eph.* 13.1). For the Didache's community, to gather frequently will help care for one's soul and will help secure personal wholeness (τελειόω; Did. 16.2). The community's time on the earth will be of no avail if they are not found as τέλειος in the last season.

## Communal Judgments and Confessions

Because the instruction in Did. 4.1–2 involves communal gatherings and reflects upon the teachings from the teacher, I assume that Did. 4.3–4 continues such communal reflections. If so, then Did. 4.3–4 communicates general instruction on how to live at peace within the communal gatherings. The communal members must not create schisms (οὐ ποιήσεις σχίσμα); they are to be peaceful with whom they are at odds (εἰρηνεύσεις μαχομένους); and they ought to judge fairly when scrutinizing communal wrongdoings (κρινεῖς δικαίως, οὐ λήψῃ πρόσωπον ἐλέγξαι ἐπὶ παραπτώμασιν). Two positive commands govern the communal gathering and intra-communal relationships: be peaceful and judge fairly.

Additionally, the community publicly confesses their sins and will remove some from the ecclesial community as a means to offer a "pure sacrifice" (Did. 14.1–2). As the community gathers on the Lord's Day, they partake of the Eucharist and publicly confess sins to one another. Furthermore, if people quarrel with their neighbor, they are prohibited to gather with the community (Did. 14.2). The purity of the sacrifice corresponds to partaking of the Eucharist and the corporate gathering.

## Role and Function of Teacher and the Teaching

### The "Teaching"

Given the name of the book "The Teaching of the Twelve Apostles" (ΔΙΔΑΧΗ ΤΩΝ ΔΩΔΕΚΑ ΑΠΟΣΤΟΛΩΝ), one should expect the motif of "teaching" to be somewhat prevalent. Although the title of the Didache in earliest Christianity is relatively unstable—see section in commentary—we are given both an incipit and inscription in H54.

Incipit: ΔΙΔΑΧΗ ΤΩΝ ΔΩΔΕΚΑ ΑΠΟΣΤΟΛΩΝ

Trans: "The Teaching of the Twelve Apostles"

Inscriptio: Διδαχὴ κυρίου διὰ τῶν δώδεκα ἀποστόλων τοῖς ἔθνεσιν

Trans: "The Teaching of the Lord to the Gentiles by the twelve apostles"

Both of these lines contain διδαχή and join this "teaching" to the twelve apostles. It is highly speculative that the Didache historically finds its origin in the actual twelve apostles. However, the two titles produce an expectation of διδαχή in the book. The book claims to continue the instruction of the Lord (i.e., Jesus) through means of the twelve apostles to the Gentiles (τοῖς ἔθνεσιν).

Διδαχή predominantly appears in the Two Ways instruction (cf. Did. 11.2). The first two uses generally relate to one other. In Did. 1.2, the way of life instruction begins with numerical terms (πρῶτον and δεύτερον) to suggest a succession of instruction. First, the wayfarers are to love God and, second, they are to love their neighbor. Then, in Did. 1.3, the instruction begins: "the teaching of these things is this." However, no numerical adverb is given in Did. 1.3, but one is listed in 2.1: δευτέρα δὲ ἐντολὴ τῆς διδαχῆς. Because Did. 1.2 includes both πρῶτον and δεύτερον and Did. 2.1 begins with δευτέρα, then the material beginning in Did. 1.3 would be considered as the "first" set of instruction. If this is so, then the love of God and love of neighbor ethic encompasses the initial meanings of διδαχή (Did. 1.3; 2.1). The ethics listed in Did. 1.3–6 fulfill one's love for God and the amended Christian Torah in Did. 2.2–7 consists of one's love for their neighbor.

As the Two Ways instruction comes to a close, διδαχή refers to the whole instruction and ethical paradigm of the Two Ways (Did. 6.1). A final set of commands exhorts the wayfarer not to be led astray from the διδαχή. The use of οὗτος and ὁδός frame the antecedent elements of διδαχή. Not to be led astray from the "teaching" maintains the instruction and ethical paradigms of Did. 1–5.

The final use of διδαχή occurs outside the Two Ways. While transient apostles and prophets continue to join the community, aberrant teaching might enter into the community. So, if a traveling teacher should join the community and subsequently teach a different teaching (ὁ διδάσκων στραφεὶς διδάσκῃ ἄλλην διδαχήν), the community must refrain from listening (Did. 11.2). However, if the teaching bears forth righteousness, then the teacher may be welcomed as the Lord. This acceptance does raise the question whether or not the ethical outcome is the basis by which "another teaching" can be accepted, or if the right διδαχή will bear both faithful instructions (cf. Did. 4.12–14) and adequate ethical orientations.

*Welcome a Teacher "as the Lord"*

As part of the *kuri-ology* of the Didache, the presence of the teacher is often welcomed as the Lord incarnated in their midst. If a teacher comes with instruction that produces righteousness, then they are welcomed as the Lord (δέξασθε αὐτὸν ὡς κύριον; Did. 11.2). A gnomic expression attributes this welcome to anyone who comes in the name of the Lord (Did. 12.1). The presence of the teachers in the community receives the same welcome as the presence of the Lord. It could be that the community elevates these itinerate teachers to embody a sacramental presence of the Lord.

Additionally, the one who teaches the word of God is to be regarded as the Lord (Did. 4.1). Those who teach receive the same honor as those who give to the Lord (τιμήσεις δὲ αὐτὸν ὡς κύριον). For Ignatius, to honor the bishop will ensure reciprocal honor from God (Ign. *Smyrn.* 9.1). Honor is an attribute often given to ecclesial officials (1 *Clem.* 21.6) and widows (1 Tim 5:3).

### *The Didachist as Teacher*

An additional implication of the "teaching" motif corresponds to how the author/redactor of the Didache's material (i.e., the Didachist) frames his self-identity. In other words, it seems that the composer(s) of the Didache places himself in a position of authority, as one who instructs the community. This posture appears more prominently in the Two Ways material than in other Didache sections.

For example, the Didachist in Did. 1.3 and 2.1 claims the "teaching is this" and the "second commandment of the teaching is this." Because this instruction in Did. 1 and 2 frames the "teaching," then it is a logical deduction to identify the redactor of the Didache, especially of the Two Ways, as a teacher.

The Didachist also portrays his voice and instruction as a teacher. As the way of life instruction closes (Did. 4.12–14), the recipients are exhorted not to abandon the commandment or modify the instruction. Rather, they must guard what has been entrusted to them (Did. 4.13). So, the way of life instruction situates its material as covenantal authority (cf. Deut 4:2; 12:32; Rev 22:18). So, if the redactor expresses this instruction, then he establishes his role as teacher and instructor.

A final example portrays the Didachist as a teacher in relation to the recipients as children in Did. 3–4. In six occurrences, τέκνον μου describes the recipients (Did. 3.1–6; 4.1). However, the recipients are not human children because they may have children of their own, they may have land and slaves, and they may have a household under their care (Did. 4.9–11). So, the "child" language creates a social-tier structure between a pupil and instructor. This social language accommodates the Didachist as a teacher.

## Ecclesial Structures

### *Community Election of Bishops and Deacons (Did. 15.1)*

Didache 15.1 portrays the community as the group who elects certain persons for their community oversight. They elect (χειροτονήσατε) for themselves both bishops (ἐπισκόπους) and deacons (διακόνους). This communal, ecclesial election likewise appears in other early second-century settings (Ign. *Phld.* 10.1; Ign. *Smyrn.* 11.2; Ign. *Pol.* 7.2). Dissimilar to canonical traditions (1 Tim 3; Tit 1), the Didache does not include explicit functions of these two ecclesial categories. Rather, the Didachist mentions that these two offices will render the service of the prophets and teachers among the community (Did. 15.2).

Additionally, the bishops and deacons exemplify qualities much like the list in 1 Tim 3 and Tit 1. For the Didachist, the two elected offices share the same qualities: (1) humility (ἄνδρας πραεῖς); (2) not greedy for money (ἀφιλαργύρους); (3) truthful (ἀληθεῖς); and (4) having been approved (δεδοκιμασμένους). Some of these qualities resemble other ethical lists in early Christianity.

Table 6. Didache 15.1 and Comparable Lists of Ethics

| 1 Tim 3:2-13 | Tit 1:5-9 | 1 Pet 5:1-4 | Did. 15.1 | Pol. *Phil.* 5.2 |
|---|---|---|---|---|
| | Not arrogant (μὴ αὐθάδη; Tit 1:7) | | Humble men (ἄνδρας πραεῖς) | |
| Not greedy for money (ἀφιλάργυρον; 1 Tim 3:3) | Not greedy for money (μὴ αἰσχροκερδῆ; Tit 1:7) | Dishonest gain (αἰσχροκερδῶς; 5:2) | Not greedy for money (ἀφιλαργύρους) | Not greedy for money (ἀφιλάργυροι) |
| Not double tongued (μὴ διλόγους; 1 Tim 3:8) | | | | Not double tongued (μὴ δίλογοι) |
| | | | Truthful (ἀληθεῖς) | Conducting according to the truth of the Lord (πορευόμενοι κατὰ τὴν ἀλήθειαν τοῦ κυρίου) |
| They first need to be approved (οὗτοι δοκιμαζέσθωσαν πρῶτον; 1 Tim 3:10) | | | Having been approved (δεδοκιμασμένους) | |

## "Teachers"

The vocation of teacher remains a bit ambiguous. I remain uncertain if this is an actual vocation and office in the community like the prophets, apostles, deacons, and overseers, or if this is an established duty that the explicit offices perform. For example, to teach is part of the function within the household codes (Did. 4.9). Anyone who teaches contrary to the Two Ways does so without regard for God (Did. 6.1). Moreover, the actual identity of the teaching figure still remains somewhat vague (Did. 4.1–2).

Additionally, the clearly identifiable offices will teach in the community. For example, the prophets will teach (Did. 11.10). If this prophet does not demonstrate proper actions that accord with their teaching, they are deemed a false prophet. Thus, the ethics of an apostle, either good or negative, will deem them as a genuine or false prophet respectively.

However, this possible *vocation* of teacher appears in two different sections of the Didache. First, the community welcomes teachers (Did. 11.1–2). Any teacher who teaches the things previously mentioned (ταῦτα πάντα τὰ προειρημένα) can be welcomed in the community. A teacher must cohere with previously known material. Additionally, if a teacher conveys a different teaching (ἄλλην διδαχήν), they must be ignored (Did. 11.2). Yet if their teaching adds to the ethical righteousness and knowledge of the Lord, then they are welcomed.

Second, in a setting about providing food for prophets, an additional instruction for a true/genuine teacher appears (διδάσκαλος ἀληθινός; Did. 13.2). This teacher, much like the laborer, is worthy of their food. The problem, however, surfaces in this literary setting as the Didachist instructs about the true/genuine prophets in Did. 13.1 and how the community provides the firstfruits for the prophets in Did. 13.3. In this way, both the prophet and teacher share a similar identity (Did. 13.2).

## Itinerate Prophets and Apostles

Another set of institutional identities concerns prophets and apostles. The identity of these figures appears predominantly in Did. 11–13. The relationship between these two identities remains a little unclear. Are the apostles and prophets a single identity? Or, are these two different offices with two distinct functions in the community? I tend to see two distinct offices that overlap in roles and duties. For example, if the apostle arrives at the community and asks for money, they are rendered a false prophet (11.6).

The identity of the apostles corresponds exclusively to the material in Did. 11. The community welcomes the apostles because they have been given by God to the church in "the decree of the gospel" (κατὰ τὸ δόγμα τοῦ εὐαγγελίου; 11.3). If an apostle enters the community, they welcome the apostle as though they were the Lord (11.4). Additionally, an apostle should receive nothing except bread. If they request and receive anything other than food, then they are rendered a false prophet (11.6).

The prophets, on the other hand, encompass the majority of the attention in Did. 11–13. The Didachist provides information concerning the ethics of the prophets and instructs the community about providing for the prophets. Finally, a list of directives informs the community about how the prophets involve themselves in the group. For example, the prophets may not request food or money (11.9, 12), act in ways contrary to their instruction (11.10), and reside more than three days within the community (12.2). The community ought not to commit the unforgivable sin by testing and judging prophets (11.7). Instead, the community provides for the prophets through housing, food, and broad provisions (11.8; 12.2). The prophets, who stay in the community, are rendered as high priests and the community offers their firstfruits to the prophets (13.3). If prophets decide to reside in the community, they must not remain idle but exercise a trade for the good of the community (12.3–4).

Next, the Didachist conveys no insight into the hierarchy of the offices within the community. In other words, what is the relationship of the bishops, deacons, and teachers with the apostles and prophets? As prophets partake of the Eucharist, they receive a concession to partake as they wish (10.7). However, do the bishops or deacons receive this same permission? The bishops and deacons perform the duties of the prophets and teachers (15.1), but does this assume unclear functions for the apostles? So, a number of questions still remain about the ecclesial structures and hierarchical features within the Didache's community.

## The "Last Days" and the Didache's Eschatological Orientation

Although a fully-fledged eschatological vision remains absent in the Didache, it should come as no surprise to observe the highly ethical, apocalyptic and eschatological vision of the Didachist. Ethics, apocalypticism, and eschatology often go together,[26] and the Didache is no exception. Although the apocalyptic and eschatological vision is incomplete, enough motifs surface to put a partial vision together. To make matters more difficult, it has

---

26. Allison, "Apocalyptic Ethics and Behavior," 295–311.

been suggested by many that Did. 16 contains a corrupt textual ending. This textual corruption limits how we assess a more holistic eschatological vision of the Didache—see section in commentary.

## Individual Eschatology

The Didache will rarely address forms of individual eschatology and typically consists of a corporate visions. However, a possible individual eschatological orientation accompanies the initial Two Ways metaphor. By using a "road" metaphor, a wayfarer heads towards one of the two polarized options, one that leads to life and one that leads to death (Did. 1.1).

However, this pure eschatological vision of the Two Ways metaphor is further complicated when the majority of the ethics portray human-to-human relationships and the reward of τέλειος is required prior to entering the community (Did. 6.2). These current elements pose a difficulty for a purely eschatological vision of the Two Ways.

## Corporate Eschatology

The corporate eschatological vision is far more prominent. With a few exceptions scattered throughout the Didache, the primary eschatological vision resides in Did. 16. So, without turning this section into commentary on Did. 16, I will only highlight a few key theological ideas from the Didache's corporate eschatological vision.

Three texts, in particular, correlate to the Church receiving the kingdom as an inheritance. I do perceive it to be a stretch to conclude that the Didache offers an early articulation of Chiliasm or pre-millennialism.[27] The eschatological vision of the Didache is not complete enough to suggest such a concept. In Did. 9.4, the Eucharist bread serves as a portrait of God gathering the church into the Kingdom (εἰς τὴν σὴν βασιλείαν). She will be gathered from the four corners of the earth, which would imply the final gathering of the church (cf. Matt 24:31; Mark 13:27; Rev 7:1). Additionally,

---

27. Charles Hill is most right, in my estimation, in that if Robert Aldridge's reconstruction of Did. 16 holds sway, then the Didache presents no temporary kingdom that is inaugurated prior to everlasting life. Rather, the return of Jesus initiates the kingdom as the final step in the eschaton. Hill, *Regnum Caelorum*, 77–78 (special attention given to 77n3); Aldridge, "Lost Ending of the Didache," 1–15. Some in Didache research argue for a Chiliastic reading of the Didache. Ladd, "Eschatology of the Didache"; Varner, "Didache 'Apocalypse,'" 309–22.

the Lord will gather the church from the four winds of the earth into the Kingdom (Did. 10.5).

Next, although the predominant motifs are ethical in nature, meekness serves as the head virtue that secures the earth as one's reward (Did. 3.7; cf. Ps. 37:11; Matt 5:5). The inheritance of the earth and the rescuing of the Church into the Kingdom of God encompass the only eschatological instruction outside of Did. 16. This "Kingdom" and "earth" language are the rewards for a faithful community.

Didache 16 presents the most cumulative material for the eschatological and apocalyptic vision of the Didache. "The last season" (Did. 16.2), "the hour when the Lord is coming" (Did. 16.1), and the apocalyptic vision of the Lord returning with the saints (Did. 16.3-8) all utilize both eschatological and apocalyptic language.

Eschatological ethics and communal preservation appropriate the vision for the return of God as the basis of eschatological motivation (Did. 16.1-2). The community must "watch" over their life, not let their "lamps" be extinguished, nor neglect to gather together. Their ethics must persevere to the end so that the time of their faith was of value (Did. 16.2). When the Lord returns in the final days, they must still be found having τέλειος (cf. Did. 1.4; 6.2).

During the final days, false prophets and corruptors will increase (Did. 16.3). As these figures increase, signs, wonders, and persecutions will increase even further (Did. 16.3-4). One particular figure will appear as the world deceiver, and they will appear like the son of man (Did. 16.4). A fire of testing, curses, and inverted moral ethics will appear and continue to increase (Did. 16.4, 5).[28]

During the Lord's return from out of the heavens, there will be three signs, a partial resurrection, and the appearance of saints. The three signs of the Lord's return will include a stretching of the sky, the sound of a trumpet, and the resurrection of the dead—all apocalyptic in orientation. The Didachist quotes material from the canonical tradition (cf. Zech 14:5; 1 Thess 3:13) in order to point out that the saints will return with the Lord (Did. 16.7).[29] The partial resurrection of the dead will occur when Jesus, as the Lord, returns with previously martyred saints—see section in commentary.

After Did. 16.8, it remains relatively difficult to discuss the apocalyptic conclusion. The ending of the Didache MS is corrupted and we are missing a definitive conclusion to the Didache—see commentary for a closer reading of a reconstructed lost ending (Did. 16.9-12).

---

28. Pardee, "Curse that Saves"; Milavec, "Saving Efficacy."

29. See section in the commentary where I argue that the saints are formerly redeemed humans who return with God forming a martyrological paraenetic.

# Part II

# Commentary on the Didache

# Title of the Didache

"The Teaching of the Twelve Apostles"

THE DIDACHE BEGINS WITH two titles: a shorter title and a longer title. These titles come from the most complete MS tradition of the Didache that dates to the eleventh century—Codex Hierosolymitanus (H54).[1] Because this MS dates to the eleventh century, questions quickly arise about the authenticity of the title. The inscriptio ("short title") and incipit ("longer title") of the Didache's titles read as follows:

| | | |
|---|---|---|
| Inscriptio: | διδαχὴ τῶν δώδεκα ἀποστόλων | The Teaching of the Twelve Apostles |
| Incipit: | διδαχὴ κυρίου διὰ τῶν δώδεκα ἀποστόλων τοῖς ἔθνεσιν | The Teaching of the Lord to the Gentiles by the Twelve Apostles |

Other text traditions of the Didache exist in fragmentary form and they do not include the title: Oxyrhynchus Papyrus 1782,[2] a Coptic Papyrus,[3] an Ethiopic version,[4] and a Latin text (*Doctr.*). According to Peradse, the Georgian tradition retains both an inscriptio and incipit.[5] Yet according to Nancy

---

1. Koch, " Debatte über den Titel," 264–88.
2. Oxyrhynchus Papyrus 1782—Did. 1.3c–4a; 2.7b–3.2a.
3. Coptic Papyrus (British Library Oriental Manuscript 9271)—Did. 10.3b–12.2a. For more on the Coptic text, consult the following articles: Horner, "New Papyrus Fragment of the *Didache*," 225–31; Schmidt, "Das Koptische Didache-Fragment," 81–99; Jones and Mirecki, "Considerations of the Coptic Papyrus," 37–46.
4. Ethiopic version—Did. 8.1–2; 11.3–13.7. The Ethiopic version, which as a whole has been lost, partially preserves some of the Did. tradition in the Ethiopian church order. Horner, *Statutes of the Apostles*, 193–94; Rordorf and Tuilier, *Didachè*, 114–15; Niederwimmer, *Didache*, 26–27.
5. According to Peradse, he happened to see the Georgian version of the Did. in

Pardee, this Georgian MS adapts "the title closely related to the inscription and incipit of H54."⁶ The Georgian version does not function as an independent witness but adapts the already extant title found in H54. The inscriptio and incipit Georgian titles read as follows:

| Inscriptio: | Lehre der zwölf Apostel, geschrieben im Jahre 90 oder 100 nach dem Herrn Christus | The teaching of the twelve apostles, having been written in the year 90 or 100 according to the Lord Christ |
|---|---|---|
| Incipit: | Lehre des Herrn, die durch die zwölf Apostel der Menschheit gelehrt worden ist⁷ | The Teaching of the Lord that had been learned by the twelve apostles for humanity |

The Georgian version not only adapts H54 but it also adds commentary to the title. The Georgian inscriptio really does not qualify as a "shorter title." Rather, it qualifies as an initial title that includes a date of composition. This Georgian version builds from and receives the H54 tradition, and it does not serve as an independent witness to the Didache.

Another question needs to be raised. How do the titles from H54 (inscriptio and incipit) correspond to a more original or earlier title? Essentially, three options exist. First, some suggest that one of the two titles in H54 generally reflects an early title.⁸ Second, some claim that both titles contain additions to the text, which do not reflect a more original reading.⁹ For example, on the basis of a simple comparison with other Two-Ways texts or similar expressions (e.g., Barn. 18.1; Doct.; Acts 2:42),¹⁰ Gunnar Garleff argues that δώδεκα most likely is not original.¹¹

---

1923. Soon after, the edition that he observed, copied by Simon Pheikrischwili, was destroyed. According to Peradse's notes, moreover, it was a copy of the entire Did. except for Did. 1.5-6 and 13.5-7—marked by *fehlen* (trans. "lacking"). It is a contested witness to the Did., regardless. For example, Rordorf and Tuilier neglect to mention this text as a direct or indirect witness to the Did. text traditions (Rordorf and Tuilier, *Didachè*, 102-28). Peradse, "Der Georgischen Überlieferung," 111-16.

6. Pardee, *Genre and Development of the Didache*, 101.
7. Peradse, "Der Georgischen Überlieferung," 115.
8. Audet, *La Didachè*, 102. Audet suggests that Διδαχαὶ τῶν ἀποστόλων is "firmly established" as the title whereas Διδαχὴ κυρίου τοῖς ἔθνεσιν is not a second title of the whole work but is a title to demarcate the moral instruction found in Did. 1.
9. Niederwimmer, *Didache*, 57; Milavec, *Didache: Faith, Hope, & Life*, vii, 55.
10. Garleff, *Urchristliche Identität*, 111-12; Also, see Rordorf and Tuilier, *Didachè*, 15-16.
11. von Harnack, *Lehre der zwölf Apostel*, Proleg. 30; Robinson, *Barnabas, Hermas and Didache*, 82, 87; de Halleux, "Ministers in the Didache," 319; Pardee, *Genre and*

Within the early Christian reception of the Didache, a variety of short titles appear with relative frequency. As seen in the following list of titles, one is able to note discrepancies between a single and plural title: Διδαχή or Διδαχαί, and *Doctrina* or *Doctrinae*. Yet this brief list of titles do not address the longer title of the Didache.[12] The following table contains Ps. Cyprian (*de Aleatoribus* 4),[13] Eusebius of Caesarea (*Hist. eccl.* 3.25.4),[14] Athanasius of Alexandria (*Ep. fest.* 39),[15] Didymus the Blind (*Comm. Ps.* 227.26-27[16]; *Comm. Eccl.* 78.22[17]), Rufinus (*Hist.* III.25.4[18]; *Symb.* 36[19]), and Ps.-Athanasius.[20]

Table 7. Titles of the Didache in Other Patristic Authors

| Patristic Author and Source | Title of Didache | Translation of Title |
|---|---|---|
| Ps. Cyprian | | |
| *de Aleatoribus* 4 | *in doctrinis apostolorum* | In the Teachings of the Apostles |
| Eusebius of Caesarea | | |
| *Hist. eccl.* 3.25.4 | τῶν ἀποστόλων αἱ λεγόμεναι Διδαχαί | Being called the "Teachings of the Apostles" |
| Athanasius of Alexandria | | |

---

*Development of the Didache*, 101–23. Pardee, however, is more settled to favor the incipit but she appears to be open to the insriptio.

12. This list of references is provided by: Pardee, *Genre and Development of the Didache*, 105.

13. Ps. Cyprian, *de Aleatoribus* 4. This is a more clear reference to the Did. because it proceeds to offer a conflated quotation of both Did. 14.2 and 15.3. "In doctrinis apostolorum est: *Si quis frater delinquit in ecclesia et non apparet legi, hic nec colligatur, donec paenitentiam agat, et non recipatur, ne inquinetur oratio vestra.*" [trans:] "It is in the *Teachings of the Apostles*, 'if some brother offends in the church and does not appear to obey the law, let him neither assemble until he gives penitence, nor be received back lest he pollutes and hinders your prayer." Niederwimmer, *Didache*, 9.

14. GCS 9.1, 253.4.

15. Péiclès-Pierre, *Fonti*, 2.75–76.

16. Gronevald, *Teil III: Kommentar zu Psalm 29–34*, 398.

17. Gronevald, *Teil II: Kommentar zu Eccl. 3–4*, 12, 70.

18. Rufinus, *Hist.* 3.25.4.

19. Rufinus, *Symb.*, 36. (CCSL 20, 171). I would still adhere to this being a reference to the Did. or a text closely resembling the Did. because Rufinus mentions Hermas (*Pastor Hermae*) in the prior clause.

20. Zahn, *Geschichte des neutestamentlichen Kanons*, 2.1.301.

| Patristic Author and Source | Title of Didache | Translation of Title |
|---|---|---|
| Ep. fest. 39 | Διδαχὴ καλουμένη τῶν ἀποστόλων | The *book* called "Teaching of the Apostles" |
| Didymus the Blind | | |
| Comm. Ps. 227.26–27 | ἐν τῇ Διδαχῇ τῇ βίβλῳ τῆς κατηχήσεως λέγεται | It says in the book of catechesis, "The Teaching" |
| Comm. Eccl. 78.22 | ἐν τῇ Διδαχῇ τῇ βίβλῳ τῆς κατηχήσεως τῶν ἀποστόλων λεγεται | It says in the book of catechesis, "The Teaching of the Apostles" |
| Rufinus | | |
| Hist. 3.25.4 | *Doctrina quae dicitur apostolorum* | Which is called, "Teachings of the Apostles" |
| Symb. 36 | *is qui appellatur Duae uiae* | It is called "Two Ways" |
| Ps. Athanasius | | |
| | Διδαχὴ ἀποστόλων | The Teaching of the Apostles |

Although some of these titles differ from H54, the non-uniformity of a title perpetuates the ambiguity of whether these patristic writers referred to the Didache, to other similar tractates, or to a "teaching" in general. In addition, because some figures know the title of the Didache in the plural, this may give more confidence to affirm quite a bit of flexibility regarding the title and, quite possibly, reconsider the plural version of the title as a more authentic version.

A number of texts in antiquity included both a shorter and longer title, even though a more well-known title would be the shorter title.[21] As Pardee notes, while some books in Greek antiquity that lacked a title would subsequently receive one after composition, some Jewish literature assumed an additional independent longer title alongside a shorter title.[22] These examples do not speak to the title of the Didache directly, but they demonstrate that the Didache is not unique in having two titles nor is the practice exclusive to the Didache's titular introduction.

---

21. The extent of my argument depends upon the findings of Pardee and her arguments. Pardee, *Genre and Development of the Didache*, 118–20.

22. Pardee, *Genre and Development of the Didache*, 118–19.

Inscriptio: Ecclesiastes

Incipit: The words of the Preacher, son of David, King of Israel in Jerusalem

Inscriptio: Song/Song of Songs/Songs of Songs

Incipit: The song of songs to Solomon

Inscriptio: The Apocalypse of Adam

Incipit: The apocalypse that Adam taught his son, Seth, in the seven hundredth year

Inscriptio: Tobit

Incipit: The book of the words of Tobit, son of Tobiel

As seen by these selected shorter and longer titles, the longer title will provide an additional descriptor. This scant evidence helps to corroborate the two titles of the Didache, even if the Didache is known more by the shorter title. Additionally, and especially as seen in the compositional history of the four-fold Gospels,[23] others in the community can provide shorter and longer titles to a given work and the additional titles reflect part of the reception history. So, to determine an original title in the original composition is quite complex, if not impossible.

Given the pieces of evidence listed above, I find it quite plausible for the Didache to have both an inscriptio and incipit early in its formation—especially referring to *when* and under *what* social circumstances these emerge. The evidence of a shorter title more often appears in patristic texts when referring to the Didache; the evidence of longer titles in ancient Jewish literature supports the plausibility of two titles appearing in ancient literature. Even if the Didache did not have these titles originally penned to the document, it may show a development to the title that serves as part of the reception history of the Didache.

The question, though, still remains as to whether or not the longer title forms part of a more original form of the Didache. The patristic evidence does help tip the scales to observe the shorter title as more authentic than not, although more research needs to uncover whether or not it should be διδαχή or διδαχαί. This two-fold difference in spelling can be

---

23. Davies and Allison recognize the Jewish patterns of a short and long title. With the Gospel of Matthew, Matt 1:1 serves an incipit-like title. Thus you have: (1) Inscriptio: Gospel of Matthew; and (2) Incipit: "Book of the New Genesis wrought by Jesus Christ, son of David, son of Abraham." Davies and Allison, *Matthew 1–7*, 153–54.

compared to how the Gospels contained ΕΥΑΓΓΕΛΙΟΝ ΚΑΤΑ ΛΟΥΚΑΝ but later patristic writers or MS evidence list ΚΑΤΑ ΛΟΥΚΑΝ or other changed forms.[24] To build upon Pardee's *Genre* work, ancient texts could use the first element in the title to depict the *genre* of literature and its modifier as the authorial source.[25] A shorter title does not negate the plausibility of a longer extant title. Rather, the longer title may provide early evidence of *how* it was read and received for the community—as a kind of διδαχή for Gentile instruction.[26]

Although I remain uncertain as to what extent the titles are authentic to an early form, the *title* still communicates and frames the text of the Didache in a particular way.[27] In a more complete form (H54), this title evokes Jesus tradition as communicated through the twelve apostles for the sake of Gentile instruction.[28] Both the incipit and inscriptio titles claim apostolic authorship. This apostolic origin is not merely the apostolic teaching of Pauline and Petrine Christianity, but rather it evokes the teachings of Jesus as provided through the twelve apostles, most likely twelve disciples of Jesus (cf. Matt 10:1–5; 11:1; 20:17). However, nothing inside the actual Didache offers any hint of apostolic authority. Plus, the Didache resembles similar Two Ways tractates.[29] So, even though the titles claim apostolic origins, the Didache is more likely a pseudepigraphal work.[30]

24. Gathercole, "Titles of the Gospels," 33–76.

25. Trobisch, *First Edition of the New Testament*, 38; Bird, *Gospel of the Lord*, 257.

26. I recognize the problem of basing this much on the title of the Did. I remain unconvinced that the title is entirely unimportant to the overall work, but the contrary is just as true. Especially in light of reception theory studies, the title could be a way for modern scholars to see *how* the Did. was received by later communities. I would like to take a moderate position on this—tentatively adhere to and interpret the longer title while prohibiting this to affect any of the internal readings of the Did.

27. According to Rordorf and Tuilier, the two titles that have survived do not help speak to the origins, the genre, or the recipients of the work. My comments do not aim to counter this suggestion at all. Rather, my comments above refer to a more final form in H54, rather than to the historical origins of the title. Rordorf and Tuilier, *Didachè*, 16–17.

28. Throughout this entire commentary, I will assume the H54 and closely related readings. I am not unaware of the complexities that this assumption now brings. Does the final form document, H54, an eleventh-century document, accurately reflect the first and second-century settings? I will make very little comment about the historical trajectory of the manuscripts and the historical critical assumptions here. Milavec documents why he affirms the validity of reading the Didache in its final form. My assumptions differ quite a bit from Milavec. I will not, however, document some of the critical concerns that I have in order to reserve my comments to a more final form document. Milavec, "Pastoral Genius of the Didache," 89–125.

29. Niederwimmer, *Didache*, 56.

30 That said, the text speaks with a *single* authorial voice (the implied author). This textual voice is not the voice of a group (the apostles). It is an I, not a we. So perhaps the titles position the text not as having been written *by* the apostles (and thus

Second, the title also reflects the supposed "Lord's teaching." Because the "teachings" are associated with the "twelve apostles," κύριος in the title corresponds to Jesus, although some have disputed this conclusion. For example, Aaron Milavec rightly notes that κύριος applies to human masters (Did. 4.11). Also, it can refer to the generic idea of "Lord-God" (cf. Did. 4.1, 12–13; 11.2; 12.1; 15.1).[31] The Didachist quotes from Malachi 1 (Did. 14.3) and attributes κύριος to the Lord-God. In another case, κύριος refers exclusively to the trinitarian Father (Did. 10.5).

However, some instances of κύριος, for the Didachist, can refer to or include a reference to Jesus (cf. Did. 6.2; 15.4). The strongest case for κύριος referring to Jesus appears in Did. 8.2 where κύριος serves as the source of a given prayer from his gospel. The listed prayer is from the Sermon on the Mount and from Jesus tradition in Matthew 6. The next instance suggests that the Eucharist exclusively may be enjoyed by those having been baptized in the name of κύριος (Did. 9.5). The Didachist already knows of the trinitarian baptismal formula (cf. Did. 7.1–3), thus Jesus can be included in the title κύριος. Furthermore, another potential Jesus tradition relates to κύριος (Did. 9.5; Matt 7:6).[32] Also, the Didache community meets κατὰ κυριακὴν κυρίου ("each Lord's day") to break bread and give thanks, which refers to the Eucharist (Acts 2:42; Did. 9.1–3).[33] In the Christian Scriptures, Jesus will return in the eschaton (Matt 24:30), yet the Didachist neglects to identify this figure (Did. 16.1, 7, 8). If Did. 16 parallels the Matthean tradition, then κύριος refers to Jesus. So, it is quite possible that the title, "The Teaching of the Lord," conveys the instruction of Jesus as administered through the twelve apostles.

The third feature of the title highlights the intended audience. The work directs its instruction "to the Gentiles." The teachings of the Lord

---

pseudepigrapha) but as communicating their teaching. This, proclaim the titles, is their teaching.

31. Milavec, *Didache: Faith, Hope & Life*, 663–66.

32. No doubt exists that this tradition remains debated and the Didachist has traditions available beyond Matt: Gos. Thom. 93; Epiphanius *Pan.* 24.5.2. See discussions in the following works that assess 1QS and other Jewish texts: Draper, "Attitude of the Didache to the Gentiles," 242–58; Davies and Allison, *Matthew 1–7*, 674–76; Betz, *Sermon on the Mount*, 493–98.

33. Early witnesses mention Christian gatherings on Sunday in association with the resurrection of Jesus. According to early ecclesial practices, the church gathered on the first day of the week (Acts 20:7). Rev 1:10 uses a similar Greek expression "κυριακῇ ἡμέρᾳ" ("Lord's day"). Another tradition, likewise, offers a similar Greek expression "κατὰ κυριακὴν ζῶντες" of not gathering on the Sabbath but according to the living Lord's *day* (Ign. *Mag.* 9.1). Ignatius likens this day to the resurrection of Jesus. It is the eighth day, as mentioned by Barnabas (Barn. 15.8–9). If the testimony of Pliny the Younger can be representative, then this day was a weekly-appointed time for early Christians: "they were in the habit of meeting on a certain fixed day before it was light" (Pliny, *Ep.* 10.96).

Jesus, as provided by the twelve apostles, aim to instruct all the nations. In this case, the Didache titles extend from the final instructions of Jesus in the Gospel of Matthew (Matt 28:18–20).

Titles help frame a piece of literature to be read in a particular way. Yet in the case of the Didache, a debate already surrounds the authenticity of the title. As previously mentioned, this literary reading of the title corresponds with minimal internal evidence to other portions of the book. Historically, the work, in its earliest form, more likely contained a version of the incipit that appears in H54. Too many additional references to the work help corroborate the Didache's title as "The Teaching(s) of the Apostles." So, although many works in antiquity can have an inscriptio and incipit, I'm more confident to suggest more authenticity to the inscriptio of the Didache than to the incipit.[34]

No other signs of apostleship exist in the Didache (cf. Did. 11.3).[35] Early communities could recognize the amount of scattered Jesus tradition to include both apostleship and Jesus in the possible titles. However, some Jesus material remains overshadowed by other instruction in the Didache. For example, the majority of Did. 2 models the second half of the Mosaic Decalogue. Even more problematic to this aforementioned literary reading of the title is the long-debated "riddle of the Didache"—*to whom* is the Didache written?[36]

So, if the title is original to the text, then it will frame the Didache in a peculiar way. More difficulty persists in interpreting and reading the Didache if it is addressed to Gentiles via the apostles's instruction. It proves difficult to affirm with certainty the authenticity of the titles—either incipit or inscriptio; and yet the final form titles may still influence one's reading of the text.

---

34. Pardee suggests, "The evidence seems to support both the antiquity and the originality of the incipit as the title of the Didache. It still does not resolve all of the problems, however, regarding the two titles, most importantly the relationship of the 'name label' of the Didache to the title of the Doctrina and to those found in patristic citations." Although much of my research is influenced by Pardee, I want to make one modification to this. I suggest that the inscriptio has much more probability as an early title of the Did. on the basis that early sources refer to a *version* of the inscriptio. However, because data of incipits appear in antiquity, this does not equally mean the Did. had an inscriptio early in its development. I would affirm the incipit of the Did. as a possibility. Pardee, *Genre and Development of the Didache*, 121.

35. I would be hard-pressed even to include the possibility of Διδαχή belonging to the instruction of the traveling apostles in Did. 11. The logical inferences of this possibility remain somewhat incoherent. For, how can the instruction about recieving the apostles (Did. 11) consist of the very group that wrote these instructions. The interpretive logic is backwards to even suggest such a possibility.

36. Vokes, *Riddle of the Didache*.

# I

## Didache 1.1—6.2

### Ethical Instruction of the Two-Ways Ethic

### I.1. Introduction to the Two Ways (Did. 1.1)

THE TWO WAYS BEGINS with a bifurcating dilemma that places a reader within a wisdom-like quandary. The reader stands at the intersection of two diverging roads. At the end each road stands one of two polarized outcomes that border the horizon: life and death. As a wayfarer, one must deeply consider the ethical posture of one's life that produces both a way to flourish in this life (namely the community) and to foretell the telic consequences.

The Didache's first six chapters constitute what scholars typically call a Two Ways tractate and serve as the oldest part of the Didache with the "most deeply embedded text-parts."[1] The Two Ways appears regularly in antiquity as a common form of wisdom, including sapiential-apocalyptic, instruction (1QS III, 13–IV, 26; Testament of Asher; Psalm 1; Gal 5:16–24; Barn. 18–20; De Doctrina; and Herm. Mand. 6.1–2 [35–36]).[2] Each road describes the set of ethical values pertinent to life or death, and humans stand before the two alternatives.[3] Instead of signifying that these roads *lead* somewhere, the reader is left to assume they do so. A "road" or "way" image activates a traveling

---

1. See the following dissertation for more on the Two Ways in antiquity: McKenna, "'Two Ways' in Jewish and Christian Writings" and Pardee, *Genre and Development of the Didache*, 162.

2. Audet, *La Didachè*, 121–66; Suggs, "Christian Two Ways Tradition," 60–74; Rordorf and Tuilier, *Didachè*, 22–34; Jefford, *Sayings of Jesus*, 27n17; Niederwimmer, *Die Didache*, 48–54, 61n72; Niederwimmer, *Didache*, 30–34, 40n73; Nickelsburg, "Origins of the Two-Ways," 95–108; Kraft, "Early Developments," 136–43; Ehrman, *Apostolic Fathers I*, 408; Del Verme, *Didache and Judaism*, 246–47; Garrow, *Matthew's Dependence on the Didache*, 67–92; Kloppenborg, "*Didache*, James, Matthew, and Torah," 195; Pardee, *Genre and Development of the Didache*, 50, 77–80, 126n148, 167.

3. Niederwimmer, *Didache*, 59.

metaphor. To use a road for the image of ethics recalls the ancient figures who "walked with God" (cf. Gen 3:8; 5:24; 6:9) and other forms of wisdom literature (cf. Ps 1:1–2). This metaphorical language permits the reader to view the journey of their life as a wayfarer traversing upon a road. The covenant community members are wayfarers upon one of the two ways of life. Thus, this image more broadly implies that the ethical life of an individual determines the telic outcome of a life. The way of life, then, consists of personal and communal ethics that facilitate an eschatological result.

This polarized ethic corresponds to other sacred and religious ancient literature. For example, a message of *Deuteronomy* affords blessings and cursings before the people of Israel (Deut 28–30) and calls forth "I have set before you life and death, blessings and cursings" (Deut 30:19). Also, the portrait of the "blessed person" depicts a metaphor road/way (Ps 1). Psalm 1:6, likewise, conveys a now/not-yet paradigm in that the eyes of the Lord perceive the way of the righteous; yet the way of death destroys such a person. Even Jesus in the Sermon on the Mount invites the hearer to walk across the threshold of a gate that will ultimately lead to life or death (Matt 7:13–14). With the language of "blessing" and "life," the Two Ways may opine on the true flourishing life.

The Treatise of the Two Spirits accentuates an apocalyptic version of the Two Ways (1QS III, 13–IV, 26).[4] This text joins together two angels (a Prince of Lights [שר אורים] and an Angel of Darkness [מלאך הושך]), who seek to influence two groups of humanity: upright or perverse humanity (1 QS III, 16–18). As the angels seek to persuade humanity, the Two Ways serves as the ethical framework for the angelic beings (1QS IV, 2–14). The ethics of humanity intertwine with the cosmological forces of these two angelic beings that eventually become manifest in a human Two Ways ethics.[5]

Other ancient Jewish and Graeco-Roman literature surely reflect this kind of Two Ways structure and apocalyptic motifs.[6] These Two Ways texts often included apocalyptic motifs,[7] angelic or otherworldly mediaries, and deterministic categories. Thus, angels or other worldly mediaries (1 En.

---

4. The Treatise is generally dated to the first century BCE (c. 100–75 BCE). Duhaime, "Dualism," 216; Leonhardt-Balzer, "Dualism," 555.

5. Stuckenbruck, *Myth of Rebellious Angels*, 93–94.

6. See a compendium of Two Ways texts in antiquity: Wilhite, *"One of Life and One of Death,"* appendix 1.

7. See the following works to observe how wisdom and apocalypticism can cohere with one another and other related features involved in apocalyptic studies: Collins, "Morphology of a Genre," 1–20; Collins, "Generic Compatibility," 165–85; Collins, "What Is Apocalyptic Literature?" 1–16; Macaskill, *Revealed Wisdom and Inaugurated Eschatology*; Goff, "Wisdom and Apocalypticism," 52–68.

100.4-5; Philo, *Sacr.* 20-40; 2 Esd 7.1-140; Silius, *Pun.* 15.20-23; Xenophon, *Mem.* 2.21-22;) influence and compel humans to convey a particular polarized Two Ways ethic (1 En. 94.1-5; 2 En. 30.14-15; T. Ash. 1.3; Philo, *Sacr.* 35-36; Ps.-Clem. H. XX.2;) that determines their ultimate outcome (Plato, *Gorg.* 524; T. Ash. 1.4-9; Clement, *Strom.* V.14). In these Two Ways, the otherworldly mediaries clash with one another and their conflict transpires through the ethical dispositions of humanity.[8]

Early Christian literature from the second century continues this apocalyptic and angelic Two Ways framework. For example, the Epistle of Barnabas includes multiple light-giving angels (φωταγωγοὶ ἄγγελοι τοῦ θεοῦ) and the angels of Satan (ἄγγελοι τοῦ σατανᾶ) that reside over the pathway of light and darkness, respectively (Barn. 18.1).[9] Similar to the larger Two Ways frame of the Didache, Barn. 19 introduces the way of life and Barn. 20 commences the way of the Black One (ἡ δὲ τοῦ μέλανος ὁδός). *De Doctrina* coheres with the Didache in terms of structure, lexical symmetry, and even textual divisions. However, *Doctr.* 1.1 frames the Two Ways so as to include two angels that reside over the cosmos. Additionally, Herm. Mand. 6.1-2 (35-36) includes two angels that reside within a single human, competing to express virtues and vices.

All of this to say, the Two Ways consists of a number of themes and a particular literary structure that transcends the Didache. This Two Ways structure and apocalyptic motif appear with relative frequency in many different ancient traditions. The Didache's Two Ways may, in fact, be one of the oldest sections in the Didache.[10] Two Ways texts include reoccurring themes, motifs, and structures to suggest that the Didache functions as a sub-genre category of the Two Ways.[11] However, the Didache uniquely expresses the Two Ways because it lacks angelic or otherworldly mediaries, contains soft determinism, and contains no cosmological structures. Common to nearly all Two Ways is some form of dualistic categories. As Huub van de Sandt

---

8. According to Loren Stuckenbruck, "All human beings, whether socially on the inside or outside of the righteous community, comprise the battleground wherein the conflict between opposing spirits is carried out." Stuckenbruck, *Myth of Rebellious Angels*, 234.

9. Draper, "Riddle of the Didache Revisited" 89-113; Tomson, "Didache, Matthew, and Barnabas," 348-82.

10. Suggs, "Christian Two Ways Tradition"; McKenna, "'Two Ways' in Jewish and Christian Writings"; Kraft, "Early Developments"; Draper, "Two Ways and Eschatological Hope," 221-51; Stewart-Sykes, *On the Two Ways*.

11. See my discussion on the Two Ways structure: 1. dualistic literary introduction; 2. sapiential invitation to consider dualized ethical paths; 3. virtue and vice lists; 4. eschatological paraenetic addressing wayfarer; 5. literary redaction and individuality of Two Ways texts. Wilhite, *"One of Life and One of Death."*

and David Flusser rightly observe, the Two Ways, and in particular the Didache, are "couched within polar tendencies of good and evil, moral and immoral qualities, and righteous and wicked people. This dualism refers to a pattern of thought which expresses two mutually exclusive categories and, as such, stresses the importance on the part of humanity making a fundamental choice between right and wrong."[12] So, a now/not-yet dualism of telic outcomes accompanies the ethical dualism. Although apocalyptic motifs color the Two Ways genre in antiquity, the Didache's version altogether lacks any apocalyptic elements in its Two Ways.[13]

As we move to interpret Did. 1.1, the Didache's Two Ways vastly differs from one another, not only in terms of the ethics but also the telic outcome. The "pathway" metaphor evokes a now/not-yet tension. Each road embodies a form of presently demonstrated ethics that also includes a telic destination of "life" or "death." As one observes the general contents of "the way of life" (Did. 1.2–4.14), nearly all ethical teaching reflects a habitual ethic of love for God or love for neighbor. Ethical dualisms emerge to portray polarized ethical opposites, good and evil, flourishing and oppression, moral virtue qualities and immoral vice categories. The Two Ways situates the reader to stand at a fork in the road and invites them to consider their ethical posture. How they move and how they reflect upon their own personal ethical disposition will determine the telic outcome of their condition. Readers and community members identify as a wayfarer where the goal is to maintain one's journey on the pathway of life.

The ethical Two Ways in the Didache reflects more often than not a present human-to-human posture, especially the way of death instruction. The way of life conveys an ethical and ideological disposition of how to relate to God and how to relate to one another so as to flourish upon the earth. The way of death, contrary and quite opposite to the way of life, leads to destruction—contrary to human flourishing. This introductory expression in Did. 1.1 sets the stage for the following six chapters. It is an introductory

---

12. van de Sandt and Flusser, *Didache*, 146.

13. Niederwimmer has presented an intriguing possibility as to why this apocalyptic and two-angels schema remains absent: "It can no longer be said with certainty whether this source spoke only of the two ways but also of the two angels or spirits who are placed over those two ways (as we now find it, *mutatis mutandis*, in the version in *Barnabas* and *Doctrina*). It is probable, though. If that is the case, the Didache would have omitted the motif of the *angeli duo*, perhaps because it plays no part in the exposition that follows. In the wake of this omission, then, anything about the 'way of life and darkness' would also have dropped out. . . . In the overall context of the *Didache*, the two-ways schema acquires an additional and concrete specification." Niederwimmer, *Didache*, 63.

summary of the proceeding material that highlights the distinct differences between the Two Ways: life and death.

## I.2. The Way of Life (Did. 1.2-4.14)

### I.2.a. First Commandment of the Way of Life (Did. 1.2-6)

The first part of the Didache's Two Ways introduces the way of life. Didache 1.2-2.7 can be summarized in two parts: (1) love for God, the one having created you (Did. 1.2b), and (2) love for one's neighbor (Did. 1.2c). This double love command occurs with relative frequency in ancient Jewish,[14] Greek and Roman,[15] and Christian traditions.[16] The Didachist, in particular, reframes this double love ethic to accord with the law of Christ (cf. Matt 22:37-39; Mark 12:30-31; Luke 10:27). Closely paralleling the Matthean Sermon on the Mount material, the double love command *christianizes* the initial way of life.[17]

The Didachist prepares the readers for what follows by using titles to frame the subsequent material in Did. 1.3 ("the teaching is this") and Did. 1.2 ("the way of life is this"). The preparatory phrase in Did. 1.3 frames the following material in 1.3-6 to express how one "loves God." Also, Did. 1.2 prepares the reader to hold together the entire way of life section (Did. 1.2-4.14). If this holds true, then Did. 1.1 initiates the frame that holds together the entire Two Ways (Did. 1.2-6.2). The repetitious use of a pronoun and δέ helps to demarcate these sections.[18] Thus, a tiered outline could look like the following:

---

14. Lev 19:18; Deut 6:5; 10:12, 19; Jub 7.20-21; 20.2-10; T. Dan. 5.3; T. Iss. 5.1-2; 7.2-6.

15. Seneca, *De Otio* 1.4; *De Beneficiis* 7, 30.2.

16. Gal 5:14; Rom 13:8-10; Ps.-Clem *Hom.* 12, 32.3-4; Gos. Thom. 25; Origen, *Comm. Rom.* 3,9 (PG 14,952-53); 4,1 (PG 14,963); 4,6 (PG 14,981); 4,7 (PG 14,986); 6,5 (PG 14,1066); 9,15 (PG 14,1221); 9,31 (PG 14,1232).

17. Niederwimmer, *Didache*, 44.

18. A pronoun may convey a cataphoric, forward-pointing, discourse function; or it may convey an anaphoric, summative, discourse function. As Pardee has argued and suggested, pronominal substitutions and renominalizations create a literary inclusio. Levinsohn offers the following, "Summary statements unite together the information they summarize and thereby indicate that the preceding material should be treated as a block, over against what is to follow." So, these ideas connect to H54 in that a combined use of μέν . . . δέ and use of cataphoric/anaphoric pronouns, Did. 1.2; 4.14; and 5.1 all relate together to create discourse segments.

Did. 1.2a: ἡ μὲν οὖν ὁδὸς τῆς ζωῆς ἐστιν αὕτη
Did. 5.1a: ἡ δὲ τοῦ θανάτου ὁδός ἐστιν αὕτη
Did. 1.2a (cataphoric): ἡ μὲν ὁδὸς τῆς ζωῆς ἐστιν αὕτη

Introduction to the Two Ways (Did. 1.1):

Introduction to the Way of Life (Did. 1.2): ἡ μὲν οὖν ὁδὸς τῆς ζωῆς ἐστιν αὕτη (trans: this is the way of life)

Introduction to the First Teaching (Did. 1.3): τούτων δὲ τῶν λόγων ἡ διδαχή ἐστιν αὕτη (trans: this is the teaching of these words)

Introduction to the Second Teaching (Did. 2.1): δευτέρα δὲ ἐντολὴ τῆς διδαχῆς (trans: the second commandment of the teaching)

As the Didachist supplies the initial features of the way of life, two elements govern the double-love command. First, the Didachist highlights God as the "one making you." "Creation" motifs reoccur as a theme to refer to those who corrupt God's creation (cf. Did. 5.2) and to attribute all created things to God (cf. Did. 10.3). In Did. 1.2, the Didachist employs creation language so as to invite one to love God—similar to Barn. 19.2.[19] With the increased ethical ideas in Did. 1–5, creation motifs also motivate personal ethics. Creation entails ownership, and thus the basis to require certain ethics and a way of life (cf. Acts 17:24)—also see a textual emendation of Wisdom of Sirach 1.5 where creation utilizes wisdom as a base.[20] Elsewhere, Athenagoras highlights creation motifs so as to beckon ethics.[21]

In the canonical tradition, God, as creator, preserves those who suffer (1 Pet 4:19). In other ancient Christian texts, creation motifs convey the faithfulness of God (1 Clem. 60.1), maintain the elect of God (1 Clem. 59.2), serve as an emblem of eschatological judgment (Barn. 15.3–5), act as a basis for personal ethics and serving God (Pol. *Phil.* 2.1), and more.[22]

---

Did. 4.14c (anaphoric): αὕτη ἐστὶν ἡ ὁδὸς τῆς ζωῆς
Pardee, *Genre and Development of the Didache*, 86–87; Levinsohn, *Discourse Features*, 277.

19. Barn. 19.2: "you shall love the one who made you, you shall fear the one who created you, you shall glorify the one who redeemed you from death."

20. Sirach 1.5: Πηγὴ σοφίας λόγος θεοῦ ἐν ὑψίστοις, καὶ αἱ πορεῖαι αὐτῆς ἐντολαὶ αἰώνιοι. "The source of wisdom is the word of God in the highest [heavens], and her ways are eternal commandments." Ziegler, *Sapientia Iesu Filii Sirach*, 128.

21. God, as creator, is a vital apologetic theme in second-century Christianity. For Athenagoras, to have a deity fashioned from human hands deters any allegiance, "If, then while marveling at the heavens and the elements for their craft, I do not adore them as gods, knowing their transient nature, how can I call those things gods which I know to have had men for their makers?" (Athenagoras, *Embassy*, 16).

22. The function of cosmology in the Apostolic Fathers would be a worthwhile endeavor. It is a frequent enough theme to note a particular set of functions in the ancient church. Consult a sampling of texts from the Apostolic Fathers: 1 Clem. 59.2–3; 60.1;

Second, the Didachist explains "loving one's neighbor" through a negative exhortation: "and whatever you do not desire to happen, do not do to another." Although Did. 1.3 refrains from repeating the numeral "first" (πρῶτον) or "second" (δεύτερον), Did. 2.1 resumes previous ideas regarding how to love one's neighbor. Didache 2.1 reminds the reader of the "second commandment" (δεθτέρα ἐντολή) and, thus, joins back to the two commands given in Did. 1.3. Chapter 2 focuses more on relational ethics and begins with "the second commandment of the teaching." In the canonical tradition, to love one's neighbor usually occurs with an additional caveat "as you would love yourself" (cf. Matt 19:19; 22:39; Mark 12:31; Rom 13:8; Jas 2:8). However, the Didachist couches the command negatively, possibly to reflect or cohere with the negative ethics in 2.1–7: "and whatever you desire not to happen to you, do not do to another" (Did. 1.3).

Love for God, as one feature of the flourishing way of life, involves personal ethics towards enemies and persecutors, personal refrain from *passions*, and a divine generous posture to give of the Father's "gifts." Much of the ethics recalls the Sermon on the Mount—namely the Matthean version—and begins what nearly all call the *sectio evangelica* (Did. 1.3b–2.1).[23] The *sectio evangelica* often generates much debate and discussion because of its relation to the Synoptic parallels, its ubiquitous absence from other Two Ways texts, and it is generally thought to be a later interpolation.[24] To love God, for the way of life, also includes blessings, prayers, and fasting on behalf of one's enemies and persecutors (Did. 1.3b; cf. Matt 5:44). According to John Welch, over 100 lines of symmetry exist between the Sermon on the Mount and the Didache, and twenty-one elements of symmetry appear with Did. 1 alone.[25] I make a few modifications to Welch's study to convey twenty-eights points of symmetry between Did. 1 and the Sermon on the Mount.

---

62.2; Herm. Vis. 1.1.6 (1.6); 2.4 (8.1); Mand. 1.1 (26.1); 9.3 (39.3); Sim. 5.6.5 (59.5); Barn. 5.5; 6.11; 15.3–5; 16.2; 19.2; Pol. *Phil.* 2.1.

23. Syreeni comments on the compositional history of the Did. and the parallels with the Sermon on the Mount in Did. 1.3b–2.1. Bentley Layton brilliantly displays the complexity of assessing the *sectio evangelica*. Layton, "Didache 1:3b–2:1," 343–83; Syreeni, "Sermon on the Mount and the Two Ways," 87–103; Nikander, "Sectio Evangelica," 287–310.

24. van de Sandt and Flusser describe the *sectio evangelica* as follows, "Section 1:3b–2:1, unlike the greatest part of the first five chapters of the Didache, undoubtedly derives from more recent sources. It clearly interrupts the connection between Did 1:3a and 2:2 and it stands out from the immediate context in Chaps. 1–6 with respect to its high number of close parallels to the gospels of Matthew and Luke.... There is a good possibility that the section was inserted into Did 1–6 at the time when the earlier Two Ways form was incorporated in the Didache as a whole." van de Sandt and Flusser, *Didache*, 40.

25. Welch, "Sermon on the Mount," 336.

## Table 8. Didache 1 and the Sermon on the Mount[26]

| | Didache 1 | | Matthew's Sermon on the Mount |
|---|---|---|---|
| 1.0 | The apostles's teaching (διδαχή τῶν δώδεκα ἀποστόλων) | 7:28 | His teaching (διδαχῇ αὐτοῦ) |
| 1.1 | Two ways (ὁδοί δύο) | 7:13–14 | Way, way (ὁδός, ὁδός) |
| | Way of life (ὁδὸς τῆς ζωῆς) | 7:14 | To life (ὁδὸς . . . εἰς τὴν ζωήν) |
| | Of life, of death (ὁδοί . . . τῆς ζωῆς, θανάτου) [inverting death-life] | 7:13 | To destruction (εἰς τὴν ἀπώλειαν) |
| 1.2 | Love (ἀγαπήσεις) the God who made you | 6:24 | Love the Master (ἀγαπήσει) |
| | Love neighbor (ἀγαπήσεις . . . τὸν πλησίον) | 5:43 | Love neighbor (ἀγαπήσεις τὸν πλησίον) |
| | All you wish won't happen to you and you to another don't do (ἄλλῳ μὴ ποίει) [inverting do-to] | 7:12 | All you wish men to do to you, and so you do to them (ποιεῖτε αὐτοῖς) |
| 1.3 | Bless those who curse you (εὐλογεῖτε τοὺς καταρωμένους) | 5:44 | Bless who curse you (εὐλογεῖτε τοὺς καταρωμένους) |
| | Pray (προσεύχεσθε) for your enemies | 5:44 | Pray (προσεύχεσθε) for those who persecute you |
| | What favor (χάρις) do you do, if you love those who love you? [inverting if-what] | 5:47 | If you love those who love you, what remarkable thing (περισσόν) do you do? |
| | Gentiles (ἔθνη) also do this (αὐτὸ ποιοῦσιν) | 5:47 | Gentile (ἐθνικοί) also do this (αὐτὸ ποιοῦσιν) |
| | Love those who hate you, have no enemy (ἐχθρῶν) | 5:43 | Love your enemies (ἐχθρούς) |
| 1.4 | Slap on the right cheek (ῥαπίζει εἰς τὴν δεξιὰν σιαγόνα) | 5:39 | Slap on the right cheek (ῥαπίζει εἰς τὴν δεξιὰν σιαγόνα) |
| | Turn to him the other also (στρέψον αὐτῷ καὶ τὴν ἄλλην) | 5:39 | Turn to him the other also (στρέψον αὐτῷ καὶ τὴν ἄλλην) |
| | You will be perfect (ἔσῃ τέλειος) | 5:48 | Be perfect (ἔσεσθε οὖν ὑμεῖς τέλειοι) |
| | Cloak (ἱμάτιον), tunic (χιτῶνά) [inverted] | 5:40 | Tunic (χιτῶνά), cloak (ἱμάτιον) |

---

26. Welch, "Sermon on the Mount," 355–61.

| | Didache 1 | | Matthew's Sermon on the Mount |
|---|---|---|---|
| | Someone compels you [to go] one mile (ἀγγαρεύσῃ σέ τις μίλιον ἕν) | 5:41 | If someone compels you [to go] one mile (ὅστις σε ἀγγαρεύσει μίλιον ἕν) |
| | Go with him two (ὕπαγε μετ'αὐτοῦ δύο) | 5:41 | Go with him two (ὕπαγε μετ'αὐτοῦ δύο) |
| | Don't ask for it back (μὴ ἀπαίτει) | 5:42 | Give to those who ask (αἰτοῦντί) |
| 1.5 | Upon all wishes to give the Father [inverting Father-all] | 5:45 | The Father's sun and rain falls on all |
| | Give to everyone who asks (αἰτοῦντί) for [thus] the Father wishes to give (δίδοσθαι) [inverting give-ask] | 7:11 | If you give to those who ask (αἰτοῦσιν) much more will the Father give (δώσει) |
| | Gifts (χαρισμάτων) | 7:10–11 | Gifts (δόματα) |
| | Blessed (μακάριος) is the giver | 5:3 | Blessed (μακάριοι) |
| | Trial, prison (ἐν συνοχῇ) | 5:26 | Judge, prison (εἰς φυλακήν) |
| | Not come out of there (ἐξελεύσεται ἐκεῖθεν) | 5:26 | Not come out (ἐξέλθῃς ἐκεῖθεν) |
| | Until he pays the last kodrantes (μέχρις οὗ ἀποδῷ τὸν ἔσχατον κοδράντην) | 5:26 | Until you pay the last kodrantes (ἕως ἔσχατον κοδράντην) |
| 1.6 | Give alms (ἐλεημοσύνη ... δῷς) | 6:3 | Give alms (ποιοῦντος ἐλεημοσύνην) |
| | Sweat in hands until you know (γνῷς) to whom to give it | 6:3 | Hands not know (γνώτω) |

When comparing the Sermon on the Mount tradition, the Didache includes a fasting ethic not initially found in Matt 5. Rather, a fasting ethic emerges in the following chapter, Matt 6, and thereby could suggest that the Didachist remains familiar with a composite Matthew Gospel or both share a similar awareness of Jesus's teaching. Albeit, it certainly increases a more focused attention to petition on behalf of enemies and certainly appears as a feature of Jesus's ethics. To "bless those who persecute you" (Did. 1.3) recalls a list of staccato ethics in the Pauline tradition (Rom 12) and the Jesus tradition of loving one's enemy (Matt 5:44).

| Matt 5:44 | Did. 1.3 | Rom 12:14 |
|---|---|---|
| ἀγαπᾶτε | Εὐλογεῖτε | εὐλογεῖτε |
| τοὺς ἐχθροὺς | τοὺς καταρωμένους | τοὺς διώκοντας |
| ὑμῶν καὶ | ὑμῖν καὶ | ὑμᾶς |
| προσεύχεσθε | προσεύχεσθε | |
| ὑπὲρ τῶν διωκόντων ὑμᾶς | ὑπὲρ τῶν ἐχθρῶν ὑμῶν | |

One's social identity in the community motivates a certain kind of behavior and posture towards those opposing them. To love those who love you back simply credits you nothing (Did. 1.3c; Matt 5:46; Luke 6:32, 34). Rather, to love those who love you will help delimit wayfarers on the way of life. "Gentiles" refers to moral outsiders. Even though the Didache shows a general awareness of Matthean values, little evidence exists to suggest that "the Gentiles" are simply an ethnic, non-Jewish identity. Rather, "Gentiles" conveys a moral outsider identity for the Didache's Christian community. Thus, to love others who simply return an act of love marks a common and shared set of morals. Even though this instruction elaborates one's love of God (Did. 1.2), to love God also includes one's love of neighbor.

According to Sermon on the Mount traditions, Jesus offers a great reward (Luke 6:35) and secures a filial relationship for those who love their enemies (Matt 5:45; Luke 6:35). The Didachist contains a different set of ethical paradigms in Did. 1.3. For the Didachist, if you love even your enemy, then you will lack all kinds of enemies. To appease hostility motivates the expression of love.

To love one's enemy, for the Didachist, results in lacking any enemies. The blessings and prayers offered earlier in Did. 1.3 directly correspond to loving those who hate them. The identity language of "enemy" and "hating you" conveys oppressive language upon the Didache's community (also see Justin, *1 Apol.* 15.9). A group, outside of their community, possesses a threat as they express the way of life. If this threat is so, then it relates to the persecution motifs also emerging in Did. 1.4 and Did. 5.2.

Next, to love requires one to abstain from particular vices (Did. 1.4). It is quite possible that the phrase "fleshly and bodily passions" (τῶν σαρκικῶν καὶ σωματικῶν ἐπιθυμιῶν) connotes multiple and varied ideas.[27] This pas-

27. Although a critical text of the Didache seems out of reach with the available MS fragments, it is here that one can be more certain of an interpolation in the Didache tradition:

sage shares textual overlap with Titus 2:12 and 2 Clem. 17.3, leaving Niederwimmer to question the reliability of H54.[28]

> Did. 1.3: ἀπέχου τῶν σαρκικῶν καὶ σωματικῶν ἐπιθυμιῶν
>
> Trans: "Abstain from fleshly and bodily passions"
>
> Titus 2:12: παιδεύουσα ἡμᾶς ἵνα ἀρνησάμενοι τὴν ἀσέβειαν καὶ τὰς κοσμικὰς ἐπιθυμίας σωφρόνως καὶ δικαίως καὶ εὐσεβῶς ζήσωμεν ἐν τῷ νῦν αἰῶνι
>
> Trans: "Training us so that by denying ungodliness and worldly passions, we may live sober, upright, and godly lives in the present age"
>
> 2 Clem. 17.3: μὴ ἀντιπαρελκώμεθα ἀπὸ τῶν κοσμικῶν ἐπιθυμιῶν
>
> Trans: "Let us not be dragged away by worldly desires"

These "fleshly and bodily passions" could refer to sexual ethics, which already appear as part of the Sermon on the Mount (Matt 5:27–30). However, the Didachist mentions nothing about sexual ethics in Did. 1, and sexual ethics will not appear until later in the Two Ways instruction (Did. 2.2; 3.2; 5.1). The command to abstain (ἀπέχου), instead, refers to the subsequent four conditional clauses.

> Conditional Clause 1: ἐάν τις σοι δῷ ῥάπισμα εἰς τὴν δεξιὰν σιαγόνα (trans: if someone gives you a blow to your right cheek)
>
> Conditional Clause 2: ἐὰν ἀγγαρεύσῃ σέ τις μίλιον ἕν (trans: if someone compels you to go one mile)
>
> Conditional Clause 3: ἐὰν ἄρῃ τις τὸ ἱμάτιόν σου (trans: if someone takes your coat)
>
> Conditional Clause 4: ἐὰν λάβῃ τις ἀπὸ σοῦ τὸ σόν (trans: if someone takes your belongings from you)

So, to abstain from fleshly and bodily passions refers not to any kind of sexual ethics, but it coheres with the subsequent set of ethics in Did. 1.4: revenge, generosity, and greediness.

---

POX 1782: ἄκουε τί σε δεῖ ποιοῦντα σῶσαι σοῦ τὸ πνεῦμα· π[ρ]ῶτον πάντων ἀπόσχου τῶν σαρκε[ι]κῶν ἐπιθυμειῶν.

H54: ἀπέχου τῶν σαρκικῶν καὶ σωματικῶν ἐπιθυμιῶν.

Apos. Con. VII, 2, 4: ἀπέχου τῶν σαρκικῶν καὶ κοσμικῶν ἐπιθμιῶν

28. Niederwimmer, *Didache*, 77.

The passions generally correspond to the anti-retaliation ethic of Matt 5:38-42 and the *lex talionis*. First, if someone strikes you on the right cheek, the Didachist exhorts to turn to them also the other cheek (Did. 1.4b; Matt 5:39). If one is able to do so, "you will be perfect" (ἔση τέλειος). Unlike Matthew's version of the Sermon on the Mount, to be τέλειος for the Didachist comes as a result of the anti-retaliation ethic and not the imitation of God (Matt 5:48). If a blow on the cheek is given, an anti-retaliation ethic not only results in a lack of enemies (cf. Did. 1.3), but also wholeness (τέλειος) results for the individual.

The theme of perfection/wholeness (τέλειος) in the Gospel of Matthew echoes a personal ethic, much like that found in the Didache. Matthew 5:48 attributes perfection as an attribute of the Father as well as a goal for personal ethics. Perfection is attained when one is able to love one's neighbor even while undergoing persecution and hatred (Matt 5:43-47). Moreover, perfection is also attained when a rich person can forgo all their riches, give to the poor, and unreservedly follow after Jesus (Matt 19:21). The Didachist, likewise, continues a similar idea to convey that a perfect person will be produced when they abstain from their passions of personal retaliation (Did. 1.4). Later in the Didache, if one is able to bear the entire yoke of the Lord, they will also attain perfection (see comments on Did. 6.2). Finally, the latter days will be useless to a person if they are not discovered as a perfect/whole person (Did. 16.2).

The following three conditional clauses move from retaliation to generosity when persecuted (Did. 1.4). As others approach you for travel, a cloak, or belongings, the Didachist calls for bountiful charity. One ought to respond with an extra mile to travel (cf. Matt 5:41) or an additional tunic to give (cf. Matt 5:40).[29] As a result, the verbs "force" (ἀγγαρεύω) and "take away" (αἴρω) signify motifs that relate to categories of persecution. Both of these terms suggest compelling someone against their will (Matt 5:41; 27:32; Mark 15:21), taking someone to their death (Luke 23:18; John 19:15; Mart. Pol. 3.2; 9.2), or the forceful capturing of personal items (Matt 13:12; 25:28; Luke 6:29; 11:22). So, when people undergo persecution, the corresponding ethic veers towards complete passivity to appease persecutors; they evoke spiritual practices on behalf of persecutors; and they extend love in response to hatred. Blessings, prayers, fasting, love, and now abundant generosity reflect the way of life ethic to satisfy persecution and to appease one's enemy.

---

29. It is interesting to note how different Matt 5:40 is from the Did.'s instruction. Matthew seems to envision a law court scene whereby a person is sued. The Didachist offers no such suggestion but hints towards thievery or request of one's cloak in Did. 1.4.

Verse 5 exhorts one to be generous with their belongings. Given the close proximity to Did. 1.4, these instructions might also continue a non-retaliation theme. The non-retaliation themes in Did. 1.3–4 cohere well with themes of generosity in Did. 1.5–6. Within both sets of instruction, those who either have items taken from them or generously give must not ask for their belongings back (1.4d; 1.5b).

Up to this point in the Didachist's argument, one's love for God solely relates to human interaction. In fact, the ethics expressed towards the oppressor may also correspond to love for one's neighbor. However, Did. 1.5 begins to clarify such an idea. Because the "Father wants from his own gifts to be given" to others (Did. 1.5c), the community must give to and act generously with persecutors. So, one's generosity to an oppressor exemplifies one's devotion to the Father, who provides for them. One must not request for the return of their belongings because the Father desires to share generously with all people. The Didachist reframes the experiences of persecution as a way to extend the gifts of the Father.

This ethic of generosity implies a few additional items. First, to evoke the name of the Father conveys either a form of early trinitarian theology (cf. Did. 7.1–4) or correspondence with the Matthean tradition of the Father.[30] Second, the belongings of each individual in the community include the gifts of the Father (ὁ πατὴρ ἐκ τῶν ἰδίων χαρισμάτων). Now, the oppressor might receive "from his own gifts." The community members, even under persecution, share the gifts of the Father to non-community members through their generosity.

Upon giving this instruction, the Didachist combines personal blessings and judicial innocence through a macarism: "Blessed is the one giving according to the commandment, for they are innocent." "Innocent" (ἀθῷος) appears in other late first and second-century settings that can overlap with soteriological categories (1 Clem. 46.3–4; 59.2) and almsgiving (Herm. Mand. 2.6 [27.6]).[31] For the Didachist, the one who gives to others lives the blessed way of life. This macarism is conditioned upon two items: one must give and one must give according to the commandment.

---

30. In particular, the Father in the Sermon on the Mount corresponds to a heavenly location (Matt 5:16, 45, 48; 6:1, 9, 14, 26; 7:11, 21), watches humanity (Matt 6:4, 6, 18), rewards and provides for humanity (Matt 6:6, 8, 26, 32), spiritually provides and nurtures humanity (Matt 5:45; 6:15), orients himself as the object of worship (Matt 5:16), serves as an exemplar of ethics (Matt 5:48), and acts and relates to humanity in secret (Matt 6:1, 4, 6, 18).

31. The term also appears in Prot. Jas., referring to the shedding of "innocent blood" (Prot. Jas. 14.1; 23.3; Matt 27:4).

Within this macarism, two additional items govern how one should read this phrase in Did. 1.5. First, "innocent" (ἀθῷος) may refer to the ethical and soteriological purity of the individual, rather than how a gift is given. In other words, ἀθῷος conveys a soteriological status to the one who gives rather than the manner of how a gift is given. There appears to be more focal interest on the person rather than how items are given, especially with the use of "blessed" as the one who gives and "woe" to the one who receives (Did. 1.5). So, the act of giving will result (ἐστιν) in personal purity. Exodus 23:7 (LXX) connects ἀθῷος with δίκαιος to suggest a kind of judicial setting. First Clement 46.3-4 joins these two words and uses "innocent" as one who is part of the elect.

However, the Didachist utilizes ἀθῷος in relation to giving to others and almsgiving. In Herm. Mand. 2.4-7 (27.4-7), a similar set of instructions correlates ἀθῷος to the act of "giving." According to David Downs, both the Didache and Hermas are not necessarily drawing from one another but most likely drawing from a similar source, either oral or written.[32]

| Did. 1.5 | Herm. Mand. 2.4-7 (27.4-7) |
|---|---|
| παντὶ τῷ αἰτοῦντί σε δίδου, καὶ μὴ ἀπαίτει· πᾶσι γὰρ θέλει δίδοσθαι ὁ πατὴρ ἐκ τῶν ἰδίων χαρισμάτων. μακάριος ὁ διδοὺς κατὰ τὴν ἐντολήν, ἀθῷος γάρ ἐστιν. οὐαὶ τῷ λαμβάνοντι· εἰ μὲν γὰρ χρείαν ἔχων λαμβάνει τις, ἀθῷος ἔσται· ὁ δὲ μὴ χρείαν ἔχων δώσει δίκην, ἵνα τί ἔλαβε καὶ εἰς τί, ἐν συνοχῇ δὲ γενόμενος ἐξετασθήσεται περὶ ὧν ἔπραξε καὶ οὐκ ἐξελεύσεται ἐκεῖθεν, μέχρις οὗ ἀποδῷ τὸν ἔσχατον κοδράντην. | (4) ἔνδυσαι δὲ τὴν σεμνότητα, ἐν ᾗ οὐδὲν πρόσκομμά ἐστιν πονηρόν, ἀλλὰ πάντα ὁμαλὰ καὶ ἱλαρά. ἐργάζου τὸ ἀγαθόν, καὶ ἐκ τῶν κόπων σου, ὧν ὁ θεὸς δίδωσίν σοι, πᾶσιν ὑστερουμένοις δίδου ἁπλῶς, μὴ διστάζων τίνι δῷς ἢ τίνι μὴ δῷς. πᾶσιν δίδου· πᾶσιν γὰρ ὁ θεὸς δίδοσθαι θέλει ἐκ τῶν ἰδίων δωρημάτων. (5) οἱ οὖν λαμβάνοντες ἀποδώσουσιν λόγον τῷ θεῷ, διατί ἔλαβον καὶ εἰς τί· οἱ μὲν γὰρ λαμβάνοντες θλιβόμενοι οὐ δικασθήσονται, οἱ δὲ ἐν ὑποκρίσει λαμβάνοντες τίσουσιν δίκην. (6) ὁ οὖν διδοὺς ἀθῷός ἐστιν· ὡς γὰρ ἔλαβεν παρὰ τοῦ κυρίου τὴν διακονίαν τελέσαι, ἁπλῶς αὐτὴν ἐτέλεσεν, μηθὲν διακρίνων τίνι δῷ ἢ μὴ δῷ. ἐγένετο οὖν ἡ διακονία αὕτη ἁπλῶς τελεσθεῖσα ἔνδοξος παρὰ τῷ θεῷ. ὁ οὖν οὕτως ἁπλῶς διακονῶν τῷ θεῷ ζήσεται. (7) φύλασσε οὖν τὴν ἐντολὴν ταύτην, ὥς σοι λελάληκα, ἵνα ἡ μετάνοιά σου καὶ ἡ τοῦ οἴκου σου ἐν ἁπλότητι εὑρεθῇ καὶ ἡ καρδία σου καθαρὰ καὶ ἀμίαντος. |

---

32. Downs, *Alms*, 249; Niederwimmer, *Didache*, 68-72; Giambrone, "According to the Commandment," 458-59; Osiek, *Shepherd of Hermas*, 26-27.

| Did. 1.5 | Herm. Mand. 2.4–7 (27.4–7) |
|---|---|
| Give to everyone who asks you, and do not ask for it back, for the Father desires to give something from his own gifts to everyone. Blessed is the one giving according to the command, for they are innocent. Woe to the one who receives: if, on the one hand, someone who is in need receives, this person is innocent, but the one who does not have need will have to explain why and for what purpose he received, and upon being imprisoned will be interrogated about what he has done, and will not be released from there until he has repaid every last cent. | (4) Clothe yourself with reverence, in which there is no evil cause for offense, but all things are smooth and joyful. Work [at that which is] good, and from your labor, which God gives to you, give generously to all who are in need, not debating to whom you will give and to whom you will not. Give to all, for God wishes that from his own gifts, gifts should be given to all. (5) So, those who receive are accountable to God regarding why and for what purpose they received; for those in distress who receive will not be judged, but those receiving with false pretenses will pay the penalty. (6) Therefore the one who gives is innocent, for as he received from the Lord a ministry to carry out, he carried it out sincerely, not worrying about to whom to give or not to give. This ministry, then, when sincerely carried out, becomes glorious in God's sight. Therefore the one who serves God sincerely in this manner will live. (7) So keep this commandment, as I have said to you, so that your repentance and the [repentance] of your family will be found to be sincere and your heart clean and unstained. |

So, if the Didache and Hermas share a similar source, then Hermas obviously provides a more extended explanation [interpretive expansion] or supplies more material from the source. Hence, the Didache and Hermas share identical phrases or nearly identical thoughts: "Give to all for God desires to give from his own gifts," "the one who gives is innocent," and give in light of the "commandment." To give results both in judicial purity ("pay a penalty"), salvific security (i.e., repentance), and the human qualities of purity, innocence, and blamelessness.

A salvific purity polarizes a parallel development of this ethic. If someone receives when they are not in need, "Woe" to that person. To give or receive corruptly contrasts the moral and soteriological status of the individual in the community. "Blessed" and "woe" contrast the divine disposition and communal reception of such a person. Because "woe" and interrogation are given to those who take and have no need and those who have need are considered "innocent," these blessed givers then are judicially innocent when giving according to the commandment. These generous ideals similarly reflect the provisions of the poor in the Deuteronomic tradition (Deut 15:7–11).

A second item concerns the phrase, "according to the commandment." What commandment does the Didachist recall? The text does not employ a quotation formula and does not supply a source or enough of a quotation to determine what source has been used. However, a few notable items hint towards a *kind* of commandment that corresponds to Jesus tradition and to almsgiving. The subsequent literary logic of the Didachist relates to proper giving and receiving. Even the quoted source in Did. 1.6 conveys proper giving. In Did. 13.5, 7 and 15.4, a similar phrase concludes the verse: "give according to the commandment" and "do this as you have in the Gospel of the Lord." Now it is debated whether or not this refers to a written gospel or if it refers to the general tenor of "Gospel."[33] Didache 13.5 and 7 relay how one might provide firstfruits, as an act of generosity, to the high priest. According to Niederwimmer, the phrase "according to the commandment" in Did. 1.5 "probably refers to a command of the Lord, but it is not clear which concrete commandment the Didachist has in mind."[34]

Anthony Giambrone notes how charity and almsgiving were a "par excellence" ethic in the early church.[35] Beyond Downs and Giambrone, research devoted to almsgiving and charity in early Christianity receives considerable focus.[36] In Tob. 4.5–11, almsgiving and "the commandment" mutually undergird each other. Testament of Asher 2.8 further associates "the commandment" with a corrupting power of wealth within a Two Ways text.[37] Poverty and alleviating the poor coincide with a commandment in Sirach:

33. Kelhoffer, "ΕΥΑΓΓΕΛΙΟΝ as a Reference to 'Gospel,'" 1–34; Kelhoffer, *Conceptions of "Gospel"*, 39–75.

34. Niederwimmer, *Didache*, 82–83.

35. Giambrone, "According to the Commandment," 450.

36. To name a few: Garrison, *Redemptive Almsgiving*; Finn, *Almsgiving in the Later Roman Empire*; Anderson, *Charity*.

37. T. Ash. 2.8: ἄλλος μοιχεύει καὶ πορνεύει καὶ ἀπέχεται ἐδεσμάτων καὶ νηστεύων κακοποιεῖ καὶ τῇ δυναστείᾳ καὶ τῷ πλούτῳ πολλοὺς παρασύρει καὶ ἐκ τῆς ὑπερόγχου κακίας ποιεῖ ἐντολάς· καὶ τοῦτο διπρόσωπόν ἐστιν ὅλον δὲ κακόν ἐστιν. ("Someone else commits adultery and is sexually promiscuous, yet is abstemious in his eating. While fasting, he is committing evil deeds. Through the power of his wealth he ravages many, and yet in spite of his excessive evil, he performes the commandments."). For more on the T. Ash, the Two Ways, and Christian influences, see the following: de Jonge, "Christian Influence," 182–235; de Jonge, "Once More: Christian Influence," 311–19; de Jonge, "Christian Influence," (1975), 193–246; de Jonge, *Twelve Patriarchs: A Critical Edition*; de Jonge, "Twelve Patriarchs and the 'Two Ways,'" 179–94; Marcus, "A Common Jewish Christian Milieu," 596–626.

Sir 29.9: Help the poor for the commandment's sake, and in their need do not send them away empty-handed.

As previously mentioned, Herm. Mand. 2.4-7 (27.4-7) includes this "commandment" in relation to almsgiving. According to Nathan Eubanks and further substantiated by David Downs, τήν ἐντολήν in 1 Tim 4:14 conveys an economic concern and almsgiving trope.[38] Giambrone convincingly concludes that ἡ ἐντολή corresponds with almsgiving "within a distinctly Jewish, Second Temple setting, in which a kind of 'parallel cult' grew up around the practice of charitable offerings."[39] Thus, for the Didachist to associate almsgiving with the commandment, Jesus tradition undergirds an already common Jewish ethic of almsgiving.

The Didachist applies a macarism to the one who generously gives, but now a divine curse concerns the person who wrongly receives. Monetary recompense and communal retribution apply to those who wrongly receive goods: "Woe to the one who receives." Because a generous disposition governs these ethical directives, a heightened sense of retribution of justice applies to those who take advantage of such generosity. They will be brought before a trial, imprisoned, and required to pay back every last cent (Did. 1.5e). Public shame through a divine "woe," imprisonment, and interrogation deter others from taking advantage of a giving community (Matt 5:25-26; 18:34; Luke 12:59). Each person who has falsely or deceivingly received must pay back every single cent. The κοδράντης was one of the smallest Roman coins in antiquity.[40] Especially as the person will undergo a court-like interrogation and imprisonment, fiscal extortionists receive no amount of leniency.

However, if community members experience any financial need, they may freely take and receive in accordance with their needs (Did. 1.5d). Likewise, these kinds of persons will be considered pure or innocent (ἀθῷος ἔσται). As the Father desires all of his earthly goods to be given to everyone, the poor are privileged to receive such alms. This ethic to provide for the poor inherently underscores Jewish and Christian provisions (Deut 15:7-8, 14; Ps.-Phocyl. 29-30; T. Zeb. 6.7; 7.2; Acts 2:45; 20:35; 1 Clem. 2.1).[41]

---

38. Eubank, "Almsgiving is 'The Commandment,'" 144-50; Downs, "Meritorious Almsgiving and the Divine Economy," 242-60.

39. Giambrone, "According to the Commandment," 465.

40. See these two volumes about coins in the Roman Empire. Harl, *Coinage in the Roman Economy*; Vagi, *Coinage*.

41. Ps.-Phocyl. 29-30: "Of that which God has given you, give of it to the needy. Let all of life be in common, and all things be in agreement."

As readers embark on Did. 1.6, a *crux interpretum* presents a few difficulties.[42] Niederwimmer suggests that the Didachist introduces a quote from sacred Scripture, although no one has been able to secure a definitive source, and the introduction formula for the quotation betrays the hand of the Didachist (Did. 9.5; 16.7).[43] The quote provides a divine prerogative to demonstrate hastiness and wisdom regarding to whom one should give alms.

Sirach 12.1 stands as the most notable possibility for the Didachist's source.[44] Other texts have been suggested, but they are often too questionable (*Ps.-Phocyl.* 23; Sib. Or. 2.79).[45] According to Richard Glover, the καὶ in Did. 1.6 connects the quote to the Jesus traditions in Did. 1.3–5.[46] However, no such Gospel phrase appears in the canonical sources, unless it reaches back to unrecorded or non-extant Jesus oral tradition. In Herm. Mand. 2.4 (27.4), a similar set of phrases appears, not to suggest that the Didache and Hermas mutually inform one another, but that probably this Sirach tradition was "popular in certain circles of the primitive church."[47]

> Sir 12.1: Ἐὰν εὖ ποιῇς, γνῶθι τίνι ποιεῖς, καὶ ἔσται χάρις τοῖς ἀγαθοῖς σου
>
> Trans: "If you do well, know [the person] to whom you are doing it, and there will be favor for your good deeds."

> Did. 1.6: Ἱδρωσάτω ἡ ἐλεημοσύνη σου εἰς τὰς χεῖράς σου, μέχρις ἂν γνῷς τίνι δῷς
>
> Trans: "Let your alms sweat in your hands, until you know to whom you may give."

---

42. Niederwimmer, *Didache*, 83.

43. Niederwimmer, *Didache*, 83–84.

44. Skehan, "Didache 1,6 and Sirach 12,1," 533–36; Draper, "Jesus Tradition in the Didache," 84; Jefford, "Glue of the Matthew-Didache Tradition," 17.

45. *Ps.-Phocyl.* 23: πληρώσει σέο χεῖρ. ἔλεον χρήιζοντι παράσχου. ("Fill your hand. Give alms to those having need").
Sib. Or. 2.79: ἱδρώσῃ σταχύων χειρὶ χρῄζοντι παράσχου. ("Give a portion of corn to each sweating hand").

46. As Glover says, "All these considerations point to the Didachist's having found this quotation in some collection of sayings attributed to Jesus." Glover, "The *Didache's* Quotations," 17.

47. Jefford, *Sayings of Jesus*, 52.

Herm. Mand. 2.4: πᾶσιν ὑστερουμένοις δίδου ἁπλῶς, μὴ διστάζων τίνι δῷς ἢ τίνι μὴ δῷς

Trans: "Give generously to all those reaching out, not wavering to whom you might give."

Interestingly, the quote frequently appears in the Latin tradition to refer to Scripture.[48] I remain a person of two minds whether or not these Latin figures refer to the Didache as Scripture or if these authors merely point to a previous source as Scripture.

Table 9. Didache 1.6 and "Giving Alms"

Augustine

| | | |
|---|---|---|
| Enarrat. Ps. 146:17 | Utrumque dictum est, fratres mei, et: Omni petenti te da modo lectum est; et alio loco scriptura dicit: Sudet eleemosyna in manu tua, quousque invenias iustum cui eam tradas. Alius est qui te quaerit, alium tu debes quaerere. Nec eum qui te quaerit relinquas inanem; Omni enim petenti te da: sed alius est quem tu debes quaerere; Sudet eleemosyna in manutua quousque invenias iustum cui des | My brothers, it is both said, "To everyone who petitions," and in another place Scripture says, "Let your alms sweat in your hands until you find a righteous person to whom you may give them [alms]." Another is one who begs of you, another seeks you out. But do not leave empty handed the one who asks of you. "Give to all the ones who beg from you." But there is another which you ought to seek out. "Let the alms sweat in your hands until you find a righteous person to whom you may give." |
| Enarrat. Ps. 103; Serm. 3.10 | Sicut enim de illo qui te quaeret dictum est: Omni petenti te, da, sic de illo quem tu debes quaerere dictum est: Sudet eleemosyna in manu tua, donec invenias iustum cui eam tradas | For it is written concerning the one who asks of you, "Give to everyone who asks of you." But concerning whom you ought to seek it has been written, "Let the alms sweat in your hand until you find a righteous person to whom you may give." |

---

48. Also see, Augustine, *Enar. in Ps.* 102:12; Cassiodorus *Expositiones in Psalterium* 40; *Expositio in Psalterium* 103; Niederwimmer, *Didache*, 84–85, 84n120.

**Gregory the Great**

| | | |
|---|---|---|
| *Regula Pastoralis* 3.20 | *Ne sub obtentu largitatis ea quae possident inutiliter spargant, audient quod scriptum est: Sudet eleemosyna in manu tua* | Lest they, under the pretext of generosity, uselessly scatter what they possess, let them hear what is written, "Let the alms sweat in your hand." |
| *Vita Chrodegangi episcopi Mettensium* 11.27 | *Memoratus est scriptum: Sudet elemosina in manu tua, donec invenias iustum cui eam tradas* | Remember the Scripture, "Let the alms sweat in your hand until you find a righteous person to whom you may give them [alms]." |

Even if identifying the source remains difficult, the Didachist quotes this expression as a proof-text to justify generous and wise giving. The image from the quote presents a person holding alms in their hand, sweating due to waiting, and then unwaveringly giving to those who have any need (also see Eph 4:28). Even though generous givers will be "blessed," the Didachist tempers and redirects unreserved generosity and causes the person to consider wisely to whom they will give.

Therefore, although some human relations reflect the instruction in Did. 1.3–6, this material echoes the first commandment of the way of life: "first you shall love God, the one who made you" (Did. 1.3). Love for God displays the "perfect" virtuous anti-retaliation and unequivocal generosity to enemies and persecutors (Did. 1.3–5; Matt 5:48). Moreover, such generosity reflects the internal abstinence of retaliation and the willingness to give belongings to persecutors. The *macarism* of giving may even be the blessings given by God when persecuted (Matt 5:10–12). Lastly, love of God reflects one who gives the divine gifts of God to those who are poor. Money and personal belongings reveal one's commitment and devotion to God—"for where your treasure is, there your heart will be also" (Matt 6:21; cf. Matt 6:19–34).

### I.2.b. Second Commandment of the Way of Life (Did. 2.1–7)

As readers move from Did. 1 to Did. 2, they likewise transition from the first commandment about the way of life to the second commandment (cf. Did. 1.2). The second commandment addresses how to love one's neighbor. Distinct from the first commandment (Did. 1.3–6), the second commandment expresses ethics much differently. Rather than offering a positive ethic, Did. 2 contains twenty-six prohibitions and exclusively reflects a negative ethic (e.g., "do not..."). Thus, to love one's neighbor, one will refrain from specific qualities and from a particular ethic that reflects much of the second half of the Decalogue.

As Did. 2.1 begins, a numeral governs how one reads the subsequent ethical instruction: δευτέρα δὲ ἐντολὴ τῆς διδαχῆς. The numeral, "second" (δευτέρα), resumes the concepts from the previous numeral in Did. 1.2.

> Did. 1.2: δεύτερον, τὸν πλησίον σου ὡς σεαυτόν
>
> Trans: "second, your neighbor as yourself"
>
> Did. 2.1: δευτέρα δὲ ἐντολὴ τῆς διδαχῆς
>
> Trans: "the second command of the teaching"

The way of life begins with two commandments, to love God and to love one's neighbor. The material in Did. 2 reflects the second commandment, a "love of neighbor" ethic. According to Jefford, the use of δεύτερον in Did. 2.1 "implies that 2.2–7, at minimum, and chaps. 2–4 at the maximum, are meant to serve as a commentary upon the theme 'love of neighbor.'"[49] The following table demonstrates that Did. 2 generally follows the order of the second half of the Decalogue too.[50]

Table 10. Decalogue and Did. 2

|  | Exod 20//Deut 5 | Did. 2 |
| --- | --- | --- |
| Decalogue Commandment #6 | Do not murder | Do not: murder (2.2), murder newly born children or fetuses (2.2), entertain a wicked plot (2.6), hate anyone (2.7). |
| Decalogue Commandment #7 | Do not commit adultery | Do not: commit adultery (2.2), pederasty (2.2), sexual immorality (2.2). |
| Decalogue Commandment #8 | Do not steal | Do not: steal (2.2). |

---

49. So, Jefford, *Sayings of Jesus*, 53.

50. van de Sandt highlights how the second table of the Decalogue in fact summarizes the essentials of the law. van de Sandt, "Matthew and the Didache," 128.

|  | Exod 20//Deut 5 | Did. 2 |
|---|---|---|
| Decalogue Commandment # 9 | Do not bear false witness | Do not: commit perjury (2.3), bear false witness (2.3), speak evil (2.3), be double-minded or double-tongued (2.4), use empty or false speech (2.5). |
| Decalogue Commandment # 10 | Do not covet | Do not: desire your neighbor's belongings (2.3), be greedy (2.6), receive an evil will against your neighbor (2.6). |

This altruistic command to "love your neighbor" follows with hints of the second half of the Decalogue in other early Christian literature as well. For example, the story of the rich young man joins together a love-of-neighbor ethic and the second half of the Decalogue only in the Matthean version (Matt 19:16–22; Mark 10:17–22; Luke 18:18–23).[51] Also, Jas 2:8 conveys that the Royal Law is fulfilled by loving one's neighbor. To love one's neighbor, one must fulfill and obey the prohibitions in the second half of the Decalogue (Jas 2:11). Paul summarizes the final half of the Decalogue as "you shall love your neighbor as yourself" (Rom 13:8–10). Interestingly, Barn. 19.5 highlights the love-of-neighbor motif, while the Decalogue material appears scattered throughout Barn. 19: do not murder (19.2 "evil plots"; 20.1); commit adultery (19.4); steal (20.1); bear false witness ("double-tongued" 19.7); covet (19.6). In fact, to love one's neighbor in Barn. 19.5 most closely corresponds to anti-abortive ethics. In Herm. Man. 8.3–6 (38.3–6), the Decalogue ethics correspond to virtues, most notably "self-control," without mentioning one's "love for neighbor." At least for some within the Christian tradition, the negative prohibitions in the second half of the Decalogue correspond to the positive ethic of loving one's neighbor.

---

51. Aland, *Synopsis of the Four Gospels*, 217–18 (§ 254).

## Table 11. Text Comparison of Did. 2.1–7, Barn. 19.1–12, Doctr. 2.2–7,[52] and Ps.-Phocyl.[53]

| Did. 2.1–7 | Barn. 19.1–12 | Doctr. 2.2–7 | Ps.-Phocyl. |
|---|---|---|---|
| 2.2: Οὐ φονεύσεις | | 2.2: *non homicidium facies* | |
| 2.2: οὐ μοιχεύσεις | 19.4: οὐ μοιχεύσεις | | 3: μήτε γαμοκλοπέειν |
| 2.2: οὐ παιδοφθορήσεις | 19.4: οὐ παιδοφθορήσεις | 2.2: *non puerum violabis* | |
| 2.2: οὐ πορνεύσεις | 19.4: οὐ πορνεύσεις | 2.2: *non fornicaberis* | |
| 2.2: οὐ μαγεύσεις | | 2.2: *non magica facies* | |
| 2.2: οὐ φαρμακεύσεις | | 2.2: *non medicamenta mala facies* | |
| 2.2: οὐ φονεύσεις τέκνον ἐν φθορᾷ | 19.5: οὐ φονεύσεις τέκνον ἐν φθορᾷ | 2.2: *non occides filium in abortum* | 150: νηπιάχοις ἀταλοῖς μὴ ἅψῃ χεῖρα βιαίως |
| | | | 184: μηδὲ γυνὴ φθείρῃ βρέφος ἔμβρυον ἔνδοθι γαστρός |
| 2.2: οὐδὲ γεννηθὲν ἀποκτενεῖς | 19.5: οὐδὲ πάλιν γεννηθὲν ἀποκτενεῖς | 2.2: *nec natum succides* | 185: μηδὲ τεκοῦσα κυσὶν ῥίψῃ καὶ γυψὶν ἕλωρα |

---

52. A few noteworthy comparisons with Did. and Doctr.: (1) *non moechaberis* and *non homicidium facies* appear as synonyms for a similar prohibition; (2) *non falsum testimonium dices* (Doctr. 2.2) appears in the middle of Did. 2.3, and not in the order of Did. 2.2–3. Especially with this observation, Did. and Barn. agree together against Doctr.; (3) Doctr. 2.6 contains additional qualities (*nec rapax nec adulator*) not found in Did. 2.6. It's very possible that these are synonymous and further elaborations of the already-present qualities.

53. For Ps.-Phocyl., all texts and translations use the following work: van der Horst, *Sentences of Pseudo-Phocylides*. According to van der Horst, Ps.-Phocyl. generally dates between 30 BCE and 40 CE in Alexandria for a Jewish Diaspora. Ps.-Phocyl. 3: "commit not adultery"; Ps.-Phocyl. 150: "Do not apply your hand violently to tender children"; Ps.-Phocyl. 184: "A woman should not destroy the unborn babe in her belly"; Ps.-Phocyl. 185: "nor after its birth throw it before the dogs and the vultures as a prey"; Ps.-Phocyl. 16: "Do not commit perjury"; Ps.-Phocyl. 7: "Tell no lies"; Ps.-Phocyl. 12: "Flee false witness."

| Did. 2.1–7 | Barn. 19.1–12 | Doctr. 2.2–7 | Ps.-Phocyl. |
|---|---|---|---|
| 2.2: οὐκ ἐπιθυμήσεις τὰ τοῦ πλησίον | 19.6: οὐ μὴ γένῃ ἐπιθυμῶν τὰ τοῦ πλησίον σου | 2.2: *non concupisces quicquam de re proximi tui* | |
| 2.3: οὐκ ἐπιορκήσεις | | 2.3: *non periurabis* | 16: μὴ δ᾽ἐπιορκήσῃς |
| 2.3: οὐ ψευδομαρτυρήσεις | | 2.2: *non falsum testimonium dices* | 7: ψεύδεα μὴ βάζειν<br><br>12: μαρτυρίην ψευδῆ φεύγειν |
| 2.3: οὐ κακολογήσεις | | 2.3: *non male loqueris* | |
| 2.3: οὐ μνησικακήσεις | 19.4: οὐ μνησικακήσεις τῷ ἀδελφῷ σου | 2.3: *non eris memor malorum factorum* | |
| 2.4: οὐκ ἔσῃ διγνώμων οὐδὲ δίγλωσσος | 19.7: οὐκ ἔσῃ διγνώμων οὐδὲ δίγλωσσος | 2.4: *nec eris duplex in consilium dandum, neque bilinguis* | |
| 2.4: παγὶς γὰρ θανάτου ἡ διγλωσσία | 19.8: παγὶς γὰρ τὸ στόμα θανάτου | 2.4: *tendiculum enim mortis est lingua* | |
| 2.5: οὐκ ἔσται ὁ λόγος σου ψευδής, οὐ κενός, ἀλλὰ μεμεστωμένος πράξει | | 2.5: *non erit verbum tuum vacuum nec mendax* | |
| 2.6: οὐκ ἔσῃ πλεονέκτης | | 2.6: *non eris cupidus* | |
| 2.6: οὐδὲ ἅρπαξ | | 2.6: *nec auarus* | |
| 2.6: οὐδὲ ὑποκριτής | 19.2: μισήσεις πᾶσαν ὑπόκρισιν | | |
| 2.6: οὐδὲ κακοήθης | | 2.6: *nec contentiosus* | |
| 2.6: οὐ λήψῃ βουλὴν πονηρὰν κατὰ τοῦ πλησίον σου | 19.3: οὐ λήμψῃ βουλὴν πονηρὰν κατὰ τοῦ πλησίον σου | 2.6: *non accipies consilium malum adversus proximum tuum* | |
| 2.7: οὓς δὲ ἀγαπήσεις ὑπὲρ τὴν ψυχήν σου | 19.5: ἀγαπήσεις τὸν πλησίον σου ὑπὲρ τὴν ψυχήν σου | 2.7: *Neminem hominum oderis, quosdam amabis super animam tuam* | |

Over twenty prohibitions compose this negative ethic. Each prohibition reflects a staccato-like cadence. Generally following the second half of the Decalogue's order, the Didachist begins by prohibiting murder (Did. 2.2) and then condemns adultery (Did. 2.2). Rather than moving on to the eighth prohibition in the Decalogue, the Didachist provides two more related prohibitions that relate to acts of adultery. To further elaborate what adultery might imply, the Didachist exhorts the community also not to commit acts of sodomy with children (παιδοφθορέω)[54] and not to partake of any acts of sexual immorality (πορνεύω).[55] According to Elizabeth Clark, "Homosexual activity, especially pederasty, was strongly condemned by early Christian writers. They were perhaps motivated in part by their rejection of pagan sexual practices, as well as by their eagerness to limit all sexual activity to the marriage couch (e.g., Justin, *1 Apol.* 27; Athenagoras, *Leg.* 34; John Chyrsostom *Oppugn.* 3)."[56] These ethics, thematically grouped together, offer a more complete prohibitive sexual ethic for the community. Following the sexual ethics, the Didachist underscores another theme that reflects the Decalogue: the prohibition of stealing. This pattern demonstrates that, although the Didachist uses the order of the Decalogue, commentary and additionally related ethics may expand a simple prohibition.

Subsequently, a collective group of ethics reflects two themes. They must abstain from magic (οὐ μαγεύσεις) and sorcery (οὐ φαρμακεύσεις).[57] According to Pliny the Elder, magic was part of religion (*Nat. Hist.* 30.1–2). According to Everett Ferguson, "magic refers to efforts to control supernatural forces for one's own ends by means that rest on some peculiar and secret wisdom."[58]

---

54. I want to suggest that the Didachist has a Graeco-Roman culture in mind here. Many of the pederasty sexual ethics relate to non-Jewish traditions. See the following: Hubbard, *Homosexuality in Greece and Rome*; Percy, *Pederasty and Pedagogy*; Williams, *Roman Homosexuality*; Skinner, *Sexuality in Greek and Roman Culture*.

55. Clement of Alexandria highlights the act of pederasty in *Paed.* 3.3.21 (FC 23): "boys are taught to renounce their own natures and play the role of a woman . . . a father, not recognizing the child he had exiled by exposure, may have frequent relations with a son turned catamite, or with a daughter become a harlot, and the freedom with which license is indulged may lead fathers into becoming husbands [of their children]." Also see: Justin, *1 Apol.* 27; Theophilus, *Ad Autolycum* 1.2; Clement of Alexandria, *Paed.* 2.10; 3.8; Athenagorus, *Leg.* 33–34; John Chyrsostom, *Oppung.* 3.8.

56. Clark, "Sexuality," 1054.

57. Benko, *Pagan Rome and the Early Christians*.

58. Ferguson, *Backgrounds of Early Christianity*, 227 (see section entitled "Magic and Maledictions," 227–35); Kahlos, "The Early Church," 148–82.

Next, another thematic grouping of ethics relates to the conduct of young children (Did. 2.2).[59] The Christian community protects newborn children. They must not kill children while in the womb (οὐ φονεύσεις τέκνον ἐν φθορᾷ) nor kill newly born children (οὐδὲ γεννηθὲν ἀποκτενεῖς). To group these two items together suggests a collective prohibition against harming children and a commitment to protect children in different stages of their development. The community protects children that are still in the womb of their mother and those who have been recently begotten. This combined prohibition forbids pre-natal and post-natal abortions. These prohibitions continue to present a clear concern for the welfare of young children (cf. Did. 4.9) and they may prepare the reader to view him- or herself as a child (cf. Did. 3.1, 3–6; 4.1). The concern for both pre-natal and post-natal abortive practices[60] emerges in both early Christian and ancient Jewish ethics.[61]

---

59. Early Christianity clearly presented a regard for children and their presence in society. Horn and Martens helpfully documents many of these concerns in the following book, including children's relation to violence in ch. 6, "Exposing Children to Violence." Horn and Martens, *Childhood and Children in Early Christianity*, 213–51.

60. In Philo (*Spec. Leg.* 3.114–15), children may be exposed to cruel deaths: "And as for their murders and infanticides they are established by the most undeniable proofs, since some of them slay them with their own hands, and stifle the first breath of their children, and smother it altogether, out of a terribly cruel and unfeeling disposition; others throw them into the depths of a river, or of a sea, after they have attached a weight to them, in order that they may sink to the bottom more speedily because of it. Others, again, carry them out into a desert place to expose them there, as they themselves say, in the hope that they may be saved by someone, but in real truth to load them with still more painful suffering; for there all the beasts which devour human flesh, since there is no one to keep them off, attack them and feast on the delicate banquet of the children, while those who were their only guardians, and who were bound above all other people to protect and save them, their own father and mother, have exposed them. And carnivorous birds fly down and lick up the remainder of their bodies, when they are not themselves the first to discover them; for when they discover them themselves they do battle with the beasts of the earth for the whole carcass."

61. These following texts lead me to suggest that abortive practices occurred with less frequency in Jewish circles than in Roman circles. Consider: Philo, *Spec. Leg.* 3.110–16; *Ps.-Phocyl.* 184–85 ("Do not let a woman destroy the unborn babe in her belly, nor after its birth throw it before the dogs and the vultures as a prey"); Sib. Or. 2.281–83; Apoc. Pet. 8; Diogn. 5.6 ("they do not expose them once they are born"); Tertullian *Apol.* 9.8 ("We are not permitted to destroy even the fetus in the womb, as long as blood is still being drawn to form a human being. To prevent the birth of a child is a quicker way to murder. It makes no difference whether one destroys a soul already born or interferes with its coming to birth."); Plato, *Resp.* V.460c–d ("I think they will take the offspring of good parents to the public nursery to some nurses who live apart in some quarter of the city. But as to the children of the lower orders, including any of those of other ranks who are born at all defective, they will conceal them in some secret out of the way spot, as is appropriate."). Also see, Plato, *Resp.* V.460e–451b which claims to provide state injunctions on the ages of men and women rearing children;

The Didachist then moves to a series of prohibitions that relate to the tongue and one's speech (Did. 2.3–5). They must refrain from swearing falsely (οὐκ ἐπιορκήσεις). The Sermon on the Mount connects this prohibition to breaking one's oath (Matt 5:33). By overlapping with the Decalogue and the New Testament instruction, the Didachist coheres with an ethic to refrain from bearing a false witness (cf. Exod 20:16; Deut 5:20; Matt 19:18; Mark 10:19; Luke 18:20; Rom 13:9). A speaking ethic addresses anyone who speaks evil (κακολογέω). Rather than directly addressing the ninth command in the Decalogue, this speech ethic may also correspond to household honor. Jesus frames evil speech in close proximity to household ethics: (1) honor your father and mother; and (2) don't speak evil (κακολογέω) of your father and mother (Matt 15:4; Mark 7:10). Thus, to prohibit evil speech closely corresponds to the ninth commandment ("do not bear false witness") and to the fifth commandment of honoring one's paternal heritage.

The Didachist transitions from speech ethics to grudge-bearing (Did. 2.3d; cf. Barn. 19.4, which includes "your brother" οὐ μνησικακήσεις τῷ ἀδελφῷ σου; Doctr. 2.4 *nec eris duplex in consilium dandum*). Although to "bear a grudge" (μνησικακήσεις) seems suggestive of longsuffering, this Greek term does not appear in the New Testament but the LXX (Gen 50:15; Prov 24:24; Ezek 25:12; Joel 4:4; Zech 7:10). Zechariah 7:10 combines together an ethic to care for sojourners while remembering no previous evils. Yet this "grudge-bearing," then, most likely evokes Sermon-on-the-Mount themes: "forgiveness" near the end of the Lord's Prayer (Matt 6:14–15) and the "blessed life" to embody a merciful way of life (Matt 5:7). In Levitical Law, to refrain from taking vengeance against one's kin relates to loving one's neighbor (Lev 19:18). To bear a grudge reflects an incommunicable feature of human nature. The contrary to the previous statement is likewise true for the Didachist, to refrain from bearing a grudge embodies the attributes of God. For example, God is unlike a human who bears a grudge, because God is rich with compassion (Herm. Mand. 9.3 [39.3]). Moreover, because the Father refrains from bearing grudges against humanity, the Father has given his Son as a ransom (Diogn. 9.2). Barnabas employs μνησικακέω in relation to the new law of Christ and to refraining from loving a "false oath" (Barn. 2.8).

---

Hippocrytus, *Nature of Children* 7–8; Aristotle, *Pol.* 1335b ("As to exposing or rearing the children born, let there be a law that no deformed child shall be reared; but on the ground of number of children, if the regular customs hinder any of those born being exposed, there must be a limit fixed to the procreation of offspring, and if any people have a child as a result of intercourse in contravention of these regulations, abortion must be practised on it before it has developed sensation and life; for the line between lawful and unlawful abortion will be marked by the fact of having sensation and being alive"); Pliny the Elder, *Natural History* 7, 20, 25, 28.

Thereafter, the Didachist warns against becoming a bipartite person and includes, for the first time, a prohibition that contains a basis for such action (Did. 2.4). To be double-minded (διγνώμων) or double-tongued (δίγλωσσος) evokes images of the double-souled person (δίψυχος) in Jas 1:8. To be double-tongued does not mean to be bilingual but to be deceitful and immoral (see Sib. Or. 3.37). The person is split in two, thereby suggesting that their internal aspects are diametrically opposed to one another. So, to be double-minded is to be fickle. To be double-tongued is to be deceitful and waver in one's speech. Much like the double-souled person, who exhibits unstable ways (Jas 1:8; 4:8), so this bipartite person brings about a snare that leads to their death (Did. 2.4). To be "double-faced" (διπρόσωποι; T. Ash. 3.1) is to embrace both good and evil dispositions (T. Ash. 2). A double mind and a double tongue simultaneously portray positive and negative dispositions, diametrically and mutually opposed to one another.[62] Redolent of the way of death (Did. 5), the Didachist beckons a virtuous way as a person who is single-minded in their ways. This concern for the whole person does not reflect mere solitude, but a matter of "otherness." As this ethic joins with the "second" component of the initial way-of-life command (see Did. 1.3; 2.1), to be double-minded and double-tongued corresponds to the second half of the greatest commandment, to love one's neighbor.

The Didachist, then, proceeds to prohibit, more explicitly, useless words (Did. 2.5). Useless words and praxis emerge together to affect the community's reputation. The metaphor of emptiness conjures up images that lack any substance (κενός). These metaphors, albeit speaking metaphors, imply words void of action. The substance of action overturns falsehood or replenishes that which is empty. Much like the ethics found in 1 John, one must love one's neighbor, not merely in words, but also in deed (1 John 3:18).

As the Didachist finishes a list of prohibitions in Did. 2, a few character traits must be avoided (Did. 2.6). The equative verb along with a negative particle (οὐκ ἔσῃ) prohibits qualities from becoming part of the essence of a person. They must not be greedy, which signifies a person unable to rule over their passions (Herm. Sim. 6.5.5 [65.5]). Furthermore, they must not become a robber (ἅρπαξ), described as a ravenous wolf in Matt 7:15 (λύκοι ἅρπαγες; cf. Gen 49:27 LXX λύκος ἅρπαξ). This trait typically appears in a list including other avoidable characteristics (cf. Luke 18:11). Paul commands to avoid such a person (1 Cor 5:11), and such a person will not inherit the kingdom of God (1 Cor 6:10). Additionally, they must not be

---

62. Although a bit dated, Seitz's article still has a number of helpful findings. Seitz, "Antecedents and Signification," 211–19.

characterized by hypocrisy, maliciousness, or arrogant qualities (ὑποκριτὴς οὐδὲ κακοήθης οὐδὲ ὑπερήφανος). To be malicious conveys the most complex emotion (4 Macc 1.25) and reflects the intentions of the Serpent in the Garden (Josephus, *Ant.* 1, 42). Although the Didachist does not further define "malicious" or "arrogant," the Didachist refrains from positively portraying the "hypocrite." The Didache's community must not assume this religious identity—see commentary on Did. 8.1–2. Hermas links false doctrine to hypocrites (Sim. 8.6.5 [75.5]; 9.19.2 [96.2]) and describes them as morally bankrupt (Sim. 9.18.3 [95.3]; 9.19.2 [96.2]).

The final prohibition is countered (ἀλλά) by a positive ethic to love one's neighbor (Did. 2.7). Especially if the second commandment in Did. 1.2 and 2.1 governs these ethical prohibitions, then Did. 2.7 serves as an inclusio and a perfect conclusion to Did. 2.

> Did. 1.2: ἀγαπήσεις ... δεύτερον, τὸν πλησίον σου ὡς σεαυτόν
>
> Trans: "love ... second, your neighbor as your yourself."
>
> Did. 2.1: δευτέρα δὲ ἐντολὴ τῆς διδαχῆς
>
> Trans: "the second commandment of the teaching"
>
> Did. 2.7: οὓς δὲ ἀγαπήσεις ὑπὲρ τὴν ψυχήν σου
>
> Trans: "love some beyond your own soul"

The ethic refrains from expressing hatred for the other person (οὐ μισήσεις πάντα ἄνθρωπον). It takes a negative view of hatred of others. So, the final ethical command in this inclusio reproves some, prays for others, and calls for some to love others more than their own soul. By framing the command with the negative first, the Didachist resembles a Levitical Law (Lev 19:17–18): "you shall not hate your brother" followed by "you shall love your brother." To love one's neighbor also implies to refrain from hating one's neighbor. And in the case of the Didachist, both the words and deeds of the person must love their neighbor *beyond* their own soul (ὑπὲρ τὴν ψυχήν σου).[63] Thus, the Didachist extends the love principle to surpass merely loving others as you would love yourself (Matt 22:39; Mark 12:31) by loving one's neighbor *beyond* yourself (cf. Phil 2:3).

---

63. BDAG, s.v. ὑπέρ §B.

### I.2.c. Teknon Sayings: Flee Every Form of Evil (Did. 3.1–6)

The rhetorical flare in the following literary section expresses an etiology of vices, whereby a chief vice stands at the head of a vice list and eventually leads to a physical expression of other vices.[64] These five, head vices segment each collective argument, and each section will begin with a vocative, "my child" (τέκνον μου), as a discourse marker—hence, others label this section as *"teknon sayings"* or a *"teknon section."*[65] "My child" groups each prohibitive ethic. In order to ward off particular vices, the Didachist presents a chief vice, followed by other vices that funnel together in order to express the same action. Thus, the list of vices subsumes the chief vice.[66] The following progression outlines the discourse structure.[67]

Did. 3.1–6 and Discourse Structure:

τέκνον μου μὴ γίνου + Chief Vice A

ὁδηγεῖ γάρ/ἐπειδή + Chief Vice A + πρός/εἰς + Vice B

μηδέ Vice C + μηδέ Vice D + (μηδέ Vice E)

ἐκ γὰρ τούτων ἁπάντων + Vice B/F + γεννῶνται[68]

Similar to the previous literary titles (Did. 1.2, 3; 2.1), the Didachist frames the genealogy of vices under a single heading (Did. 3.1). Here, the Didachist modifies the following five vice lists under a single literary title that summarizes the entire section (Did. 3.1). According to Kloppenborg, "This kind of discourse, which seeks to establish family resemblances among certain behaviors, and which operates from and seeks to illustrate

---

64. Kloppenborg, "Poverty and Piety," 219.

65. Niederwimmer, *Didache*, 94; van de Sandt, "James 4, 1–4," 43; van de Sandt, "Reorientation of Halakah," 316.

66. Some suggest that these symmetrical ethics pattern after the Noahide laws. Some of these ethics appear as similar commands given to the sons of Noah as recorded in bYoma 67b and Sifra, Aharei Moth 9,10 on Lev 18:4. van de Sandt and Flusser comment well on a few additional Jewish texts concurrent with the Noahide commands. van de Sandt and Flusser, *Didache*, 133–34.

67. Pardee rightly notes, "a four-part statement (τέκνον μου, μὴ γίνου ... γὰρ [ἐπειδὴ] ... μηδὲ ... γὰρ ...) that is repeated five times gives an integrity to this sub-section and sets it apart from the instruction which precedes and follows it." Pardee, *Genre and Development of the Didache*, 163.

68. Of the five sayings, four maintain a similar form, whereas the other one differs. Sayings 1, 3–5 correspond to the following in the last line. The final vice is a repeated vice from the second line of Did. 3.2, 4, 5, and 6: ἐκ γὰρ τούτων ἁπάντων + Vice B + γεννῶνται. Saying 2 (Did. 3.3) corresponds to the following in the last line. It introduces a new vice lexeme, although somewhat related to its corresponding Vice B (πορνεια): Did. 3.3: ἐκ γὰρ τούτων ἁπάντων + (New Vice) μοιχεῖαι + γεννῶνται.

the theoretical claim of the unity of the Torah, belongs to a fairly sophisticated moral speculation, hardly consonant with addressees far down the social ladder."[69]

> Did. 3.1: My child, flee from every form of evil and from everything that resembles it.

The community ought to flee all forms of evil. Not only must they flee evil, but they must flee all such items that merely represent evil (ἀπὸ παντὸς ὁμοίου αὐτοῦ).

A social identity undergirds each prohibitive ethic. As each prohibition begins with "my child," the Didachist assumes the role of a father or mother to the recipient. To use "my child" implies a self-identified, more mature instructor who plays a nurturing role to a beloved family member. Familial language reflects other Jewish wisdom instruction. For example, Prov 1:8 begins with a father instructing his son on the ways of wisdom. 1 John 2 creates a three-tiered familial ethical instruction (cf. Mark 3:31–35). This kind of sapiential instruction appears in other ancient settings, too (T. Reu. 1.2; T. Sim. 2.1; 3.1; T. Lev. 10.1). So, the familial structure and instruction reflect forms of wisdom as they intersect with communal purity.[70]

Another question needs to be raised that concerns the identity of "my child." Is the "child" an actual child or adolescent? Or is the child a grown adult? How might they be perceived in the community? The child-like label does not reflect one's age, per se, but one's lived experiences in the new way of life. They most likely function as grown adults in civilization at large, while their communal identity may exhibit more childish ethics and experiences of the way of life. "My child" occurs a few times in the Didache's Two Ways (Did. 3.1, 3, 4, 5, 6; 4.1), whereas "child" occurs much less (Did. 2.2; 5.2 [2x]). "My child" addresses the familial wisdom-like instruction, whereas the simple use of "child" appears in ethical commands to abstain from abusing children—except the final call in Did. 5.2, "may you, child, be delivered from these things." So, within the Didache's Two Ways, each reference to "my child" reflects a physically grown person who resides in a pupil-teacher relationship receiving instruction about the Two Ways. Each τέκνον μου most likely possesses some form of financial stability so that they may be able to give freely of their goods (Did. 4.5, 8). They too have a full household with physical sons and daughters (Did. 4.9) and servants (Did. 4.10). So, it is quite possible that "my child" (τέκνον μου) functions as an

---

69. Kloppenborg, "Poverty and Piety," 219.
70. Del Verme, *Didache and Judaism*, 244.

identity marker for their spiritual status within the community as well as their spiritual naiveté in the Two Ways teaching.

The first chief vice prohibits anger because anger will lead to murder (Did. 3.2; ὁδηγεῖ γὰρ ἡ ὀργὴ πρὸς τὸν φόνον). The anger of humanity eventually drives one to murder. This particular line of logic likewise appears in the Matthean Sermon on the Mount (Matt 5:21–22). Anger and murder emerge as companions. However, as Luz suggests, "we must abandon the thesis of a general progression,"[71] which coheres with the Didachist's logic—no intensifying progression, but an etiology. In addition to anger, the Didachist also considers jealousy (ζηλωτής), contentiousness (ἐριστικός), and a hot temper (θυμικός) to beget murder. This logic might cause one to raise a few questions about the vice list. Is anger the chief vice that the community must avoid in order to perpetuate communal safety? Are the subsequent vices (jealousy, contention, etc.) subsumed under a category of "anger," or do these vice categories stand on their own merit? Either way, murder stands at the head of a list of vices that will beget the physical action of murder. The way of life invites the wayfarer to a life of virtue to perpetuate the life of a community.

The second list of vices prohibits a host of sexual ethics (Did. 3.3). Here, "lust" (ἐπιθυμητής) stands as the chief character trait that undergirds physical adultery, for unchecked lust eventually leads to adultery (πρὸς τὴν πορνείαν). Much like the previous anger-murder paradigm appearing in the Sermon on the Mount, the lust-adultery pattern likewise appears in the Matthean Sermon on the Mount. Adultery, in this case (Did. 3.3), manifests itself as a physical act of adultery (πορνεία), unlike the internal realized adultery as part of Jesus's instruction (Matt 5:27–28). Moreover, to contain a foul mouth (αἰσχρολόγος) and wanton eyes (ὑψηλόφθαλμος) will also beget adultery (ἐκ γὰρ τούτων ἁπάντων μοιχεῖαι γεννῶνται). The Didachist switches from πορνεία to μοιχεία to convey a totality of sexual impropriety. Hermas combines πορνεία with μοιχεία (Herm. Mand. 4.1.5 [29.5]; 8.3 [38.3]; cf. Sir 23.23), the Didachist later employs four of the five vices in Did. 3.3 again in Did. 5.1 (μοιχεῖαι, ἐπιθυμίαι, πορνεῖαι, αἰσχρολογία), and μοιχεία frequently occurs in other vice lists that function similar to πορνεία (T. Ash. 2.8; 1 Clem. 30.1; 2 Clem. 6.4; Barn. 20.1). These examples indicate that when πορνεία and μοιχεία appear together, both sexual activities and sexual desires are combined within a comprehensive understanding of sexual wantonness. Because the primary ethic reflects sexuality, the Didachist may not refer to a "foul mouth" in general, but to a foul mouth similar to the sexual and deviant speech in Eph 5:4 and 5:12. According to Jeremy

---

71. Luz, *Matthew 1–7*, 235.

Hultin, "Perhaps the fact that the Didache warns against being a speaker of indecent words gives some small indication that the concern is with words as a means of communicating sexual interest rather than with hearing—and being aroused by—lewd talk."[72] Shameful and reckless sexual speech will normalize sexuality and thereby cause the community members to engage in sexually deviant infidelity. Similarly, to possess eyes that wander could refer to pride; but eyes that lift up portray eyes that lose the focal attention of the path and correlate to a careless gaze of sexual desire.[73]

The third chief vice prohibits soothsaying (οἰωνοσκόπος) because it will lead to idolatry (Did. 3.4). This vice prohibits any omen from the behavior of birds. The one who would interpret the birds would be considered an "augur."[74] Furthermore, the Didachist also lists an enchanter (ἐπαοιδός), an astrologer (μαθηματικός), and the one providing magical washing rites (περικαθαίρω) as activities that lead to idolatry.[75] Additionally, they must not even desire to see or to hear such things being performed (μηδὲ θέλε αὐτὰ βλέπειν [μηδὲ ἀκούειν]).[76] The Didachist has already prohibited other kinds of magic and potion mixing (Did. 2.2; οὐ μαγεύσεις, οὐ φαρμακεύσεις) and will prohibit similar acts of magic and potion mixing as evil (Did. 5.1; μαγεῖαι, φαρμακίαι).[77] However, the material in Did. 3.4 appears to be both more specific than these other examples in the Didache and aims to address even the desire to see such actions. Although idolatry, in general, reflects a Christian critique of or Jewish concern with Hellenism, the actions more predominately

---

72. Hultin, *Ethics of Obscene Speech in Early Christianity*, 144 (see 136–45).

73. To lift the eyes waywardly also appears in other early Christian and ancient Jewish texts: "O Lord, Father and God of my life, do not give me haughty eyes, and remove evil desire from me" (Sir 23.4–5); "I have not had intercourse with any woman other than my wife, nor was I promiscuous by a lustful look (ἐν μετεωρισμῷ ὀφθαλμῶν)" (T. Iss. 7.2); "He does not find delight in pleasure, nor does he grieve his neighbor, nor does he stuff himself with delicacies, nor is he led astray by visual excitement (οὐ πλανᾶται μετεωρισμοῖς ὀφθαλμῶν): the Lord is his lot" (T. Benj. 6.3); "For the person with a mind that is pure with love does not look on a woman for the purpose of having sexual relations (οὐχ ὁρᾷ γυναῖκα εἰς πορνείαν)" (T. Ben. 8.2).

74. See: Philo *Mut.* 202; *Spec.* 1.60; *Spec.* 4.48; Dionysius of Halicarnassus *Ant. rom.* 3.70, 71; 4.62; 8.38; Euripides *Suppl.* 500. Within Christian literature, see the following: Clement of Alexandria *Protr.* 2.11 (SC 2); Cyril of Alexandria *Comm. Isa.* (PG 70:397, 417, 1013, 1016); John Chrysostom *Exp. Pss.* (PG 55:273).

75. Ps.-Phocyl. 149: "Make no potions, keep away from magical books."

76. The Georgian MS contained this additional expression, "nor to hear" (μηδὲ ἀκούειν). Also, *Doctr.* 3.4 contains this two-fold "see and "hear" expression. However, *Doctr.* lacks any augur-like prohibition and uses "mathematics" as the chief vice: *noli esse mathematicus neque delustrator, quae res ducunt ad uanam superstitionem; nec uelis ea uidere nec audire.* See Niederwimmer, "Textprobleme der Didache," 114–30.

77. Irenaeus connects magic, gnostic doctrine, and blasphemy in *Haer.* 2.31.

reflect ancient Roman culture than Christian or Jewish concerns.[78] Outside the abortive concerns in Did. 2, the polemic against *kinds* of magic and superstition reflects the cultural concerns the clearest.

The fourth saying warns against lying because deceit leads to thievery (Did. 3.5; ἐπειδὴ ὁδηγεῖ τὸ ψεῦσμα εἰς τὴν κλοπήν). Two additional vices subsequently beget thievery, love of money (φιλάργυρος) and vanity (κενόδοξος). It may be easier to ascertain how "love of money" and vanity correspond to thievery than the act of lying. Hermas joins ψεύστης with internal luxury, allowing free rein to one's passions, and indulging in wanton actions (Sim. 6.5.5 [65.5]). Similarly, those who lie defraud the deposit entrusted to them by the Lord (Mand. 3.2, 5 [28.2, 5]). Yet it remains more difficult to join the ethics of lying to thievery from other texts in early Christianity. In the canonical tradition, lying and stealing are loosely joined together in Eph 4:25–28. The Didachist, without commenting on literary dependence, coheres with the motifs in Eph 4:28, where the motifs of honesty link together with stealing. Additionally, those who love money (φιλάργυρος) act contrary to natural ways (4 Macc 2.8) and are frequently associated with other vices (T. Lev. 17.11; 2 Tim 3:2). To be vain (κενόδοξος) can coincide with exorbitant amounts of money or the pleasure derived from gold (Ep. Arist. 8), and it counters the work of the Spirit of God (Gal 5:26). It still remains rather difficult to ascertain the specific ways that lying, love of money, and vanity directly correspond to thievery, but for the Didachist's argument, it seems quite natural.

The fifth and final chief vice prohibits grumbling (μὴ γίνου γόγγυσος) because it leads to blasphemy (Did. 3.6; ὁδηγεῖ εἰς τὴν βλασφημίαν). Additionally, a self-willed obstinate posture (αὐθάδης) and evil-mindedness (πονηρόφρων) likewise beget blasphemies. Such a grumbling posture may reflect a careless utterance about God or one's circumstances thereby leading one to say something blasphemous about God. Hermas mentions this pompous disposition as a result of believers knowing nothing at all (Sim. 9.22.1 [99.1]; cf. Sim. 5.4.2 [57.2]; Sim. 5.5.1 [58.1]). Those who act self-willed are compared to irrational animals and they lack reverential fear, so they blaspheme against God (2 Pet 2:10–12). To reflect an evil mind (πονηρόφρων) still clearly references "to be intent on evil, to give voice to a wicked intent."[79]

These negative vices, the actions they lead to, and the interconnection of vices are all encapsulated in the opening line: "My child, flee from every form of evil and from everything that resembles it" (Did. 3.1). These

---

78. Milavec, *Didache: Faith, Hope & Life*, 150–51.
79. Niederwimmer, *Didache*, 99.

prohibited ethical behaviors directly oppose the way of life. As these various vice lists all "lead" to a particular telos, the Didachist still evokes a "pathway" metaphor. The Didachist's list of vices leading toward death reflects the ethical and moral dilemmas of evil in the flourishing life. Certain characteristics or actions will subsequently "lead" one off the way of life to a particular end that is unwelcomed.

### I.2.d. Be Humble and Virtuous to Inherit the World (Did. 3.7–10)

After finishing an outline of vices, the Didachist offers a brief counter-ethic. The Didachist does not leave the reader only with a list of vices from which to abstain. Rather, he exhorts the reader/community to embody a virtuous way of life. Prohibitive ethics prove problematic in so far as they provide no definitive corrective for their adherents. They negatively clarify what readers are *not* to become (μὴ γίνου) but neglect to suggest what they should become (ἴσθι). A perpetual negative ethic lacks any vision for a flourishing life. As in Diognetus, a negative ethic serves as a moral boundary marker (Diogn. 5). So, those who abstain from a particular set of behaviors reflect a particular identity to outsiders, but such a negative ethic provides no positive way to flourish within the community.

Although the Didachist does not assume the parental-child paradigm (Did. 3.1–6; 4.1), the structure loosely follows the previous section and still embodies the "air" of a parental-child sapiential instruction. Now, as a corrective to the previous set of ethics (Did. 3.1–6), the Didachist exhorts the child to be (ἴσθι) humble and to embody other virtuous qualities.

Humility, similar to the previous section (Did. 3.1–6), functions as the chief virtue (Did. 3.7) and will lead to a host of other virtues (Did. 3.8). The etiology of interconnected virtues resembles a flourishing life and replaces an etiology of vices.

Didache scholars regularly appeal to Ps 36:11 LXX and Matt 5:5 as probable solutions to questions of source dependency.[80] "The saying 'the meek shall inherit the earth' in Did 3:7," explains Christopher Tuckett, "could derive from Mt 5:5 though position and presence of that beatitude in Matthew is textually uncertain and common dependence of the *Didache*

---

80. According to van de Sandt and Flusser, "This expansion is dependent upon Ps 37:11a (MT), 'and the meek shall inherit land/earth' (=36:11a, LXX), a text which has been used in Matt 5:5 too, but presented there in the form of a macarism" (van de Sandt and Flusser, *Didache*, 134). Also see: Jefford, "Milieu of Matthew, Didache, and Ignatius," 40; Niederwimmer, *Didache*, 100; Niederwimmer, *Die Didache*, 131; Welch, "Sermon on the Mount," 345; Myllykoski, "Without Decree," 441–42.

and Matthew on Ps 36:11 is equally likely."[81] Both Ps 36:11 LXX and Matt 5:5 generally correspond to this Didache tradition.[82]

| Ps 36:11 LXX | Did. 3.7 | Matt 5:5 |
|---|---|---|
|  |  | μακάριοι |
|  | Ἴσθι δὲ |  |
|  | πραΰς, | οἱ πραεῖς, |
|  | ἐπεὶ | ὅτι |
| οἱ | οἱ |  |
| δὲ |  |  |
| πραεῖς | πραεῖς | αὐτοὶ |
| κληρονομήσουσιν | κληρονομήσουσι | κληρονομήσουσιν |
|  | τὴν | τὴν |
| γῆν | γῆν | γῆν |

To inherit the earth motivates one to exhibit humility. The Didachist refrains from framing this Jesus tradition as a *macarism*, which prevails in the initial teachings of the Matthean Sermon on the Mount. Also, the expression "the meek will inherit" (πραεῖς κληρονομήσουσι) and the second half of Did. 3.7 align more closely with Ps 36 LXX. Thematically, Ps 36 LXX places the wicked persons in contrast to the meek/oppressed, this theme somewhat correlating to the social oppression in Did. 5.1–2.[83] Yet themes from the Sermon on the Mount motifs halt identifying Ps 36 LXX as a particular social background: meekness (Did. 3.7//Matt 5:5), patience (Did. 3.8), mercifulness (Did. 3.8//Matt 5:7), innocence (Did. 3.8), gentleness (Did. 3.8//Matt 5:9), goodness (Did. 3.8//Matt 5:48), being listeners (Did. 3.8//Matt 7:24), non-personal exaltation (Did. 3.9//Matt 6:1), and association with the upright and humble (Did. 3.9; cf. Matt 6:1–18). Thus, I suggest that Did. 3.7 is more textually connected to Ps 36:11 LXX, whereas Did. 3.7 more thematically corresponds to both Psalmic and Matthean traditions in

81. Tuckett, "Synoptic Tradition in the Didache," 108.
82. Jefford, *Sayings of Jesus*, 73–77.
83. Niederwimmer, *Didache*, 100.

different ways: broader contextual concerns of Ps 36 LXX and shared lexeme and virtue concerns of Matt 5–7.[84]

While humility functions as the chief virtue, the community must also exhibit patience, mercy, innocence, gentleness, goodness, fear of God's words, and corporate humility (Did. 3.8–9). With the previous etiological vice list, the Didachist now counters with a different etiological virtue list. "Patience" (μακρόθυμος) characterizes those whom the Spirit of God indwells (Herm. Mand. 5.1.1–2 [35.1–2]). "Merciful" (ἐλεήμων) qualifies the nature and character of God (1 Clem. 60.1), Jesus (Heb 2:17), and presbyters (Pol. Phil. 6.1). "Innocent ones" (ἄκακος) describes children who do not know evil (Herm. Mand. 2.1 [27.1]) and the innocent qualities of Jesus as he takes the place of the guilty (Diogn. 9.2). "Gentleness" (ἡσύχιος) coheres with the one who remains meek and mild (Herm. Mand. 5.2.3 [34.3]) and who trembles at God's word (1 Clem. 13.4, quoting Isa 66:2).

The meek (πραΰς; Matt 5:5), the merciful (ἐλεήμων; Matt 5:7), and the guiltless (ἄκακος; Matt 5:8 καθαρός) similarly correspond to the virtues in the Sermon on the Mount. These virtues reflect "ways of being" in the world. To embody such attributes may describe how the Didachist envisions the blessed way of life. Thus, to obtain human flourishing, these traits must be embodied. If these character traits reflect the Sermon on the Mount *macarisms*, then the Didachist appears to use these traits as a way to obtain a blessed way of life.

Particular character traits determine social and communal boundaries (Did. 3.9). As one exhibits humility, one ought to refrain from self-exaltation and from permitting one's soul to be arrogant (οὐχ ὑψώσεις σεαυτὸν οὐδὲ δώσεις τῇ ψυχῇ σου θράσος). The Didachist presents a humility-pride dichotomy that appears in other Jewish-Christian ethics (Jas 4:6; 1 Pet 5:6; Prov 3:34; 1 Clem. 59.3; Barn. 19.3). This binary ethic serves as a social boundary marker to disassociate with the haughty and to join one's soul to the humble (οὐ κολληθήσεται ἡ ψυχή σου μετὰ ὑψηλῶν). The community must not associate with those who imbibe such arrogance; rather, they must join themselves to the righteous and humble.

As gentleness or humility begin an etiology of virtues, they also help to accept personal determinism as good (Did. 3.10). For the Didachist, this cursory comment stands as the first substantial doctrinal statement regarding God and his actions in the world. The Didachist guides the reader to receive all these personal events as good (ὡς ἀγαθὰ προσδέξῃ), whether persecution (Did. 1.3–4) or other such events in life (τὰ συμβαίνοντά σοι ἐνεργήματα). I

---

84. Garrow, *Matthew's Dependence on the Didache*, 84–85. Alan Garrow suggests that the *teknon* teachings of Did. 3.1–6 may be an exposition of Ps 36 LXX. Did. 3.7 operates as a sapiential exposition of Ps 36 LXX.

do not perceive the Didachist blindly ignoring tragedy or moral evils (Did. 2.2). Rather, humility provides the moral quality for a person to recognize that nothing happens apart from God (ἄτερ θεοῦ). Arrogance (αὐθάδης), the antithesis of humility, will produce blasphemies against God (Did. 3.6). So, humility functions as a necessary virtue that permits others to speak accurately about God and to affirm rightly how he acts within the world.

As Did. 3 comes to a close, the way of life now provides some personal depth beyond "thou shalt not." Meekness or humility anchors the way of life. Such humility will allow persons to inherit an eschatological world, to become merciful to others, to exhibit other virtuous qualities, and to relate properly to the world. Additionally, humility serves as a proper virtue to receive all personal events, either good or bad, as happening from the hand of God.[85]

## I.2.e. Communal Ecclesial Ethics (Did. 4.1–4)

As readers now continue their trek towards Did. 4, the Didachist presents a set of ethical commands that does not explicitly connect with the previous sections. By this point in the Didache's narrative, the ethical flow remains relatively unconnected with previous sections, but all undergird the way of life. The material in Did. 4 contains the final set of training that portrays the ethical way of life and contains four relatively independent units. In other words, at a grammatical and discourse level, very few literary cues progress the thought process; rather, thematic discontinuity helps to segment the literary work into four ethical themes.

The first set of ethical instruction relates to ecclesial gatherings (Did. 4.1–4). The parent-child construct once more activates wisdom-like categories as "my child" characterizes the recipients. Rather than offering warnings about what to avoid, of the kind we saw with the previous use of "my child" (Did. 3.1–6), the Didachist here provides a positive ethic via parental wisdom. As new members join the community, they must know how to behave during ecclesial gatherings. Four kinds of commands govern their ecclesial ethics: (1) Remember the one speaking (i.e., teaching them); (2)

---

85. To "accept all things that happen from God" is an aphorism that appears in Jewish, early Christian (Rom 8:28), and Stoic literature (Seneca, *Ep.* 107.9). For example, "Accept whatever befalls you, and in times of humiliation be patient" (Sir 2.4); "All that shall be, He foreknows, all that is, His plans establish; apart from Him nothing is done" (1QS XI, 11). In early Christianity, some suggest that Origen quotes from the Did.: "Therefore the divine Scripture teaches us to accept all that happens to us as sent by God, knowing that nothing happens without God" (*Princ.* 3.2.7).

honor the teacher; (3) seek out the presence of the saints; (4) give fair and unfavorable judgments.

First, they must remember (μιμνήσκω) the person speaking the words of God to them. To remember one's teacher can refer to prayer, especially as seen in a number of examples from the New Testament (Eph 1:16; Col 4:18; 1 Thess 1:3; 2 Tim 1:3-4; Phlm 4). However, this phrase corresponds to a similar statement in Heb 13:7, whereby the recipients remember their leaders, "those who spoke to you the word of God."

> Did. 4.1: τοῦ λαλοῦντός σοι τὸν λόγον τοῦ θεοῦ μνησθήσῃ
>
> Trans: "Remember the one speaking to you the word of God."
>
> Heb 13:7: Μνημονεύετε τῶν ἡγουμένων ὑμῶν, οἵτινες ἐλάλησαν ὑμῖν τὸν λόγον τοῦ θεοῦ
>
> Trans: "Remember the one's leading you, those who spoke to you the word of God."

Thus, the Didachist's instruction does not exclusively refer to prayer, although prayer would surely not be discouraged. Rather, to "remember" may also refer to adhering to ethical instruction. In other words, both Hebrews 13:7 and Did. 4.1 may also summon, for the reader, a motif of ethical mimesis: remember the life and teachings of the one instructing you.

Additionally, the people must also honor (τιμήσεις) their teachers. Rather than bestowing a simple honor as teachers, they honor them "as the Lord" (ὡς κύριον). According to Ignatius, those who honor the bishop receive honor from God (Ign. *Smyrn.* 9.1). To fear the Lord Jesus Christ also corresponds to one's honor of an elder (1 Clem. 21.6). So, to honor a communal teacher directly influences how one may receive blessings from God. Furthermore, the community must remember and honor these teachers, as they represent the Lord himself to the community. Throughout the Didache at large, teachers are received as the Lord (Did. 11.2; 12.1). Those who teach experience a similar reception as the incarnate Lord.

Furthermore, with "remember" and "honor" paralleling one another, the "child" must exhibit these qualities night and day. Barnabas 19.9b–10 includes very similar expressions to Did. 4.1–2, but the text includes two notable differences:

| Did. 4.1-2 | Barn. 19.9b-10 |
|---|---|
| (1) Τέκνον μου, τοῦ λαλοῦντός σοι τὸν λόγον τοῦ θεοῦ μνησθήσῃ νυκτὸς καὶ ἡμέρας, τιμήσεις δὲ αὐτὸν ὡς κύριον· ὅθεν γὰρ ἡ κυριότης λαλεῖται, ἐκεῖ κύριός ἐστιν. (2) ἐκζητήσεις δὲ καθ' ἡμέραν τὰ πρόσωπα τῶν ἁγίων, ἵνα ἐπαναπαῇς τοῖς λόγοις αὐτῶν. | (9b) ἀγαπήσεις ὡς κόρην τοῦ ὀφθαλμοῦ σου πάντα τὸν λαλοῦντά σοι τὸν λόγον κυρίου. (10) μνησθήσῃ ἡμέραν κρίσεως νυκτὸς καὶ ἡμέρας, καὶ ἐκζητήσεις καθ' ἑκάστην ἡμέραν τὰ πρόσωπα τῶν ἁγίων, ἢ διὰ λόγου κοπιῶν καὶ πορευόμενος εἰς τὸ παρακαλέσαι καὶ μελετῶν εἰς τὸ σῶσαι ψυχὴν τῷ λόγῳ, ἢ διὰ τῶν χειρῶν σου ἐργάσῃ εἰς λύτρον ἁμαρτιῶν σου |
| My child, remember night and day the one speaking the word of God. You shall honor him as Lord. For whenever the Lord's nature is spoken, there the Lord is. You shall seek each day the presence of the saints so that you may find comfort in their words. | You shall love, as the apple of your eye, all those speaking to you the word of the Lord. Remember the day of judgment night and day and you shall seek the presence of the saints according to each day, either laboring through the word and going out to comfort and endeavoring to save the soul by the word, or you shall work with your hands so as *to provide* a ransom for your sins. |

The Didachist exhorts a perpetual remembering and honoring of the teacher, whereas Barnabas exhorts a perpetual remembering of pending judgment. Rather than remembering the teachers, Barn. 19.10a records the "day of judgment" (ἡμέραν κρίσεως) as the object of their memory. As Ferdinand Prostmeier reflects, "Durch den Gegenstand des μιμνήσκειν, nämlich die ἡμέρα κρίσεως, ist dieses tägliche (καθ'ἑκάστην ἡμέραν) Nachsinnen auf das Eschaton ausgerichtet." ("Through the object of the μιμνήσκειν, namely the ἡμέρα κρίσεως, this daily [καθ'ἑσκάστην ἡμέραν] contemplation of the eschaton is oriented.")[86] Also, the Didachist recalls the christological category of the teacher, whereas Barnabas utilizes the "apple of your eye." Matti Myllykoski also notes that Barn. 19.10 is formulated without reference to Jesus (i.e., ὡς κύριον) and also adds the command to love the teacher "as the apple of your eye."[87] He subsequently suggests that the differences between Did. 4.1 and Barn. 19.9-10 occur "because the author [i.e., Barnabas] has moved the reader's attention toward responsibility in the day of the eschatological judgment."[88]

As the teacher and their instruction are presented to the community, a sacramental presence of the incarnated Lord serves as the basis to remember

---

86. Prostmeier, *Der Barnabasbrief*, 552-53.

87. Myllykoski, "Without Decree," 437.

88. Myllykoski, "Without Decree," 445.

and honor the teachers. Both the presence of the teacher and the content of the teaching provide a sacramental presence of "the Lord" (κύριος). When the instructor speaks God's word, the nature of the Lord is present, and thus the Lord himself becomes present (ὅθεν γὰρ ἡ κυριότης λαλεῖται, ἐκεῖ κύριός ἐστιν). The use of κυριότης and κύριος cumulatively suggest both nature and presence. The term κυριότης appears elsewhere in settings that point to cosmic powers (1 En. 61.10; Eph 1:21; Col 1:16) and can convey the power of the Lord through his presence (Herm. Sim. 5.6.1 [59.1]; Jude 9). As the teacher teaches, a theophany-like experience occurs. When the Lordship of Jesus is proclaimed by the teacher, the incarnate Lord's presence appears in and through the one who teaches.[89]

The perpetual presence of the saints preserves the community (Did. 4.2). To join this Didache community will result in communal comfort and will secure perfection in the final season (Did. 16.1–2). For the community to gather frequently, the wayfarer will be nourished and sustained. Similar to remembering the one who teaches multiple times in a single day, so too the community member seeks out the presence of the saints in the community. The daily presence of the saints accentuates and secures the community.[90]

Considering the final form of the Didache for a moment, I perceive an inner logic of "saint" (ἅγιος) in other portions of the Didache. We first see this inner logic here in Did. 4.2 and then again in the Eucharistic liturgies.[91] The identity of οἱ ἅγιοι in Did. 4.2 refers to baptized community members (Did. 7.1–4), who are permitted to take the Eucharist (Did. 9.5). For the Didachist, the ritual baptism is a necessary condition for participating in the Eucharist. Consequently, anyone not baptized is excluded from the meal.

Did. 9.5: μηδεὶς δὲ φαγέτω μηδὲ πιέτω ἀπὸ τῆς εὐχαριστίας ὑμῶν, ἀλλ' οἱ βαπτισθέντες εἰς ὄνομα κυρίου, καὶ γὰρ περὶ τούτου εἴρηκεν ὁ κύριος· Μὴ δῶτε τὸ ἅγιον τοῖς κυσί

---

89. According to Niederwimmer, "Κυριότης ("lordship") here probably refers to the characteristic of *Jesus* as κύριος. Thus the Didache text means that the place from which the proclamation about the κυριότης of Jesus goes forth is at the same time the place of his presence. There, in the mouth of the teacher and in his teaching, the *Kyrios* himself is present. Thus the teacher himself should be honored as if the *Kyrios* himself were standing before you. In the word of the teacher, the *Kyrios* is present." Niederwimmer, *Didache*, 105.

90. Milavec suggests that rest is to be found "in the words of a community living the Way of Life." Milavec, *Didache: Faith, Hope & Life*, 161.

91. This is a good example of how *Wirkungsgeschichte* may be a helpful way to assess the development of the Didache's textual development. At one point Did. 1–6 was unconnected to the other portions of the Didache. So, it is possible that the identity of the saints (οἱ ἅγιοι) could express a different identity throughout its compositional development.

Trans: "Let no one eat or drink from your Eucharist except those having been baptized into the name of the Lord, for the Lord has also spoken concerning this: 'Do not give the holy things to dogs.'"

Furthermore, the parallel liturgical expression joins together ἅγιος and μετανοέω as a prerequisite to approach the Eucharist (Did. 10.6).

Did. 10.6: Εἴ τις ἅγιός ἐστιν, ἐρχέσθω· εἴ τις οὐκ ἐστί, μετανοείτω

Trans: "If any are holy, let them come. If any are not, let them repent."

Thus, ἅγιός operates as a mandatory status for participation in the Eucharist liturgies and is secured through ritual washing and repentance.[92] So, if this is the case and the final form of the Didache can be considered for a moment, then the "child" and community member in Did. 4.2 finds rest in οἱ ἅγιοι, who have previously experienced the ritual washing and expressed public repentance.

The final communal theme warns against creating schisms in the community (Did. 4.3–4). The warnings appear to include early signs of communal discipline, too. The new wayfarers must not create schism or cause division; rather, they must strive for communal peace (cf. Matt 5:9). Schism (σχίσμα) opposes peace (Barn. 19.5) and one's love for neighbor (1 Clem. 49.5). Communal schisms cause some to leave the faith altogether, plunge many into doubt and despair, and lead to perversion (1 Clem. 46.9).

Thus, if communal members seek to divide the community, the remaining ones must join together to judge righteously (Did. 4.3). The Didachist neglects to inform what such a judgment should entail. Is it dismissal from the community? Is it public or private reproof? Regardless of the decision, the community must act with resolve and unwavering commitment to such a decision (οὐ διψυχήσεις). Verse 4 consists of a *crux interpretum* regarding what exactly is intended here.[93] This corporate action is reminiscent of ecclesial discipline and expulsion on the basis of relational divisions and quarrels (cf. Matt 18:17–20; 1 Cor 5:3–5; 2 Cor 2:5–11). Given that the new member may find support in the words of the whole community, quarrels and divisions will ward off such communal support. Therefore, the community will lead to some form of undefined, yet resolved, corporate judgment (Did. 4.4).

---

92. John Chyrsostom conveys a similar idea: τὰ ἄγια τοῖς ἁγίοις "the holy things for holy persons" (*Hom. Heb.* 17.5; PG 63:133).

93. Niederwimmer, *Didache*, 106.

### I.2.f. Giving to Those in Need (Did. 4.5–8)

The Didachist, once more, revisits the concept of almsgiving and generosity. The community will become a generous people, giving alms and sharing their communal goods. In the span of a few verses, the Didachist simultaneously opts for a generous giving of goods and a prohibition of parsimony. The motifs of almsgiving are a familiar idea in ancient Judaism or early Christian culture, even appearing in a previous section of the Didache (cf. Did. 1.5–6). The Didachist, not unlike others in antiquity, joins together ransom and soteriological categories with almsgiving.

As the literary logic progresses, the Didachist does not prohibit anyone from receiving. Rather, the ethics prohibit those from receiving who then close their hand when others are in need. The community member must not be one who receives while withholding from others with a closed fist (Did. 4.5; πρὸς δὲ τὸ δοῦναι συσπῶν). This ethic does not entirely prohibit receiving. Rather, it condemns stinginess or a refusal to likewise give.

Additionally, those who acquire good through their labors now may give alms as a ransom for their sins (Did. 4.6; δώσεις λύτρωσιν ἁμαρτιῶν σου). The labors and incomes of a single individual will benefit the entire community and will contribute to personal soteriology. Thus, if one works diligently to acquire possessions (ἐὰν ἔχῃς διὰ τῶν χειρῶν σου), they freely give of their goods so as to help reprieve the needs of the community. Moreover, as they give, they will acquire a "ransom for your sins" (λύτρωσιν ἁμαρτιῶν σου).[94] Barnabas likewise conveys a similar ethical motif in that persons may generously give so as to obtain a ransom of their sins (Barn. 19.9–10). Ransom, although still joined to soteriological categories, exclusively relates to almsgiving in this setting (cf. Pol. Phil. 10.2).

To provide for the poor and sojourner reflects covenantal provisions in Israel. No one will be left desolate (Deut 15:4). Similar to the ethical vision of the Didachist, Israel was to give with an open hand to those in need (Deut 15:8). Essentially, all forms of financial needs were satisfied, and the economic needs of the community fulfilled. To love one's neighbor directly corresponded with the generosity shown to the poor and the sojourner (Lev 19:9–10). Through the covenantal blessings, Israel was to provide for those in need.

What remains intriguing about the Didachist's ethics is the tie to soteriological categories. Didache 4.6 joins together ransom and almsgiving. This combined ransom and almsgiving language likewise appears in later Jewish

---

94. According to Stephen Finlan, "ransom" is an ethical idea. As the word connects with sacrifice, "ransom" bears an abstract and ethical meaning and is not necessarily related to sacrifice and atonement. Finlan, "Identity in the Didache Community," 21.

literature. For example, Dan 4:27 LXX joins together almsgiving and ransom categories (τὰς ἁμαρτίας σου ἐν ἐλεημοσύναις λύτρωσαι) so that sins will be ransomed through giving alms and by extending compassion to the poor. Furthermore, almsgiving will save from death and purge sin (Tob 12.9), and garner attention from the face of God, lay up treasures, and serve as an excellent offering to the Most High (Tob 4.7–11). To give alms will also atone for sin (Sir 3.30; ἐλεημοσύνη ἐξιλάσεται ἁμαρτίας).

These themes continue within early Christian literature, too. Almsgiving, which provides repentance for sins, is better than both fasting and prayer (2 Clem. 16.4; ἐλεημοσύνη ἀμαφοτέρων). Alms will liberate a person from death (*eleemosyna de morte liberat*; Pol. *Phil.* 10.2). As previously mentioned, Barnabas likewise combines the labor of one's hands, giving alms, and providing a ransom for sins (Barn. 19.9–10). Generally related, 1 Peter notes how the love of one's neighbor "covers" (καλύπτω) sins (1 Pet 4:8).[95] Alms serve as a memorial to God (Acts 10:4, 31). A final example to consider appears in Herm. Sim. 2 (51). As Hermas considers an elm tree and a vine, the Shepherd explains how they serve as a symbol for the servants of God (Sim. 2.2 [51.2]). A "rich/poor" binary paradigm serves to "allow these two groups to exist in symbiosis, and the nature of that complementary relationship limits the active agency of the poor to their spiritual act of prayer."[96] The rich person gives to the poor without hesitation (Sim. 2.5 [51.5]) and so enables the poor person to fulfill their prayerful obligation. The one who does these things "will not be abandoned by God" (ὁ ποιῶν οὐκ ἐγκαταλειφθήσεται ὑπὸ τοῦ θεοῦ) and their works will be recorded "in the books of the living" (ἔσται ἐπιγεγραμμένος εἰς τὰς βίβλους τῶν ζώντων; Sim. 2.9 [51.9]). According to Downs, these phrases, though sounding meritorious are not soteriological, but "2.9 affirms that the righteous prayers of the poor and the righteous charity of the rich will be inscribed in a heavenly book of deeds," and so "almsgiving in Sim. 2 is *meritorious* but not *atoning* (or salvific)."[97]

Therefore, the Didachist's tradition of ransom and almsgiving matches well with a number of traditions. The Didachist adds to this tradition by declaring that if one works with his hands, he will make ransom for his sins when he gives generously (Did. 4.6). Then, the Didachist adds that one should not doubt or hesitate (διστάζω) when giving, nor should one

---

95. Downs explores the reception of 1 Pet 4:8 in early Christianity, including 1 Clem. 49.2–6; 2 Clem. 16.1–4; Clement of Alexandria (*Quis div.* 32, 37; *Strom.* 4.18); *Didasc.* 2.3–4; Tertullian (*Scorp.* 6.10–11); Origen (*Hom. Lev.* 2.4.4–5). Downs, *Alms*, 175–201.

96. Downs, *Alms*, 251.

97. Downs, *Alms*, 254.

grumble (γογγύζω) when giving (Did. 4.7). The theme of hesitatating when giving also appears in other almsgiving settings (Barn. 19.11) or requests for needs from God (Herm. Sim. 5.4.3 [57.3]). The grumbling here in Did. 4.7 seems different from the grumbling that leads to blasphemies (Did. 3.6), although a similar term appears. To hesitate and then to grumble seems like a personal regret of previous actions. The Didachist wards off such responses on the basis of God being the one who provides recompense (τίς ἐστιν ὁ τοῦ μισθοῦ καλὸς ἀνταποδότης). Why must the community not waver in giving alms? Because God will even repay and give good gifts to those who give alms. Not to hesitate reflects a complete trust in God, who supplies reward. Not only does a reward pay back the alms, but also the metaphor portrays the one who repays as good (Did. 4.7). This reflects a similar, though not identical, tradition to Jesus's teaching. Money and devotion to money reflect one's spiritual piety (Matt 6:24).

This view of alms naturally reflects how to care for members of the community (Did. 4.8). Economic stability is the sum of all its parts. That is, all persons take their goods and share equally with their brothers and sisters in the community (cf. Acts 2:44–46). By mentioning the "brother or sister" (τῷ ἀδελφῷ), the Didachist helps reorient to whom alms are given. Up to this point, nothing hints at prior familial relationships in Did. 4.5–7. But now, generous almsgiving does not merely reflect general generosity, but generosity focused upon its community members. Thus, the Didachist frames this ethic in such a way that the community members generously give of their goods, and the act of giving corresponds closely to soteriological motifs and is a proper way to reflect the God who repays. The community, if functioning properly, will be self-sustaining, having no poor person among them.

This ethical section concludes with a greater to lesser comparison to motivate such generosity (Did. 4.8d). If the community shares in all spiritual and imperishable items, must they not also share all things of lesser value? If you are united with the imperishable (i.e., the greater thing), are you also not united and sharers of the perishable (i.e., the lesser things)? This *qal-wahomer* conclusion to almsgiving similarly appears in Rom 15:27 ("For if the gentiles have come to share in their [Israel's] spiritual things, they ought also to serve them in physical things"). Union and corporate solidarity (κοινωνοί ἐστε) serve as the corporate basis to share goods with other brothers and sisters in need. This communal living further shapes and further substantiates the social association with those that are righteous and humble (Did. 3.9). Only as members embody the virtues extolled here can the economic needs of the community be met.

## I.2.g. Household Code (Did. 4.9–11)

Household codes (*haustafeln*) are reminiscent of structured family cells and basic society. Within these cursory household code instructions, three primary commands address two sets of social strata. Especially, if "my child" still remains as the intended audience (cf. Did. 4.1), this title helps to substantiate the spiritual tutelage of the way of life wayfarer rather than indicating an actual age. Two of the three commands address the primary family units: (1) do not withhold from but teach your children; and (2) do not command your slaves harshly. Additionally, a final command addresses the slaves in the household structure: submit to your master. Even though the Didachist only addresses two social categories, three social categories appear: (1) a parental and master unit; (2) children; and (3) slaves. However, the husband-wife instruction is altogether and strikingly absent in this *haustafel*.[98]

As the Didachist transitions from almsgiving into the household code, he changes topics while continuing a "giving" metaphor (Did. 4.9). Rather than "giving" monetary goods, parents must not withdraw their hand (οὐκ ἀρεῖς τὴν χεῖρά σου) from their child. Given the already-passive disposition and non-violent patterns elsewhere in the Didache's Two Ways, to withdraw a hand does not correspond to withholding corporal punishment. Rather, the opposite of withdrawing a hand is teaching one's children (ἀλλὰ ἀπὸ νεότητος διδάξεις). So, to withdraw a hand refers more to provisions and instruction than to corporal punishment. As the previous sets of instruction portray an extended hand either to give or to receive, this similar metaphor now depicts how parental roles function in the home. Parents must generously give to their children, not necessarily monetary goods, but instruction.

From their youth (ἀπὸ νεότητος), children will receive the sapiential instruction of "the fear of God" (τὸν φόβον τοῦ θεοῦ). The fear of God functions as the base of wisdom. This theme commonly appears in Jewish sapiential instruction, especially as depicted in Prov 1:7: "the fear of the Lord is the beginning of wisdom." Thus, parents who pursue the way of life will secure the wisdom of their progeny. Consequently, the next generation will begin their life with a sapiential foundation in the way of life. To fear God

---

98. Draper suggests that this omission can be explained via rabbinical principles. "So," Draper continues, "the continued subjection of the women and children to their male patriarch was implied in the instruction on the continued subjection of slaves." Draper, "Children and Slaves in the Community," 121. I recognize that we need to make some guesses and historical assumptions when assessing the historical features of the Did. However, this example is one that needs more historical research. As the Didachist distances the community from rabbinic practices on fasting and prayer (cf. Did. 8.1–3), why would they maintain rabbinical household customs?

corresponds to how Christians function in the Empire (1 Pet 2:17). Communal mutual submission bases itself in the "fear of Christ" (Eph 5:21). The fear of the Lord also influences the ethos of οἱ δοῦλοι in other household codes (Eph 6:5; Col 3:22). Polycarp instructs the wives specifically to walk in faith, love, and purity, to love all without favor, and to train their children in the fear of the Lord (παιδεύειν τὴν παιδείαν τοῦ φόβου τοῦ θεοῦ; Pol. Phil. 4.2). And likewise, Clement regards the "fear of God" as the base of child discipline (παιδεύσωμεν τὴν παιδείαν τοῦ φόβου τοῦ θεοῦ; 1 Clem. 21.6). So, to train and to instruct children in the "fear of God" represents a common Christian appropriation of Jewish parental instruction.

Second, the Didachist addresses the parental unit once more, now addressed as servant owners, not to give orders out of bitterness (Did. 4.10; cf. Barn. 19.7). To command (ἐπιτάσσω) reflects one who resides in an authority position and gives orders to be followed (Phlm 8; 1 Clem. 20.3; 37.3). Now, not only do wayfarers teach their children, but also they are expected to treat their male and female servants (δούλῳ σου ἢ παιδίσκῃ) in a particular way. The Didache refrains from condemning or encouraging the acquisition of new servants; so, I am unsure whether or not the Didache's community would perpetuate servant ownership.

The primary command for these servant owners possesses two additional implications. They must refrain from commanding their slaves in an angry or harsh spirit (πικρία). Such a quality must not be part of the Christian's life but appears in a vice list (Eph 4:31). It describes bitter speech (πικρίας γέμει) and fits within a larger list of universal depravity (Rom 3:14). Πικρία appears in a list of vices to avoid as it describes the "evil spirit" (Herm. Mand. 5.2.8 [34.8]). As this term appears with ὀξυχολία ("a bad temper"), πικρία also occurs within Hermas in an etiology of vices (Herm. Mand. 5.2.4 [34.4]). Additionally, πικρία reflects much of the harsh language and the vices in Did. 5.1 and so to command one's servants with πικρία does not reflect the virtuous life.

If masters harshly command their servants, then such language may damage the potential spiritual future of their slaves. In order to motivate the masters, the Didachist warns them not to command harshly, "lest they [the slaves] stop fearing God, who is over both" (μήποτε οὐ μὴ φοβηθήσονται τὸν ἐπ' ἀμφοτέροις θεόν). The ethics of a superior figure will affect those over whom they have authority. If those in position of power possess vices, it may adversely influence the spiritual outcome of their subordinates. According to the Didachist's framework, the servant possesses a similar religious devotion as their owner. For Did. 4.10 mentions, in a passing comment, the religious identity of the slaves/servants: "those hoping in the same God." A harsh and angry tone can lead to the spiritual demise of the servants. They may no longer fear God, who rules over both the owner and servant. By neglecting to fear God, the servants will neglect the foundational elements of wisdom (cf. Prov 1:7) and the very sapiential base of the owner's children (Did. 4.9). If owners are to pass along wisdom as the fear of God, their anger can deter their slaves from this life of wisdom.

The Didachist includes an additional soteriological comment about the Spirit of God. He calls women and men to himself, not based upon social classes, but with regard to those whom the Spirit has prepared (τὸ πνεῦμα ἡτοίμασεν).[99] Part of this preparation, then, is the wisdom-like example of the master. God generously gives prepared items to those who wait upon him (1 Clem. 35.3). God has prepared certain items in the beginning (Diogn. 8.11). Also, this is the first mention of the Spirit (τὸ πνεῦμα) in the Didache, and most likely refers to the Holy Spirit, who prepares people to respond to the call of God. Although such a statement is missing in the Apostolic Constitutions, Barnabas likewise expresses the work of the Holy Spirit (Barn. 19.7). In Did. 4.10, God calls both women and men, without regard for social class, and calls those whom the Spirit of God has prepared. By connecting this predestinarian theological idea with a speech vice of the master, the ethics of the master may impede those whom the Spirit of God has prepared for salvation. Also, to speak harshly of another contributes to how a person perceives another. Pleasing speech from the master is required because the Spirit of God calls from all social strata. To speak harshly may, in fact, speak more to how a person perceives the status of a human (also see Jas 3:9–10). Therefore, speak well to all persons, regardless of their social condition, because they receive the same preparation from the Spirit of God.

The final ethical command breaks focus from an apprenticeship wisdom (i.e., pupil to "my child") and the manner in which they speak to masters. The Didachist now addresses the slaves (Did. 4.11). Regardless of the actions of the slave owners, each servant must submit to their owners (Did. 4.11). It remains unclear if the Didachist addresses the religious devotion of slaves directly or indirectly. That is, does the Didachist generally address slaves and their exclusive submission to way-of-life masters? Or does the Didachist specifically address a way-of-life ethic for the servants? If the previous instruction points out the work of the Spirit of God regardless of the social strata, then it would seem natural to address more generally a way-of-life ethic exclusive to the servants. To the servant, a master functions as a *type* (τύπος) of God himself. In the *Letters of Ignatius*, bishops served as a symbol of the Father (*Tral.* 3.1) or of God (*Magn.* 6.1). So, as the servants

---

99. Niederwimmer appeals to the "predestinarian motifs" that reside in this text. "In the first, the elect are prepared for salvation by the Spirit, and in the second instance the Spirit is given as eschatological gift to the elect." Niederwimmer, *Didache*, 111.

engage with their earthly masters, they encounter the emblematic heavenly God.[100] Thus, to submit with modesty and fear directly addresses a *type* of God. Αἰσχύνη may correspond to a negative quality, but with φόβος the term may convey a sense of modesty (Barn. 19.7). By serving as a type, masters join a similar rank with teachers (Did. 4.1-2) as they too are to be revered as a divine figure. These two figures assume a priest-like role that serves as a conduit to the divine figure, and they may sacramentally embody the divine figure upon the earth in their hierarchical status.

### I.2.h. Covenant Renewal (Did. 4.12-14)

As the Didachist arranges the final set of way-of-life instruction, he concludes with notable directives that recall an ecclesial covenant (Did. 4.12-14). All forms of hypocrisy (πᾶσαν ὑπόκρισιν) should be hated. All items displeasing the Lord (πᾶν ὃ μὴ ἀρεστὸν τῷ κυρίῳ) should also be hated. Hypocrisy has already appeared in the Didache's Two Ways (Did. 2.6) and occurs in the way-of-death vice list (Did. 5.1). Interestingly, Barnabas similarly shares much of this teaching and yet places both the hypocrisy ethic (Did. 4.12) and abandoning the commandment (Did. 4.13) in a different contextual Two-Ways setting (Barn. 19.2). Barnabas places the hypocrisy ethic with the material that similarly parallels Did. 1.2 and 3.9. As the way of life concludes in the Didache, the Didachist places hypocrisy last to ward off any form of duplicitous display of the way of life. To please (ἀρεστός) God appears as a common ethic (Isa 38:3; Tob 4.21; 1 John 3:22) in religious literature and especially joins with covenantal obedience: "You shall diligently keep the commandments of the LORD your God . . . and you shall do what is right and good in the sight of the LORD" (Deut 6:17-18).

To abhor hypocrisy and to please God with one's ethics naturally corresponds with the covenant-renewal language (Did. 4.13). The recipients of the way of life must not forsake the teaching, nor add to it, nor subtract from it. They must guard it. Two items emerge from Did. 4.13 that require additional comment: (1) "commandments of the Lord" and (2) covenant-renewal language. First, the Didachist sees his teaching as an extension of the "Lord's commandments" (ἐντολὰς κυρίου). As the wayfarers abide by the way of life, they also abide by the Lord's commandments. By making this connection, the Didachist may not perceive a difference in the Lord's instructions and the ethical descriptions of his own writings. To deter from the way of life, then, is to deter from the Lord's own instruction.

---

100. Niederwimmer, *Didache*, 111.

Second, to guard and to prohibit any addition or subtraction from the aforementioned ethics demarcate a form of covenant renewal. These precepts similarly correspond to other forms of covenant stipulations. In this case, Deut 4:2 may serve as the prime example: "You shall not add to the word that I command you, nor take from it, that you may keep the commandments of the Lord your God that I command you."[101] Other examples take the form of courtroom commitments or a divine voice that remains immutable:

> Jer 26:2 (33:2 LXX): Thus says the Lord: Stand in the court of the Lord's house, and speak to all the cities of Judah that come to worship in the house of the Lord all the words that I command you to speak to them; do not hold back a word.

> 1 En. 104.10–13: And now I know this mystery: For they (the sinners) shall alter the just verdict and many sinners will take it to heart; they will speak evil words and lie, and they will invent fictitious stories and write out my Scriptures on the basis of their own words. And would that they had written down all the words truthfully on the basis of their own speech, and neither alter nor take away from the words, all of which I testify to them from the beginning! Again know another mystery!: that to the righteous and the wise shall be given the Scriptures of joy, for truth and great wisdom. So to them shall be given the Scriptures, and they shall believe them and be glad in them, and all the righteous ones who learn from them the ways of truth shall rejoice.

> Ep. Arist. 310–11: As the books were read, the priests stood up, with the elders from among the translators and from the representatives of the "Community," and with the leaders of the people, and said, "Since this version has been made rightly and reverently, and in every respect accurately, it is good that this should remain exactly so, and that there should be no revision." There was general approval of what they said, and they commanded that a curse should be laid, as was their custom, on anyone who should alter the version by any addition or change to any part of the written text, or any deletion either. This was a good step taken, to ensure that the words were preserved completely and permanently in perpetuity.

> Josephus, *Ant.* 1.17: As I proceed, therefore, I shall accurately describe what is contained in our records, in the order of time

---

101. Also see Deut 12:32: "Everything that I command you, you shall be careful to do. You shall not add to it or take from it."

that belongs to them; for I have already promised so to do throughout this undertaking, and this without adding anything to what is therein contained, or taking away anything therefrom.

Any warning to refrain from adding to the material presents a divine and legal weight that demands obedience from the community. In both *Epitome* 11 and *Canons* 14.3, the Two Ways includes "guard what you have received, neither adding nor subtracting [from it]," and then again in *Canons* 30 "to guard the commandments, neither taking away nor adding anything, in the name of our Lord, to whom be glory forever, Amen." These warnings convey the complete teaching, and thus they must not be modified (cf. Rev 22:19). To ward off modifying the text aids its perpetuity. So, to add something to the material would convey that the material, as it stands, remains incomplete; to ward off any addition to the material communicates the severity of such actions; and to disobey these commands often leads to covenantal curses.

As the Didachist concludes and shapes a covenant-like community, and if pleasing God and the absence of hypocrisy remain as chief concerns for the way of life, then the covenant community is now synonymous with the gathered community (ἐν ἐκκλησίᾳ; Did. 4.14). According to the Didachist's logic, corporate confession of sin precedes participation in corporate prayers. Therefore, the previous covenant stipulations imply a particular way of being within this local assembly. They must confess sins publically prior to approaching prayer (also see Dan 9:20; Matt 5:23–24; Jas 5:16). Prayer must not be offered with an evil conscience (cf. Heb 10:22), which is caused by unconfessed sin—which also prohibits any participation in the Eucharist (Did. 14.1-2).

The final statement, "this is the way of life,"[102] serves as a *conclusio*. It marks the end of the way-of-life exposition. These ethics—conveyed through Jesus tradition, a Christianized Torah, and other macarisms—form the basis for a flourishing life, both individually and within the corporate community. Within a local-assembly covenant, to adhere to this form of wisdom will provide blessings and security in the way of life and upon the road that culminates in true life.

---

102. Barnabas coheres with its focus on light and darkness: αὕτη ἐστὶν ἡ ὁδὸς τοῦ φωτός (Barn. 19.12).

## I.3. The Way of Death (Did. 5.1–2)

Now, the Didachist turns to complete the Two Ways instruction by finally commenting upon the way of death (Did. 5.1–2). Much like the way of life, the metaphor of a road expresses the wayfaring experiences for the person. As Did. 1.1 expresses the vast differences between the Two Ways, so now the way of death expresses the polar opposite of the way of life. Much of what appears in Did. 5.1–2 also materializes as part of a negative ethic within the way of life. This metaphor of travel conveys both the present life and the telic outcome. In this way-of-death instruction, the structure develops in three segmented features:

a. An introductory description of the way of death (5.1a)
b. Catalogue of vices (5.1b–2a)
   b1. twenty-three vices (5.1b)
   b2. nineteen groups of evildoers (5.2a)
c. A call to be delivered from the way of death (5.2b)

The Didachist begins the way of death in much the same way that the way of life begins. A few preliminary statements introduce the content of the ways of being. In Did. 5.1, the Didachist introduces the way of death with a simple predication (εἰμί), in a highly complementary manner as to the way of life in Did. 1.2. This notable symmetry is too proportioned to suggest any kind of accidental inclusion. Instead, I suggest that this symmetry is not only intentional on behalf of the Didachist, but this symmetry suggests an internal textual coherence. Observe the following symmetry:

Did. 1.2a: ἡ μὲν οὖν ὁδὸς τῆς ζωῆς ἐστιν αὕτη

Trans: "The way of life is this:"

Did. 5.1a: ἡ δὲ τοῦ θανάτου ὁδός ἐστιν αὕτη

Trans: "The way of death is this:"

This text reflects a μέν . . . δέ relationship. Within discourse, a μέν . . . δέ structure creates an anticipatory element whereby μέν introduces an initial clause that anticipates a clause as introduced by δέ.[103] That is, the μέν clause constrains and anticipates the resolve as found in the δέ clause.[104]

---

103. Runge observes the following: "μέν signals the presence of one common constraint: anticipation of a related sentence that follows. . . . I view μέν as always prospective, even in instances where δέ does not follow." Runge, *Discourse Grammar*, 75–76.

104. Levinsohn may overstate the function of μέν in narratives. As μέν functions

These discourse markers suggest that the way-of-life material anticipates a resolve. So, the way-of-death instruction provides the second and necessary section and, according to this discourse marker, the two sections can and should be read together.

As the way-of-death instruction begins (Did. 5.1), a summary statement expresses an all-encompassing and universal maxim to describe the way of death: "above all, it is evil and completely cursed." "Above all" (πρῶτον πάντων; 1 Tim 2:1; Herm. Mand. 1.1 [26.1]) more likely refers to prominence rather than a numerical list.[105] As the way of life begins, the Didachist offers a numerical list that begins with "first" (Did. 1.2) and then "second" (Did. 1.2; 2.1). No such numerical list exists in the way of death. Altogether, this way-of-death instruction lacks any moral compass, reflects wickedness, and consists thoroughly of curses. Because Did. 5.1a possesses some material parallel with Did. 1.2a, the utter demise in 5.1a also reflects a lack of love for the creator and for one's neighbor.

As the way of life describes communal flourishing and the ultimate life, the Didachist creates a social category of inner death that includes telic destruction. Even though a "bless" phrase remains absent in the way-of-life introduction, the "curse" language coheres with the covenantal ideas in Did. 4.12–14. If this covenantal parallel proves valid, then a blessing/cursing paradigm emerges. The blessed and flourishing life is to live in the ways of life. However, the covenantally cursed life (Gal 3:10) is to live in the ways of death.

Human injustice and its relation to the flourishing life circumvents a particular divine worldview. For example, Ps 73 conveys a particular set of lenses to view human injustice, an oppressive social group, and a perceived framework for human flourishing. The outcome of the psalm conveys a different goal for the individual. Much like this way of being, the way of death affords a vision of inner destruction—from the perspective of those traveling on the way of life. The way of death patterns a way of being as seen from the perspective of those on the way of life. So, those already traveling upon a way that leads to life receive a protreptic call to forsake their ways and to engage a new way of life: "children, be delivered from all these things" (Did. 5.2b).

---

in Did. 1.2, by no means is downgraded or of any less importance. Due to the size comparison of what the μέν clause introduces, the way of life far exceeds the way of death in terms of length, structure of material, and development of thought. Stephen Levinsohn offers the following: "The term *prospective* is used in connection with μέν to mean that it anticipates, or at least implies, a corresponding sentence containing δέ.... In particular, the information introduced with μέν is often of secondary importance in comparison with that introduced with δέ." Levinsohn, *Discourse Features*, 170.

105. BDAG, s.v. πρῶτος § 2.a.α.

The initial part of the way of death parallels the second half of the Decalogue, as reflected in Did. 2 and the ethic of Did. 3.1–6.[106] This instruction simply records twenty-three vices. Many of the negative ethics also appear as prohibitive ethics in the way of life and appear to model the order of the fifth, sixth, and seventh Decalogue commands. For example, the way of death also consists of murders (cf. Did. 2.2; 3.2), sexual deviancy (cf. Did. 2.2; 3.3), thievery (cf. Did. 2.2; 3.5), idolatry (cf. Did. 3.4), magic and sorcery (cf. Did. 2.2; 3.4), and false testimonies (cf. Did. 2.3, 5; 3.5). Even the "double-minded" and "double-tongued" ethical prohibition corresponds to the duplicitous or "double-heartedness" (διπλοκαρδία) ethic. Furthermore, the converse of the ethical implications in Did. 3 is humility and blessedness, which counters arrogance and the pompous flairs within the way of death (Did. 5.1).

Hypocrisy appears as an ethical feature that creates social division within the whole of the Didache. It characterizes the wayfarer on the way of death (Did. 5.1) and it must be avoided by those on the way of life (Did. 2.6). As the Didachist gives final remarks regarding the way of life, as a covenant renewal, hypocrisy must be hated by "my child" (Did. 4.12). Furthermore, by invoking Matthean language, the Didachist portrays a social separation in Did. 8 between the community and the "hypocrite." To adhere to different religious practices also implies avoiding the identity of the hypocrites. For example, the community will avoid fasts on particular days to elude a corporate identity with the hypocrites (Did. 8.1) and the Didache community presents a different set of prayers to relinquish solidarity with the religious hypocrites (Did. 8.2).[107]

Furthermore, this way of death creates a social system whereby those considered part of the way of death are described as social oppressors (Did. 5.2a). Followed by a lengthy list of participles—with a few exceptions—the Didachist conveys the continued actions (nineteen in total) of those journeying on the way of death. By doing so, the Didachist creates a social identity for "the other"—those not part of the way-of-life community

The Didachist frames the reader—and subsequently the community—as the victim of those on the oppressive way of death. First, those on

---

106. Did. 5.1 rarely parallels the way of death material in Barn. 19 and *Doctr.* 5. It is not until Did. 5.2 that Did. and Barn. once more begin to parallel one another.

107. Nothing in the Did. text offers a similar social historical identity with the Matthean view of "the hypocrites." In Matt, "hypocrites" is an ethical label given to the Pharisaical system. There does not appear to be a diatribe against Pharisees or an anti-Pharisaical message in the Did. Thus, even though it evokes similar language, it does not appear to equate the same historical referent. The Did. is often pro-Torah and veers quite counter to any explicit anti-Jewish sentiment.

the way leading to death persecute the good (διῶκται ἀγαθῶν; cf. 1 Clem. 45.4). The Didachist, especially harkening back to the Sermon on the Mount's ethics, invites the reader to prepare for such persecution (cf. Did. 1.3–4). Moreover, the ethical vigilance to persevere also appears in the final set of instructions as the Didache's community will face trouble and persecution in the final days (Did. 16.4).

Next, unlike the fair judgments characteristic of the way of life (Did. 4.3–4), the way of death is marked by a failure to judge morally and fairly—in either legal or personal judgments. Third, the travellers on the way of death continue to separate the social classes systematically. They offer no mercy to the poor (οὐκ ἐλεοῦντες πτωχόν). They offer no reprieve or justice for the oppressed (ἀποστρεφόμενοι τὸν ἐνδεόμενον; Did. 4.8). They turn their back upon the needy. They continue to oppress those already afflicted.

Furthermore, the way of death perpetuates the dominance of the affluent. In the way-of-death ethic, those already possessing wealth judicially and publicly advocate for the wealthy (πλουσίων παράκλητοι). Last, the way of death maintains its wayferers' social prowess as they continue to oppress children. In this manner, the way of life secures a safe haven for the life of an unborn (Did. 2.2), completely countered in the way of death. They murder children (φονεῖς τέκνων). As the Didachist continues, the phrase "corrupters of *what is* formed *by* God" (φθορεῖς πλάσματος θεοῦ) follows, and it may correspond to the corruption of children. Also, the way of life prohibits abortion φθορά in Did. 2.2, corresponding to the verbal idea φθορεύς in Did. 5.2.

As wayfarers on this way are unable to know the one who made them, the Didachist has a few consecutive phrases that express the creative works of God. To corrupt God's creation conveys a moral approach to children. With abortion already mentioned in Did. 5.2, the way of death may offer the moral demise of sexual corruption (cf. Did. 2.2; παιδοφθορέω). Wayfarers on the way of death use their dominion over children to perpetuate their own social positions.

Beyond perpetuating a variety of socially oppressive features, the way of death also lacks the moral and philosophical abilities to view the world rightly. First, these participants have an unaligned epistemology. They hate the truth (μισοῦντες ἀλήθειαν) and love lies (ἀγαπῶντες ψεῦδος). Those traveling along the way of death may think they have the correct lens to observe the truth. Second, they lack any moral character, including forms of gentleness and patience (ὧν μακρὰν πραΰτης καὶ ὑπομονή). This counters the blessed life to pursue humility (Did. 3.7). Next, they offer inchoate decisions by not clinging to that which is good (οὐ κολλώμενοι ἀγαθῷ οὐδὲ κρίσει δικαίᾳ). Last, the way of death possesses a form of mixed telic affections. Those on that way pursue worthless things and pursue the rewards that follow.

It is important to see that the author employs a powerful rhetorical strategy in seeking to persuade his readers, and in a different rhetorical context might express his views with more nuance. The Didachist portrays the way of death as awful and destructive—which it is—but to this end he presents the ethical lives of those on this path in very stark ways, ways that likely do not reflect the how those he speaks of would characterize them. The Didachist may use excessive language in order to help offer moral clarity to the way of life and to invite others to abstain from the way of death. So, the Didachist may portray the wider community that surrounds his readers to the extreme, which may not accurately portray all their experiences. If the Didachist self-identifies as a way-of-life participant, does he rightly portray the way of death? In other words, can the Didachist rightly convey the ethics, actions, and intents of the participants on the way of death as a non-participant? In Social Identity Theory (SIT), "group polarization has been characterized as a group decision-making bias, in which groups make judgments which are more extreme than the average initial position of the group members."[108] Moreover, group polarization conveys one group to an extreme that does not represent the whole. "From the point of view of intra- and intergroup social perception, we must remember that there is a tendency towards perceiving the ingroup as better in certain attributes."[109] It appears, then, that the Didachist uses stereotypical way-of-death material to secure in-group loyalty among his readers.

The Didachist protreptically appeals to the destructive ways of death. The way of life far surpasses and reflects a far superior way of being in the world. Although the Didachist portrays the community as a victim of the way-of-death oppressors, the way of life offers a better way of being in the world. True human flourishing, according to the Didachist, is patterned after the way of life, not the way of death. A child (τέκνον), as a particular social stratum within the way of life (cf. Did. 3.1, 3, 4, 5, 6; 4.1), receives the final beckoning call to forsake the way of death. The Didachist ends the way of death by calling the "child" to be rescued from the way of death. The Didachist extends a protreptic call to forsake one way of being in the world and to join oneself to another way, namely the way of life (cf. Tob 4.5). By invoking "child," the Didachist offers a term only reserved for those on the way of life, a term that invites familial images and thereby creates a new social status for them in the community.

Thus, the inferior social status of the Didache community offers a superior way of being to those on the way of death. "O children," invites the

---

108. Hogg and McGarty, "Self-Categorization and Social Identity," 15.
109. Páez et al., "Constructing Social Identity," 214.

Didachist, "may you be delivered." Although the way of death destroys one's life, the way of life presents the blessed and new way to experience true human flourishing.

## I.4. Conclusion to the Two Ways (Did. 6.1–2)

Didache 6.1–2 now concludes the Two Ways. The Didachist carefully structures the final elements of the Two Ways.[110] Consider the cohesive features that frame the actual Two Ways content:

1. Introduction to the Two Ways (Did. 1.1)

    1.a. The Way of Life Instruction (Did. 1.2—4.14)

        1.a.1. Introduction to the Way of Life (Did. 1.2a): "The way of life is this:"

        1.a.2. Conclusion to the Way of Life (Did. 4.14b): "This is the way of life:"

    1.b. The Way of Death Instruction (Did. 5.1–2)

        1.b.1. Introduction to the Way of Death (Did. 5.1a): "The way of death is this:"

        1.b.2. Conclusion to the Way of Death (Did. 5.2b): "Children, be delivered from all these things."

2. Conclusion to the Two Ways (Did. 6.1–2)

These discourse features help provide cohesion to the two individual ways. The pronoun in Did. 4.14b has an anaphoric function to link back to Did.

---

110. van de Sandt and Flusser reconstruct the Two Ways as a whole, and in particular, I want to document how they complete the Two Ways. GTW serves as the "Greek Two Ways" reconstruction and ETGTW serves as the "English translation of the GTW." van de Sandt and Flusser, *Didache*, 128, 130.

GTW 6:1: Ὅρα, μή τίς σε πλανήσῃ ἀπὸ ταύτης τῆς διδαχῆς, ἐπεὶ παρεκτὸς τῆς διδαχῆς σε διδάσκει.

GTW 6:4: Ἐὰν μὲν συμβουλεύων ταῦτα ποιῇς καθ'ἡμέραν, ἐγγὺς θεοῦ ζῶντος ἔσει· ἐὰν δὲ μὴ ποιῇς, μακρὰν ἀπ'ἀληθείας ἔσει.

GTW 6:5: Ταῦτα πάντα εἰς τὸ πνεῦμα σου ἐνβάλλων οὐ πεσεῖ τῆς ἐλπίδος σου (ἀλλὰ διὰ τουτούς ἁγίους ἀγῶνας στέφανον λήψει).

ETGTW 6:1: *See to it that no one leads you astray from this instruction, since [the person who would do so] teaches apart from the [right] instruction.*

ETGTW 6:4: *If you will act with this in mind every day, you will be near to the living God, [but] if you will not act so, you will be far from the truth.*

ETGTW 6:5: *Put all this in your mind and you will not be deceived in your hope (but through these holy contests you will reach a wreath).*

1.2a.¹¹¹ Also, the imperative, vocative, and the summative pronoun in Did. 5.2b help to cohere with the final elements within this section.¹¹²

I want to suggest that Did. 6.1–2 concludes the Didache's Two Ways and Did. 6.3 begins a new section.¹¹³ My discourse argument consists of two items: (1) Did. 6.1–2 provides two essential features for constrained material and (2) Did. 6.3 begins with περί δέ + genitive, which denotes a topic change. First, Did. 6.2 includes a post-positive γάρ, which does not introduce a new section but constrains and supports the material found in Did. 6.1.¹¹⁴ The clause that includes γάρ "does not advance the discourse but adds background information that strengthens or supports what precedes."¹¹⁵ Related, a μέν . . . δέ construction governs the two primary clauses in Did. 6.2. As previously discussed (see commentary section on Did. 5.1–2), a μέν . . . δέ structure creates an anticipatory element to the discourse whereby μέν introduces an initial clause that anticipates a clause as introduced by δέ.¹¹⁶ So, in this way, all of Did. 6.2 functions as constrained material that builds upon and strengthens the preceding material in Did. 6.1. Second, Did. 6.3 introduces the new clause with περί δέ + genitive to denote a new topical break. Throughout the Didache's next section (Did. 6.3—10.7[8]), περί δέ

---

111. Pronouns occupy an anaphoric function, unless they have no antecedent, then they will have a forward-pointing function. According to Pardee, the pronouns in both Did. 1.2a and 4.14b have an anaphoric and cataphoric function, respectively, and thereby create a literary inclusion (Pardee, *Genre and Development of the Didache*, 87). Also see: Levinsohn, *Discourse Features*, 277; Runge, *Discourse Grammar*, 64; Smyth § 1247; BDF § 290.3.

112. Pardee, *Genre and Development of the Didache*, 88.

113. At least three positions comprise Did. scholarship as it seeks to segment this literary division. Either Did. 5.2a, 6.1, or 6.3 conclude the Two Ways. For example, Garrow suggests that the Two Ways in the Did. exclusively refers to the material in Did. 1–5, and more specifically Did. 1.1—5.2a. Whereas, Did. 6.1–3 is a Christian interpolation to cohere with the baptism section. Draper surveys early Christian scholarship to speak of Did. 6.1 and 6.2–3 as the divisions whereby 6.2–3 refers to an "original Jewish substructure of the Two Ways," an independent tradition to bridge the gap between a Jewish Two Ways and Christian liturgy, or a redaction by the Didachist to join a Jewish Two Ways with Christian liturgy. Garrow, *Matthew's Dependence on the Didache*, 67, 97; Syreeni, "Sermon on the Mount and the Two Ways," 90; Draper, "A Continuing Enigma," 106–23; Jefford, "Tradition and Witness in Antioch," 75–89; Draper, "Torah and Troublesome Apostles," 347–72.

114. Pardee, "Visualizing the Christian Community," 73; Smyth § 2803.

115. Levinsohn additionally suggests, "The presence of γάρ constrains the material that it introduces to be interpreted as strengthening some aspect of the previous assertion, rather than as distinctive information." Runge, *Discourse Grammar*, 52; Levinsohn, *Discourse Features*, 91.

116. Runge, *Discourse Grammar*, 75–76.

+ genitive frequently appears to signal either a new topic (Did. 7.1; 9.1; cf. 11.3) or additional instruction (9.2, 3).[117]

(1) Constrained Discourse Material

1.a. γάρ constrains Did. 6.2 with Did. 6.1: εἰ μὲν γὰρ δύνασαι βαστάσαι ὅλον τὸν ζυγὸν τοῦ κυρίου

1.b. μέν . . . δέ constrains two clauses together within Did. 6.2: εἰ μὲν γὰρ δύνασαι . . . εἰ δ' οὐ δύνασαι

(2) Disjunctive Discourse Material

2.a. περί δέ signals a new topic in Did. 6.3: περὶ δὲ τῆς βρώσεως

So, even though much of Didache scholarship suggests a literary division between Did. 5.2 and Did. 6.1–3 or Did. 6.1 and 6.2–3, the discourse features in Did. 6.1–3 suggest otherwise. Even if this text division may not reflect the initial composition and the process of interpolations, the discourse features in H54 divide the two sections between Did. 6.1–2 and 6.3. From this cursory discourse analysis and from the text delimitation of Nancy Pardee, I will build from the premise that Did. 6.1–2 concludes the Didache's Two Ways and Did. 6.3 begins the next section altogether.[118]

In Did. 6.1, the Didachist begins the concluding section. These summary statements frame the Two Ways and most likely still assume the "child" as the recipient. The "child" must vigilantly keep "this way of teaching" (Did. 6.1). Without specifying which way, the pronoun ταύτης conveys a summative role both to commend a way of life and to abhor a way of death. "This way of teaching" summarizes all the material in Did. 1–5.

The concepts in Did. 6.1–2 echo the self-reflective voice of the speaker. The Didachist offers an epistemological foundation for their words—or at least a philosophical foundation—and they include part of the teaching of God (ἐπεὶ παρεκτὸς θεοῦ σε διδάσκει). If anyone teaches contrary to the Didache's Two Ways, then he or she will lead someone astray (μή τις σε πλανήσῃ). The Didachist perceives his own instruction as bearing some form of divine authority. Enough authority is present to equate any teaching not coherent with the Two Ways as teaching done apart from God. The Two Ways maintains an ethical orthodoxy. Those who teach others contrary to the Two Ways fail to consider God (παρεκτὸς θεοῦ). From the Didachist's

---

117. Mitchell explores the ways in which περί δέ indicates new topics within a variety of ancient Greek literature. Mitchell, "Concerning ΠΕΡΙ ΔΕ," 229–56; Pardee, *Genre and Development of the Didache*, 135.

118. Pardee suggests that the material in Did. 6.3 most likely originated "at a stage later than the Two Ways text of 1.1—6.2" and consists of the baptismal text later in the textual history of the Didache. Pardee, *Genre and Development of the Didache*, 139–40.

frame of reference, the ethical instruction coheres with the divine teachings of God and he condemns all teachers who veer from the Two Ways as teaching without regard for God.

As we move into Did. 6.2, it will be helpful to raise a few questions. According to Niederwimmer, one's reading of "yoke" (τὸν ζυγὸν τοῦ κυρίου) influences possible readings of "wholeness/perfection" (τέλειος ἔσῃ) as a *crux interpretum*.[119] So, to what does "the yoke of the Lord" refer? Second, how is the yoke related to the obedience-reward paradigm of τέλειος? Third, given the ethical rigors of the Two Ways, why does the Didachist permit partial obedience? At a basic literary level, four essential features govern the conditional elements in Did. 6.2. If the wayfarers can bear under "the whole yoke of the Lord," then they will be τέλειος. However, if they are unable to bear under the whole yoke, then they bear what they are able.

In order to maintain these ethical rigors of orthodoxy, the wayfarer faces a possible reward of wholeness/perfection as a result (Did. 6.2). The Didachist combines two Matthean motifs: the "yoke of the Lord" and perfection. I turn to these two concepts next.

In order to receive τέλειος, wayfarers must bear under and keep "the whole yoke of the Lord" (ὅλον τὸν ζυγὸν τοῦ κυρίου). Yoke (ζυγός) appears in a variety of ancient settings, including religious and non-religious contexts. Its use in ancient Jewish literature (specifically in LXX) reflects the balance of scales (Isa 46:6; Ezek 5:1; Jer 39:10; Sir 28.25), joins animals together in cooperation (Deut 21:3; Josephus, *Ant.* 12.194), and is used in apocalyptic judgment settings (Ps 61:10 LXX; Isa 40:15; 4 Ezra 3.34; 2 En. 41.1; 61.8). In religious settings, it refers to covenantal relationships (Gen 27:40), obedience (Zeph 3:9), oppression (Lev 26:13; Isa 14:5), and religious subordination (Jer 2:20; 5:5).[120]

Graeco-Roman literature bears similar resemblances of conjoining animals (Homer, *Il.* 5.799; 24.576) or humans (Philostratus, *Vit. Apoll.* VI.40; Achilles Tatius, *Leuc. Clit.* V.6.4) together, religious connotations (Arisitaenetus, *Er. Ep.* 2.7), and military and nautical features (Polybius, *Hist.* I.45.9; Pindar, *Nem.* 5.51).

However, in Christian literature, ζυγός assumes a nearly exclusive religious meaning. Pharisees place an unbearable yoke upon their forbearers (Acts 15:10); the Mosaic Law is likened to a yoke of slavery (Gal 5:1). Jesus offers a gentle and easy yoke[121] and desires to exchange the yoke (Matt

---

119. Niederwimmer, *Didache*, 121.
120. Bertram and Rengstorf, "Ζυγός, Ἑτεροζυγέω," 896–98.
121. Luz recalls this yoke as a form of benevolency. Luz, *Matthew 8–20*, 171.

11:29-30).[122] Barnabas compares the yoke to the new law of Jesus (Barn. 2.6). Justin Martyr associates the yoke with the message of Christ (*Dial.* 53.1)—whereby a yoke also coheres with a virtuous allegorical reading, "thereby giving us symbolic lessons of the necessity of leading a just and active life" (*Dial.* 88.8).

Therefore, within these broader trajectories, to what does the "yoke" refer in Did. 6.2? Given that the material in Did. 6.2 further elaborates upon the material in Did. 6.1, I note how the term generally connects between "this teaching" and the "yoke." Some in Didache scholarship relegate the yoke to sexual asceticism,[123] to the *sectio evangelica* (Did. 1.3b—2.1),[124] or to Christian instruction of the Jewish Law.[125] Because "this teaching" (Did. 6.1) and "yoke" (Did. 6.2) connect together, the Didachist uses yoke (ζυγός) to help form the religious and ethical identity of the Didache community so that the yoke refers to the Jesus tradition in Did. 1.3b—2.1, to the entire way-of-life instruction (Did. 1.2—4.14), and a disavowal of the way of death (Did. 5.2b). Therefore, the yoke wholly corresponds to the Didache's Two Ways.

If the yoke (ζυγός) refers to the whole ethical guidance in the Didache's Two Ways, then τέλειος corresponds to the covenental reward system. Perfection/wholeness is a highly complex lexical term throughout antiquity.[126] David Peterson rightly distinguishes the lexical possibilities between personal and non-personal, and religious and non-religious nuances. "In such contexts," explains Peterson, "it is important to determine the particular writer's measure of τέλειος, whether it is a physical, moral, philosophical, or religious concept."[127]

Within Hebrew literature, τέλειος consistently corresponds to two Hebrew terms: שלם and תמים.[128] In the first century CE, Philo relates τέλειος to

122. See Deutsch, *Hidden Wisdom and the Easy Yoke*.

123. von Harnack, *Lehre der zwölf Apostel*, 19-21; Knopf, *Die Lehre der Zwölf Apostel*, 21; Bertram and Rengstorf, "Ζυγός, Ἑτεροζυγέω," 901.

124. Niederwimmer, *Didache*, 122; Rordorf and Tuilier, *Didachè*, 32-33; Schröter, "Jesus Tradition," 238.

125. Draper, "A Continuing Enigma," 112; van de Sandt, "'Bearing the Entire Yoke of the Lord,'" 331-44.

126. LSJ s.v. τέλειος; GE s.v. τέλειος; Delling, "τέλος, τελέω, κτλ," 49-87.

127. Peterson, *Hebrews and Perfection*, 46.

128. Of its nineteen uses: שלם (cf. Judg 20:26; 21:4; 1 Kgs 8:61; 11:4; 15:3, 14; Jer 13:19) and תמים (cf. Gen 6:9; Exod 12:5; Deut 18:13; 2 Sam 22:26; Song 5:2; 6:9). As τέλειος refers to people, it conveys the sense of internal and undivided wholeness. The term appears alongside moral attributes of blamelessness and righteousness (Gen 6:9; cf. Sir 44.17), and mercy (2 Sam 22:26). It conveys complete and undivided devotion to God (cf. 1 Kgs 8:61; 1 Chr 28:9). Within the Dead Sea scrolls, שלם and תמים convey

virtue and a religious value system.¹²⁹ In *De sacrificiis Abelis et Caini*, Philo joins τέλειος with ἀρετή (*Sacr.* 43). Furthermore, virtues such as "understanding" (φρόνησις), "bravery" (ἀνδρεία), and "righteousness" (δικαιοσύνη) can be deemed "wholly noble and perfectly good" (*Sacr.* 37). Noah was τέλειος (*Deus* 117, 118). The Father of perfect nature (τῆς τελείας φύσεως) sows happiness into the hearts of humanity (*Leg.* 3.219). God possesses a perfect nature (τέλειος φύσις) and humanity ought to acquire a perfect nature for themselves (cf. *Cher.* 9), free from all passions (*Ebr.* 135). Τέλος, τέλεος, and τέλειος relate to happiness, virtue, and a road metaphor in *Plant.* 37. For Philo, τέλειος characterizes God's character and can be found in certain humans. When it applies to humanity, the features of perfection and virtue are present, while all evil passions are absent.¹³⁰

Graeco-Roman literature relegates τέλειος to humanity and virtuous qualities. A moral and virtue value-system appears within Greek philosophy. As Gerhard Delling notes, "τέλειος takes on special significance for the Gk. understanding of man; the point is that total humanity and the full ἀρετή which are to be achieved."¹³¹ The τέλειος person in Plato and Aristotle combines together τέλειος with "virtue" (ἀρετή). In other words, virtue plays an integral part in the wholeness of a person (e.g., Plato, *Tim.* 30d; 41c; 92c; Plato, *Phileb.* 61a; cf. *Leg.* 647d). Aristotle likewise combines τέλειος and ἀρετή. Justice (Aristotle, *Eth. nic.* 1129b.30), friendship (Aristotle, *Eth. nic.* 1156b.34), and nobility (Aristotle, *Eth. nic.* 1149a.11) are perfect virtues. To be τέλειος is to have no insufficiency outside of oneself or possessing any deficiency (*Metaph.* V.XVI.1, 5). Perfection in virtue is attained when an object or person attain their end—with no more room for advancements (*Metaph.* V.XVI.4).

Within first- and second-century Christian literature, τέλειος most closely corresponds to Graeco-Roman virtue concepts and refers to humanity.¹³² Matthean and Jacobean literature mutually undergird a similar

---

ethical patterns and Torah observance. Each person must walk in the way of perfection (תמים), not neglecting Torah (1QS XIII, 20–21), the council will reflect a house of perfection (תמים) that establishes covenant ethics (1QS XIII, 10). Furthermore, one is to walk perfectly in all the ways of Torah (1QS III, 9–11; cf. II, 2, 20). To walk and to observe Torah often occurs with 1) תמים QH I, 36; 1QSb I, 2; V, 22; 1QS I, 8; III, 9; IX, 19; XI, 17), and שלם conveys wholeness without division (1QH XVI, 7, 17).

129. Philo uses τέλειος over four hundred times in his literature, and so his use of τέλειος is quite complex.

130. See the following for a fuller treatment of τέλειος in Philo: Delling, "τέλος, τελέω, κτλ," 70–72.

131. Delling, "τέλος, τελέω, κτλ," 69.

132. Wisdom (σοφία) is only taught to the τέλειος (1 Cor 2:6) and in order to maintain a τέλειος quality, one must be persuaded of the whole will of God (Col 4:15).

trajectory and relate the term to Torah and persons. If you are able to love your enemy, then "you will be perfect" like the heavenly Father (Matt 5:48). Torah obedience and almsgiving relate to τέλειος (Matt 19:21). The law is τέλειος (Jas 1:25) and the Father gives good and τέλειος gifts (Jas 1:17). The perfect person will persevere (Jas 1:4) and control their whole body (Jas 3:2; ὅλον τὸ σῶμα). Congruent with the Matthean and Jacobean tradition, the *Letters of Ignatius* likewise correspond with the Didache. Those who possess the word of Jesus are τέλειος (Ign. *Eph.* 15.2). The musical metaphor in Ign. *Phld.* 1.2 joins the commandments of God with a virtue list. Ignatius reflects upon his soul and blesses his mind fixed in God, knowing these actions to be virtuous and wholesome (Ign. *Phld.* 1.2; ἐπιγνοὺς ἐνάρετον καὶ τέλειον οὖσαν). In Ign. *Smyrn.* 10-11, τέλειος appears in four consecutive verses. Jesus is τέλειος hope (Ign. *Smyrn.* 10.2; cf. Ign. *Smyrn.* 4.2). Ignatius asks that the gracious gift of God may be given to him completely (Ign. *Smyrn.* 11.1), so that the work of the Smyrneans may be perfect in the entire heaven and earth (Ign. *Smyrn.* 11.2). Finally, perfect people think upon perfect things (Ign. *Smyrn.* 11.3).

As some of the early Christian literature displays, the τέλειος ἀνήρ portrays a person wholly committed to Christian Torah observance and who displays virtue. The Didache uses τέλειος in a few ways. Two uses appear in the Two Ways (Did. 1.4; 6.2) whereas two verbal forms appear in the liturgical section (Did. 10.5) and in the final section of the Didache (Did. 16.2). The Didachist conjoins τέλειος with a non-retaliation ethic from Jesus tradition (Matt 5:39-42; Luke 6:29-30).[133] The final ethical command of the Didachist demands vigilance and ethical perfection (Did. 16.1-2). Last, Did. 10.5 presents perfection as a needed condition prior to entering the prepared kingdom.

Now, Did. 6.2 is better understood in light of this broader summary of ζυγός and τέλειος. "Yoke" refers to the moral Two-Ways stipulations and "perfection" refers not to moral perfection but to a Graeco-Roman virtue system. To be perfect means to lack any deficiency. Thus, to bear fully under the yoke of the Lord demonstrates that this person lacks nothing as a person. Didache 6.2 explains how community members obtain personal wholeness and true *shalom*. As the Didachist combines a virtue and vice list with the outcome of τέλειος, the Didache links arms with part of the Graeco-Roman τέλειος ἀνὴρ setting and with part of the Jewish inner-*shalom* tradition.

As the Didachist finishes the Two Ways, readers are now presented with ethical freedoms to bear what they are able (ὃ δύνῃ, τοῦτο ποίει).

---

Pauline tradition reflects a τέλειος person (Eph 4:13; Col 1:28).

133. Hartin, "Ethics in the Letter of James," 300.

What should we make of the partial obedience? It is striking to note that although the Didachist offers a rather rigorist ethic, the final comments offer permissive and concessive qualities. As the Didachist details this ethical permission, another yoke is not presented. So, the community may partially abide by the same Two-Ways yoke. In other words, they need not perform the entire yoke of the Lord to inherit the quality of τέλειος. The Didachist does not suggest that the community performs a counter-ethic, but they may partially perform the current yoke. To receive personal wholeness is not a reward after death, but is a personal quality given to the community who bear the "yoke of the Lord."

The Didachist concludes that this Two Ways instruction continues the divine authoritative teaching. If the individuals cling to the teachings of the Two Ways, they will acquire the necessary ethical perfection to acquire communal acceptance and secure an eschatological life (cf. Did. 16.1–2). For the way of life is both an invitation to live a superior ethical life whereby persons achieve moral and personal flourishing, and a rejection of an inferior way of life.

# II

## Didache 6.3–10.7

### Liturgical Rituals

As we embark into section two of the Didache, a few remarks are in order regarding the use of δέ and the use of περί (δέ) + genitive. Each use of δέ or περί δέ + genitive will serve as a discourse marker to help progress and to segment the list of arguments.

Table 12. δέ + prepositional phrase (περί δέ or μετά + inf.) literary structure for Did. 6.3–10.7

Section I: Περὶ δὲ τῆς βρώσεως: Now concerning food (Did. 6.3)

Section II: Περὶ δὲ τοῦ βαπτίσματος: Now concerning baptism (Did. 7.1)
Secondary instruction: Fasts (Did. 8.1)
Secondary instruction: Prayer (Did. 8.2)

Section III: Περὶ δὲ τῆς εὐχαριστίας: Now concerning the Eucharist (Did. 9.1)
Secondary instruction: Concerning the cup (Did. 9.2; περὶ τοῦ ποτηρίου)
Secondary instruction: Concerning the broken bread (Did. 9.3)
Secondary instruction: Prohibiting the Eucharist (Did. 9.5)

Section IV: Μετὰ δὲ τὸ ἐμπλησθῆναι: Now after being filled (Did. 10.1)
Secondary instruction: Concession given to the Prophets (Did. 10.7)

In Did. 6.3—10.7, δέ details the logical and structural series of ideas in three distinct ways (e.g. Did. 6.3; 7.1; 9.1, 3; 10.1). At the structural discourse level, δέ, when accompanied by a prepositional phrase, will provide structure to the entire discourse. In this way, if περί δέ + genitive or μετά δέ + infinitive appear, they will each function as a topical divider for II. Liturgical Rituals.[1] Thus, each of the four major sections divides among the following topics: food, baptism, Eucharist, and second instruction on the Eucharist.

The other two uses of δέ either advance a secondary topic within the major segments or they logically develop a given topic.[2] For example, δέ (+discontinuity) will offer a mild break to the major discourse section and will introduce subsidiary or secondary instruction. These mild breaks introduce fasting (Did. 8.1) and prayers (Did. 8.2) following the baptismal instruction. Within the first Eucharist section (Did. 9), περὶ τοῦ ποτηρίου (Did. 9.2) advances the exchange through περί + genitive. Didache 9.3 includes περί δέ + genitive. The single use of περί δέ + genitive, in this case, advances not the structural development but offers a secondary development to the Eucharist instruction. Δέ introduces the clause to prohibit a non-baptizand from the Eucharist in Did. 9.5. The final section concludes as with a concession given to the prophets also introduced by δέ (Did. 10.7). The final use of δέ (-discontinuity) logically develops the discourse rather than introducing a new section or set of ideas (e.g. Did. 7.2, 3, 4, 5; 8.1b).

## II.1. Concerning Food (Did. 6.3)

Christian communities developed their own food laws (Col 2:16), and the Didachist gives some freedom to his community (ὃ δύνασαι, βάστασον). This initial section comments on the food customs: περὶ δὲ τῆς βρώσεως.[3] Even

---

1. Mitchell, "Concerning ΠΕΡΙ ΔΕ."

2. Runge, *Discourse Grammar*, 28–36. Smyth regards this feature by stating, "Copulative δέ marks transitions, and is the ordinary particle used in connecting successive clauses or sentences which add something new or different, but not opposed, to what precedes, and are not joined by other particles" (Smyth § 2836).

3. Did. 6.3 serves as a complex feature of the Did.'s composition. I don't pretend to solve these problems, in fact I've purposely avoided being fixated on such conundrums throughout the Did. However, here and a few other places do deserve an additional comment. I've been quite influenced by Pardee's textual reconstruction of the Did., and I assume her argument about Did. 6.3. She comments, "Yet the MS and SA of 7.1 indicate that all of chs. 1–6 are to be included in the recitation prior to baptism so that it is evident that 6.3, though originating at a stage later than the Two Ways text of 1.1—6.2, was at some point considered part of the catechetical/baptismal text." She further regards, "The use of the marker περὶ δέ and the fact that the instruction on food laws was not included with the rest of the Two Ways teaching seems to indicate that the material

with the more controversial food customs transitioning during the first century (cf. Rom 14:1–23; 1 Cor 8:1–13), no hint of controversy appears here.

The Didachist does prohibit, especially (λίαν), someone from eating meat offered to idols. The ethical basis of such comment remains absent in the Didachist's argument. Additionally, to prohibit others from consuming falsely offered food may not relate to physical or spiritual defilement per se, but the actions may hint towards religious identity. In other words, to eat this food will not harm the physical body. Within the Corinthian literature, food does not commend a person to God but can offend a weak conscience (1 Cor 8:8). For the Didachist, a different line of reasoning emerges as the food is contaminated, and thereby, consists of false service. To prohibit sacrificed food is a cultic act and may relate to one's social identity within the religious community. The reason bases itself in ministry or service (λατρεία) given to dead gods (θεῶν νεκρῶν)—plural and non-living, two features diametrically contrary to Christian worship.

It remains unclear to what "dead gods" might refer. The "dead" deity critique is a long-sustained Jewish monotheistic criticism of the seemingly superstitious worship of pagans (cf. Isa 44:9–20). However, the plural feature of dead deities suggests something other than Jewish monotheism. As observed in Diogn. 2, pagan worship consists of dead objects made by human hands. Idolatrous worship, from a Christian vantage point, also includes fat and meat sacrifices (cf. Diogn. 2.8). Jewish and Roman religious identities express their worship through meat sacrifices to dead idols.

It is possible that the material in Did. 6.2–3, and more specifically Did. 6.3, corresponds to material in Acts 15.[4] If this is so, then this set of instruction about food corresponds to cultic ethics in response to Christian and Jewish relations in the first century.[5]

---

was added at a time when a respect for the integrity of the Two Ways had arisen." I would encourage readers to engage Pardee's work far more thoroughly. Pardee, *Genre and Development of the Didache*, 139–40 (also see n198).

4. I suggest that Did. 6.3, historically, amends the Two-Ways conclusion in Did. 6.1–2. However, the vast majority of Did. scholarship suggests otherwise. van de Sandt and Flusser, in ch. 7 "A Jewish-Christian Addition to the Two Ways: Did 6:2–3," supplies a helpful and up-to-date reading of Did. 6.2–3 as a Christian amendment to the Did. text (van de Sandt and Flusser, *Didache*, 238–70). Also consider Jefford's three articles on the topic: Jefford, "Ancient Witness to the Apostolic Decree," 204–13; Jefford, "Tradition and Witness in Antioch," 75–89; "Tradition and Witness in Antioch" (1992), 409–19.

5. See Richard Bauckham's work on Acts 15 and the apostolic decree. Bauckham argues that the gentiles are able to be included with the people of God through the Mosaic Law making provisions for them. Thus, this idea may corroborate that the Didachist has a gentile audience in view for Did. 6.2–3. After all, which Jew would need reminding not to eat idol food? Bauckham, "James and the Jerusalem Church."

Table 13. Did. 6.2–3 and the Jerusalem Council

| Did. 6.2–3 | Acts 15 |
|---|---|
| "Yoke of the Lord" (6.2) | ". . . by placing a yoke on their necks" (15:10) |
| "Bear what you are able" (6.2, 3) | "Neither our fathers nor us are able to bear" (15:10) |
| "Abstain from food offered to an idol" (6.3) | ". . . abstain from the things polluted by idols" (15:20, 29) |

Thus, if one consumes sacrificial meat, one's conscience may remain undefiled, but one compromises one's religious identity. In line with the concession of Did. 6.2, the community most likely practices other forms of cultic food rituals—although they remain absent in this instruction. To concede ritual practices frees the members to "bear as they are able" so that they may eat and practice other rituals in accordance with their conscience.

## II.2. Concerning Baptism, Fasts, and Prayer (Did. 7.1—8.3)

### II.2.a. Baptismal Instructions (Did. 7.1–4)

The Didachist then proceeds to discuss the baptismal ritual (περὶ δὲ τοῦ βαπτίσματος). As the material unfolds, it naturally progresses from catechism to modal scenarios, and finally to communal involvement with the baptizand. A circumstantial clause conditions the baptismal event (ταῦτα πάντα προειπόντες; cf. Did. 11.1). Prior to the primary command, "to baptize" (βαπτίσατε), the Didachist (as a mentor) reviews the Two Ways with the catechumen.[6]

As we assess the final form of the Didache text, we may assume a few elements while interpreting "all these things" (ταῦτα πάντα).[7] Prior to the ac-

---

6. An anarthrous participle that precedes the primary verb will often offer background information to support the primary command. In the case of Did. 7.1, it appears that the participle provides material to suggest preverbal recitation of material prior to the baptismal act. Runge, *Discourse Grammar*, 249–50.

7. I mention this final-form assumption because the majority of Did. scholars observe redaction between Did. 6 and Did. 7 within the compositional history of the tradition. Thus, my purpose is not necessarily to assess the compositional history but to make a judgment about the final form of the Did. It is quite important to assess the Two Ways as its own independent tradition and its own moral framework. At some point in the compositional history of the Did., the Two Ways assumes an additional function as

tual baptismal act, Did. 1.1—6.2 functions as catechism material.[8] Although this may not be the explicit or sole function of the Two Ways in antiquity,[9] the Didache's use of the Two Ways assumes a particular function in Did. 7 to prepare catechumens for baptism and eventually to prepare them to enter the community rituals (cf. Did. 9.5; 10.6). Regardless of an original form, a final-form reading of H54 substitutes the Didache's Two Ways for "all these things" (ταῦτα πάντα). To "say beforehand" conveys an act of communication, and the pronoun ταῦτα substitutes material and acts as a placeholder for the preceding material. Furthermore, even Pardee notes that Did. 1.1—6.3 "is itself a separate text" to warrant this antecedent function for ταῦτα πάντα.[10] Furthermore, and especially given the placement of Did. 7.1, it is difficult to deduce if Did. 6.3 and food customs become part of the reviewed material.[11] Because the material in 6.3—10.7 is structured with the predominant use of δέ + prepositional phrase, and more predominately περί δέ + genitive, I am more inclined to suggest that the reviewed material passes over 6.3 and refers to the material exclusively visible in the Two Ways (Did. 1.1—6.2).

If the final form of the text presents Did. 7.1 to be read with Did. 1.1—6.2, are there other internal features in the Two Ways that hint towards a catechesis instruction? The verbal idea of προειπόντες has an antecedent time referent to "tell beforehand" or "having said something previously"—either written in a text (Diogn. 3.2; Herm. Mand. 9.4 [39.4]) or audibly spoken (Gal 5:21; 1 Thess 4:6; Heb 10:15).[12] Here in the Didache, I would suggest that this term conveys the idea of audibly telling or publically declaring[13] because the catechumen does not appear to memorize the Two Ways but recalls the Two

---

prebaptismal ethical catechesis.

8. I acknowledge the problem of this interpretation if we are assessing the composite structure of the Didache. This is one area where assessing Did. and *Wirkungsgeschichte* will prove quite helpful. For example, the Two Ways did not carry a Two-Ways baptismal catechesis as its primary and original operative. It is not until it is attached to Did. 7.1 that this reading takes shape. Moreover, prior to the attachment of the Two Ways in the composite form, does ταῦτα πάντα προειπόντες appear in the earlier form or was it added when Did. 1–6 was added? Furthermore, was there any catechesis operative in Did. 7 prior to the addition of the Two Ways material? Other than this phrase, baptism could merely continue with ritual washings for communal entrance.

9. McKenna, "'Two Ways' in Jewish and Christian Writings."

10. Pardee, *Genre and Development of the Didache*, 84.

11. Ian Henderson observes the unique ways in which the Didache should be described as "oral," especially when compared to other texts. See the following article for more arguments. I find his conclusion and three senses quite insightful. Henderson, "Didache and Orality," 283–306.

12. BDAG, s.v., προεῖπον.

13. LSJ s.v., προεῖπον.

Ways as a confession of repentance (cf. Did. 10.6). Especially if this verb is chosen over other possibilities, then there may be some likelihood of a verbal and public recitation during the baptismal ritual. A community of onlookers is present at the baptismal event (Did. 7.4).

Thus, a catechumen preforms the Didache's Two Ways as a prerequisite for baptism and other communal rituals (cf. Did. 9.5), and, ultimately, repents (Did. 10.7) to enter the community. Even if the Two Ways were not used for pre-baptismal catechism, might there be anything within the Didache's version of the Two Ways that would permit such practice?

First, the διδαχή (Did. 1.3; 2.1; 6.1) presents itself as a corpus of teaching and instruction.[14] The contents are generally composed of ethics, whereas doctrinal features assume a secondary role. Thus, the διδαχή may be viewed holistically to prepare catechumens in the basic ethical paradigms and to exhort them to desist from particular vices (cf. Did. 5.2). Second, the Two Ways contains a figure that offers proverbial instruction (cf. Prov 1–9). By addressing the reader as τέκνον μου (Did. 3.1, 3, 4, 5, 6; 4.1; 5.2), the Didachist creates a familial hierarchy. They become teacher/parent of the pupil/child. The baptismal instruction continues this hierarchical thread by including "the one baptizing" (Did. 7.4). This single figure, quite possibly, can embody both the catechesis instructor that the Two Ways envisions as well as the active agent in the baptismal event.

Third, although the recipients in the Two Ways are often addressed as τέκνον μου (Did. 3.1, 3, 4, 5, 6; 4.1; 5.2), some of these persons are portrayed as wealthy adults. For example, the "child" gives doctrinal instruction and wisdom to their own "son and daughter," and must not command their slaves in anger (Did. 4.9–11). Therefore, τέκνον μου in the previous sections could refer to their spiritual state as children in the faith. The baptismal recipient must have the ability to recite this instruction, either through practice or at least verbatim. So, the term "child" indicates nothing of the audience's actual age but their spiritual childishness, which expresses their need for a tutor/mentor.

The last final-form idea that I want to raise joins the covenant features of the Two Ways and the washing ritual. Baptism corresponds with community initiation and includes soteriological overtones (Did. 7.4; 9.5). If Did. 4.12–14 occupies a treaty/covenant *proviso* for the community, then baptism operates as a sacred ritual to confirm one's identity with the

---

14. The use of imperatival instruction permeates the Two Ways (Did. 1–6). Within Did. 1–6, over a hundred commands are found. Some are prohibitions (μή + *aorist subjunctive*; οὐ(κ) + *future indicative*) or positive commands (*present imperative*; *future indicative*). The predominant form for the Didachist's instruction is the *future indicative*, which is also reminiscent of Matthew's imperative use of the future indicative.

covenant. Baptism corresponds to the corporate identity and covenantal requisites of the community. Furthermore, as seen below, baptism not only enables the new participant to partake in the second religious symbol (i.e., the Eucharist) but baptism may also sanctify one's status (cf. Did. 9.5). Therefore, in order to identify with the community, baptism is the sacred sign of committing oneself and the initial covenantal washing to participate in a covenant community.

On the basis of these cumulative features, the Didache's Two-Ways material, in its final textual form, functions as a pre-baptismal catechesis. Upon reviewing the aforementioned material (Did. 1–6), the Didachist presents a list of baptismal instructions that include a trinitarian confession, modes of baptism, and pre-baptismal communal instructions. First, similar to Matt 28:19, the trinitarian name accompanies the washing ritual (εἰς τὸ ὄνομα τοῦ πατρὸς καὶ τοῦ υἱοῦ καὶ τοῦ ἁγίου πνεύματος; Did. 7.1).[15] With the trinitarian formula, the Didache's expression reflects a distinct Christian theology (cf. Justin, 1 Apol. 61.3). The formula precedes any of the forthcoming third- or fourth-century trinitarian debates, and minimal theological categories detail where the Didache fits within second-century debates.[16]

Next, the baptismal order progresses with precise modes of operation, which may depend more upon the physical and geographical circumstances. Even if the modal concessions do not denote geographical circumstances, these baptismal descriptors soften the ethical rigors. The ritual should include running water (ἐν ὕδατι ζῶντι; Did. 7.1).[17] With the already-present Gospel tradition, it remains quite difficult not to relate Did. 7.1 and "living water" with the trinitarian language in the Gospel of John and "living water" (John 4; 7:37–39).[18] Next, if cold running water

---

15. The Apos. Con. provides a different reading and a variant to this tradition. As a fourth-century witness, the Apos. Con. may demonstrate some form of modification to the Did. tradition. This problem is well beyond the scope of the current commentary in that it raises the following questions: (1) if we have H54, does the Apos. Con. reflect a more primitive and reliable witness? (2) does H54 reflect an amended witness given the different readings in Apos. Con.? (3) what might the text tradition look like prior to Apos. Con.?

16. See the following on trinitarian discussion in the second century, especially pneumatology. Barnes, "Beginning and End of Early Christian Pneumatology," 169–86; Bucur, *Angelomorphic Pneumatology*.

17. Nathan Mitchell regards the "living water" as a Hebraism for "fresh, flowing water which has been taken from a spring." Mitchell, "Baptism in the Didache," 251–52.

18. Another possibility of "living water" reflects the Levitical cultic ritual in Lev 14:5–9, 50–53 whereby "living water" was used for leprosy in the house and purification rituals. Additionally, Num 19:17 highlights the use of "living water" for purification rituals. By the time we reach Tertullian (*d.* 220), these water ethics no longer are needed: "it makes no difference whether a man be washed in a sea or a pool, a stream

remains unavailable, stagnant cold water is the next option (Did. 7.2a). Subsequently, if any cold water is not available, then warm water will suffice (Did. 7.2b). If neither of the aforementioned options avail, then pouring water upon the head of the individual properly expresses baptism.[19] If pouring water is the mode of choice ("sprinkling" 1QS III, 9), then pouring water must be on the head (Did. 7.3) and in accordance with the trinitarian name (Did. 7.3b).[20] As the final concession permits one to pour water, the previous expressions entail a full-body cleansing. Tertullian, in *Prax.* 26.9, mentions that one will be baptized three times in accordance to the trinitarian name. Also, Hippolytus, in *Trad. Ap.* 21, documents a rather lengthy process for a community baptism ritual.[21]

The text does not indicate the *why* of such progression. It does not explain *why* cold running water is preferred over warm stagnant water. Furthermore, it does not indicate *why* immersion is preferred over pouring water. Because the mode fluctuates with either geographical or in some cases physical circumstances, the ritual of cleansing is prized more highly than modal expressions. To be washed with water is the necessary requirement to enter the community. Moreover, the cleansing (either via immersion or pouring) enables one to enter the community and to partake of other sacred practices (Did. 9.5).

If the Didache's baptismal teaching, namely the trinitarian confession, exclusively corresponds to the Matthean Jesus tradition (Matt 28), then what other material emerges in its cultural and literary repertoire to inform the baptismal teaching? In other words, how did the Didachist and the community know to use the trinitarian formula and a full-body cleansing as the modal procedure?[22] Because no instruction is given on the *why* in Did. 7, one may assume that other early Christian communities were familiar with a Matthean Jesus tradition and washing rituals in their cultural and religious heritage.

---

or a fount, a lake or a trough" (*Bapt.* 4).

19. In *Bapt.* 4.3, Tertullian mentions that it makes no difference where one acquires the water for baptisms.

20. Mitchell mentions three possible variants of the baptismal formulas in the Did.: Did. 7.1c; 7.3; 9.5. Mitchell, "Baptism in the Didache," 252–53.

21. Both Lawrence and Thomas explore "Living Water" in the DSS. "Living Water" is used in the Damascus Document to describe people of the covenant. If the Didachist evokes this language, it could be quite possible to echo this language to portray people who walk in the way as a covenantal ritual. Lawrence, *Washing in Water*, 81–154; Thomas, "Living Water," 375–92 (most notably, 380–83).

22. Draper, "Ritual Process and Ritual Symbol in Didache," 121–58.

The last set of baptismal directives anticipates the ensuing material about fasting (Did. 8.1). Pre-baptismal fasts included the baptizer, the baptizand, and anyone else in the community. Pre-baptismal fasts were not out of the ordinary in early Christianity (Acts 9:9–19; Justin, *1 Apol.* 61.2; Tertullian, *Bapt.* 20.1; *Ps.-Clem. Rec.* 7.37.1).[23] If the community could join in, they were encouraged to do so. This communal involvement possibly aided the acceptance of the catechumen into the community. Moreover, the present community acts as the audience to the audible recitation of the Two Ways (Did. 7.1). This further confirms baptismal washing as a sacred symbol and as a ritual to enter into a covenant community. Only the catechumen and baptizer receive further instruction to fast for one to two days prior to the ritual event (Did. 7.3).

## II.2.b. Fasting Instructions (Did. 8.1)

Following the teaching on baptism, the Didachist develops two additional, subordinate themes—fasting and prayer. Even though Did. 7.1–4 predominantly focuses upon baptism, the section concludes with the topic of communal fasting. So, the use of δέ in Did. 8.1 helps to progress an argument, and the topic of fasting provides a simple topical change. Furthermore, the Didachist will combine the motif of fasting with hypocrisy in Did. 8.1. By introducing the topic of hypocrisy, the use of δέ in Did. 8.2 also helps to present an additional argument; yet it thematically remains linked to the subsequent section. In these next few verses that include three topic changes, the Didachist will predominately focus on a topic and subtly introduce the following topic.

Topic 1: Baptism (Did. 7.1–4) and subtle introduction of Fasting (7.4)

Topic 2: Fasting (Did. 8.1) and subtle introduction of Hypocrisy (8.1b)

Topic 3: Hypocrisy and Prayer (Did. 8.2–3)

So, the Didachist links the three sections by δέ and an anaphoric use of themes. The Didachist will introduce the subsequent section by briefly mentioning a subordinate theme during the preceding section.

Didache 8.1 revisits the theme of fasting. The community must not fast on specific days. The hypocrites fast on Monday, literally the "second from the Sabbath" (δεύτερος σαββάτων), and Thursday, implied by the "fifth from the Sabbath" (πέμπτος). To counter and avoid fasting on these two selected

---

23. Justin and Tertullian accompany baptism rituals with prayers and fasting. A three-month fast is alluded to in *Ps.-Clem. Rec.*

days, the Didachist instructs the covenant community to fast on Wednesday (τετράς) and Friday, literally "the day of preparation" (παρασκευή).

These exhortations slightly differ from the Matthean Jesus tradition (Matt 6:16–17). There, Jesus concerns himself with the external appearance of those fasting (Matt 7:16–17). Both the hypocrisy and fasting motifs give ethical instruction to conceal external appearances. If persons fast and display a disfigured or gloomy face, then they have received their reward.

However, the Didachist shows no concern for physical appearances. Rather, his concern is far more about the specific days to fast. Thus, the ethic in Did. 8.1 refrains from criticizing fasting, but rather it assumes the continued practice. The community must still fast twice a week, but on different days from the hypocrites. Why does the concern for different days rather than the hypocrisy of focusing on external features become the prominent feature? As they fast on different days, the Didache community members concern themselves far more with their religious identity and social distinctions. Fasting itself is not the problem; rather, to be associated with the hypocrites or to confuse the Didache's covenant community with the hypocrites emerges as the problem. Even the fasting ethic coheres with the Two-Ways ethic to avoid hypocrisy (Did. 2.6; 5.1). Therefore, to fast on different days provides both a religious and social practice aimed at distancing their community from the hypocrites, who may have an otherwise similar religious practice. The Didachist and his community may have considered fasting an important act of piety, but that is not the focus of this instruction. The concern here is on fasting as *a social-identity marker*, differentiating the audience from "the hypocrites."

A few questions need to be raised. First, who are the hypocrites? If the Didachist aims to separate two religious identities, from whom does the community separate? Second, what remains particularly unique about Monday, or the "second from the Sabbath" (δευτέρᾳ σαββάτων) and Thursday, or "fifth *from the Sabbath*" (πέμπτῃ)? And, third, what remains particularly unique about the two new days for the Didache's Christian community—Wednesday (τετράδα) and Friday as the "day of preparation" (παρασκευήν)?

The first question that needs to be raised concerns the identity of the "hypocrites" in Did. 8.1. If the Didachist distinguishes between his readers and "hypocrites" and requires a day change, who resides in this latter group? Hypocrisy and fasting are inextricably linked together in Matthew 6:16–18 and most likely refer to the scribes and Pharisees, who practice their righteousness publically (Matt 5:20; 6:1). In the Gospel of Matthew, hypocrisy (ὑπόκρισις) or being a hypocrite (ὑποκριτής) characterizes the Pharisees (Matt 15:7; 22:18; 23:13–29), scribes (Matt 15:7), Herodians (Matt 22:18), and those living with inconsistent demands upon others

(Matt 7:5). Thus, "hypocrites" carries a consistent vision of the Jewish leaders in the Gospel of Matthew, but that does not seem to bear out necessarily in the Didache. Within the Mishnah, Jewish fasts ensue on Monday and Thursday (*m. Ta'an.* 1.6; 2.9; *m. Meg.* 3.6).[24] These three Mishnah texts in particular point to customs for a two-day-per-week fast, instruct participants to read from the law, and stipulate market customs. So, it seems that the Didache utilizes similar Matthean language (Matt 6:16–18) but targets nacent forms of rabbinic Judaism.[25]

To distinguish these two particular days, the Didachist still works from a Jewish calendar of days and practices an already-available custom. For example, the Didachist's framework for days counts the days after Sabbath—"second from the Sabbath." Furthermore, Luke 18:12 already presents a custom of two fasts per week. So, the number of fasts per week, either individual or corporate, remains unchanged, but to count from the Sabbath still underscores a Jewish framework.

To fast on Wednesday and on Friday may associate the Didache's community with the life of Jesus.[26] For example, *Didasc.* 21 suggests Wednesday as the day of Jesus's betrayal in the garden and Friday as the day Jesus was put to death. *Didascalia* provides a two-fold day of fasting for Christian liturgy and provides the life of Jesus as a rubric for these specific days (cf. Apos. Can. 69).

## II.2.c. Prayer Instructions (Did. 8.2–3)

The second conjoined theme recites a liturgical form of the Lord's Prayer (cf. Matt 7:9–13).[27] Much like the previous sections on baptism and fasting, a thematic chain links these three sections. As I already mentioned, the baptism section concludes with a passing comment about fasting (Did. 7.4);

---

24. Zangenberg, "Social and Religious Milieu of the Didache," 55.

25. Goodman, *History of Judaism*, 229–310.

26. Paul Bradshaw and Maxwell Johnson briefly document how Wednesday and Friday became meaningful days to the Christian tradition. Clement of Alexandria (*Strom.* 7.12), Origen (*Hom. Lev.* 10.2), Tertullian (*De ieiunio* 10; *De oratione* 23) likewise connect Wednesdays and Fridays to days of fasting. In the fourth century, Socrates Scholasticus records Origen's practice that the Scriptures were read on Wednesdays and Fridays in a service. Epiphanius held services on Wednesday, Friday, and Sunday, yet it remains unclear if the Eucharist was part of all three (*Adv. haer.* 3.22). Ambrose, on the other hand, does not include a full Eucharist meal but a partial Eucharist ceremony during the week (*Sermones in psalmum* 118 8.48; 18.28). Bradshaw and Johnson, *Origins of Feasts*, 29–36.

27. David Clark's work provides a theological reading of the prayer in the Did. All of chap. 4 explores these theological concepts. Clark, *The Lord's Prayer*, 109–34.

then, the fasting section combines and intertwines a motif about hypocrisy (Did. 8.1); and this final section regarding prayer joins together a hypocrisy motif and the liturgy of prayer (Did. 8.2).

So, not only must the community refrain from fasting like the hypocrites, now they refrain from praying like the hypocrites (cf. Matt 6:5–8). Little information is provided in Did. 8.2–3, let alone in the whole Didache, to help identify these hypocrites. If the final-form text joins together other sections of the Didache, then, literarily, the hypocrites represent wayfarers who are not a part of the way of life. The Two-Ways instruction provides an ethical identity and thereby creates a communal identity. The way of life details hypocrisy negatively (Did. 2.6; 4.12), and it informs part of the ethical identity for the way-of-death wayfarer (Did. 5.1). Historically, there may not be enough literary details to identify this group. Yet if the fasting custom (Did. 8.1) corresponds with the customs of prayer (Did. 8.2), and the identity of the hypocrite acts similarly in both sections, then it is quite possible to identify the hypocrite as the same one who fasts on "Monday" and "Thursday" as a form of Judaism in the second century. These two liturgical practices reflect the complexities of Jewish and Christian social identity.

Rather than praying like the hypocrites, the community prays "just as the Lord commanded in his Gospel" (ὡς ἐκέλευσεν ὁ κύριος ἐν τῷ εὐαγγελίῳ αὐτοῦ). This is the one explicit section where I remain a bit more persuaded of an existing Matthean text to construct this Didache practice. Although "Gospel" (εὐαγγέλιον) appears in other Didache sections (11.3; 15.3–4), those examples may not necessitate a concrete written tradition, but more of an oral tradition of "gospel."[28] According to Simon Gathercole, the term εὐαγγέλιον appears relatively early as a title on the canonical Gospels.[29] The use of the divine name (ὁ κύριος) can refer to Jesus (cf. Did. 9.5; 16:1, 7, 8).[30] Via a cumulative argument, I suggest that "Gospel" and the "prayer" help identify ὁ κύριος as Jesus. Next, the Didachist anchors the prayer in a divine directive, "the Lord has commanded." Fourth, the divine command contains an actual appearance of material tangibly found "in his Gospel," namely the Gospel of Matthew. Fifth, the Didache's prayer reflects nearly

---

28. I agree with Niederwimmer's sentiment: "By εὐαγγέλιον, the Didachist means either the living voice of the Gospel or a written gospel. It is difficult to decide." Niederwimmer, *Didache*, 135.

29. Gathercole, "Titles of the Gospels." Also see: Hengel, *Four Gospels and the One Gospel*.

30. Smith rightly counters many of Milavec's arguments, who suggests that "all instances of 'Lord' in the Didache ought to be understood as referring to the Lord God." Smith, "Lord Jesus and His Coming," 363–407; Milavec, *Didache: Faith, Hope & Life*, 665.

verbatim the Matthean Lord's Prayer and not the Lucan version of the prayer (Matt 6:9–13; cf. Luke 11:2–4). Last, the present motifs of hypocrisy, prayers, and fasting match similar motifs found in the Sermon on the Mount Jesus tradition (Matt 6:1–18). Thus, based upon a collective set of smaller arguments, this section might give credence to a burgeoning presence of a physical Matthean text or to the oral retelling of material that is quite close to a Matthean text (cf. Did. 8.3). Given that the prayer forms part of a daily liturgy, the community's oral memory is not a remote possibility by any means.

When compared with a critical New Testament text (NA28), Did. 8.2 coheres quite closely to Matt 6:9–13.[31] Below, I will merely document and mark the differences.

| Did. 8.2 | Matt 6:9–13 |
|---|---|
| Πάτερ ἡμῶν ὁ ἐν <u>τῷ οὐρανῷ</u>, | Πάτερ ἡμῶν ὁ ἐν <u>τοῖς οὐρανοῖς</u>· |
| ἁγιασθήτω τὸ ὄνομά σου, | ἁγιασθήτω τὸ ὄνομά σου· |
| ἐλθέτω ἡ βασιλεία σου, | ἐλθέτω ἡ βασιλεία σου· |
| γενηθήτω τὸ θέλημά σου, | γενηθήτω τὸ θέλημά σου, |
| ὡς ἐν οὐρανῷ καὶ ἐπὶ γῆς. | ὡς ἐν οὐρανῷ καὶ ἐπὶ γῆς· |
| Τὸν ἄρτον ἡμῶν τὸν ἐπιούσιον δὸς ἡμῖν σήμερον, | τὸν ἄρτον ἡμῶν τὸν ἐπιούσιον δὸς ἡμῖν σήμερον· |
| καὶ ἄφες ἡμῖν <u>τὴν ὀφειλὴν</u> ἡμῶν, | καὶ ἄφες ἡμῖν <u>τὰ ὀφειλήματα</u> ἡμῶν, |
| ὡς καὶ ἡμεῖς <u>ἀφίεμεν</u> τοῖς ὀφειλέταις ἡμῶν, | ὡς καὶ ἡμεῖς <u>ἀφήκαμεν</u> τοῖς ὀφειλέταις ἡμῶν· |
| καὶ μὴ εἰσενέγκῃς ἡμᾶς εἰς πειρασμόν, | καὶ μὴ εἰσενέγκῃς ἡμᾶς εἰς πειρασμόν, |
| ἀλλὰ ῥῦσαι ἡμᾶς ἀπὸ τοῦ πονηροῦ· | ἀλλὰ ῥῦσαι ἡμᾶς ἀπὸ τοῦ πονηροῦ. |
| <u>ὅτι σοῦ ἐστιν ἡ δύναμις καὶ ἡ δόξα εἰς τοὺς αἰῶνας.</u> | |

Only two of these four parallels convey any significant meaning. And both variants do have reasonable answers as to why they appear in these two accounts. First, Matt 6:9 includes a plural form of heaven (ὁ ἐν <u>τοῖς οὐρανοῖς</u>), whereas Did. 8.2 only contains a singular form (ὁ ἐν <u>τῷ οὐρανῷ</u>). Jonathan Pennington has argued for an idiolectic use of heaven and earth pairs in

---

31. An additional study may consider what kind of gospel text existed in the late first or early second centuries that could even cohere with these readings in Did. 8.2.

the Gospel of Matthew.³² Thus, the plural form in Matthew's Gospel speaks more to an idiolectic use of the Matthean redactor than to highlight a textual variant between the Didache and Matthew.

The second difference substantially adds to the Didache's version of the prayer—a final benediction (ὅτι σοῦ ἐστιν ἡ δύναμις καὶ ἡ δόξα εἰς τοὺς αἰῶνας). Within this primary literary unit (II. Liturgical Rituals [Did. 6.3—10.7]), two different liturgical expressions frequently appear in the prayers with repeatable patterns: a shorter and longer liturgical doxology.

Table 14. Shorter and Longer Liturgical Doxologies

| | |
|---|---|
| Longer Doxology: Conclusion to Prayer Liturgy (Did. 8.2) | ὅτι σοῦ ἐστιν ἡ δύναμις καὶ ἡ δόξα εἰς τοὺς αἰῶνας |
| Shorter Doxology: After Cup and Bread in First Meal Liturgy (Did. 9.2, 3) | σοὶ ἡ δόξα εἰς τοὺς αἰῶνας |
| Longer Doxology: Conclusion to First Meal Liturgy (Did. 9.4) | ὅτι σοῦ ἐστιν ἡ δόξα καὶ ἡ δύναμις διὰ Ἰησοῦ Χριστοῦ εἰς τοὺς αἰῶνας |
| Shorter Doxology: After Cup and Bread in Second Meal Liturgy (Did. 10.2, 4) | σοὶ ἡ δόξα εἰς τοὺς αἰῶνας |
| Longer Doxology: Conclusion to Second Meal Liturgy (Did. 10.5) | ὅτι σοῦ ἐστιν ἡ δύναμις καὶ ἡ δόξα εἰς τοὺς αἰῶνας |

The longer and shorter doxologies offer a topical structure to the prayers. Each of the longer liturgical sayings concludes a larger liturgical unity. For example, Did. 8.2 concludes the ritual daily prayers; Did. 9.4 concludes the Eucharist prayers; and Did. 10.5 concludes the final-meal Eucharist prayers. Each of the shorter benediction sayings provides topical arrangements within the liturgical prayers. For example, Did. 9.2 concludes the prayers about the cup; Did. 9.3 concludes the prayers about the broken bread; Did. 10.2 concludes the prayers for giving thanks to the Father; and Did. 10.4 concludes the prayers about giving thanks for the Father's gifts.

So, the final liturgical doxologies amended to the Didache's version of the daily prayers is itself idiolectic and includes an amended expression to the community's structure of the liturgy. The community frequently and collectively voices together, "For to you is the power and the glory unto the ages." At the end of the day, no fundamental theological difference exists between Matthew's version and the Didache except these few idiolectic phrases.³³

---

32. Pennington, *Heaven and Earth*.
33. Tomson, "The Lord's Prayer (Didache 8)," 186.

The community offers these prayers three times a day (Did. 8.3). By using this prayer as part of the liturgical repetition of the community, a liturgical formation more than likely underscores the community. That is, to pray this prayer three times a day would require a structure to one's day, and a structure to one's piety, and would assist in the cultural memory of the prayer. As Niederwimmer notes, "The prayer that follows, the Lord's Prayer, would have been found already in the liturgy that served the Didachist as a source, but it is utterly impossible to decide whether the Didachist modified the given wording (perhaps according to the liturgical tradition familiar to him, or according to the wording of a gospel text before him)."[34] By averring this prayer three times a day, individuals distinguish their practice and piety from the hypocrite. As Hans Kvalbein notes, "They had received a new prayer from their Lord and Master, that became their distinctive mark."[35] This prayer slowly morphs into Christian liturgy at large and regularly informs the creedal development and personal piety.[36]

## II.3. Concerning the Eucharist (Did. 9.1–10.7)

### II.3.a. Initial Eucharist Prayer and Stipulations (Did. 9.1–5)

The Eucharist liturgies in chapters 9–10 possess more theological reflection than any other literary section in the Didache.[37] In the Eucharist liturgies, one will hear nascent trinitarian and binitarian theology, Davidic and servant motifs, epistemological categories, eschatological-ecclesial gathering, temple and dwelling motifs, and the idea of God as creator. With a possible exception in Did. 16, the Didachist deeply and theologically reflects more in these two chapters than anywhere else in the book.

---

34. Niederwimmer, *Didache*, 135.
35. Kvalbein, "Lord's Prayer," 245.
36. Pelikan, *Credo*, 161–66, 388–96.
37. Much of my understanding about Did. 9–10 derives from Jonathan Schwiebert's work. I will not aim to build from these works, but merely to summarize and highlight a variety of helpful arguments from the following two works: Schwiebert, *Knowledge and the Coming Kingdom*; Schwiebert, "Pray 'in This Way,'" 189–207.

It remains relatively debated how Did. 9 and Did. 10 are related to one another.³⁸ Do these two chapters reflect:³⁹ (1) an agape meal, denoting a fellowship meal; (2) only the bread and wine instituted by the Lord; (3) a Eucharist meal, whereby a community simultaneously eats a meal and celebrates the Eucharist;⁴⁰ (4) a celebration of the Eucharist followed by an agape feast; or (5) "table prayers, reworked out of Eucharistic prayers, used in ascetic circles."⁴¹

My literary reading of Did. 9–10 inclines me toward option (3).⁴² A few liturgical cues and literary markers may suggest two forms of a liturgical expression stated prior to and after a corporate meal. I will elaborate upon this concept as I comment upon the text. Regardless of how someone may historically reconstruct this communal event, the Eucharist involves the two elements administered by Jesus in the upper room (cf. Matt 26:26–29; Mark 14:22–25; Luke 22:17–20);⁴³ an expression of thanksgiving (εὐχαριστήσατε; Did. 9.1; 10.1); liturgical prayers associated with the cup, bread, and meal; and a large meal to satisfy the hunger of the communal gathering (μετὰ δὲ τὸ ἐμπλησθῆναι; Did. 10.1).⁴⁴

---

38. Niederwimmer helpfully documents seven different developments and variations within critical Didache scholarship: Did. 9–10 reflects (a) a Eucharist celebration, followed by an *agape*; (b) only an *agape* meal; (c) only the "Lord's Supper" whereas Did. 14 more truly reflects Sunday Eucharist celebrations; (d) only the prayers followed by the Eucharist in Did. 10.6; (e) a vigil celebration; (f) Eucharist prayers with a meal because Eucharist and *agape* have not been fully separated just yet; (g) a full-course meal, but with no correspondence with the Christian Lord's Supper. Niederwimmer, *Didache*, 141–42; Riggs, "Sacred Food of Didache 9–10," 256–83.

39. According to Rouwhorst, three primary issues arise in Didache scholarship: (a) "the shape and the content of the ritual meal, the 'Eucharist,' underlying the extant text of the Didache which is commonly assumed to be the work of a redactor who made use of older sources"; (b) "the development of the chapter prior to their final redaction or compilation, especially the antiquity of the sources employed and the milieu, Jewish or Christian, from which they were derived"; (c) "the place of the rituals underlying the final stage of the Didache as well as the sources in the overall development of the Eucharist and other ritual meals in early Christianity." Rouwhorst, "Didache 9–10," 144.

40. My view is fairly close to this position. So, Betz, "Eucharist in the Didache," 247.

41. Garrow, *Matthew's Dependence on the Didache*, 13–14.

42. Schwiebert suggests that, due to the highly structured parallels between Did. 9 and 10, the Didachist presents three repeated items: one prayer for the cup, one prayer for the bread, and one post-meal prayer. Schwiebert, *Knowledge and the Coming Kingdom*, 64.

43. Charles Bobertz reads the rituals in Did. 9–10 alongside Mark 6 and 8. Bobertz, "Ritual Eucharist within Narrative," 93–99.

44. Willy Rordorf highlights a few elements that relate to the prayers in Did. 9–10, especially since his *Sources chrétiennes* volume twenty years prior to this article. He comments on the text critical problems and about the rituals in Did. 9–10. Rordorf, "Mahlgebete in Didache Kap. 9–10," 229–46.

The Eucharistic liturgy follows a particular order (οὕτω εὐχαριστήσατε; Did. 9.1) and begins with the cup (πρῶτον περὶ τοῦ ποτηρίου; Did. 9.2). As the cup appears first, it remains distinct from the bread-cup (cf. Matt 26:26–29; Mark 14:22–25) or the cup-bread-cup order (cf. Luke 22:17–20). To present the cup first, the Didachist breaks from recorded Jesus tradition—and denotes some fluidity in the early Christian liturgy.[45]

Fixed and variable elements exist within the liturgical recitations. According to Schwiebert, the fixed elements demonstrate that "the prayer leader does not, strictly speaking, have the option to say one thing and not another: certain phrases and expressions are set in advance."[46] Accordingly, four fixed liturgical features appear: (1) a verbal clause "we thank you, Father"; (2) relative clauses "which you made known to us . . ."; (3) a petition to "gather"; and (4) shorter and longer doxologies.[47] The remaining expressions, according to Schwiebert, "evidently have been supplied by the composer of this portion of the Didache for some other reason."[48]

Three broad topics govern this initial "cup" liturgy. First, the participants offer thanksgiving to the Father when presenting the cup. To offer thanks to the Father implies a form of worship to one member of the Trinity. Yet the use of "Father" theologically implies a Son and also conveys, at the least, an incipient form of binitarianism.

The Didachist presents a two-fold reason for the Thanksgiving.[49] First, they express thanks "on behalf of the holy vine of David." Second, Jesus undergirds the means through which they express thanksgiving. The theological logic seems rather confusing at first glance. "The holy vine of David" does not

---

45. Jefford rightly notes, "One is hard pressed to believe that the words of the Didache would ever have found general acceptance within a non-messianic branch of Judaism, considering their focus on the name of Jesus, reference to a select assembly of the ancient ἐκκλησία and the concluding messianic context of the final μαραναθα proclamation." Jefford, "Didache and Eucharist," 34.

46. Schwiebert, *Knowledge and the Coming Kingdom*, 78.

47. Schwiebert, *Knowledge and the Coming Kingdom*, 78.

48. Schwiebert, *Knowledge and the Coming Kingdom*, 88.

49. The Did.'s blessing of the bread parallels quite simply the triparte structure of a Rabinninc blessing (m. *Brachot* 6.1).

| Did. 9.3 | m. Brachot 6.1 |
|---|---|
| We thank you, our Father | Blessed are you, O Lord, our God, King of the universe, |
| for the life and knowledge which you have made known to us through Jesus, your servant; | who brings bread out of the earth |
| to you be the glory forever | Amen. |

seem synonymous with Jesus, because Jesus acts as the means through which the thanksgiving occurs. Otherwise, the community offers thanksgiving *on behalf of Jesus* and *through Jesus*. Although having two referents for a single phrase in early Christian readings is not unusual,[50] this dual referent for the Didachist does seem quite illogical.

Thus, "the holy vine of David" symbolically refers to something else. According to Niederwimmer, "holy vine of David" coheres with eschatological salvation.[51] I am not ruling out the eschatological component, but I would suggest a form of eschatological *presence*. Simply, wine resides inside the cup from a "vine." The "holy vine" may speak to the element itself that resides within the cup. The wine within a Eucharist cup gives a reason for the thanksgiving. To combine the "holy vine" and David recalls the wine in the kingdom of David. For example, to rebuild David's booth in the kingdom will produce abundant wine (Amos 9:11–15). Furthermore, Jesus expresses a sentiment that he will not drink of the "fruit of the vine" until he drinks it within his Father's kingdom (Mark 14:25; Matt 26:19; Luke 22:18). As wine and Davidic themes coalesce, the Didachist may connect motifs of the kingdom, eschatological features, and the identity of David. So, although Niederwimmer offers a helpful notion of "eschatological salvation," I'm more inclined to suggest that the community extends thanksgiving because of the Davidic eschatological kingdom *presence*.

While the Holy Vine signifies such eschatological presence, the Father through means of the Son reveals the eschatological presence. Although the text refrains from explaining how Jesus makes this presence known, it does express that Jesus functions as a revealer of such presence. Jesus may be revealed through a verbal retelling of the liturgy, or the presence of the "Holy Vine" acts as the presence of Jesus himself. If the presence emerges through verbal recitation, then this teaching could harken back to the kingdom instruction of the Last Supper (cf. Matt 26:26–29; Luke 22:14–23). Or the presence of Jesus reveals this presence. The "servant" language suggests such a connection:

Did. 9.2

. . . for the holy vine of *David, your servant*

. . . through *Jesus, your servant*

Because David and Jesus parallel one another and because they share the same title of "servant" (τοῦ παιδός σου), then Jesus, David, "servant,"

50. See the inaugural chapters in the following work on early Christian exegetical patterns: Kannengiesser, *Handbook of Patristic Exegesis*, 115–269.

51. Niederwimmer, *Didache*, 146.

kingdom, and wine thematically interrelate. The wine in the chalice symbolically refers to the Davidic kingdom of God that is now made manifest in the person of Jesus, which is revealed in and through the chalice.

Next, the liturgical prayers focus upon the broken bread (κλάσμα; Did. 9.3). This liturgy follows a similar cadence, especially noting how the community gives thanks to the Father through Jesus (cf. Jewish prayers in *m. Ber.* 6.1). "Life and knowledge" have been revealed to the community through Jesus. A similar idea likewise appears in Did. 10.2 whereby knowledge, faith, and immortality have been made known through Jesus.

If we assess a final form of the Didache to read across the composite sections, then it remains quite difficult not to connect the "life" that appears in the broken bread to the way of life in Did. 1–4. Moreover, the broken bread and its relation to life and knowledge also provide Eucharistic epistemological categories. That is, through the broken bread comes knowledge. Although the Didachist shows little knowledge of Gospel material outside of the Sermon on the Mount, to connect the Eucharist with knowledge resembles Luke 24, when the eyes of the two travelers open after the breaking of bread (Luke 24:30–31). Thus, "life" in Did. 9.3 may refer to the ethical Two Ways, to Jesus himself, or to the freedom that comes through knowledge (cf. Luke 24). The broken bread gives life and knowledge/understanding. Life may now correspond to the freedom that comes about because of knowledge.

The binitarian relationship reveals this "life and knowledge" to the community. The Father serves as the primary revealer of this life and knowledge through the means of Jesus, his servant. This binitarian relation does not explicitly express Father and Son, but Father, Jesus, and servant categories. Although these categories do not necessarily denote Son and Father roles, to employ the language of "Father" implies the theological category of divine relationship: Father and Son.[52] Instead, the identity of "servant" (παῖς) primarily frames the Didache's perception of Jesus in the Eucharist. "Servant" modifies the identity of Jesus on multiple occasions in this liturgical section (Did. 9.2, 3; 10.2; cf. 10.3). Additionally, David receives the title of "servant," which also establishes a David-Jesus identity (Did. 9.2).

To employ "servant" language does not exclusively relate to a "suffering" metaphor (cf. Isa 42–54; Matt 12:18; Mark 10:45). Rather, for the Didache's liturgy, Jesus' role as "servant" solely relates to his being the means through which things are revealed.[53] So, Jesus as *revealer* corresponds to

---

52. See David Yeago's article about theological language. Yeago, "New Testament and the Nicene Dogma," 152–64.

53. Besides these Acts traditions, Jesus or the Lord appears as a παῖς in 1 Clem. (59.2, 3, 4), Mart. Pol. (14.1, 3; 20.2), and Barn. (6.1; 9.2).

servanthood and the servant actions of Jesus for the Father. In other early Christian literature, Jesus also receives the title of God's "servant" in association with his glorification (Acts 3:13), his resurrection (Acts 3:26), spoken revelation through the Spirit of God (Acts 4:25; Ps 2:1–2), his experience of political hostility (Acts 4:27), his practice of miracles (Acts 4:30), and other factors. So, in early Christological identity, Jesus receives the title and portrays the function of a servant and the Didache's liturgy contributes to this rich Christological diversity. Aside from the Didache, only Luke 1:69 and Acts 4:25 join both Christological and Davidic identity with servant language. Yet oddly enough, cross theology and a suffering Jesus remain altogether absent in the Didache's Eucharistic liturgy. In agreement with Schwiebert, to note how much diversity exists between the canon traditions and the Didache suggests that "we are dealing with two ritual paths, both beginning at roughly the same point and both moving metaphorically toward a comparable eschatological future, the kingdom of God, bound up with the figure of Jesus."[54]

Furthermore, the breaking of the bread contains an additional liturgical element (Did. 9.4). Didache 9.4 likens this gathering of the ἐκκλεσία to the Eucharist and, more specifically, to the process of making the Eucharistic bread:

> Just as this broken bread (κλάσμα) was scattered upon the hills and having been gathered together it became one, thusly, let your church (ἐκκλεσία) be gathered from the corners of the earth into your kingdom. (Did. 9.4)[55]

Here, the bread reflects both exilic imagery (cf. Jer 31:10; Ezek 28:25) and eschatological hope. Alistair Stewart joins the elements in Did. 9.4 to the eschatological ingathering of the church in Matt 15 and John 11.[56] The Didachist provides a making-of-bread allegorically that represents the exiled community, eventually gathered into the kingdom. The bread is at first scattered all across the mountains, a phrase that refers to the wheat and other separate

---

54. Schwiebert, *Knowledge and the Coming Kingdom*, 104.

55. van de Sandt and Flusser rightly and creatively observe that the symmetries between Did. 9 and 10, quite notably between 9.4 and 10.5, "suggest that these prayers refer to a single meal." The authors further elaborate, "[the prayers] encircle the actions which occur between them. Rather than representing two different kinds of meals (first a Eucharist and then an *agape*, or first an *agape* and then a Eucharist), the prayers apparently frame a satiating meal. This supper, including the prayers, is called the 'Eucharist.'" van de Sandt and Flusser, *Didache*, 301.

56. Stewart, "Fragment on the Mountain," 175–88; Also consult the following article on the background of John for Did. 9.4: Vööbus, "Liturgical Traditions in the Didache" 81–87.

ingredients. The necessary items were "gathered" together to become "one." In like manner, the church, which is scattered, will gather together into the kingdom.[57] The Didachist uses exile imagery with eschatological hope to help communicate the ideas indicated by the broken bread.[58]

A similar idea appears in Did. 10.5, and this tradition evokes more of an eschatological setting.[59] There, a plea directs the "Lord" to remember (μνήσθητι) and to deliver (τοῦ ῥύσασθαι) the church from all forms of evil (cf. Matt 6:13) to set up a gathering motif:

> Did. 10.5: "And gather it from the four winds (ἀπὸ τῶν τεσσάρων ἀνέμων) into your kingdom, which you have prepared for it"

According to Wim Weren, the use of ἐκκλησία in Did. 9 and 10 portrays at least two different elements: (1) an imperfect church, needing protection from evil, and (2) the preparation of the kingdom for the church.[60] Especially in Did. 9.4, the gathered church from the four corners implies a community that is currently scattered, an exile motif (Isa 11:12; Jer 49:36) that similarly resembles the scattered bread on the hillside. And to gather the ἐκκλησία conveys an eschatological, potentially apocalyptic setting (2 Esd 13.5; Rev 20:8), whereby the church will be gathered into God's eschatological kingdom (Matt 24:31).

A number of explicit teachings from Jesus tradition are glaringly missing in the Didache's Eucharist setting. For example, Did. 9.1–4 continues an early Christian Eucharist liturgy that neglects to include the new covenant (Mark 14:24; Matt 26:28; Luke 22:20), anything about the death and blood of Jesus (Mark 14:24; Matt 26:28; Luke 22:20–22),[61] any inauguration or remembrance language (Matt 26:28; Luke 22:19), any soteriological language (Matt 26:28), and any joining of the breaking of the bread to the body of Jesus (Mark 14:22; Matt 26:26; Luke 22:19). Rather, Did. 9.1–4 joins David, Jesus, and eschatological kingdom language to the vine (Did. 9.2); includes servant and epistemological categories (Did. 9.2–3); and combines the church as emblematic of the broken bread (Did. 9.4).[62]

This first Eucharistic liturgy ends after Did. 9.4. Didache 9.5 additionally instructs *how* and *to whom* to administer the Eucharist. So, this material in Did. 9.5 instructs the community and remains excluded from the liturgy.

---

57. Vogt, "'One Bread Gathered from Many Pieces,'" 377–91.
58. Draper, "Eschatology in the Didache," 569–72.
59. Draper, "Irrevocable Parting of the Ways," 237.
60. Weren, "Ideal Community," 182.
61. van de Sandt and Flusser, *Didache*, 304.
62. Larsen, "Eucharistic Prayers in Didache 9–10," 252–74.

To use περί + genitive provides secondary instruction about the cup (Did. 9.2) and the bread (Did. 9.3–4) within the larger section on the Eucharist (περὶ δὲ τῆς εὐχαριστίας; Did. 9.1). Also, three liturgical benedictions in Did. 9.1–4 aid to segment the recitations.

> Shorter liturgical doxology (Did. 9.2): σοὶ ἡ δόξα εἰς τοὺς αἰῶνας
>
> Shorter liturgical doxology (Did. 9.3): σοὶ ἡ δόξα εἰς τοὺς αἰῶνας
>
> Longer liturgical doxology (Did. 9.4): ὅτι σοῦ ἐστιν ἡ δόξα καὶ ἡ δύναμις διὰ Ἰησοῦ Χριστοῦ εἰς τοὺς αἰῶνας[63]

The shorter doxologies segment a given topic within the liturgy whereas the longer doxology concludes the liturgy. Thus, Did. 9.5 additionally instructs the community and precedes the next full section (Did. 10.1), and most likely is not part of the communally recited material.

In Did. 9.5, the Didachist highlights *who* may partake of the Eucharist. The text completely restricts anyone from partaking of the Eucharist, except for one group of persons.[64] No one may eat or drink of this sacred meal except (ἀλλά) those who have been baptized.

Because of this additional instruction, the baptism section (Did. 7.1–4) joins with this first Eucharist section (Did. 9.1–4). To partake of the Eucharist meal, community members must first receive a baptism into the name of the Lord (εἰς ὄνομα κυρίου). This "name" refers to the trinitarian formula in Did. 7.1. As the Didachist fences off the Eucharist and prohibits some from partaking of this meal, it does convey an order and the absolute necessity of ritual washing that results in cleansing for the community. The ritual cleansing precedes the meal.

The Didachist anchors such an idea (περὶ τούτου εἴρηκεν) with a divine impetus (ὁ κύριος) from a partial Jesus-tradition quote (Matt 7:6).[65] "Lord," in the preceding line (Did. 9.5a), refers to the trinitarian name (Father, Son, and Spirit), but this second use of "Lord" more likely denotes Jesus. The Didachist prohibits the non-baptized from partaking of the Eucharist because "the Lord has spoken concerning this." Because a partial quote appears from Matt 7:6a,[66] "Lord" refers to Jesus, who spoke the Sermon-on-the-Mount tradition.

---

63. According to Schwiebert, the order of this expression and rhythmic cadence might reveal a need to amend the Did. text by removing διὰ Ἰησοῦ Χριστοῦ and switch the order of ἡ δόξα καὶ ἡ δύναμις. Schwiebert, *Knowledge and the Coming Kingdom*, 65–66.

64. Runge, *Discourse Grammar*, 92–100.

65. Stephen Llewelyn highlights the complexity of understanding Matt 7:6a. Llewelyn, "Mistranslation or Interpretation?" 97–103.

66. Gos. Thom. also presents a similar expression. The Gospel of Matt is not the

| Did. 9.5b | Matt 7:6 |
|---|---|
| περὶ τούτου εἴρηκεν ὁ κύριος· | |
| Μὴ δῶτε τὸ ἅγιον τοῖς κυσί | Μὴ δῶτε τὸ ἅγιον τοῖς κυσὶν |
| | μηδὲ βάλητε τοὺς μαργαρίτας ὑμῶν ἔμπροσθεν τῶν χοίρων, μήποτε καταπατήσουσιν αὐτοὺς ἐν τοῖς ποσὶν αὐτῶν καὶ στραφέντες ῥήξωσιν ὑμᾶς |

By quoting this tradition, the Didachist reappropriates the Matthean tradition. Instead of "dogs" referring to gentiles, as reflected in Matthean themes (Matt 15:26–27), and instead of "holy things" portraying a vague referent, "dogs" and "holy things" now refer to the Eucharistic customs.[67] For the Didachist, "dogs" now refers to the non-baptized and the "holy things" now refers to sacred elements of the Eucharist. This language reflects inner- and outer-group polarization whereby the Didachist frames the outsider as embodying particular characteristics very different from those exemplified by the people welcomed to partake of the Eucharist. It would be a horrifying event to have dogs eating sacred food (cf. 4QMMT 58–62).[68]

To apply this Matthean tradition to the Eucharist sanctifies the elements in the Eucharist. Persons now need to acquire the status of ἅγιός as a mandatory quality to participate in the Eucharistic liturgy.[69] For, holy things are only given to holy people. The chalice wine is given the status of ἅγιος (Did. 9.2). The parallel liturgical expression in Did. 10.6 joins together ἅγιος and μετανοέω as a prerequisite to participate in the Eucharist. Therefore, repentance (Did. 10.6) and baptism (Did. 7.1–4; 9.5) enable a person to enter into the community, and only at that moment may

only material that the Didachist could be drawing from: "Do not give holy things to dogs, or they might throw them on the dung heap. Do not throw pearls to swine, or else they might [bring it to naught], [grind them to bits], or [make mud of it]" (Gos. Thom. 93). Ehrman and Pleše note the three different textual reconstructions. Ehrman and Pleše, *Apocryphal Gospels*, 330–31.

67. Draper has helpfully highlighted that this meal reflects "Temple food reserved for the priests in the first instance, which is then extended to the whole eschatological community understood as the Temple." Furthermore, "dogs" corresponds to a similar image in the Qumran community whereby a dog refers to the "quintessential source of defilement of the holy Temple food." Draper, "Attitude of the Didache to the Gentiles," 246–48.

68. van de Sandt, "Eucharistic Food of the Didache in Its Jewish Purity Setting," 236–39; van de Sandt, "Baptism and Holiness," 147.

69. John Chyrsostom conveys a similar idea: τὰ ἅγια τοῖς ἁγίοις "the holy things for holy persons" (*Hom. Heb.* 17.5; PG 63:133).

they partake of the sacred meal.⁷⁰ "Baptism and appropriate behavior," as Jürgen Zangenberg remarks, "has replaced circumcision as a criterion for belonging to the group, and participation in the community meal has substituted for taking part in the sacrificial cult in the temple."⁷¹ Baptism and repentance fundamentally change one's soteriological condition to ἅγιος so they may partake of the sacred meal.⁷²

## II.3.b. Final Eucharist Prayer and Stipulations (Did. 10.1–7)

Didache 10 details the final liturgical recitation (εὐχαριστέω; Did. 10.1) after the gathering finishes the Eucharist meal (μετὰ δὲ τὸ ἐμπλησθῆναι). As we make assumptions about the order between Did. 9 and 10, it will affect the historical reconstruction of the Didache's Eucharistic liturgies. I will predominantly focus upon the final form of the document. If the final form of H54 can help reconstruct second-century settings, then the liturgy offers what I perceive to be the following order: (1) initial or opening Eucharist remarks; (2) immediately followed by or accompanied with the cup and broken bread; (3) followed by or accompanied with a corporate meal; (4) upon finishing the meal, closing Eucharist comments; (5) a concluding corporate liturgy with Μαραναθά. Ἀμήν.

As the Didachist uses μετά + infinitive, it marks a literary division between Did. 9 and Did. 10. A temporal succession and sequence of events are indicated by μετά + τό infinitive.⁷³ So, *after* people have had their fill of a meal (μετὰ δὲ τὸ ἐμπλησθῆναι), they give thanks with the liturgical recitations found in Did. 10.2–6.⁷⁴ To be full or fully satisfied (ἐμπίπλημι) easily combines with the other culinary images in Did. 9–10. Beyond the chalice and bread in Did. 9 and 10, the master (δέσποτης) gives food and drink to humanity (Did. 10.3).

Quite similar to the previous liturgy (Did. 9.2, 3), the community offers thanks. This thanksgiving differs slightly from Did. 9.2 in that they give thanks to "the Holy Father" (Did. 10.2), differing from "our Father" (Did.

---

70. van de Sandt highlights the many Jewish traditions that undergird the cultic meal. van de Sandt, "Eucharist as a Holy Meal," 1–20.

71. Zangenberg, "Social and Religious Milieu of the Didache," 62.

72. This idea is not unfamiliar to others in the second century. For example, Justin, *1 Apol.* 66: "No one is allowed to partake of the Lord's Supper except the one who believes what we teach to be true, and who has been washed."

73. BDAG, s.v. μετά B.2.d.α.

74. So Niederwimmer, "The phrase μετὰ δὲ τὸ ἐμπλησθῆναι suggests that the preceding meal was a full meal for satisfaction of hunger (cf. John 6:12: ὡς δὲ ἐνεπλήσθησαν)." Niederwimmer, *Didache*, 155.

9.2). This "holy" adjective underscores two reasons for thanksgiving. First, they give thanks because of the indwelling divine name. The "holy name" dwells within the people. Because "Holy Father" precedes this expression, the divine "name" (ὄνομα) conveys both the name of the Father (Did. 8.2; cf. 14.3 κύριος) as well as the united name of the Father, the Son, and the Spirit (Did. 7.1, 3; 9.5). Because Did. 8.2 can reflect previous source material, the divine "name" more likely refers to the trinitarian name.

Either the name of the Father or the Triune persons dwell (κατασκηνόω) within those partaking the Eucharist (cf. Ign. *Phld.* 4.1). If this is so, at what point does this dwelling occur? Might this be incipient *theosis* and Johannine union with God? According to the Didache's theological vision, the Didachist provides no clear idea of when this dwelling might occur. Yet to baptize "into the name of God" could result in the trinitarian name dwelling inside a person. Baptism and the inner dwelling of God necessarily transform the community so they can partake of the Eucharist meal. Within the early development of second-century theology, the Didachist coheres with others by depicting participatory related themes—e.g. Pauline literature, Johannine themes, and Ignatius of Antioch.[75]

Second, the community gives thanks for the knowledge, faith, and immortality that are made known through Jesus. In some undefined way, knowledge, faith, and immortality connect to this Eucharist event. The liturgy for the broken bread conveys a similar idea:

| Did. 9.3 | Did. 10.2 |
|---|---|
| We give thanks to you, our Father, for the life and knowledge | We give thanks to you, O holy Father, |
|  | and for knowledge and faith and immortality |

So, knowledge becomes a vital component that Jesus reveals in and through the Eucharist. Part of the Didache's epistemology depends upon an embodied participation of the community with the Eucharist. In the meal, more knowledge is discovered.

Immortality, however, functions very differently. Jesus reveals immortality and the trinitarian persons offer immortality in the Eucharist.

---

75. I am aware of these arguments found in Jefford's article. My comment about participatory themes does not sit in opposition to or in conflict with this article. Rather, I am noting the similar themes, even if Ignatius and Didache do not ultimately cohere. Jefford, "Conflict at Antioch," 262–69.

But what does the Didachist attempt to convey? The Eucharist kingdom liturgy already implies some form of afterlife (Did. 9.4; 10.5). Furthermore, is immortality only offered to those who partake of the Eucharist? Does this imply that the way-of-death wayfarers do not experience immortality? A number of anthropological questions still remain unresolved by exclusively considering the Didache.

Second-century Christianity presents a vision of the Eucharist that extends immortality to the participant. This Didache tradition serves as one text of a few to associate immortality with the Eucharist.

> Ign. *Eph.* 20.2: "All of you, individually and collectively, gather in grace, by name, in one faith and one Jesus Christ . . . breaking one bread, which is the medicine of immortality, the antidote we take in order not to die but to live forever in Jesus Christ."[76]

> Acts of John 109: "And having asked for bread, he gave thanks saying, '. . . For you alone, O Lord, are the root of immortality and the fountain of incorruption, and seat of the ages; you have been called all these names for our sakes, so that now we, calling upon you through them, may recognize your greatness, which we cannot see at the present, but which is only visible to the pure, solely in the image of the man portrayed in you.'"[77]

These two Eucharist traditions interrelate the bread with the immortality of the participant. In fact, Ignatius calls the bread "the medicine of immortality" (Ign. *Eph.* 20.2). If you partake of the medicine, then you will have life in Jesus Christ as the antidote. Even in the Acts of John, the author places the immortality in the broken-bread liturgy and features Jesus as the root of immortality. Still, Jesus joins together with the bread, and immortality can be received through the bread elements.

As Did. 10.2 completes a smaller unit, it will be helpful to comment briefly on the structure of Didache 10. After the initial giving of thanks, a shorter benediction finishes the first of three small liturgical expressions (Did. 10.2). Additionally, Didache 10 will include the following doxologies:

> Shorter Doxology: Did. 10.2: σοὶ ἡ δόξα εἰς τοὺς αἰῶνας
>
> Shorter Doxology: Did. 10.4: σοὶ ἡ δόξα εἰς τοὺς αἰῶνας
>
> Longer Doxology: Did. 10.5: ὅτι σοῦ ἐστιν ἡ δύναμις καὶ ἡ δόξα εἰς τοὺς αἰῶνας

The Didachist also uses vocatives to begin each smaller liturgical unit in Did. 10. For example, "O Holy Father" begins Did. 10.2, "almighty master"

---

76. Translation from Holmes, *Apostolic Fathers*.
77. Elliott, *Apocryphal New Testament*, 336.

(δέσποτα παντοκράτορ) begins Did. 10.3, and "O Lord" (κύριε) begins Did. 10.5. These literary cues help to segment the text according to smaller ideas. So, a vocative will begin a new smaller thematic idea whereas the shorter/longer doxology will conclude the smaller literary units.

The next liturgical section (Did. 10.3-4) addresses God, more likely the Father (Did. 10.2), as δέσποτα παντοκράτορ. Within some Christian traditions, δεσπότης referred to humans who rule over slaves (1 Pet 2:18; Herm. Sim. 5.2.2 [55.2]), someone who possesses subjects (Herm. Vis. 2.2.4 [6.4]; Sim. 1.6 [50.6]), or a generic name given to God or the Father (1 Clem. 7.5; 36.4; Mart. Pol. 19.2). Some traditions, more coherent with the use in Did. 10.3, use this term in contexts that depict God as creator (Acts 4:24; Diogn. 8.7; Prot. Jas. 11.2). Within the Didache's liturgy, God, as the Father, serves as the creator in whom all things have their source.

The Didachist bases an argument in a creator motif to explain how God provides for people. For God is the creator of all things on behalf of his own name (Did. 10.2; 1.2). The ubiquitous creation motif portrays God as funneling food to all persons. So the Father's creator identity relates to his provision for humans (cf. Matt 6:32; Luke 12:30). Food and drink were created so as to give humans enjoyment and thus ultimately cause them to give thanks to God (cf. Eccl 9:7; 10:19). The general provisions of God affect all peoples, who are therefore obligated to give thanks to God as their provider. But the wayfarers upon the way of death are characterized as those who do not know the one who created them (Did. 5.2).

The food motif affects, once more, one's identity. Food, in general, is given to all humans, but the *spiritual* food is given to those partaking the Eucharist (Did. 10.3). As part of the Eucharistic liturgy, the "spiritual food and drink" (πνευματικὴν τροφὴν καὶ ποτόν) further embed themselves into the community's social identity. "Them" and "us" language attaches itself to the food elements. "They" receive general food so that ultimately they will give thanks to God; but "we" have been given spiritual food so that "we" will receive immortality and life. This identity language depicts the social and religious privilege of the Eucharist's participants. Eternal life, moreover, is also provided, possibly in connection with the spiritual food elements. It is the servant Jesus (cf. 9.2, 3; 10.2) who provides eternal life.

This second, shorter liturgical recitation concludes with a general idea of thanksgiving (Did. 10.4). Although the Father consists of the all-providing God who creates humans (Did. 1.2) and gives food (Did. 10.3), the powerful quality of God anchors the basis for thanksgiving (ὅτι δυνατὸς εἶ; cf. 1 Clem. 61.3). Through his powerful nature, God provides the means for persons to express thanks.

In the final liturgical recitation (Did. 10.5), prior to the close of the whole Eucharist liturgy (Did. 10.6), two prominent ideas govern this third and final benediction. The liturgy invokes God to remember (μνήσθητι) and to gather (σύναξον) the church. The call for God to remember the church beckons a concern to deliver and to perfect her. "Deliverance" often accompanies early Christian prayers (1 Clem. 18.14; 60.3) and it appears in the Lord's Prayer itself (Matt 6:13; Did. 8.2). Here in Did. 10.5, a plea to rescue will deliver her from "every form of evil." Without the article governing "evil" (ἀπὸ παντὸς πονηροῦ), this prayer refers to general evil as opposed to "the Evil One" directly (cf. ῥῦσαι ἡμᾶς ἀπὸ τοῦ πονηροῦ; Did. 8.2).

The prayer of Did. 10.5 shares a few elements in the Two Ways, namely the "perfection" theme in Did. 6.2. To be delivered from every form of evil may correspond to the inverse of "to be perfected in your love" (τελειῶσαι αὐτὴν ἐν τῇ ἀγάπῃ σου; Did. 10.5). Full deliverance from evil may in fact consist of complete perfection of the church. In the Eucharistic liturgies, this deliverance corresponds to an eschatological vision; yet to be delivered from all forms of evil similarly describes the way of death: "first of all, it is evil" (πρῶτον πάντων πονηρά ἐστι; Did. 5.1), and to bear the yoke of the Lord brings wholeness and perfection (τέλειος; Did. 6.2). So, to remember the church may depict eschatological deliverance more directly and may implicitly correspond to the continued perfection of the community as depicted in the Two Ways.

Next, the liturgy invokes God to gather the church. Eschatological overtones encapsulate this prayer. To gather from the four winds and to mention "kingdom" cumulatively evoke the eschatological motifs. Especially with the paralleled expression in Did. 9.4, the kingdom and gathering motifs permeate an eschatological deliverance as part of the Eucharistic customs:

| Did. 9.4 | Did. 10.5 |
|---|---|
| οὕτω συναχθήτω σου ἡ ἐκκλησία | σύναξον αὐτὴν |
| ἀπὸ τῶν περάτων τῆς γῆς | ἀπὸ τῶν τεσσάρων ἀνέμων, |
|  | τὴν ἁγιασθεῖσαν, |
| εἰς τὴν σὴν βασιλείαν | εἰς τὴν σὴν βασιλείαν, |
|  | ἣν ἡτοίμασας αὐτῇ |
| Thusly, let your church be gathered from the corners of the earth into your kingdom. | Gather her from the four winds, whom you have sanctified, into your kingdom, which you have prepared for her. |

Angelic and non-angelic traditions often accompany "four corners" or "four winds" traditions in both Jewish and early Christian eschatological settings (cf. Ezek 37:8-9 LXX; 3 En. 26.9; Rev 7:1). Hermas especially portrays how the apocalyptic events involve angels (Sim. 9.2.1-3 [79.1-3]; cf. Sim. 9.10.7 [87.7]; 9.15.1-6 [92.1-6]).[78] Some early Christian traditions join angelic beings with a gathering-into-the-kingdom motif (Matt 24:31; Mark 13:27). Still, other early traditions refrain from including angelic involvement within the gathering motif, and the Didache continues these specific trajectories (Isa 11:12; Jer 49:36; 2 Esd 13.5; Gr. Apoc. Ezra 3.6; Rev 20:8).

The final two verses end quite oddly (Did. 10.6, 7). Because they exist as part of the final form, they influence the liturgies and make it difficult to reconstruct their historical function. The longer liturgical benediction supplies a simpler conclusion (Did. 10.5). As Did. 10.6 moves rather abruptly away from the kingdom and eschatological motifs, the closing prayer calls for grace to come and the world to end. The coming of one item (grace) and the passing away of another (the world) overlap with the prior few phrases of the liturgy (10.5). The coming "kingdom" and the coming "grace" overlap to replace the passing earth. Although an original plea for help,[79] "Hosanna" seems to be used in a positive sense of offering praise to God.[80]

The final call to repent presents a few difficulties, especially in light of the antecedent topics. "If some are holy," which already functions as one of the requirements to partake the Eucharist, they may approach the meal. But "if some are not [holy]," the community excludes them from the Eucharist and beckons them to repent.

If this phrase serves as a prerequisite to partake of the Eucharist, it appears in an odd setting. Why would this call to repent serve as part of a liturgy that only "holy people" recite as they partake of the Eucharist? In other words, a call to repent is placed in an environment of people already possessing holiness, given through baptism, to participate in the Eucharist (Did. 9.5). Now, this idea does cohere with the teaching given in Did. 9.5, but that still does not answer *why* it is part of the liturgical recitations.

Verse 7, in particular, presents a handful of problems, both in terms of its tradition-history and internal literary ideas. Up to this point in the Didache, prophets have not received any attention. So, they oddly appear here without any formal introduction or previous instruction. The mention

---

78. According to Mark Grundeken, Hermas offers very few comments to distinguish between "spirits" and "angels." In fact, Grundeken suggests they are one and the same. Grundeken, *Community Building*, 62; cf. Osiek, *Shepherd of Hermas*, 32.

79. Niederwimmer, *Didache*, 162.

80. It is quite possible that these Eucharistic prayers contain corporate responses. So, Schwiebert, *Knowledge and the Coming Kingdom*, 67-69.

of prophets emerges in an already-coherent literary collection, and the insertion about prophets breaks a literary pattern already found in Did. 7–10. The Didachist grants the prophets to partake of the Eucharist in any way they deem necessary (ὅσα θέλουσιν). After Did. 9–10 has offered structured liturgies and specific social-identity language (insider and outsider), the prophets receive quite a concession. Instruction about the prophets will not appear until Did. 10.3–12 and again in Did. 13. The prophets may celebrate the Eucharist and offer liturgical prayers in whatever fashion they see fit. It is not until later in the Didache that readers receive additional instruction about true and genuine prophets.

As we finish exploring the Eucharistic teachings, I want to quote Schweibert's conclusion at more length:

> In sum, we have two meal rituals taking two distinct paths but sharing significant common ground [Didache and canon tradition]: two "eucharistic" or meal traditions growing, without mutual influence, in a common environment, and performing comparable functions for their participants. Both look to Jesus, but for different reasons and, one might say, with different purposes. On the other hand, both also aim toward a common goal, the "kingdom of God", although the means to that common end once again appear quite different. . . . Both traditions appear only in Greek; both are attested only in the diaspora. Both have plausibly taken shape in roughly the same early period, and plausibly coexist within the years 50–70 CE.[81]

## II.4. [Coptic Addition]: Concerning the Ointment (Did. 10.8)

One more item I would like to raise concerns the so-called *Myron* (μύρον) prayer.[82] It remains quite difficult to discuss a "hypothetical" final form of the Didache Greek text due to (1) a lack of a modern critical edition and (2) the modern base Didache text builds upon H54, an eleventh-century document. So, here in Did. 10.8 and in Did. 16.9(–12), I will briefly comment upon a reconstructed text.

Besides being found in the Apostolic Constitutions (VII, 27, 1–2), Did. 10.8 appears in a Coptic translation. Br. Mus. Or. 9271 is a Coptic papyrus text that includes Did. 10.3b—12.2a. F. Stanley Jones and Paul A. Mirecki

---

81. Schwiebert, *Knowledge and the Coming Kingdom*, 110.
82. Gero, "So-Called Ointment Prayer," 67–84.

have offered a readable Coptic text, translation, and commentary on the text.[83] Unlike Jones and Mirecki and Niederwimmer,[84] who title this addition as Did. 10.7, I will cohere more with van de Sandt and Flusser,[85] as well as Jefford,[86] by enumerating this Coptic version as Did. 10.8. In my mind, this distinction better enables us to distinguish the ointment addition from H54 without confusing the material in Did. 10.7 (H54). The following table includes the Greek provided from Klaus Wengst's edition[87] and the Coptic translation from Jones and Mirecki.[88]

| Klaus Wengst Grk Did. 10.8 | Did. 10.8 Trans. | Apos. Con. VII, 27, 1–2 |
|---|---|---|
| περὶ δὲ τοῦ μύρου οὕτως εὐχαριστήσατε· εὐχαριστοῦμέν σοι, πάτερ, ὑπὲρ τῆς εὐωδίας τοῦ μύρου οὗ ἐγνώρισας ἡμῖν διὰ Ἰησοῦ τοῦ παιδός σου· σοὶ ἡ δόξα εἰς τοὺς αἰῶνας· ἀμήν. | Concerning the saying for the ointment, give thanks just as you say: "We give thanks to you, Father, concerning the ointment which you showed us, through Jesus your Son. Yours is the glory forever! Amen" | And concerning the ointment, give thanks in this way: "We give thanks to you, O God creator of all things, also on behalf of the sweet fragrance of the oil and on behalf of immortality, which you have made known through Jesus your servant, because yours is the glory and the power forever. Amen." |

For one community of Didache readers, especially for whoever used what is now catalogued as Br. Mus. Or. 9271, Did. 10.8 functioned as part of a final form text. I'm not commenting upon whether or not Did. 10.8 needs to be included in a modern edition of the Didache. I assume the critical position of Jefford via Niederwimmer:

> The "ointment" prayer was likely interpolated either around the year 200 CE or slightly earlier, was then incorporated into ApCon

---

83. Jones and Mirecki, "Considerations of the Coptic Papyrus."

84. Niederwimmer, *Didache*, 165–67.

85. van de Sandt and Flusser, *Didache*, 299.

86. Jefford, *Teaching of the Twelve Apostles*, 56–57.

87. Wengst, *Didache*, 82; for the Coptic, see Jones and Mirecki. Given the readership of this commentary, I deemed Greek to be more helpful for my readers than providing the Coptic. Jones and Mirecki, "Considerations of the Coptic Papyrus," 52.

88. This translation is from Jones and Mirecki based off of the Coptic version. I saw no reason to offer a modified translation after translating the Coptic. Jones and Mirecki, "Considerations of the Coptic Papyrus," 53.

with alterations, and the "noninterpolated" text continued in the forms now known from the witnesses of H and Geor.[89]

So, the critical discussions often consider a *Vorlage*,[90] whereas I want to suggest that some second-century community (more likely a Coptic community) understood this *Myron* prayer as part of the Didache's Eucharist liturgy.[91]

Yet I would suggest that Didache scholars as a whole may need to reconsider how to comment upon and assess this Coptic version of Did. 10.8. If, as Jefford and Niederwimmer suggest, the Coptic version is a second-century interpolation, why is an eleventh-century MS (H54) viewed as more reliable for modern readings of the Didache, especially in this instance?[92] In other words, what specific reasons exclude Did. 10.8 as part of a modern critical text? Didache 10.8, in fact, could qualify by some of the basic standards in text criticism: (1) harder reading; (2) earlier reading via date of Coptic MS. Given this concern, I invite the majority of Didache scholarship to revisit the questions of *whether* and *how* Did. 10.8 may influence a modern critical edition.

If I can join Br. Mus. Or. 9271 version of Did. 10.8 with H54 for a thought experiment, what kind of interpretive possibilities arise? The *Myron* prayer coheres with the liturgical discourse features by including the following:

1. an expression similar to "we give thanks" (εὐχαριστοῦμέν)

2. an opening line "concerning the ointment" to cohere with the Greek περί δέ + genitive (περὶ δὲ τοῦ μύρου)

3. a specific "Thanksgiving" given to the Father

4. Jesus, as the servant, serving as the means by which something is revealed

5. the shorter doxology (σοὶ ἡ δόξα εἰς τοὺς αἰῶνας· ἀμήν)

Although there may be no direct or clear interpretation for Did. 10.8, to consider other traditions will greatly inform the Didache's tradition. I foresee a few possible options. Given the Didache's general coherence with

---

89. Jefford, *Teaching of the Twelve Apostles*, 57; Niederwimmer, *Didache*, 167.

90. A là Wengst, *Didache*, 82.

91. Joseph Ysebaert suggests not an ointment prayer but to give thanks for a sweet/pleasing smell. Ysebaert, "So-Called Coptic Ointment Prayer," 1–10.

92. Niederwimmer suggests, "The result is that . . . it is still preferable to hold to the judgment that the Coptic prayer of blessing is secondary, and that it was probably a prayer over the oil of anointing." Niederwimmer, *Didache*, 167.

James, the use of oil is in a prayer of blessing for the sick (Jas 5:14–15; Mark 6:13). Next, in Apos. Con. VII, 44, 1, ointment occurs within the process of baptism. The ointment is placed upon the baptizand as an aroma of Christ and to identify with his death and resurrection. Another second-century example appears in Justin Martyr. He presents an allegorical reading of Ps 44:8 whereby the oil consists of a figure of Christ. None of these previous interpretive options are totally outside the scope of what Did. 10.8 might imply. Ointment for sickness, preparation for death, association with Jesus, or a sacramental presence of Christ himself all entail possible readings for Did. 10.8.[93]

---

93. Dominika Kurek-Chomycz undertakes a different line of reasoning. She incorporates notions of aroma from 2 Cor 2:14–16 and underscores a wisdom and fragrance background. Kurek-Chomycz, "Sweet Scent of the Gospel," 323–44.

# III

## Didache 11.1—15.4

Ecclesial and Communal Order

### III.1. Conduct for Reception of Outsiders: Teachers, Apostles, and Prophets (Did. 11.1—13.7)

#### III.1.a. Concerning Teachers (Did. 11.1-2)

ONE OF THE MANY problems that present themselves in Did. 11.1—13.7 is that the section contains a generally incoherent message. Some have documented well the literary instability and a non-unified vision for "the one who teaches," prophets, and apostles, as well as many features of the textual coherence.[1]

This initial brief section on teachers raises a few questions. It does not explicitly present an identity for these teachers, but the text seems to address the idea of general instructors (ὁ διδάσκων; Did. 11.2). What is the relationship that these teachers share with the subsequent instruction about the apostles and prophets (Did. 11.3)? Do both the apostles and prophets simultaneously self-identify as teachers or has the Didachist created a generic third category? Additionally, how might "the one who teaches" relate to the Didachist or the bishops and deacons (Did. 15.1)? Their relationship to the community still remains relatively unknown.

Answers to these previous questions will remain relatively vague, but three essential literary ideas emerge in this brief section. The Didachist instructs (1) *how* to welcome traveling teachers; (2) *when* to refrain from

---

1. Rordorf and Tuilier, *Didachè*, 104-20; Jefford and Patterson, "Note on *Didache* 12.2a," 65-75; Draper, "Torah and Troublesome Apostles"; Draper, "Torah and Troublesome Apostles (1996)," 340-63; Draper, "Weber, Theissen, and 'Wandering Charismatics,'" 541-76; van de Sandt and Flusser, *Didache*, 331-64; Tuilier, "Les charismatique itinérants dans la Didachè," 157-72; Rothschild, *Essays on the Apostolic Fathers*, 175-84.

listening to the traveling teachers; and (3) *why* to welcome teachers who contribute to the virtue of the community.

The Didachist first exhorts the community to welcome particular traveling teachers (Did. 11.1). They must welcome those who teach "all these things that have previously been mentioned" (ταῦτα πάντα τὰ προειρημένα). A similar phrase appears in Did. 7.1: ταῦτα πάντα προειπόντες. A few questions come to mind with regard to this expression. How do the nearly identical phrases in Did. 7.1 and 11.1 relate to one another? And, to what does Did. 11.1 refer? If Did. 11.1 points the reader back to the material in 7.1, then to welcome teachers must also cohere with the liturgical and pietistic practices of the Didachist. Furthermore, if Did. 7.1 refers to the Two-Ways material, then Did. 11.1 now refers to all of Did. 1.1—10.7. Thus, to welcome any teacher must cohere with the previous material as provided by the Didachist.

However, the Didache does mention a particular time not to listen to a teacher (Did. 11.2). If any veer from the previous teachings and "teach another teaching" (διδάσκῃ ἄλλην διδαχήν), then the community must not listen to them (μὴ αὐτοῦ ἀκούσητε). Within this brief conditional prohibition, "to welcome" in Did. 11.1 seems to cohere synonymously with "to listen" in Did. 11.2. Additionally, to welcome a teacher in Did. 11.1 also implies that the community will listen/obey such a teacher. Yet given the customs in Did. 11.3—13.7, "to welcome" and "to listen" will also include offering lodging, food, and other provisions from the community.

Additionally, if a teacher not only veers from these previous teachings but also "teaches another teaching," the community will reckon them as false teachers by ignoring their teachings (Did. 11.2). Neglecting to listen will bestow a *scarlet letter* of "false teacher" upon this individual.

These two previous instructions leave readers to infer a *kind* of self-perceived authority prescribed in the Didachist. A true teacher will cohere with the already-present instruction in the Didache. The Didachist does not claim inspiration or a divine source; rather, the Didachist claims to possess the "right" teaching. The standard to accept or to reject another extols the instruction already provided in the Didache. The Didachist uses their teaching as the standard of community orthodoxy. If any teachings contradict the Didachist's instruction, they reside outside the bounds of proper teaching.

This self-reflective perception is not particularly unique to this section (Did. 11.1–2). For example, the recipients of the Two Ways must not add to or subtract from the way of life (Did. 4.13). The person who leads astray from the Two Ways instructs without reverence to God (Did. 6.1). These cumulative comments leave readers to infer a self-acclaimed and self-perceived authority of the Didachist's instruction. I'm not sure the Didachist perceives his writing as Holy Writ, but he does provide a clearly authoritative norm for the community's moral and doctrinal training.

Last, the Didachist wards off the community from listening to the errant teachers (Did. 11.2b). Here, the community will welcome these instructors as the Lord himself (ὡς κύριον). Likewise, this reverential honor, given to teachers, appears in the way of life (Did. 4.1). Anyone who teaches the word of God likewise will be revered as the Lord (ὡς κύριον). Yet the instruction to welcome a teacher actually reflects nothing about the content of the teacher's instruction (contra Did. 11.1). Instead, the Didachist focuses upon *the result* of one's instruction. If they teach in such a way that adds to righteousness and to more knowledge of the Lord, then they may be welcomed. If a teacher contributes to the ethical morals and knowledge of the Lord, then the community must welcome them as the Lord (Did. 11.2b). The result of one's teaching contributes to the authenticity of the teacher. This does raise a question that the Didache does not seem to answer. If a teacher instructs something different, but not counter to the Didache's previous instruction, and if it contributes to the increase of virtue, might they still be accepted into the community? Additionally, as the Didache rarely revisits the "teacher" again, "this seems to suggest that the established right of the teacher to a permanent home is extended here to the prophets."[2]

### III.1.b. Concerning Genuine and False Itinerate Apostles and Prophets, and Traveling Christians (Did. 11.3—13.7)

#### III.1.b.α. Concerning Apostles and Prophets (Did. 11.3-12)

After educating about true teachers, the Didachist turns next to advise about genuine traveling apostles and prophets. For the Didachist to separate between teachers and apostles and prophets, one may assume they function differently in the community. Their permanent residency recalls their only, visible distinction. They both teach (cf. Did. 4.1; 11.1, 2, 10; 13.2), but they both receive scrutiny for false teaching in slightly different ways.

It is exceptionally difficult to discern the precise difference in function, if there is one, between the apostles and prophets (Did. 11.3). For, this section concerns both of them as governed by the single preposition and single article (περὶ δὲ τῶν ἀποστόλων καὶ προφητῶν)—so a close relationship exists grammatically between the two, even if they historically comprise of two different groups of people. As Draper relates, "Not all apostles, then, would necessarily have been prophets, but perhaps coming from outside

---

2. van de Sandt and Flusser, *Didache*, 343.

the community would have fit in the category of apostles, those arriving and claiming to be delegated representatives of the Lord and so to be received 'as the Lord.'"[3] Furthermore, if an apostle comes, they are welcomed (Did. 11.4). But if this apostle stays beyond an allocated time, then they become a "false prophet" (Did. 11.5). Also, if an apostle requests money as they leave the community, then they become a "false prophet" (Did. 11.6). After 11.6, the Didachist exclusively uses the language of "prophets" and no longer refers to the two groups. So, some overlap between the groups is evident, but I remain unconvinced by the suggestion that they are alternative names for the same people. I am more inclined to think of these apostles and prophets as two groups, but the customs for the community remain relatively the same, and if either group crosses an ethical or custom line, then they receive the same title: "false prophet."

The primary way to respond to these apostles and prophets appears as a set of ordinances or formalized set of rules (δόγμα)[4] as found in the gospel. "Gospel" (εὐαγγέλιον) appears a total of four times in the Didache (Did. 8.2; 15.3, 4). Other than Did. 8.2 with the related Matthean Jesus tradition, these uses of "gospel" do not necessitate a text or oral tradition of a specific canonical Gospel. Especially in Did. 11.3, the conduct reflects the general conduct of the "gospel." In Did. 15.4, one's practice of prayers and charity follows "the gospel of our Lord." No additional modifiers govern the use of "gospel" in Did. 11.3 to suggest a specific Gospel text, a specific Gospel ordinance, or a specific Gospel tradition. Instead, it seems that whatever is operative of this "gospel," it reflects the general tenor of the gospel of the Lord. If anything would disrupt this *gospelizing* tenor, then the community must deal accordingly.

Once more, the community welcomes a figure "as the Lord" (ὡς κύριος; Did. 11.4). An apostle who comes to the Didache's community is welcomed as one would accept the Lord. This phrase (ὡς κύριος) appears in two other settings (Did. 4.1; 11.2). In both situations, teachers of the community are exalted to a particular level and accepted as the Lord himself. This phrase gives a kind of authority to the figures within the community who teach and instruct rightly.

Within this initial instruction about the apostles and prophets, more space is devoted to instruction concerning false prophets than good or acceptable prophets. First, a prophet is false if they stay too long in the community (Did. 11.5). The community permits a prophet to reside only

---

3. Draper, "Apostles, Teachers, and Evangelists," 157.
4. BDAG, s.v. δόγμα I.

one day, unless a need arises that requires him or her to stay a second day.[5] However, if a prophet resides three days within the community, he or she is a false prophet (contra Did. 12.2).

Next, prophets are false if they request financial assistance (ἀργύριον; Did. 11.6). These people must not accept anything but food until they find their next location for lodging (ἕως οὗ αὐλισθῇ). If upon departure they ask for money, they are false prophets. These comments reflect the Jesus tradition, which prohibits taking money (Luke 9:3), a money belt (Mark 6:8), gold and silver (Mark 10:9), or a purse with them (Luke 10:4). These itinerant individuals entrust themselves to poverty and to the generous communities, and ultimately to God, who will nourish and provide for them.

Third, if prophets order and partake of a meal, they are false prophets (Did. 11.9). Even if prophets order "in the spirit" (Did. 11.7, 8, 12), they still may not partake of this meal. To do something "in the spirit" speaks of the genuineness of their activity. So, even with purity and in the right way, prophets may still not request and partake of food. Rather, these ethical prohibitions refer to the rewards given to a genuine prophet through the community. If they are true prophets, then they will have no lack of food (cf. Did. 11.6; 13.1–7).

Finally, if they live by a contrary ethic to their teaching, then they are false prophets (Did. 11.10). Thus, to possess the right dogma still may not ward off the concerns of the community about their status as true prophets. Slightly different than Did. 6.2 and 11.2, a person must not teach counter to the Two Ways or to the previous teachings. Didache 11.2 also suggests that a teacher's instruction may still be valued if their teaching contributes to virtue. The inverse, though, occurs in Did. 11.10, whereby one's virtue can make or break one's perception of truth.

Sprinkled throughout this section are comments on how to treat and welcome the apostles and prophets. First, the community must not put to test (οὐ πειράσετε) or judge (οὐδὲ διακρινεῖτε) the prophets (Did. 11.7). This verse seems problematic on multiple levels. Although the general communal virtue falls in line with the ordinances of the gospel (Did. 11.3), the community must not prohibit one from judging or testing the teaching or character of the prophet. Any prophet, who speaks "in the Lord," is *de facto* protected from judgment (cf. 1 John 4:1–6). Furthermore, to receive them with no judgment will further undergird their divine-like quality of being received "as the Lord" (Did. 11.4).

---

5. According to Niederwimmer, "The strikingly rigorous rule shows that (1) radical homelessness is one of the factors in the existence of apostles in the Didache, and (2) they did not appear as ongoing or even temporarily resident functionaries in these communities. Instead, their life is itinerancy." Niederwimmer, *Didache*, 176.

Furthermore, if the community does test the prophets, they commit an unpardonable sin. The Didachist assures his audience that any and all sin will be forgiven (πᾶσα γὰρ ἁμαρτία ἀφεθήσεται), but to judge these traveling prophets will result in an unpardonable consequence: "this sin will not be forgiven."[6] Observe this similar expression in Matt 12:31–32:

| Matt 12:31–32 ESV | Did. 11.7b |
|---|---|
| Therefore I tell you, every sin and blasphemy will be forgiven people, but the blasphemy against the Spirit will not be forgiven. And whoever speaks a word against the Son of Man will be forgiven, but whoever speaks against the Holy Spirit will not be forgiven, either in this age or in the age to come. | For all sins will be forgiven, but this sin will not be forgiven |

This Matthew tradition further corroborates how the Didachist perceives these traveling prophets "as the Lord." To cast any form of testing or judgment lands on par with speaking a word against the "Son of Man." According to Matthew's version of the blasphemy of the Spirit, to speak against the Son of Man—Jesus—speaks against the Holy Spirit, and thus it permits no room to receive forgiveness. These paralleled ideas fully correspond to the Didache's perception of the unpardonable sin. To test a prophet—who speaks in the Spirit, who is received "as the Lord," and who portrays the presence of Jesus—results in an unpardonable sin.

Rather than openly testing or judging a prophet, it seems that the community must wait for false prophets to expose themselves (Did. 11.8). The community should judge temperately, as the fruits of the prophet will manifest themselves—for their good or for their demise. Although a prophet may only stay one or two days (Did. 11.5; contra Did. 13.1), this time will be enough to expose their conduct. The ethics and conduct of the prophet validate whether or not they are a true prophet. At least in this close literary section, ethics and virtue determine the validity of one's instruction (Did. 11.2, 5, 6, 9, 10; cf. 6.1).

Likewise, to expose a prophet through their works combines elements from two sections in the Matthean Sermon on the Mount. First, not everyone who speaks "in the Lord" is a true prophet. To speak "in the Lord"

---

6. Other expressions of unforgable sin: Gospel Tradition, Gos. Thom. 44; Questions of Bartholomew V.4.

is a mark of genuine prophecy (Did. 11.7, 12). Second, the conduct of the prophet will produce the marks of a false prophet.

| Matt 7:21 ESV | Did. 11.8 | Matt 7:16, 20 ESV |
|---|---|---|
| Not everyone who says to me, "Lord, Lord," will enter the kingdom of heaven, but the one who does the will of my Father who is in heaven. | Not everyone who speaks in the spirit is a prophet, except if they (sg.) exhibit the ways of the Lord. | |
| | Thus, from their ways, a false prophet and a prophet will be made known. | [16]You will recognize them by their fruits.<br><br>[20]Thus you will recognize them by their fruits. |

Thus, the conduct and fruits of the person reveal their nature as a true or false prophet.[7] Especially now in light of Matt 7:15-23, Herm. Mand. 12.3.1 (46.1), and Act. Thom. 79, the behavior or ways of the Lord (τοὺς τρόπους κυρίου) do not exclusively refer to an ascetic way of life but to a legitimate concern for an ethical posture.[8]

Next, the Didachist in Did. 11.11 presents a set of ideas that are difficult to interpret. How does the community relate to genuine prophets, who must not be judged by the community (οὐ κριθήσεται ἐφ' ὑμῶν)? They must not be judged because *God* judges them: "for they have the judgment with God" (μετὰ θεοῦ γὰρ ἔχει τὴν κρίσιν). This idea expresses rather simple logic: if all prophets and teachers are welcomed as the Lord, then God serves as their judge. The community remains hopeful that God will judge any and all prophets.

However, an additional description about the genuine prophets further perplexes the meaning. Michael Holmes writes the following about Did. 11.11:

> The phrase has never been explained satisfactorily. It may refer to some symbolic action intended to convey spiritual truth, analogous to those performed by some of the OT prophets (e.g.,

---

7. Tuilier assesses the Matthean and Did. traditions about the itinerant figures. Tuilier, "Les charismatique itinérants dans la Didachè."

8. van de Sandt and Flusser, *Didache*, 345; Draper, "Social Ambiguity and the Production of Text," 284-312.

Hosea's marriage to Gomer), which may have seemed to some members of the community to be of doubtful propriety.⁹

I do not pretend to satisfy the concerns about the meaning of this verse or to offer something that will change the way it is read. Part of the exhortation given to the community prohibits any imitation of the genuine prophet. The secondary Greek clause reads: μὴ διδάσκων δὲ ποιεῖν ὅσα αὐτὸς ποιεῖ. The preceding verbs (δεδοκιμασμένος, μὴ διδάσκων) provide backgrounding information to the primary clause (οὐ κριθήσεται ἐφ' ὑμῶν) not to judge these prophets. Thus, the community avoids a complete imitation of the prophet: "lest teaching *you* to do what he himself does." It remains rather unclear why the community should not imitate a prophet, especially when he or she is a genuine prophet.

Moreover, the nearly indiscernible clause concerns how the genuine prophet "acts in accord with the earthly mystery of (God's) assembly."¹⁰ The *crux interpretum* within this clause consists of the phrase: "to an earthly mystery of the church/assembly (ἐκκλησία)."¹¹ To further exacerbate this problem, two different text traditions present some difficulty. Consider the following translations that cohere with Did. 11.11, a Coptic recension, and an Ethiopic Church Order:¹²

| Did. 11.11 | Did. 11.11 (Coptic) | Ethiopic Church Order |
|---|---|---|
| But any prophet having been deemed true/genuine, manifesting the earthly mystery of the church, lest teaching *you* to do what he himself does, will not be judged by you; for, their judgment is with God. | Every true prophet, having been approved, having taught and testified to an orderly tradition in the church, those among you should not judge him, but his judgment is with God. | Every prophet proved in truth, who acts in the assembly of men and acts unlawfully, shall not be judged by you for his judgment is from God. |

Thus, given the difficulty, any comments given often build upon H54 rather than these other traditions. Some observations help to interpret Did. 11.11. First, whatever the genuine prophets perform, it reflects a cosmic

---

9. Holmes, *Apostolic Fathers*, 363.

10. BDAG, s.v. μυστήριον 2.c. Even the editors of the lexicon further explain that this Didache phrase is quite a difficult phrase to explain.

11. Draper relates the *cosmic mystery* to an apocalyptic kingdom-oriented *ecclesia*. Draper, "Performing the Cosmic Mystery of the Church," 37–57.

12. Horner, *Statutes of the Apostles*, 22–25.

mystery before the assembly. Second, the cosmic mystery serves as a basis not to judge the genuine prophets. And, third, the prophets of antiquity did this as well, thus hinting at the longevity and acceptance of such practice.[13]

The final command to refrain from judging bases itself upon the prophets' generous disposition (Did. 11.12). If prophets request money/silver, "or any such thing" (ἢ ἕτερά τινα), then they must be ignored. However, if they ask for these items in order to give to others in need, then they are free to give and not receive judgment.

### III.1.b.β. Examining Traveling Christians (Did. 12.1–5)

The second of three larger sections on itinerant apostles and prophets portrays three essential ideas. This section, along with the three ideas, also conveys some inconsistencies when compared to the previous section (Did. 11.3–12).[14] The three ideas include the following: (1) welcoming any traveler (πάροδιος) coming in the name of the Lord (Did. 12.1);[15] (2) assisting those who pass by (Did. 12.2); and (3) how to evaluate those who stay in the community (Did. 12.3–5).

Given that Did. 12 refrains from specifying who the travelers are, it remains vague whether they are Christian people in general or prophets and apostles in particular. However, given that Did. 13 resumes the thread of prophets and apostles from Did. 11, readers may infer that the wayfarers

---

13. Niederwimmer examines two lines of reasoning and concludes, "If these suggestions are correct, the passage should be interpreted as follows: it may happen that the prophet will not arrive alone but accompanied by a Christian woman with whom he lives in a spiritual marriage" (Niederwimmer, *Didache*, 180–81). My primary contention with the "spiritual marriage" view is how it conceives the prophet as acting for the cosmic mystery. The prophet acts on behalf of the "bride" and Jesus, as the bridegroom. Cosmology and marriage, yes, appear together in canonical traditions (Gen 1:27; 2:24; Eph 5:22–32). However, the prophets *work on behalf of* the cosmic and earthly mystery, they do not *embody* the "cosmic mystery." Thus, the prophets tie themselves to the ecclesial gathering; they do not reflect spiritual marriage. Also see: Draper, "Wandering Charismatics and Scholarly Circularities," 43.

14. Draper documents much of the redaction that appears in Did. 11–13. According to Draper, some of Did. 12 parallels and potentially employs the same language in Did. 11.4–6. Draper, "Weber, Theissen, and 'Wandering Charismatics.'"

15. Rothschild includes an extended discussion about πάροδιος and its relation to χριστέμπορος. She proposes, "this unique insiders' expression, πάροδιοι, suits such visitors perfectly (i.e., visiting non-members) because, according to the Didachist, they are not 'on the way,' but literally *alongside* it; and not 'alongside the *way*,' but 'alongside' '*belonging* to the way' παρα- + ὅδοις." Rothschild suggests once more that these persons are non-Christians, non-baptizands, non-community members, and possibly parasites to the community. Rothschild, *Essays on the Apostolic Fathers*, 184–88.

in Did. 12 are these same itinerate prophets and apostles. I suggest that one may not need to choose between the options. The Didachist most likely has both Christian travellers in general and the prophets in particular in mind. The main reason rests in the phrase, welcome "anyone who travels *in the name of the Lord*" (Did. 12.1), which is similar to the phrase to "welcome every apostle . . . as if they were the Lord" (Did. 11.4; cf. 11.2). Yet "anyone who comes in the name of the Lord" can also refer to anyone merely living "as Christians" in Did. 12.4. So, to travel "in the name of κύριος" probably refers to traveling in the name of Jesus as a Christian.

If this section comments on how to receive a traveling prophet, then Did. 12 presents some clear and identifiable discrepancies with Did. 11. First, the community examines all who are welcomed "in the name of the Lord" (Did. 12.1); yet commands in Did. 11.7, 11, and 12 condemn even the possibility of judging a prophet. Second, travelers may stay up to three days, if needed (Did. 12.2); yet a prophet is deemed false if they stay up to the three days in Did. 11.5. And, third, if these persons choose to settle, then Did. 12 marks a transition in the customs dealing with prophets (Did. 12.3; 13.1; cf. 11.5).

The Didachist begins by having the community welcome *all* of those traveling in the name of the Lord (Did. 12.1). The ethic seems to welcome *any* outsider who claims the name of the Lord. It appears it would rather the community welcome a false prophet than turn away a genuine Christian. A difference between Did. 12.1 and Did. 11 reflects how the community tests these persons coming into the community. As they approach, the community examines and tests their legitimacy (δοκιμάσαντες). Upon doing so, the community will have enough insight to judge what is right and what is false (lit., "the right and the left"; δεξιὰν καὶ ἀριστεράν).

Second, if the traveler coming in the name of the Lord only intends to pass by, then the community will offer much hospitality (Did. 12.2). Here, the community helps in whatever way they are able (βοηθεῖτε αὐτῷ ὅσον δύνασθε). So, although they generously extend hospitality with their goods and supplies, they limit the duration of these travelers. They extend up to two total days with a third as needed.

The final set of instructions address *if* and *how* the community might assimilate wayfarers permanently into their community (Did. 12.3–5). If they come in the name of the Lord, two options present themselves to wayfarers. If they are craftspeople (τεχνίτης; cf. Diogn. 2.3), then they work for their living. The community expects that the wayfarers now labor for their own daily food—"let them work and let them eat."; ἐργαζέσθω καὶ φαγέτω (Did. 12.3 cf. 2 Thess 3:10, 12).

However, if the wayfarer is not a craftsperson, then the community will decide how they will contribute to the community (Did. 12.4). The term τεχνίτης conveys an idea of self-sustaining work. If they can work for themselves with a particular trade for the good of the community, then they can provide for themselves. Yet if they are unable to do so, the community will judge among themselves (κατὰ τὴν σύνεσιν ὑμῶν προνοήσατε; cf. Did. 12.1) how to assimilate this newly established wayfarer.

The community immediately requires certain expectations from the individual. He or she must dwell in the community as a Christian and not as one who is idle (Did. 12.4). This use of the title "Christian" contains a positive religious identity, whereas in early literature the title still referred to an outsider or one receiving persecution (Acts 11:26; 1 Pet 4:16; Suetonius, *Nero* 16.2). This new person works diligently for whatever they receive. Furthermore, it might be suggested that to be a Christian entails working with one's hands, or at least to possess a particular ethic to work with one's hands. Idleness is not used here to indicate laziness, but refers to unemployment (ἀργός; Matt 20:3, 6; 1 Tim 5:13).

However, if someone desires not to work with the employment given, then he or she is considered a "Christmonger" (χριστέμπορος; Did. 12.5). Such a person, who joins the community but neglects to contribute to the communal work, must be avoided. To beware of such a person is also reminiscent of one's complete abstinence and removal from meat sacrificed to idols (cf. Did. 6.3). Contextually, it appears that a χριστέμπορός describes a person who wrongly uses the name of "Christ" to join a community and to receive its benefits without contributing to the needs of the community (cf. Did. 12.1, 4). Later Christians use "Christmonger" to refer to heretics or to reproach opponents.[16] This neologism, which does not appear in Greek literature prior to the Didache, is not a favorable identity and more than likely refers to one who wrongly uses the name of the Lord for personal gain and communal acceptance.[17]

---

16. Lampe s.v. Χριστέμπορος. Cf. Gregory of Nazianzus, *Or.* 21.31; John Chrysostom, *Hom.*6.1 in 1 Thess.

17. Niederwimmer brilliantly lists a few texts in antiquity that either use this neologism or reflect similar ideas (Niederwimmer, *Didache*, 187): Ps.-Clem. *Ep. ad virg.* 1.10.4; Hippolytus, *Frag. Ruth.* (GCS 1.2.120); Athanasius, *Frag. Matt.* (PG 27.1381A); Basil, *Ep.* 240.3 (PG 32.897A); Gregory of Nazianzus, *Or.* 40.11 (PG 36.372C).

### III.1.b.γ. Settling of Genuine Prophets and Provisions for High Priests (Did. 13.1–7)

The Didachist concentrates one more section on how to treat genuine prophets. Like the previous two chapters, Didache 13 seems to convey, again for an additional time, different customs. Now, a genuine prophet may reside, stay, and establish him- or herself permanently within the community (Did. 13.1; cf. 11.5). Along with these new customs, the Didachist also introduces how to be hospitable to the poor. It is in this section, particularly, that Jewish covenantalism and Jewish ideas come to bear more clearly.[18]

If genuine prophets "desires to settle" within the community (θέλων καθῆσθαι; cf. Did. 12.3), the community welcomes them to do so (Did. 13.1). As such people settle, the community recognizes them as prophets. They, likewise, receive credit as genuine teachers (Did. 13.2), which permits them to collect food. This custom distinguishes the communal actions in Did. 12.3–4. For, the titles "prophet" and "teacher" sanction them worthy of communal provisions.

People in the community provide for their prophets by giving all of their firstfruits (πᾶσαν ἀπαρχήν; Did. 13.3). They take their products, more specifically, from their wine and the threshing floor (Deut 18:3–4; Num 18:8–32; Ezek 44:30; Neh 10:32–39), to the prophets. From these brief Hebrew Bible examples, the Didachist simply continues the Jewish practices of a community bringing forth their firstfruits as provisions. Furthermore, they give their cattle and sheep as firstfruits. These customs reflect similar customs from the Levitical Law. The covenantal community of Israel provided wine, wheat from the threshing floor, cattle, and sheep to the Levitical priests (Deut 18:1–8; cf. Num 18:12). If these similarities prove deliberate, then it further corroborates how the Didachist perceives his community: as a covenantal community that receives blessings and cursings from God and provides for their priests (Did. 13:3). Interestingly, Apos. Con. II, 26, 3 overlaps the identity of high priests with bishops, priests, with presbyters, and Levites with deacons.

Furthermore, the Didachist provides the basis for these practices (Did. 13.3b). The prophets, and possibly the teachers (Did. 13.2), receive an additional title of high priests in verse 3 (αὐτοὶ γάρ εἰσιν οἱ ἀρχιερεῖς ὑμῶν). The title of high priest does not reflect a temple cult or any kind of sacrificial

---

18. Patterson suggests that "a careful analysis of these chapters reveals a developing conflict between local leaders and the itinerants who frequently visited the community which made use of the Didache and, further, that this conflict was resolved through the regulation of the authority and behavior of the itinerants." Patterson, "Didache 11–13," 313–29.

system. The prophets within the Didache focus on teaching, instruction, and ethics, and do not focus upon the temple cult, nor form part of the larger Sanhedrin, nor offer individual sacrifices. The Didachist attributes the name "high priest" to the traveling prophets. Thus, these high priests quite possibly possess no Jewish lineage and no familial tie to the Levitical or Zadokite priesthood (1 Chr 24:1–19)—historically, the hereditary high priest lineage concluded with Onias III in 174 BCE.[19]

However, if no resident prophets or teachers, and subsequently no high priests, reside within the community, the people must still set aside their firstfruits to provide for the poor (Did. 13.4–7).[20] If the community makes any bread (Did. 13.5), if they open any jar of wine or oil (Did. 13.6), if they acquire money or clothes (Did. 13.7), they must give of their firstfruits to the poor. Through a firstfruit offering, the community provides for both the poor (cf. Deut 15:11) and the high priests/prophets/teachers (cf. Deut 18:1–8; 1 Tim 5:18).

A guiding commandment governs how the community ought to give: give "according to the commandment" (Did. 13.5, 7). This commandment seems to be already assumed, especially since no such explicit command expresses these ideas. "Give according to the commandment" (δὸς κατὰ τὴν ἐντολήν) likewise appears in Did. 1.5. Even in Did. 1.5, the commandment similarly is not mentioned; yet the premise still remains the same. To "give in accordance with the commandment" explicitly relates to hospitality and the giving of one's goods. This commandment may reflect the Deuteronomic ideal of provisions for the poor (Deut 15:7–8) and the communal tithe (Deut 14:28–29).

These habits extend a hand of generosity as a common ethic. Even if no prophets present themselves to the community, the same firstfruits help to provide for the poor (cf. Did. 13.4). These combined themes of high priest and provision for the poor reflect covenant ideals and a community that flourishes with covenant obedience and blessings (cf. Lev 23:22; Deut 15:4, 7–11; 24:19–22).

---

19. Instone-Brewer, "Temple and Priesthood," 201.

20. Zachary Smith creatively reads Did. 13 and provides a Roman social setting as a background. Smith, "Of Firstfruits and Social Fixtures," 251–68.

## III.2. Conduct for Communal Order (Did. 14.1—15.4)

### III.2.a. Additional Instructions for the "Lord's Day": Communal Confession and Eucharist Sacrifice (Did. 14.1–3)

The Didachist altogether changes the focal point from communal instructions about "outsiders" to communal instructions for the "inward" community (Did. 14.1—15.4). The instruction depicts how the inward community may partake of the Eucharist and live with peace and charity. This move to the "inward" community will close the ethical instruction for the Didachist, pending the eschatological section (Did. 16.1-8).

During the Lord's Day, the community will gather to break bread, having formerly confessed their sins (Did. 14.1).[21] The Didachist describes the "Lord's Day" as follows: κατὰ κυριακὴν δὲ κυρίου.[22] This term (κυριακός) appears elsewhere to depict the idea of belonging to the Lord. For example, the term attributes a quality given to the bread in the Eucharist (1 Cor 11:20). The term also describes the "Lord's Day" (Rev 1:10; cf. Gos. Pet. 9.35). And κυριακός counters the Sabbath Day (Ign. *Mag.* 9.1). The Apostolic Constitutions similarly express this Didache text and reads as follows: "The resurrection day of the Lord, *which* we call 'the Lord's day'" (τὴν κθριακήν φαμεν; Apos. Con. VII, 30, 1). The term applies to either Eucharist features or the resurrection day of an ecclesial gathering.

To give further evidence of an ecclesial gathering on the Day of the Lord, they gather in order to break bread and give thanks (κλάσατε ἄρτον καὶ εὐχαριστήσατε). The combined use of breaking bread and giving thanks evidences a meal, and more likely, a Eucharist setting. If each time the community gathers together they break bread, then this also communicates the frequency of the Eucharist meal (cf. Acts 2:42).[23] I have no problem with seeing this section as additional material when the Didachist raises the concerns of the Eucharist once more (Did. 9-10). Not that the Didachist repeats

---

21. Draper has commented upon all of Did. 14. His reading leads him to conclude, "this study has attempted to show that the short instruction in Did. 14 represents a Christian Jewish *aggadah* on sacrificial atonement, underpinned by the interpretation of Mal. 1:11, 14. It distinguishes between offences against God (perhaps understood as ritual offences?) and offences against fellow members of the community (certainly understood as moral offences)." Draper, "Pure Sacrifice in Didache 14," 247.

22. Tidwell, "Didache XIV:1," 197–207.

23. Resurrection day, first day of the week, and local gatherings occurred on Sunday: John 20:1, 19; 1 Cor 16:2; Barn. 15.9; Pliny, *Ep.* 10.96; Justin, *1 Apol.* 67.3; *Dial.* 24.1; 41.4; 138.1.

the same or similar instruction as in Did. 9–10, but these two sections can reflect a similar setting.[24]

Prior to partaking the Eucharist, the community first confesses their communal sins so that they will offer a pure sacrifice.[25] The purity of the sacrifice rests upon the corporate confession. This language does raise a question as to the phrase, "your pure sacrifice" (καθαρὰ ἡ θυσία ὑμῶν ᾖ). (1) The pure sacrifice may refer to the general corporate gathering. In this way, the gathering itself in purity from sin represents a cultic practice. Or (2) the pure sacrifice may refer to the confession of the people and their reconciliation. Or, finally, (3) the sacrifice could refer to the actual breaking of bread. The "pure sacrifice" most likely reflects a combined idea of position 2 and 3: a reconciled gathering of the community breaking bread. The pure sacrifice does not exclusively refer to the communal confession of sins, because the "pure" quality results from corporate confession (Did. 14.1, 2). Moreover, the primary commands to break bread (κλάσατε; Did. 14.1) and to "Eucharist" (εὐχαριστήσατε; Did. 14.1) underscore the "pure sacrifice." Additionally, the corporate exclusion of a single person (Did. 14.2) coheres with the idea of a purified community that partakes of the Eucharist. Thus, the pure sacrifice relates to a purified community that both has no unconfessed corporate sin and partakes of the Eucharist corporately.[26]

Confessed sin is the ethical prerequisite to partake of the Eucharist (Did. 14.1, 2). Because the Didachist does not mention baptism in this setting (cf. Did. 9.5), we may assume that corporate confession does not inaugurate one's participation in the Eucharist but accentuates community

---

24. I assume the position and sentiment of van de Sandt and Flusser: "Did 14, therefore, obviously refers to the same reality as that described in Did 9–10. In addition to these actions, Did 14 speaks of 'sacrifice' but there is no compelling reason for believing that 'breaking bread,' 'giving thanks' and the 'sacrifice' refer to separate rituals. It is also beside the point to contend that, since Did 14 is concerned with the Eucharist, Did 9–10 must deal with the *agape* celebration because the editor cannot have discussed the same subject twice. For, although the Eucharist depicted in Did 14 is none other than that of 9–10, it is not a mere repetition." van de Sandt and Flusser, *Didache*, 303–4.

25. "In the Didache," notes Finlan, "purity no longer has a *national* or a *temple* dimension, which makes it profoundly different from both Pharisaic and Sadducean thinking. Purity in the Didache has no connection with temple cult or priestly rules. Therefore, to my mind, it is misleading to speak of 'cultic purity,' which usually implies cultic purification rites and a sharp separation between Jew and gentile. 'Purity' is far more abstract in the Didache than it is in a community where gentiles are considered impure." Finlan suggests that "purity" language distinguishes the Did.'s communal identity from other religious groups due to the term being used in a different way. Finlan, "Identity in the Didache Community," 21.

26. Niederwimmer similarly suggests that sacrifice refers to, in a special sense, the εὐχαριστήσατε. Niederwimmer, *Didache*, 197.

maintenance for corporate Eucharistic purity. The community will exclude any members with unreconciled quarrels (Did. 14.2). This lack of reconciliation results in a defiled sacrifice (Did. 14.2; cf. Matt 5:23-24). Unconfessed relational sins directly correlate to communal cultic practices. Excluding selected members will result in a pure sacrifice. They prohibit them from partaking the Eucharist until members reconcile with other community members.

A divine basis governs this practice: "for this is the sacrifice being spoken by the Lord" (Did. 14.3). Of the few possible quotations in the Didache, two exclusively relate to the Eucharist practices (cf. Did. 9.5). The quotation freely recites Mal 1:11 and Mal 1:14,[27] whereby the Didachist imparts a *fuller sense* of the Malachi traditions and lexically connects these concepts to a "pure sacrifice."[28]

| Mal 1:11 LXX | Did. 14.3 | Mal 1:14 LXX |
|---|---|---|
| διότι ἀπὸ ἀνατολῶν ἡλίου ἕως δυσμῶν τὸ ὄνομά μου δεδόξασται ἐν τοῖς ἔξνεσι, | | |
| καὶ ἐν παντὶ τόπῳ <u>θυμίαμα</u> προσάγεται τῷ ὀνόματί μου καὶ θυσία καθαρά, | Ἐν παντὶ τόπῳ <u>καὶ χρόνῳ</u> προσφέρειν μοι θυσίαν καθαράν· | |
| διότι μέγα τὸ ὄνομά μου ἐν τοῖς ἔθνεσι, λέγει κύριος παντοκράτωρ. | ὅτι βασιλεὺς μέγας εἰμί, λέγει κύριος, καὶ τὸ ὄνομά μου <u>θαυμαστὸν</u> ἐν τοῖς ἔθνεσι. | διότι βασιλεὺς μέγας ἐγώ εἰμι, λέγει κύριος <u>παντοκράτωρ</u>, καὶ τὸ ὄνομά μου <u>ἐπιφανὲς</u> ἐν τοῖς ἔθνεσιν. |

The loose textual connection suggests that the Didachist more freely quotes these two Malachi texts, probably through a homeoteleuton (διότι in Mal 1:11 and 14). Additionally, the Didachist substitutes incense as a pure sacrifice (Mal 1:14). A pure sacrifice exclusively refers to a reconciled

27. All LXX texts from the Twelve Prophets are based on Ziegler, *Duodecim Prophetae*.

28. This will be the first of many occurrences in early Christian theology that use Mal 1 to underscore Eucharistic instruction. Malachi 1 occurs in the following texts as a scriptural basis for the Eucharist: Justin, *Dial.* 28.5; 41.2; 116.3; 117.1, 4; Irenaeus, *Haer.* 4.17.5-6; Tertullian, *Adv. Iud.* 5.4, 7; *Adv. Marc.* 3.22.6; 4.1.8.

community partaking in the Eucharist. As the sacrifice reflects a weekly partaking of the Eucharist, the Didachist refrains from hinting about the sacrifice's efficacy. The sacrifice expresses cultic worship instead of atoning actions. By conflating these two texts, the Didachist correlates the Eucharist to a pure sacrifice being made to a king in every place. This sacrifice also reflects the locale and purity of the cultic expression.

### III.2.b. On the Appointment of Bishops and Deacons (Did. 15.1–2)

The ecclesiology within the Didache is rather multi-dimensional. Prior to describing the final ecclesial order, the Didachist has already recalled a high concern for the community's sacred symbols. Both baptism (Did. 7.1–4) and the Eucharist (Did. 9–10) are regarded as among the highest sacred practices in the community. Both rituals contain some form of liturgical and communal significance. Moreover, the community possesses teachers (Did. 11.1–2)—even if their identity is relatively unknown—and they welcome traveling prophets and apostles (Did. 11.3—12.7). Now, as we near the close of the Didache as a whole, the Didachist adds two more official positions to the ecclesial cohort: bishops and deacons (Did. 15.1).

The responsibility resides within the ecclesial community to appoint both bishops and deacons (Did. 15.1). It seems that early Christian literature presents a few ways to elect officials. At times, both other elders (cf. Acts 14:23; Titus 1:5) and the ecclesial community (cf. Acts 6:3) will appoint for themselves additional leaders. The Didachist, however, depicts the entire community gathering to elect and to appoint (χειροτονήσατε) for themselves certain bishops and deacons (Did. 15.1; cf. Ign. *Phild.* 10.1; 1 Clem. 42.5). Yet many notice that the office of presbyter is not mentioned.[29]

Although no clarity governs how many officials may be elected, the Didachist does delineate the gender (ἄνδρας) and personal character of these offices (Did. 15.1). Quite similar to the New Testament (cf. Acts 6:3; 1 Tim 3:1–7, 8–13; Titus 1:6–9; 1 Pet 5:1–3), these two offices require a number of qualifications. As the Didachist displays, these two offices need men who are "worthy of the Lord," humble, lack a love for money or rapaciousness (cf. 1 Tim 3:3; 1 Pet 5:2), are true, and have been tested (δεδοκιμασμένους; cf. 1 Tim 3:6, 10).[30]

---

29. See Jefford's article on the very topic. Stewart notes Jefford's work but differs in his conclusions. Jefford, "Presbyters in the Community of the *Didache*," 122–28; Stewart, *Original Bishops*.

30. Although the Pastoral Epistles and Did. 8–15 may reflect a similar concern for

Rather than beginning with a repeated positive ethic of "welcome them as the Lord" (cf. Did. 11.1, 2, 4), the Didachist frames the command negatively: "do not despise (ὑπεροράω) them" (Did. 15.2). The community regards these bishops and deacons on the basis of their equal status with the prophets and teachers (Did. 15.2). These appointed men carry out the ministry of the prophets and teachers (Did. 15.1). It remains rather unclear as to what extent the bishops and deacons fulfill the ministries of prophets and teachers. Do they perform the duties of a prophet and teacher if none present themselves to the community? Or, do the bishops and deacons function as the ministerial hands of the prophets and teachers by extending their teachings and ethics?

So, the Didache's community seems to present a fivefold ecclesial leadership that includes a particular hierarchy—though it remains explicitly unclear if one person may bear more than one title (cf. Did. 11.6). The prophets, apostles, and teachers function as upper leadership and seem to receive more regard than the bishops and deacons. These two additional roles, the bishops and deacons, seem to preserve and maintain the ministry of the teachers and the prophets through their service. Yet the bishops and deacons receive some honor along with the prophets and teachers (Did. 15.2).

### III.2.c. Ethical Orientation in Accordance with the Gospel (Did. 15.3–4)

The final section extends broad ethical instruction that accords with the gospel of the Lord (Did. 15.3, 4). As the ethics vaguely refer to "the gospel of the Lord," this gospel component governs both sets of ethics in this final section. It has been debated if the ethic that is bound up "in the gospel of the Lord" refers to an actual, tangible Gospel text or if the ethic demonstrates a tenor of what one has in the general message of the Lord. For the following section (Did. 15.3–4), the two uses of "the gospel" do not convey a tangible document but a message congruent with the *kerygma* of the gospel.

The first ethic corrects any member who has committed wrongdoing, the *correctio fraterna* (Did. 15.3). Peace guides the ethic during correction (cf. Col 3:15). Anger must not govern the correction and must be avoided (cf. Jas 1:20). Moreover, the ethic that concerns peace and anger is an ethic appearing "in the gospel of the Lord." The community strictly adheres to communal harmony: to correct sin in peace and without anger (Did. 15.3).

---

the ethics and identity of the community leaders, "the instructions themselves apparently are changed and amplified to meet the different situations." van de Sandt and Flusser, *Didache*, 340.

Additionally, if someone harms another, then the entire community helps to defend the harmed one. The one harming another (ἀστοχέω) is nearly ostracized from the community until they repent. To describe them as ἀστοχέω requires an additional comment because the term elsewhere alludes to those who deviate from their faith or deny the words of the Lord (cf. 1 Tim 1:6; 6:21; 2 Tim 2:18; 2 Clem. 17.7). This person could either cause others to deviate from their faith or, by their ethic, they adversely affect the community (ἀστοχοῦντι κατὰ τοῦ ἑτέρου).

The Didachist does not instruct how to care for the oppressed or recipient of wrongdoing. Instead, the Didachist instructs how to regard offenders. First, the community excludes them and, essentially, shuns them (Did. 15.3). Second, the offenders may not defend themselves or speak to another in the community. Third, if they repent, then the ban may be overturned. If the Pauline tradition and material from 2 Clement can offer insight, then the offender may be on the verge of deviating from their faith. To ostracize the offender protects and preserves the faith of the community. These actions communicate a concern for communal harmony and the gravity of a covenantal breach. Huub van de Sandt reads Matt 18:15–17 and Did. 15.3 as windows into communal reproof practices.[31]

The final set of ethics concerns prayers, almsgiving, and a universal "all of your practices" (Did. 15.4). These ethical operatives base themselves "in the gospel of the Lord." They must continue their communal and individual prayers, almsgiving, and all other practices after the pattern set forth "in the gospel of the Lord." Prayer already signals a covenant member. They must not pray as the hypocrites do (Did. 8.2). They recite the "Lord's Prayer" thrice daily (Did. 8.3). Furthermore, they recite prayers during the Eucharist at each community gathering (Did. 9–10). Here, however, the Didachist provides no content to follow but the regular act of prayer. Their prayers (τὰς εὐχάς) follow what appears "in the gospel" (Did. 15.4).

Second, all acts of charity model what they have received "in the gospel" (Did. 15.4). This charitable giving may differ from a general command to be generous (cf. Did. 1.4–5; 4.5–8). These acts of charity (τὰς ἐλεημοσύνας) reflect "almsgiving" as similarly given in Did. 1.6 (cf. 4.6). Rather than a general observance, this command more likely refers to giving alms to the poor. The New Testament and early church materials regularly instruct others to give alms. Almsgiving is good, better than prayer, and relieves the burden of sin (2 Clem. 16.4). Almsgiving marks godly character (Acts 10:2, 4, 31). Some of the early apostles gave alms or refrained from giving alms

---

31. van de Sandt, "Developing Jewish-Christian Reproof Practice," 173–92.

(Acts 3:2-3, 10; 24:17). Furthermore, Jesus tradition provides instruction about this practice (Matt 6:2-4; Luke 11:41; 12:33).

Before I finish this section, I need to comment on the "in the gospel" phrase once more. What does "in the gospel" mean? What can "gospel" refer to and what might be obviously excluded? Especially in this present text, anger and peace, prayers, and almsgiving reflect what ought to be done "in the gospel [of the Lord]." Does this "gospel" refer to a written document[32] or to oral tradition?[33] The Didache references "in the gospel (εὐαγγελίον)" a total of four times (cf. Did. 8.2; 11.3; 15.3, 4). Three of the uses directly correspond to the Gospel of Matthew. For example, Did. 8.2 mentions "gospel" and then quotes from Matt 6:9-13. By vaguely referring to the "ordinances of the gospel," the Didachist inexplicitly refers to the material in Matt 7:15-20 to adjudicate between false and genuine prophets. Furthermore, even this section discusses anger (Matt 5:21-26), almsgiving (Matt 6:2-4), and prayer (Matt 6:5-13). So, to refer to "gospel" exclusively insinuates Sermon-on-the-Mount material.[34]

However, a single problem quickly exposes the weakness of any argument desiring to attribute these Didache traditions to an actual Matthean text.[35] The Didachist quotes no explicit Matthew material related to "in the gospel." The community prays the Prayer thrice daily (Did. 8.2-3). Thus, the liturgy imbeds ideas into the very fabric and memory of the community. The liturgy can answer why Did. 8.2 appears as a quotation. Moreover, "in the gospel" exclusively refers to the Sermon-on-the-Mount material in all four references. So, to use the phrase "in the gospel [of the Lord]," the Didachist rarely shows any awareness of non-Sermon-on-the-Mount Matthean material.

---

32. Tuckett, "Didache and the Writings," 105-6; Kruger, *Canon Revisited*, 213.

33. Milavec, *Didache: Faith, Hope & Life*, 720-23.

34. van de Sandt rightly suggests that the phrase "as you have in the gospel" may refer to some written gospel or more likely to a circulating oral tradition. He does conclude, "It might be appropriate, therefore, to suggest that Matthew was not used as a source for Did. 15.3a. Instead, 'the gospel' which is referred to may be a source which shows a marked correspondence with 1QS 5:24b-25." I have some difficulty ascribing "gospel" language to Qumran material, but I would be more open to saying Qumran traditions influence the Matthean community and Matthew's Gospel, and thereby, influence the Did. In this way, "gospel" goes through Matthew into the Qumran traditions. van de Sandt, "Developing Jewish-Christian Reproof Practice," 187.

35. Taras Khomych rightly notes, "The Didache is not centered on Christology. Accordingly, the term εὐαγγέλιον, which reappears four times in this short document, can hardly be associated with the birth, death, and resurrection of Jesus Christ. Instead, it is found predominantly in the paraenetical context." Khomych, "Another Gospel," 469.

Though a Matthean text may exist at the time of the Didache's composition, I remain unconvinced that a comprehensive Matthean document *must be* present in the hand of the Didachist or in the community. I am of the persuasion that the Didachist and the Matthean redactor share some material and the interchange of material reflects the more lengthy composite forms of the Didache. Sermon-on-the-Mount motifs appear near the "in the gospel" phrase and the nature of the evidence does lend itself to the idea that at least the Sermon on the Mount (and possibly the Olivet Discourse [cf. Did. 16.3–8; Matt 24–25]) have shaped the identity of the Didachist and their teaching. So, at some point, the Didachist and the community may have become proprietors of a small text in Matthew. The connection to a Matthean Gospel is more attuned with Did. 16, the section we turn to next. What this tells me is that the Didachist or Didache community is generally aware of Matthew, they share similar material during and/or after the composition of Matthew, or the Didachist redactor utilizes a Matthean text quite variedly for each section of the Didache throughout a lengthy composition—as one Didache scholar commented to me, "the Didache was not written during a Saturday evening."[36]

---

36. I remember Clayton Jefford expressing this sentiment to me many times.

# IV

## Didache 16.1-8

### Eschatological Ethics and Teaching

THE CONCLUDING CHAPTER OF the Didache closes with a final, ethical exhortation and a substantial, doctrinal excursus on the last things.[1] A longer note on the structure and genre warrants some further comment. First, much of the ethics in the Didache as a whole reflects their current circumstance. Ethical directives inform the community how to live in their current situations and to reflect communal standards. Second, due to the prevailing ethical injunctions, Did. 16 stands as the second most theologically saturated section in the Didache (cf. Did. 9–10). Didache 16.3-8 includes the most sustained apocalyptic teaching. Last, if the document ended at Did. 16.2, instead of 16.8, the Didache's conclusion would not really be affected because Did. 16.3-8 serves as the theological basis to motivate the ethics in Did. 16.1-2.

Didache 16.2 contains the final ethical appeals in the Didache. The passage calls for a vigilant ethic. That is, Did. 16 presents an ethic that focuses on the future as opposed to current situations—a fitting conclusion to the book. The Didachist coalesces ethics about an eschatological future, having been disjoined from the previous section on charitable living. Didache 16.1 signals a new section and concludes the final ethical instruction

---

1. van de Sandt and Flusser rightly note, "The eschatological section, concluding the Didache in chap. 16, consists of two distinct parts. First there is a parenetic passage, which includes two concrete admonitions, i.e. a call for vigilance (16:1a) and an admonition to meet 'frequently' (16:2a). Both incentives are substantiated eschatologically." van de Sandt and Flusser, *Didache*, 35.

of the Didache as asyndeton connects Did. 15.4 and 16.1.² Asyndeton and a new ethical theme permit a change in topics.³

The second half of Did. 16 focuses upon apocalyptic and eschatological motifs (Did. 16.3-8). It, however, anchors the ethical instruction and is grammatically subservient to the final vigilant call in Did. 16.1-2. Initially marked with γάρ, Did. 16.3-8 provides the basis for its immediate antecedents.⁴ Although grammatically functioning as the basis for the final ethical paraenesis (Did. 16.1-2), it might influence one's reading of the Two Ways—noted by the use of ζωή—to observe sapiential and ethical themes within Jewish apocalypticism.⁵

This doctrinal digression serves as the theological impetus to motivate the ethics in Did. 16.1-2—marked by γάρ. Within the doctrinal section (Did. 16.3-8), five sets of progressive events narrate the series. Four temporal adverbs (τότε) seemingly progress five apocalyptic and eschatological scenes.

Some have even suggested that the original form of the Didache's Two-Ways instruction (Did. 1-6) concluded with Did. 16, thereby suggesting that Did. 7-15 is inserted material⁶—or vice versa, the Two Ways and apocalypse

---

2. Niederwimmer rightly observes that the introduction of Did. 16.1 presents a warning grammatically. One would anticipate, at least, γρηγορεῖτε οὖν. Niederwimmer, *Didache*, 214.

3. Smyth § 2167d. According to Levinsohn, "Strictly speaking, the absence of any conjunction between sentences of a Greek text should imply only that the author offered no processing constraint on how the following material was to be related to its context. . . . Asyndeton is the norm between *paragraphs* with different topics when the topic of the new paragraph is not considered to strengthen, develop from, be associated with, or be inferred from that of the previous one." Levinsohn, *Discourse Features*, 118-19.

4. Levinsohn comments, "Background material introduced by γάρ provides explanations or expositions of the previous assertion. The presence of γάρ constrains the material that it introduces to be interpreted as *strengthening* some aspect of the previous assertion, rather than as distinctive information." Runge suggests, similarly, "The information introduced does not advance the discourse but adds background information that strengthens or supports what precedes. . . . Γάρ introduces explanatory material that strengthens or supports what precedes. This may consist of a single clause, or it may be a longer digression. Although the strengthening material is important to the discourse, it does not advance the argument or story. Instead, it supports what precedes by providing background or detail that is needed to understand what follows" (Levinsohn, *Discourse Features*, 91). Also see: Runge, *Discourse Grammar*, 52-54.

5. So, Del Verme, *Didache and Judaism*, 226; Allison, "Apocalyptic Ethics and Behavior," 295-311; Collins, "Generic Compatibility."

6. Bammel, "Schema und Vorlage"; Kamlah, *Form der katalogischen Paränese*, 210-14; Kraft, *Barnabas and the Didache*, 12-16; McKenna, "'Two Ways' in Jewish and Christian Writings," 185-86; Del Verme, *Didache and Judaism*, 243-51; Syreeni, "Sermon on the Mount and the Two Ways," 88; Pardee, *Genre and Development of the Didache*, 164n85.

were added to the rituals material. Four probable solutions appear regarding the relationship between Did. 1–6 and Did. 16.[7] First, Did. 1–6 along with Did. 16 formed a Jewish prototype *Vorlage*.[8] Second, Did. 1–6 formed the complete edition of the Didache's Two Ways—though it remains debated whether or not Did. 6.1, 2, or 3 concludes the Two Ways.[9] Third, according to Hans Seeliger, Did. 16 functions as a polemic directed against the false prophets within Did. 11–15.[10] No contemporary Didache scholar has suggested this third option in recent times. And, fourth, Did. 16 remains unrelated to and disjointed from Did. 1–6.

For Marcello Del Verme, Did. 16 functions as the final section to an initial Two-Ways treatise.[11] Others, such as Bammel, Kamlah, Kraft, and McKenna, likewise appeal to Did. 16 as the ending of the Two Ways for the Didache.[12] Matti Myllykoski notes a literary seam between Did. 5.1 and 6.1, a change from a plural verb form (Did. 5.2) to a singular (Did. 6.1), and the brevity of the apocalypse (Did. 16). Accordingly, he suggests, "it is possible that the salutation in the plural once had a natural connection to the beginning of the apocalypse. Also, the shortness of the apocalypse is best explained with its original connection to the Two Ways treatise."[13]

The fourth option suggests that Did. 16 remains unrelated to the conclusion of the Didache's Two Ways. In this manner, Did. 1–6 serves as a whole complete unit and without regard for the apocalyptic ending of Did. 16.[14] According to Rordorf and Tuilier, the beginning chapters of the Di-

---

7. The following section is further elaborated in the chapter "'The Meek Shall Inherit the Earth': Apocalypticism and Internal Readings of the Didache's Two Ways": Wilhite, *"One of Life and One of Death."*

8. Tuckett, "Didache and the Writings," 84.

9. See van de Sandt and Flusser, *Didache*, 128, 130, 138–39, 238–70.

10. Seeliger, "Background and Purpose of the Apocalyptic," 381–82; contra Balabanski, *Eschatology in the Making*, 200–201.

11. Del Verme, *Didache and Judaism*, 243. Del Verme articulates three essential retorts to Rordorf and Tuilier's arguments. (1) It is implausible to separate Did. 1–6 and 16 on the basis of presumed eschatological traits; (2) A close connection exists between apocalyptic and sapiential literature in antiquity. Thus, Did. 16.1 and 1.1 link sapiential and apocalyptic traditions together; (3) Did. 16 and Did. 1–6 may continue to represent the community. In this way, the Didachist's composition of Did. 1–6 may fuse together the similar concerns in Did. 16. By connecting the Two Ways and the Apocalyptic sections, this joint relationship may corroborate an "Enochic matrix."

12. Bammel, "Schema und Vorlage"; Bammel, "Pattern and Prototype"; Kamlah, *Form der katalogischen Paränese*, 210–14; Kraft, *Barnabas and the Didache*, 12–16; McKenna, "'Two Ways' in Jewish and Christian Writings," 185–86; Draper, "A Continuing Enigma," 108.

13. Myllykoski, "Without Decree," 447.

14. Kloppenborg, "Transformation of Moral Exhortation," 90–92.

dache already contain some eschatological passages and do not require a new conclusion to the Two Ways[15]—even though γρηγορεῖτε ὑπὲρ τῆς ζωῆς ὑμῶν (Did. 16.1) may allude to Did. 1–6.[16]

As source and redaction criticism will continue to reflect upon the tradition-history of the Didache's development, I offer a few literary arguments to suggest that Did. 16 may not conclude Did. 1–6. So, even if Did. 16 at one time concluded Did. 1–6, we still need to account for the following literary features:

1. Two-Ways texts in antiquity often include a literary frame that appropriates a variety of apocalyptic motifs. For example, 1 En. 91.1 frames the Two Ways with angelic presence. Barnabas 18.1–2 utilizes cosmological dualisms. Barnabas, in fact, concludes the Two Ways with a reward of the kingdom (Barn. 21.1). Testament of Benjamin 6.1 contains the evil way under the auspice of Beliar. Even if other Two-Ways texts contain an extended apocalyptic or eschatological instruction as some form of conclusion, this glaring absence accentuates the lack of apocalyptic instruction in the Didache's Two Ways.

2. Even if a composite addition or original text of Did. 6 contained eschatological and apocalyptic concepts, it still does not answer *how* and *why* these features are entirely absent within the Didache's Two Ways. In other words, even if Did. 16 formed part of the Didache's version of the Two Ways, it does not adequately answer for the missing apocalyptic features within the contents of the Two Ways.

3. Even if Did. 16 concludes the Didache's Two Ways, it still lacks common apocalyptic features found in other ancient Two-Ways texts. The presence of angels (cf. Did. 16.7), light-darkness dualism, and explicit cosmological differences are all lacking in Did. 16. Thus, even if Did. 16 resolves Did. 1–6, signs of redaction are readily visible due to its break from other ancient Two-Ways texts. If this is so, then it will further complicate the future of Didache studies until other MSS are discovered.

4. Finally, although a Two-Ways text frequently concludes with an eschatological paraenetic, it individualizes the instruction. If Did. 16 concludes the Didache's Two Ways, then the Didache would still be an anomaly by offering a corporate eschatological conclusion. The Two Ways convey individualized eschatology, frequently based upon a

---

15. Rordorf and Tuilier, *Didachè*, 82.
16. Rordorf and Tuilier, *Didachè*, 82.

rewards system, whereas Did. 16 explores more corporate and global eschatology.[17]

Much of the thematic material in Did. 16 likewise appears in the Matthean Olivet Discourse (Matt 24-25).[18] The following merely highlights the thematic similarities and dissimilarities between Did. 16 and the Matthean Olivet Discourse.[19]

Table 15. Similarities between Did. 16.1-8 and Matt 24-25

| Didache 16.1-8 | Matthew 24-25 |
| --- | --- |
| Be vigilant (16.1) | Be vigilant (24:42; 25:13) |
| Lamps (16.1) | Lamps (25:1-13) |
| Be ready (16.1) | Be ready (24:44) |
| Increased lawlessness (16.4) | Increased lawlessness (24:12) |
| Increased hatred (16.4) | Love will grow cold (24:12) |
| Persecution (16.4) | Delivered to tribulation and death (24:9) |
| Betrayal (16.4) | Betrayal (24:10) |
| World deceiver will commit "signs and wonders" (16.4) | False christs and false prophets will commit signs and wonders (24:24) |
| Many will fall away (16.5) | Many will fall away (24:10) |

17. For a consideration on the lost ending of the Didache, see arguments in the following: Aldridge, "Lost Ending of the Didache," 1-15.

18. Pardee considers the presence of Gospel material in both Did. 1 and 16. She notes that "this material comes from a stage prior to the recognition of the 'gospel' mentioned elsewhere in the work, likely to be identified as the Gospel of Matthew." The presence of gospel-like material and parallels in Did. 1 and 16 pose tremendous difficulty as we assess the compositional history—concerning which, I offer none in this commentary. Pardee, *Genre and Development of the Didache*, 191.

19. I remain rather convinced by and depend greatly upon Verheyden's assumptions. He notes, "If a good case can be made for the hypothesis that Did. 16.3-8 shows traces of the use of Matthew's version of the discourse, it is a priori rather than implausible that this can be taken in a minimalistic way, as if Did. recalled or borrowed a couple of expression from Matt and then forgot about the rest of the discourse or the gospel. It is therefore a reasonable assumption to consider reading the eschatological scenario of Did. 16 with an eye on Matt. I do not want to argue that Matthew's Gospel was Did.'s only source of inspiration for each and every detail of its composition. But I do think Matthew's discourse in chap. 24 has guided and inspired the author/compiler of chap. 16 to a greater extent than the somewhat oblique verbal paralells would suggest." Verheyden, "Eschatology in the Didache," 201.

| Didache 16.1-8 | Matthew 24-25 |
|---|---|
| One who endures will be saved (16.5) | One who endures will be saved (24:13) |
| Signs will appear (16.6)[20] | Sign will appear in heaven (24:30) |
| Sound of a trumpet (16.6) | Angels and a loud trumpet (24:31) |
| Will see the Lord coming (16.8) | Will see the Son of Man (24:30) |

Table 16. Differences between Did. 16.1-8 and Matt 24-25

| Didache 16.1-8 | Matthew 24-25 |
|---|---|
| Exhortation about lamps (16.1) | Kingdom of heaven simile about lamps (25:1-13) |
| Gather together (16.2) | |
| Ethical and eschatological perfection (τελειόω; 16.2) | Eternal fire and eternal life (25:41-46) |
| "Last days" are a future time (16.3) | Fig tree and the time is near (24:32-35) |
| Sheep turned into wolves (16.3) | Persecution and wolves in the midst of sheep (Matt 10:16) |
| Deceiver of the world (16.4) | Abomination of desolation standing in the holy place (24:15) |
| Heavens will open (16.7) | Cosmological darkening and appearance in heaven (24:29-30) |
| Lord will come with saints (16.7) | Jesus comes with angels (24:31) |
| World will see the Lord on the heavens (16.8) | Tribes of earth will mourn when they see (24:30) |

From this cursory analysis, it becomes readily obvious that Did. 16 both agrees and disagrees with the Olivet discourse. Vicky Balabanski observes the following about the relationship between Did. 16 and Matt 24: "Didache 16, like other Christian writings from this era, shows a remarkable freedom to rearrange, interpret and omit material drawn from Matthew 24 and elsewhere in the Gospel, as well as the freedom to supplement it from other sources."[21] Thus, in no way does the Didachist

---

20. Kloppenborg, "Special Matthaean Tradition," 54-67.
21. Balabanski, *Eschatology in the Making*, 197.

seek to supplant the teachings of Matthew,[22] but the Didache reflects early eschatological instruction.

Although the Didache may show thematic, and at times verbal, symmetry with the Gospel of Matthew, the Didache does not appear to be bound to the teachings of Matthew or, for that matter, does not reflect another "Matthew." The symmetry may show a common Jesus tradition and a general familiarity with first-century eschatological traditions. The thematic differences nuance how the Didachist uses a Matthean tradition (textual or oral). There remains a considerable amount of freedom to reshape the material. As the two columns reflect, the Matthean parallels appear quite scattered all throughout Matt 24-25. The Didachist, even if purposely using Matthew, demonstrates considerable freedom to rearrange, to modify, and to interpret the Matthean tradition.

## IV.1. Eschatological Moral Conduct (Did. 16.1-2)

The final two literary sections complete the Didache. The first is an eschatological paraenetic (Did. 16.1-2). The second is a brief doctrinal treatise that notes the persons and events of the final days (Did. 16.3-8). Within the first ethical paraenetic, two motifs emerge: corporate vigilance and purposed corporate gathering.

The first motif relates to corporate vigilance. The community must watch over their souls. "Watch" (γρηγορέω) commonly appears in prayer settings (Matt 26:38, 40; Mark 13:34, 37; 14:38; Acts 20:31;) and cosmic alertness (Bar 2.9; Matt 24:43; 1 Thess 5:6; 1 Pet 5:8; Rev 3:2-3; cf. 1 Macc 12.27). To mention lamps (cf. Matt 25:1-13), to include a similar *logion* of the Lord (γρηγορέω), and to note the return of κύριος all evoke an apocalyptic literary setting.[23] According to Niederwimmer, the Didachist utilizes traditional paraenetic material that is often "associated with the Christian anticipation of the end."[24]

The pending eschatological realities motivate the commands to "watch over" one's life, not to let their lamps "go out" (cf. Matt 25:8), nor to be unprepared. These pending "last days" (Did. 16.3) and the approaching eschatological martyrdom events serve to motivate the community towards a specific

---

22. Balabanski, *Eschatology in the Making*, 197.

23. According to Del Verme, Did. 16 is both apocalyptic and eschatological. It is apocalyptic in terms of the worldview that it reflects and is eschatological in terms of its contents. Del Verme, *Didache and Judaism*, 223-24.

24. Niederwimmer, *Didache*, 214.

ethic of personal and corporate vigilance.[25] The secret hour of the Lord's return motivates them to "watch," to prohibit their lamps from going out, and to prepare—"for you do not know the hour in which our Lord shall return" (Did. 16.1c). These ethics all convey a similar idea: to keep up their ethical vigilance. In order to maintain ethical purity, the Didachist instructs the community about eschatology to motivate each community member.

The second motif regards corporate gathering (Did. 16.2). The community helps to stimulate personal perseverance.[26] Moral safeguards govern the corporate gathering (Herm. Sim. 9.26.3 [103.3])—Ign. Eph. 13.1-2 describes how the corporate gathering involves a cosmic conflict with Satan. The Didache's community seeks the things that benefit the soul (ζητοῦντες τὰ ἀνήκοντα ταῖς ψυχαῖς). To "gather together" also considers the breaking of bread, giving of thanks, and personal confession (cf. Did. 14.1). Thus, to gather, joined with corporate confession, focuses upon ethical vigilance and corporate purity (cf. Heb 10:24-25). In Barn. 19.10, "to seek out daily" also invites one to remember the eschatological judgment.[27] If the corporate community functions properly, then they will work to preserve the individual and corporate purity until the final days.

It remains quite difficult not to join together literarily the Two Ways (Did. 1–6) with this final call for vigilance. As ζωή (Did. 16.1) and a verbal form of τελειόω (Did. 16.2) appear, these ideas reverberate with the way of life (cf. Did. 1.1-2) and the acquiring of perfection (cf. Did. 1.4; 6.2).[28]

Acquiring perfection (τελειόω) in the final days is predicated upon the maintainance of personal and corporate vigilance (Did. 16.2b). If the community falters, then the "time of belief" will be of no use. Faith or belief (πίστις) does not necessarily reappear throughout the Didache. In the Eucharistic liturgies, the Father reveals faith (Did. 10.2). The "time of belief" alludes to the entire time of one's wayfaring journey on the way of life. Eschatological wholeness undergirds a person to persevere.

---

25. See Draper, "Resurrection and Zechariah 14.5," 155–79.

26. Khomych presents a few readings for Did. 16.2 and concludes that this eschatological gathering also includes some Eucharist overtones. Khomych, "Admonition to Assemble Together," 121–41.

27. So Niederwimmer, *Didache*, 215.

28. "Given the variety of opinions on the tenuous arguments for dependency," suggests Pardee, "nothing prevents one from seeing both Did. 1.3b—2.1 and ch. 16 as completely independent of the Synoptic Gospels. Both of these sections perhaps attest a period when the tradition was still transmitted in smaller textual units. . . . A direct connection of the Two Ways with ch. 16 is also supported by the references to *perfection* in 1.4, 6.2 and 16.2, references that are not part of the Two Ways texts in *Barnabas* or *Doctrina*." Pardee, *Genre and Development of the Didache*, 183.

However, this rigid ethic proves quite difficult to reconcile with the permissive ethic in Did. 6.2. At the conclusion of the Two Ways, if wayfarers are unable to "bear the whole yoke of the Lord," then they may do what they can. Either the Didachist permits a softened commitment to the way of life that neglects to fulfill all the stipulations or the Didachist maintains rigid standards in order to accentuate communal purity—even if some falter. Due to the immediate apocalyptic tradition, the rigid standards most likely secure loyalty in the face of pending persecution (Did. 16.5).

## IV.2. Motivation: Eschatological Descriptions and Apocalyptic Return of the Lord (Did. 16.3–8)

### IV.2.a. Introduction to the False Prophets and Corrupters (Did. 16.3–4a)

These final verses in Did. 16 underscore the previous ethical dogmas and motivate the community (Did. 16.1–2). Marked by an explanatory conjunction (γάρ), the Didachist describes early apocalyptic ideas that echo the Olivet Discourse (Matt 24–25; Mark 13). Four temporal adverbial markers divide five successive scenes that narrate the final events (τότε; Did. 16.4, 5, 6, 8). As explain van de Sandt and Flusser, "The description of the apocalyptic disturbances and calamities in 16:2–8 is neatly ordered in subsequent periods by the use of the temporal adverb τότε (then)."[29] To help clarify this final section, the "apocalyptic drama" introduces characters and slowly unfolds their activity within the narrative.

Prior to mounting this apocalyptic drama, the Didachist begins to inform about key figures and their respective characteristics. First, many false prophets and corrupters will increase, sheep will apostatize, and morals will decline (Did. 16.3). To seduce or corrupt (φθορεύς) also extends to the patterns within the way of death. These terms exclusively relate to one who corrupts children: οὐ φονεύσεις τέκνον ἐν φθορᾷ (Did. 2.2) and φονεῖς τέκνων (Did. 5.2). To corrupt, along with the moral demise, also extends to the increasing disarray of the social order and an increase of lawlessness during the last days (cf. 2 Tim 3:1; 2 Pet 3:3).

These two characters take the "good" and demoralize it. "Sheep" and "love" become corrupted and transformed into their counterpart. The metaphor of a sheep, who transforms into a wolf, slightly differs from the Sermon-on-the-Mount tradition (Matt 7:15; cf. 2 Clem. 5.2–4). False prophets are not veiled wolves presenting as sheep (as in Matt 7:15).

---

29. van de Sandt and Flusser, *Didache*, 36.

Rather, the false prophets (Did. 16.3) may legitimately be, but are not limited to, those who transform good sheep into fellow wolves. Furthermore, to corrupt the "good" also transforms love into hatred, as a counterpart. An increase of moral lawlessness may transform this hatred (Did. 16.4a). A parallel in Matt 24:14, "the love of many shall grow cold," slightly differs in meaning. Rather than spiritual apathy, "love" initially shapes the way of life (Did. 1.2). Therefore, to turn from love to hatred is to move from the way of life to the way of death.

Deceived community members transform from supposed sheep to wolves (Did. 16.3). The metaphor of sheep, especially in Matthean contexts, refers to true disciples (cf. Matt 25:31–46). Within the Didache, no such idea appears. Didache 13.3 mentions sheep, yet in a cultic setting. The identity category of "sheep" regularly indicates a metaphor that refers to herds of people who follow a particular religious officiate or leader (cf. Ezek 34; 1 Pet 5:1–2; Acts of Peter 4.8). So, sheep, in Did. 16, most likely serve as the antithesis to wolves. They adhere to the way of life, bound by lawful deeds, and marked with love. The false prophets will succeed, however, in taking sheep and turning them into wolves. This anarchical vision recalls Matthew's portrait of an increase in false prophets, leading others astray, in betrayal, and a decrease in love (Matt 24:10–12).

It appears that certain people will emerge who devote themselves to false teachings and prophecy. They also will promulgate the moral corruption of societal norms. These corruptors, ultimately, turn the highest moral of love from the way of life (cf. Did. 1.2–3) and corrupt it.

The presence of increasing lawlessness (ἀνομία) will result in further social confusion (Did. 16.4a). As this lawlessness grows during the "last days," hatred and persecution will characterize common relationships. Hatred toward one another and persecution will emerge regardless of social class or religious identity. Even some false prophets and corruptors will turn to persecute their own (ἀλλήλων).[30]

### IV.2.b. Introduction to the World Deceiver (Did. 16.4b)

This second literary scene—marked by τότε—highlights a worldwide figure (Did. 16.4b). As righteousness has already decreased because of false prophets and corruptors already prevailing, a dominating figure finally enters the scene. The worldwide deceiver (κοσμοπλανής) appears. This

---

30. Lindemann notes that ἀλλήλους does not refer to Christians. I, likewise, concur and suggest that it refers to the "eschatological outsider." Lindemann, "Endzeitrede in Didache 16," 162–63.

*hapax legomenon* is similar to the "deceiver" and "anti-Christ" in 2 John 7 (ὁ πλάνος καί ὁ ἀντίχριστος) and to "the one deceiving the entire inhabited earth" in Rev 12:9 (ὁ πλανῶν τὴν οἰκουμένην ὅλην).[31] This term is also quite similar to Apoc. Pet. 2, "this is the deceiver who must come into the world and do signs and wonders in order to deceive." Whomever this word refers to, the figure possesses some form of global and cosmic influence to deceive mass amounts of people. According to Verheyden, "this character calls forth associations with traditions on the Antichrist and Satan; . . . the Deciever is a parody of Christ."[32]

This deceiver will display a particular set of abilities, different than the previous group of false prophets and corrupters. He will perform signs and wonders as one mimicking the "Son of Man." This messianic-like term may help spread and perpetuate his influence (cf. Dan 7:13–14). Apocalyptic discourse already expects some form of messianic deliverance. He may mimic Jesus as the "Son of God." The miraculous signs and wonders will capture the attention of many. The Didachist does not, however, present this figure in opposition to God. Rather, the "world-deceiver" may think he is continuing the work of God and taking his rightful place as God's messianic son.

This person resembles the final anti-Christ figure, who will perform signs and wonders and will embody an apocalyptic figure of rebellion and lawlessness. The rest of chapter 16, however, never revisits this figure to describe their final outcome, successes, or fate.

When the world (ἡ γῆ) eventually falls into his hands, he will commit unspeakable abominations (ἀθέμιτος)—some of which have never been seen or performed before (Did. 16.4). It remains unclear, however, what these actions will be. Will they consist of deeds that he alone performs? Will he alone commit these deeds or will the world join him? Or do these unseen deeds only consist of personifying the "Son of God" and deceiving the world?

The idea behind ἀθέμιτος appears to relate to breaking norms or customary tradition. It relates to idolatry (1 Pet 4:3), anger and jealousy (1 Clem. 63.2), and breaking customs (Acts 10:28). Thus, to determine what kind of acts this world-deceiver will commit seems quite difficult. The language simply conveys an act that no one has yet committed. Contextually, these abominations do not include the institution of anti-Christ worship but consist of the persecution of Christians (Did. 16.5).[33] But if the abominable acts refer to the persecution of Christians, then they

---

31. Other apocalyptic figures of similar description are found in Dan 7:25; 11:36–39; 2 Thess 2:3, 8; Rev 13; Justin, *Dial.* 110. Also consult Hippolytus, *De Antichr.* 6 and *Apoc. Pet.* 2.

32. Verheyden, "Eschatology in the Didache," 204.

33. Niederwimmer, *Didache*, 220.

will consist of *unspeakable* persecutions because Christians had already experienced forms of persecution in the first and second centuries.[34] It thus may not refer to institutional persecution itself but the expression of broader acts of persecutory acts (Justin, *Dial.* 110—"unlawful deeds"). Alternatively, if the other text traditions bear weight, then deceitful acts are the most prominent (see *Apoc. Pet.* 2).

### IV.2.c. The Fiery Test, Persecution, and Salvation (Did. 16.5)

The third literary scene, once more, is marked by τότε (Did. 16.5). A "fiery test" emerges that will fall upon all of humanity. Additionally, this new scene introduces a new character and a means of salvation.

The fire of testing falls upon every person, irrespective of religious piety or social strata. With the *in toto* expressions, "earth" (Did. 16.4) and "all creation of humanity" (ἡ κτίσις τῶν ἀνθρώπων),[35] a global event emerges. Nothing in Did. 16 requires that this event reflects a final end-time apocalyptic judgment—yet in the light of other text traditions, it quite possibly describes the final apocalyptic events. In fact, the Didachist mentions nothing of divine judgment or vindication from God. The Didachist, instead, portrays God as one who rescues rather than one who judges (cf. Did. 1.5; 3.10; 9.4; 10.5; 16.7–8).

The "fiery trial," secondly, may refer to a purgatorial fire whereby it will purify those who experience the event.[36] However, some will die by this fire and some will persevere through this fire. Although "fire" may denote a purifying process (Isa 1:25–26; Jer 6:29; Ezek 22:20; 24:11; Zech 13:9; 1 Pet 1:6–7), God may serve as both a divine judge for the wicked and a purifier of the redeemed.[37]

However, this reading proves textually problematic for three reasons. First, God does not bring about the "fiery trial." Rather, the fiery trial appears through the actions of both the false prophets and world-deceiver (Did. 16.4). The Didachist does not frame God as a punitive character. The literary logic, especially in Did. 16, refrains from depicting God as such. In fact, the Didachist does not introduce God into these scenes until Did.

---

34. Even consider a more critical appraisal of early Christian martyr events. Moss, *Ancient Christian Martyrdom*.

35. This phrase also appears in Mark 16:15; Herm. Mand. 7.5 (37.5); and Col 1.23 and conveys a similar notion.

36. Milavec, "Birth of Purgatory," 91–104; Milavec, "Pastoral Genius of the Didache," 131–55.

37. So, Milavec, *Didache: Commentary*, 82.

16.7. As already revealed in a different eschatological setting, God gathers the church and acts as one who rescues (Did. 9.4; 10.5). Moreover, nothing in Did. 16 suggests that God retributively presents justice to those who lack any form of piety. Rather, the Didachist depicts God as one who returns to rescue those slain by the persecution (Did. 16.6c–7).

Second, if the fiery test possesses a purifying component, then death ought not to be an outcome (ἀπολοῦνται; cf. Prov 27:21 LXX). If so, then it lacks a true purifying feature (Isa 48:9–10). For, the "fiery trial" brings about the death of those who apostatize (σκανδαλισθήσονται). Also, unlike other forms of cosmological fire and destruction (cf. Matt 24:29–30), some survive such an experience—i.e., those who endure (cf. Rev 13:10; 14:12).

Third, πύρωσις can refer to persecution. First Peter 4:12 links "fiery trial" together with Christian persecution (1 Pet 4:12–15), the only such reference in Christian Scripture. With the false prophets and corrupters persecuting one another in Did. 16.4, it remains quite possible that the "fiery trial" befalls all of humanity (Did. 16.5).

I advocate this third interpretive option. The "fiery trial" is the experience of persecution. To experience fire also correlates to testing and persecution in 1 Pet 4:12. The "fire" represents persecution befalling Christians (cf. Herm. Vis. 4.3.4 [24.4]). This persecution will fall upon all persons irrespective of social status. Already, the false prophets and corrupters persecute one another (Did. 16.4a), as well as those belonging to the Didache community. This fire, if a reference to persecution, also corresponds to other apocalyptic events that increase end-time persecution (cf. Matt 24:9–11, 21–22).

As persecution falls upon all persons, two outcomes may occur (Did. 16.5b). Either a person will experience the "fire," will be led to sin (σκανδαλίζω), and will fall away to destruction. Or a person will persevere in their faith and be saved by the "accursed one" (κατάθεμα). This accursed figure is Jesus (cf. Gal 3:13),[38] rather than an accursed place—i.e., grave or death.[39] To be saved by the "accursed one" will cohere with apocalyptic salvation (Mark 13:13). So, to "fall away" relates to death, "endurance" to salvation, and Jesus to "the accursed one" who will rescue. Verheyden rightly observes, "To describe the period that precedes the end Did. does not refer to earthquakes or political and military disasters. Instead it has selected a tribulation that forms a constant threat for the community: the dangers of betrayal and of apostasy."[40]

---

38. Consult Pardee on this argument. She argues, exceptionally, for the "accursed" expression to refer to Jesus as the accursed figure. Pardee, "The Curse That Saves," 156–76.

39. Holmes, *Apostolic Fathers*, 369.

40. Verheyden, "Eschatology in the Didache," 209.

## IV.2.d. The Signs of Truth and a Partial Resurrection (Did. 16.6–7)

The next literary scene reflects upon the "signs of truth" (Did. 16.6–7). As the literary logic unfolds, the amount of deceit, lawlessness, and corruption in the first few scenes accompanies a change of characters.

Three events seem to occur in successive staccato fashion. The "signs of truth" occupy the opening of the heavens, the sound of a trumpet, and a partial resurrection of the dead saints.[41] These events partially correlate to other apocalyptic traditions (cf. Matt 24:30–31; Mark 13:26–27). The opening of the heavens in the canonical tradition typically conveys the sight and return of Jesus (cf. Matt 24:30) and the tearing of the temple veil (Matt 27:51).[42] A trumpet, likewise, gathers the saints (Matt 24:31; 1 Thess 4:16). A partial resurrection similarly corresponds to the trumpet tradition in 1 Thess 4:15–17.[43] The "signs of truth" move the Didachist's focal point from the destructive deceit of a pseudo-Christ figure and his prophets towards God who will redeem and rescue the saints.

The Didachist does not speak of a general resurrection. Instead, the resurrection is partial and extends exclusively to the saints (Did. 16.7)—as indicated by the expression "but not of everyone." As a basis for this partial resurrection, the Didachist quotes Zech 14:5 LXX (cf. 1 Thess 3:13). This proof-text secures hope for those slain by the hands of persecutors. The return of God with "his saints" participates in a martyrological tradition. Other biblical traditions vaguely refer to the "saints" that return with God; thus, leaving it to the interpreter to read ἅγιοι as "saints" or "holy ones" (Zech 14:5; 1 Thess 3:13; cf. Rev 19:14). As Christian tradition suggests that changing of substance occurs at the resurrection (cf. 1 Cor 15:40, 42, 44), it remains quite viable to argue that "saints"—resurrected saints ὡς

---

41. Draper underscores the "sign of the Son of Man" as part of the Totem of the cross and the Isaianic portrait of a Messiah. Draper, "Development of 'the Sign of the Son of Man,'" 13–19.

42. According to Gurtner, the tearing of the veil in Matthew is twofold. For our concerns here, the first purpose helps corroborate Did. 16 as apocalyptic in nature. The opening of the heavens, with the accompanying earthquake and resurrections, is an apocalyptic event that signifies the death of Jesus. Given Didache's proclivity to utilize Matthew's traditions, the opening of the heavens functions as an apocalyptic event that begins the resurrection process with the martyrs. Gurtner, *Torn Veil*, 138.

43. Although I disagree with Garrow's assessment of a Did. tradition undergirding the Thessalonian correspondence, he nonetheless provides helpful historical work and parallels between 1 Thess and Did. 16. Garrow, "Eschatological Tradition behind 1 Thessalonians," 191–215.

ἄγγελοι (cf. Mark 12:25)—and "angels" may be indistinguishable.[44] For example, Jesus, when instructing the Sadducees about the resurrection, concludes that resurrected persons will be ὡς ἄγγελοι (Mark 12:25). This partial resurrection might also contribute to the Didachist not yet knowing of the general resurrection.[45]

If the Lord returns with glorified saints to rescue those saints who have been persecuted, Zech 14:5 operates as a paraenesis for the hearers. This tradition similarly relates to Rev 19, where an army dressed in white and pure linen returns with the Lord (Rev 19:14).[46] White robes adorn the saints, pieces of clothing received after martyrdom (Rev 7:13–14). Thus, when they return with God (Did. 16.7; cf. Rev 19:14), they vindicate those who have died by the hands of their oppressors (Did. 16.3, 5; cf. Rev 6:9–11). Draper documents a number of Jewish and early Christian readings of Zech 14:5. He concludes that early Christian and Jewish martyrdom theology evokes Zech 14:5 often as a proof-text.[47]

This scene in the Didache, then, conveys the rescuing events of God. The heavens open, and God resurrects the martyred saints. Zechariah 14:5 serves both as a proof-text to support a partial resurrection and to encourage those about to be slain. Didache 16.7 presents a martyrological tradition whereby God returns with glorified saints to rescue saints that have died during the final apocalyptic persecution.

### IV.2.e. The Revelation of the Coming Lord (Did. 16.8)

The final scene and final verse in the extant form of the Didache depict the return of the Lord within the clouds. In the biblical testimony, God coming upon the clouds is both his retribution and his rescue of the saints (cf. Zech 12:10; Rev 1:7; Matt 24:30; Luke 21:27). However, the Didachist portrays

---

44. Also Draper, "Resurrection and Zechariah 14.5," 165. Cf. Cyril of Alexandria, *Comm. Zach.* 14. Consider the reading from Didymus the Blind: "He comes also with great 'power,' however, because *holy ones* accompany him, not men only but also angels. It is logical, in fact, that 'those who have been eyewitnesses and servants' and 'ministering spirits assigned to his service' by him should with him be resplendent, so that he should be acknowledged as their king, and they as his powers, that is, his forces" (*Comm. Zach.* 14).

45. van de Sandt and Flusser comment, "The limitations of the resurrection to only the saints suggests that the Didache does not know (yet) a general resurrection." van de Sandt and Flusser, *Didache*, 36.

46. I am not advocating a form of dependency or awareness between Did. and Rev. Rather, I am noting two similar traditions.

47. Draper, "Resurrection and Zechariah 14.5," 178.

God exclusively returning to rescue the saints. The text might be taken as implying retributive wrath upon the wicked, but the prevailing focus in this setting is on God as a deliverer.

As God returns on the clouds, the Didachist concludes the eschatological paraenetic in Did. 16.1–2. God returns to rescue the people who walk within the way of life. This apocalypse offers a paraenetic voice of hope, detailing how the way-of-death wayfarers—oppressors—will not have the final victory. So the Didachist begins the apocalypse with the eschatological demise of apostasy, deceit, and false prophets and then concludes with victory and hope. Didache 16.3–8 begins with the destructive demise of false prophets, increased lawlessness, persecution, and a Son-of-God impersonator. Now, it ends with divine victory, a divine victory that is neither retributive nor vindictive, but a divine victory of martyrological rescue.

## IV.3. [Lost Ending] (Did. 16.9–12)

The conclusion of the Didache has caused quite a bit of difficulty. The extant Greek manuscript (H54) concludes with Did. 16.8 and thus all the following material is merely hypothetical until more substantial evidence is found. Unless an older Didache MS emerges, the ending of Did. 16.8 will more than likely complete the Didache's teaching.[48]

Two primary reasons, at least, help us to affirm that Did. 16.8 does not reflect the complete ending. First, H54 contains missing space in the MS near Did. 16.8. This may reflect an incomplete ending or space to complete the ending. Second, other traditions that appear in the tradition-history of the Didache contain additional material that corresponds with the Didache's ending. If these observations prove suggestive, then it will be the work of further historical labors to adjudicate *why* the MS was abbreviated. Some suggest that the Didache was abbreviated in order to portary anti-chiliasm tendencies in the early second century.[49] I'm less inclined to think that the text was abbreviated on account of chiliast elements in the Didache.

---

48. van de Sandt and Flusser influenced me early on in my reading of the Didache. As we approach the final verses of Did. 16, we are presented with an abrupt ending, a "conclusion of the apocalypse is unfortunately lost in the Jerusalem Manuscript." As van de Sandt and Flusser caution, it remains rather difficult to accept Apos. Con. readings, although I want to suggest they point to a disparity in the tradition. The Georgian translation, likewise, might not supply a clear conclusion to the Did. van de Sandt and Flusser, *Didache*, 36–37, esp. 37n89.

49. Varner, "Didache 'Apocalypse,'" 318–20; Ladd, "Eschatology of the Didache," 177; contra Hill, *Regnum Caelorum*, 77.

Robert Aldridge offers research on the matter that is worth considering. In his article, "The Lost Ending of the Didache,"[50] Aldridge identifies three versions of eschatological endings that cohere with the Didache literary tradition: (1) Apostolic Constitutions;[51] (2) the Georgian Version of Didache, now non-extant; and (3) *De abrenuntiatione in baptismate*, by St. Boniface. After reviewing these three versions, he then suggests a possible reconstruction of the Didache's lost eschatological ending.

Table 17. A Lost Ending to the Didache Reconstructed in Apos. Con., Georgian Version, and St. Boniface

| Apostolic Constitutions VII, 32 | Georgian Version (Didache) | *De abrenuntiatione in baptismate*, St. Boniface |
|---|---|---|
| . . . with the angels of his power, in the throne of his kingdom, to condemn the devil, the deceiver of the world, *and to render to every one according to his deeds. Then shall the wicked go away into everlasting punishment, but the righteous shall enter eternal life*, to inherit those things which *eye hath not seen, nor ear heard, nor have entered into the heart of man, such things as God hath prepared for them that love him*; and they shall rejoice in the kingdom of God, which is in Christ Jesus. | Then the world will see our Lord Jesus Christ, the Son of Man who is [simultaneously] Son of God, coming on the clouds with power and great glory, in his holy righteousness to repay every man according to his works before all mankind and before the angels. Amen | Believe in Christ's coming, the resurrection of the flesh, *and the judgment of all men. Evil men will be assigned to eternal fire and righteous men to eternal life.* In that place there is life with God without death, light without shadows, health without sickness, fullness without hunger, happiness without fear, joy without sadness; there eternal glory [is]; there the righteous will shine like the sun, since *eye hath not seen, nor ear heard, nor has arisen in man's heart that which God has prepared for them that love him.* . . . |

From these versions and variants of the Didache's lost ending, Aldridge suggests the following as a reconstructed conclusion to the Didache—what I likewise desire to label as Did. 16.8–12:

50. Aldridge, "Lost Ending of the Didache."

51. Aldridge regards the following about the Apos. Con.: "*Constitutions'* conclusion, however, has not received widespread acceptance as the *Didache's* true ending but is generally regarded as a variant." Aldridge, "Lost Ending of the Didache," 6.

> ⁸ Then the world will see the Lord coming upon the clouds of heaven with the angels of his power, in the throne of his kingdom,
> ⁹ to condemn the devil, the deceiver of the world, and to render to every one according to his deeds.
> ¹⁰ Then shall the wicked go away into everlasting punishment, but the righteous shall enter eternal life,
> ¹¹ to inherit those things which eye hath not seen, nor ear heard, nor have entered into the heart of man, such things as God hath prepared for them that love him.
> ¹² And they shall rejoice in the kingdom of God, which is in Christ Jesus.

Although this ending helpfully contributes to the additional study of the Didache, I will refrain from offering an interpretation of this reconstruction. I choose to do so because the ending does not form part of a final edition of the Didache. Additionally, I am not fully convinced that the reconstruction coheres as a compatible ending with the Didache's teaching.

No doubt, Aldridge provides a very helpful service to Didache scholarship by supplying this amended ending. However, I do want to offer a few reasons why this suggested ending may not fully cohere with the rest of the Didache and thereby still needs further editing. I humbly, however, have nothing to offer as a replacement—other than to say, let us hope for an older MS of the Didache to appear that contains a fuller ending of Did. 16.

I remain in much agreement with Aldridge, especially regarding the need to offer a text reconstruction of the ending of Did. 16. However, I desire to suggest a few reasons why the above text reconstruction still needs attention. First, the divine language that the Didachist often chooses to refer to Jesus is κύριος (cf. Did. 16.12). Moreover, the Didachist may use υἱός to relate Jesus to the trinitarian name (Did. 7.1–3) and to servitude in the Eucharist liturgies (Did. 9.2, 3; 10.2). "Jesus Christ" appears in the longer Eucharist doxology (Did. 9.4). So, theological and Christological clarity, and explicit Christological titles are often not given to Jesus throughout the Didache. This amended ending further depicts an obvious place that "Jesus" should be used instead of κύριος (cf. Did. 8.2; 9.5; 16.1).

Second, the language of "everlasting punishment" and "eternal life" reflects an explicit eschatological outcome for humanity. The Didachist certainly uses the language of "eternal life" (10.3) and "immortality" (10.2) in the Eucharistic liturgies. Yet the language of eternal destruction and condemnation is altogether lacking. The Didache, as a whole, generally offers exclusive comments to inner community outcomes and not to the outer community.

Third, to use "devil" is too explicit (Did. 16.9). The names of the outsiders or the evildoers are limited to false prophet, corrupters, wolves, and the deceiver of the world (Did. 16.3, 4). An explicit title of the devil does not cohere with general titles of the opposition. Why not consider the "deceiver" or the "Evil One" (cf. Did. 8.2)?

Fourth, the reconstruction of Did. 16.11 follows too closely the material in Apos. Con. VII, 32. The Didachist does not develop a habit of quoting large amounts of Scripture, let alone quoting sacred material without a quotation formula (Did. 8.2; 9.5; 14.3; 16.7). Additionally, if this verse adequately reconstructs the Didache's ending, then this will be the first place that the Didache is aware of any Pauline tradition (cf. 1 Cor 2:9).

| 1 Cor 2:9 ESV | Did. 16.11 | Apos. Con. VII, 32 |
| --- | --- | --- |
| But as it is written, "What no eye has seen, nor ear heard, nor the heart of man imagined, what God has prepared for those who love him" | to inherit those things which eye hath not seen, nor ear heard, nor have entered into the heart of man, such things as God hath prepared for them that love him | to inherit those things which *eye hath not seen, nor ear heard, nor have entered into the heart of man, such things as God hath prepared for them that love him* |

Because this Pauline tradition expands upon Isa 64:4, the Isaianic tradition lacks a number of features that appear in 1 Cor 2:9. So these additional emendations reflect more a Pauline tradition than the Isaianic tradition.

Last, recompense, as a theme, is altogether absent from the Didache (cf. Did. 16.9). To "render to every one according to his deeds" reflects a theme that does not appear in Did. 16, and the Two Ways do not reflect this tenor. For example, τέλειος applies to those who bear the yoke of the Lord (Did. 6.2). Furthermore, Did. 16.3–8 does not focus on any forms of judgment for the religious outsider or their eternal condition. Rather, the statement "many will fall away and perish" reflects their death, whereas the Didachist does not comment about their judgment (Did. 16.5). The eschatological portrait in Did. 16 focuses upon rescue and deliverance, not coming judgment for the world—although these ideas may be assumed. The recompense theme in Did. 16.9 appears to offer a new concept that is not adequately anticipated by the previous theology of the Didache as a whole.

# Bibliography

Aland, Kurt, ed. *Synopsis of the Four Gospels: Greek-English Edition of the Synopsis Quattuor Evangeliorum*. 15th ed. Stuttgart: German Bible Society, 2013.
Albright, W. F., and C. S. Mann. *Matthew*. AB 26. New York: Doubleday, 1971.
Aldridge, Robert E. "The Lost Ending of the Didache." *VC* 53 (1999) 1–15.
———. "Peter and the 'Two Ways.'" *VC* 53 (1999) 233–64.
Allen, David M. "Introduction: The Study of the Use of the Old Testament in the New." *JSNT* 38 (2015) 3–16.
Allison, Dale C., Jr. "Apocalyptic Ethics and Behavior." In *The Oxford Handbook of Apocalyptic Literature*, edited by John J. Collins, 295–311. Oxford: Oxford University Press, 2014.
———. *Studies in Matthew: Interpretation Past and Present*. Grand Rapids: Baker Academic, 2005.
Anderson, Gary. *Charity: The Place of the Poor in the Biblical Tradition*. New Haven, CT: Yale University Press, 2013.
Arzi, Abraham. "Terefah." In *Encyclopaedia Judaica*, 2nd ed., edited by Fred Skolnik and Michael Berenbaum, 19:647. Farmington Hills, MI: Keter, 2007.
Ascough, Richard S. "An Analysis of the Baptismal Ritual of the Didache." *SL* 24 (1994) 201–12.
Audet, Jean-Paul. "Affinités Littéraires et Doctrinales du 'Manuel de Discipline.'" *RB* 59 (1952) 219–38.
———. *La Didachè: Instructions des Apôtres*. EBib. Paris: Gabalda, 1958.
Ayres, Lewis. "Continuity and Change in Second-Century Christianity: A Narrative against the Trend." In *Christianity in the Second Century: Themes and Developments*, edited by James Carleton Paget and Judith Lieu, 106–21. Cambridge: Cambridge University Press, 2017.
Balabanski, Vicky. *Eschatology in the Making: Mark, Matthew, and the Didache*. SNTSMS 97. Cambridge: Cambridge University Press, 1997.
Bammel, Ernst. "Pattern and Prototype of *Didache* 16." In *The Didache in Modern Research*, edited by Jonathan A. Draper, 364–72. AGJU 37. Leiden: Brill, 1996.
———. "Schema und Vorlage von *Didache* 16." StPatr 4 (1961) 253–62.
Barnes, Michel René. "The Beginning and End of Early Christian Pneumatology." *AugStud* 39 (2008) 169–86.
Bauckham, Richard. "James and the Jerusalem Church." In *The Book of Acts in Its First-Century Setting. Volume 4: Palestinian Setting*, edited by Richard Bauckham, 415–80. Grand Rapids: Eerdmans, 1995.

———. *Jesus and the God of Israel: God Crucified and Other Studies on the New Testament's Christology of Divine Identity*. Milton Keynes, UK: Paternoster, 2008.

Beaugrande, Robert de, and Wolfgang Dressler. *Introduction to Text Linguistics*. LLL 26. London: Routledge, 1981.

Benko, Stephen. *Pagan Rome and the Early Christians*. Bloomington, IN: Indiana University Press, 1984.

Bertram, Georg, and Karl Heinrich Rengstorf. "Ζυγός, Ἑτεροζυγέω." In *TDNT* 2:896–98.

Betz, Hans Dieter. *The Sermon on the Mount: A Commentary on the Sermon on the Mount, Including the Sermon on the Plain (Matthew 5:3—7:27 and Luke 6:20–49)*. Hermeneia. Minneapolis, MN: Fortress, 1995.

Betz, Johannes. "The Eucharist in the Didache." In *The Didache in Modern Research*, edited by Jonathan A. Draper, 244–75. AGJU 37. New York: Brill, 1996.

Bihlmeyer, Karl. *Die apostolischen Väter*. Tübingen: Mohr, 1970.

Bird, Michael F. *Evangelical Theology: A Biblical and Systematic Introduction*. Grand Rapids: Zondervan, 2013.

———. *The Gospel of the Lord: How the Early Church Wrote the Story of Jesus*. Grand Rapids: Eerdmans, 2014.

Bloch, Maurice. "Symbols, Songs, Dance and Features of Articulation: Is Religion an Extreme Form of Traditional Authority?" *EuroJS* 5 (1974) 55–81.

Blomberg, Craig L. *Matthew*. NAC 22. Nashville, TN: Broadman, 1992.

Blowers, Paul M. "Patristic Interpretation." In *The Oxford Encyclopedia of Biblical Interpretation*, edited by Steven L. McKenzie, 2:81–89. New York: Oxford University Press, 2013.

Blumell, Lincoln H., and Thomas A. Wayment, eds. *Christian Oxyrhynchus: Texts, Documents, and Sources*. Waco, TX: Baylor University Press, 2015.

Bobertz, Charles A. "Ritual Eucharist within Narrative: A Comparison of Didache 9–10 with Mark 6:31–44; 8:1–9." *StPatr* 45 (2010) 93–99.

Bockmuehl, Markus. *Seeing the Word: Refocusing New Testament Study*. STI. Grand Rapids: Baker Academic, 2006.

Boersma, Hans. *Heavenly Participation: The Weaving of a Sacramental Tapestry*. Grand Rapids: Eerdmans, 2011.

———. *Nouvelle Théologie and Sacramental Ontology: A Return to Mystery*. Oxford: Oxford University Press, 2009.

———. *Scripture as Real Presence: Sacramental Exegesis in the Early Church*. Grand Rapids: Baker Academic, 2017.

Boersma, Hans, and Matthew Levering, eds. *The Oxford Handbook of Sacramental Theology*. Oxford: Oxford University Press, 2018.

Bokedal, Tomas. "Scripture in the Second Century." In *The Sacred Text: Excavating the Texts, Exploring the Interpretations, and Engaging the Theologies of the Christian Scriptures*, edited by Michael Bird and Michael Pahl, 43–61. GPP 7. Piscataway, NJ: Gorgias, 2010.

Boring, M. Eugene. "The Gospel of Matthew: Introduction, Commentary, and Reflections." In *New Testament Articles, Matthew, Mark*, 87–505. *NIB* 8. Nashville, TN: Abingdon, 1995.

Bradshaw, P. F. "Yet Another Explanation of Didache 9–10." *SL* 36 (2006) 124–28.

Bradshaw, Paul F., and Maxwell E. Johnson. *The Origins of Feasts, Fasts and Seasons in Early Christianity*. ACC 86. Collegeville, MN: Liturgical, 2011.

Breed, Brennan W. *Nomadic Text: A Theory of Biblical Reception History*. ISBL. Bloomington, IN: Indiana University Press, 2014.

Brooks, E. Bruce. "Before and after Matthew." In *The Didache: A Missing Piece of the Puzzle in Early Christianity*, edited by Jonathan A. Draper and Clayton N. Jefford, 247–86. ECL 14. Atlanta: Society of Biblical Literature, 2015.

Brooks, Stephen H. *Matthew's Community: The Evidence of His Special Sayings Material*. JSNTSup 16. Sheffield, UK: Sheffield Academic, 1987.

Brown, Raymond E. "The Pater Noster as an Eschatological Prayer." TS 22 (1961) 175–208.

Bucur, Bogdan Gabriel. *Angelomorphic Pneumatology: Clement of Alexandria and Other Early Christian Witnesses*. VCSup 95. Leiden: Brill, 2009.

Butler, B. C. "The Literary Relations of Didache, Ch. XVI." *JTS* 11 (1960) 265–83.

Carruthers, Mary. "Memory, Imagination, and the Interpretation of Scripture in the Middle Ages." In *The Oxford Handbook of the Reception History of the Bible*, edited by Michael Lieb, Emma Mason, and Jonathan Roberts, 214–34. Oxford: Oxford University Press, 2011.

Carson, D. A. "Matthew." In *Matthew, Mark, Luke*, edited by Frank E. Gæbelein, 1–599. EBC 8. Grand Rapids: Zondervan, 1984.

Clark, David. *The Lord's Prayer: Origins and Early Interpretations*. STTEEMT 21. Turnhout, Belgium: Brepols, 2016.

Clark, Elizabeth A. *Reading Renunciation: Asceticism and Scripture in Early Christianity*. Princeton, NJ: Princeton University Press, 1999.

———. "Sexuality." In *Encyclopedia of Early Christianity*, edited by Everett Ferguson, 2nd ed., 1053–54. New York: Routledge, 1999.

Claussen, Carsten. "The Eucharist in the Gospel of John and in the *Didache*." In *Trajectories through the New Testament and the Apostolic Fathers*, edited by Andrew F. Gregory and Christopher M. Tuckett, 135–63. Oxford: Oxford University Press, 2005.

Clerici, Agostino, ed. *Didachè Letter di Ignazio d'Antiochia A Diogneto*. 8th ed. Milan: Figilie di San Paolo, 2014.

Collins, John J. "Introduction: Towards the Morphology of a Genre." In *Apocalypse: The Morphology of a Genre*, edited by John J. Collins, 1–20. Semeia 14. Atlanta: Society of Biblical Literature, 1979.

———. "What Is Apocalyptic Literature?" In *The Oxford Handbook of Apocalyptic Literature*, edited by John J. Collins, 1–16. Oxford: Oxford University Press, 2014.

———. "Wisdom, Apocalypticism, and Generic Compatibility." In *In Search of Wisdom: Essays in Memory of John G. Gammie*, edited by Leo G. Perdue, Bernard Brandon Scott, and William Johnston Wiseman, 165–85. Louisville, KY: John Knox, 1993.

Corwin, Virginia. *St. Ignatius and Christianity in Antioch*. New Haven, CT: Yale University Press, 1960.

Crossley, James G. *Reading the New Testament: Contemporary Approaches*. RRTS. London: Routledge, 2010.

Davies, W. D., and Dale C. Allison Jr. *Matthew 1–7: Volume 1*. Vol. 1. ICC. London: T. & T. Clark, 1988.

———. *Matthew 8–18: Volume 2*. Vol. 2. ICC. London: T. & T. Clark, 1991.

———. *Matthew 19–28: Volume 3*. Vol. 3. ICC. London: T. & T. Clark, 1997.

Dawson, John David. *Christian Figural Reading and the Fashioning of Identity*. Berkeley: University of California Press, 2002.

de Halleux, André. "Ministers in the Didache." In *The Didache in Modern Research*, edited by Jonathan A. Draper, 300–320. AGJU 37. New York: Brill, 1996.

Delling, Gerhard. "τέλος, τελέω, κτλ,." In *TDNT* 8:49–87.

Del Verme, Marcello. "The Didache and Judaism: The Ἀπαρχή of Didache 13:3–7." StPatr 26 (1993) 113–20.

———. *Didache and Judaism: Jewish Roots of an Ancient Christian-Jewish Work*. London: T. & T. Clark, 2004.

Deutsch, Celia. *Hidden Wisdom and the Easy Yoke: Wisdom, Torah and Discipleship in Matthew 11.25–30*. JSNTSup 18. Sheffield, UK: Sheffield Academic, 1987.

Downs, David J. *Alms: Charity, Reward, and Atonement in Early Christianity*. Waco, TX: Baylor University Press, 2016.

———. "The God Who Gives Life That Is Truly Life: Meritorious Almsgiving and the Divine Economy in 1 Timothy 6." In *The Unrelenting God: Essays on God's Action in Scripture in Honor of Beverly Roberts Gaventa*, edited by David J. Downs and Matthew Skinner, 242–60. Grand Rapids: Eerdmans, 2013.

Draper, Jonathan A. "Apostles, Teachers, and Evangelists: Stability and Movement of Functionaries in Matthew, James, and the Didache." In *Matthew, James, and Didache: Three Related Documents in Their Jewish and Christian Settings*, edited by Huub van de Sandt and Jürgen K. Zangenberg, 139–76. SBLSS 45. Atlanta: Society of Biblical Literature, 2008.

———. "The Apostolic Fathers: The Didache." *ExpTim* 117 (2006) 177–81.

———. "Barnabas and the Riddle of the Didache Revisited." *JSNT* 58 (1995) 89–113.

———. "Children and Slaves in the Community of the Didache and the Two Ways Tradition." In *The Didache: A Missing Piece of the Puzzle in Early Christianity*, edited by Jonathan A. Draper and Clayton N. Jefford, 85–121. ECL 14. Atlanta: Society of Biblical Literature Press, 2015.

———. "Christian Self-Definition against the 'Hypocrites' in *Didache* 8." In *The Didache in Modern Research*, edited by Jonathan A. Draper, 223–43. AGJU 37. Leiden: Brill, 1996.

———. "Conclusion: Missing Pieces in the Puzzle or Wild Goose Chase? A Retrospect and Prospect." In *The Didache: A Missing Piece of the Puzzle in Early Christianity*, edited by Jonathan A. Draper and Clayton N. Jefford, 529–43. ECL 14. Atlanta: Society of Biblical Literature, 2015.

———. "A Continuing Enigma: The 'Yoke of the Lord' in Didache 6.2–3 and Early Jewish-Christian Relations." In *The Image of the Judaeo-Christians in Ancient Jewish and Christian Literature*, edited by Peter J. Tomson and Doris Lambers-Petry, 106–23. WUNT 158. Tübingen: Mohr Siebeck, 2003.

———. "The Development of 'the Sign of the Son of Man' in the Jesus Tradition." *NTS* 39 (1993) 1–21.

———. "The *Didache*." In *The Writings of the Apostolic Fathers*, edited by Paul Foster, 13–20. London: T. & T. Clark, 2007.

———. "The Didache." In *The Apostolic Fathers: An Introduction*, edited by Wilhem Pratscher, 7–26. Waco, TX: Baylor University Press, 2010.

———, ed. *The Didache in Modern Research*. AGJU 37. Leiden: Brill, 1996.

———. "The *Didache* in Modern Research: An Overview." In *The Didache in Modern Research*, edited by Jonathan A. Draper, 1–42. AGJU 37. Leiden: Brill, 1996.

———. "Do the Didache and Matthew Reflect an 'Irrevocable Parting of the Ways' with Judaism?" In *Matthew and the Didache: Two Documents from the Same*

*Jewish-Christian Milieu?* edited by Huub van de Sandt, 217–41. Minneapolis, MN: Fortress, 2005.

———. "Eschatology in the Didache." In *Eschatology of the New Testament and Some Related Documents*, edited by Jan G. van der Watt, 567–82. WUNT 2/315. Tübingen: Mohr Siebeck, 2011.

———. "First-Fruits and the Support of Prophets, Teachers, and the Poor in *Didache* 13 in Relation to New Testament Parallels." In *Trajectories through the New Testament and the Apostolic Fathers*, edited by Andrew Gregory and Christopher Tuckett, 223–43. NTAF. Oxford: Oxford University Press, 2005.

———. "The Holy Vine of David Made Known to the Gentiles through God's Servant Jesus: 'Christian Judaism' in the *Didache*." In *Jewish Christianity Reconsidered: Rethinking Ancient Groups and Texts*, edited by Matt Jackson-McCabe, 257–83. Minneapolis, MN: Fortress, 2007.

———. "The Jesus Tradition in the Didache." In *The Jesus Tradition Outside the Gospels*, edited by David Wenham, 5:269–87. GP. Sheffield, UK: JSOT Press, 1984.

———. "The Jesus Tradition in the *Didache*." In *The Didache in Modern Research*, edited by Jonathan A. Draper, 72–91. AGJU 37. Leiden: Brill, 1996.

———. "Lactantius and the Jesus Tradition in the Didache." *JTS* 40 (1989) 112–16.

———. "Mission, Ethics, and Identity in the *Didache*." In *Sensitivity towards Outsiders: Exploring the Dynamic Relationship between Mission and Ethics in the New Testament and Early Christianity*, edited by Jacobus Kok, Tobias Nicklas, Dieter T. Roth, and Christopher M. Hays, 470–89. WUNT 2/364. Tübingen: Mohr Siebeck, 2014.

———. "The Moral Economy of the Didache." *HTS TheoStud* 67 (2011) 1–10.

———. "The Old Testament in the *Didache* and in Subsequent Church Orders." In *Die Septuaginta—Orte und Intentionen*, edited by Siegfried Kreuzer, Martin Meiser, and Marcus Sigismund, 743–63. WUNT 361. Tübingen: Mohr Siebeck, 2016.

———. "Performing the Cosmic Mystery of the Church in the Communities of the *Didache*." In *The Open Mind: Essays in Honour of Christopher Rowland*, edited by Jonathan Knight and Kevin Sullivan, 37–57. LNTS 522. London: T. & T. Clark, 2015.

———. "Pure Sacrifice in Didache 14 as Jewish Christian Exegesis." *Neot* 42 (2008) 223–52.

———. "Resurrection and Zechariah 14.5 in the Didache Apocalypse." *JECS* 5 (1997) 155–79.

———. "Ritual Process and Ritual Symbol in Didache 7-10." *VC* 54 (2000) 121–58.

———. "The Role of Ritual in the Alternation of Social Universe: Jewish-Christian Initiation of Gentiles in the Didache." *List* 32 (1997) 48–67.

———. "Social Ambiguity and the Production of Text: Prophets, Teachers, Bishops, and Deacons and the Development of the Jesus Tradition in the Community of the *Didache*." In *The Didache in Context: Essays on Its Text, History, and Transmission*, edited by Clayton N. Jefford, 284–312. NovTSup 77. Leiden: Brill, 1995.

———. "Torah and Troublesome Apostles in the Didache Community." *NovT* 33 (1991) 347–72.

———. "Torah and Troublesome Apostles in the *Didache* Community." In *The Didache in Modern Research*, edited by Jonathan A. Draper, 340–63. AGJU 37. Leiden: Brill, 1996.

———. "The Two Ways and Eschatological Hope: A Contested Terrain in Galatians 5 and the *Didache*." *Neot* 45 (2011) 221–51.

———. "Vice Catalogues as Oral-Mnemonic Cues: A Comparative Study of the Two-Ways Tradition in the *Didache* and Parallels from the Perspective of Oral Tradition." In *Jesus, the Voice, and the Text: Beyond the Oral and the Written Gospel*, edited by Tom Thatcher, 111–33. Waco, TX: Baylor University Press, 2008.

———. "Walking the Way of Life or the Way of Death in the Present Existence as the Beginning of Eschatological Life or Death in the Renewed Earthly Kingdom: The Rationale for the Limitation of the Resurrection to the Righteous Departed in *Didache* 16,6–8." In *Resurrection of the Dead: Biblical Traditions in Dialogue*, edited by Geert van Oyen and Tom Shepherd, 383–401. BETL 249. Leuven: Peeters, 2012.

———. "Wandering Charismatics and Scholarly Circularities." In *Whoever Hears You Hears Me: Prophets, Performance, and Tradition in Q*, edited by Richard A. Horsley and Jonathan A. Draper, 29–45. Harrisburg, PA: Trinity, 1999.

———. "Weber, Theissen, and 'Wandering Charismatics' in the *Didache*." *JECS* 6 (1998) 541–76.

———. "'You Shall Not Give What Is Holy to the Dogs' (*Didache* 9.5): The Attitude of the *Didache* to the Gentiles." In *Attitudes to Gentiles in Ancient Judaism and Early Christianity*, edited by David C. Sim and James S. McLaren, 242–58. LNTS 499. London: T. & T. Clark, 2013.

Draper, Jonathan A., and Clayton N. Jefford, eds. *The Didache: A Missing Piece of the Puzzle in Early Christianity*. ECL 14. Atlanta: Society of Biblical Literature, 2015.

Draper, Jonathan Alfred. "A Commentary on the Didache in the Light of the Dead Sea Scrolls and Related Documents." PhD diss., University of Cambridge, 1983.

Duhaime, Jean. "Dualism." In *Encyclopedia of the Dead Sea Scrolls*, edited by Lawrence H. Schiffman and James C. VanderKam, 1:215–20. Oxford: Oxford University Press, 2000.

Edwards, James R. *The Hebrew Gospel & the Development of the Synoptic Tradition*. Grand Rapids: Eerdmans, 2009.

Edwards, J. Christopher. *The Ransom Logion in Mark and Matthew: Its Reception and Its Significance for the Study of the Gospels*. WUNT 2/327. Tübingen: Mohr Siebeck, 2012.

Ehrman, Bart D. *The Apostolic Fathers I*. LCL 24. Cambridge: Harvard University Press, 2003.

———. *The Apostolic Fathers II*. LCL 25. Cambridge: Harvard University Press, 2003.

Ehrman, Bart D., and Zlatko Pleše. *The Apocryphal Gospels: Texts and Translations*. Oxford: Oxford University Press, 2011.

Elliot, J. K., ed. *The Apocryphal New Testament: A Collection of Apocryphal Christian Literature in an English Translation*. Oxford: Oxford University Press, 1994.

Elliot, Mark W. "Effective-History and the Hermeneutics of Ulrich Luz." *JSNT* 33 (2010) 161–73.

Eubank, Nathan. "Almsgiving Is 'The Commandment': A Note on 1 Timothy 6.6–19." *NTS* 58 (2012) 144–50.

Eusebius. *Die Kirchengeschichte*. Vol. 2, part 1 of *Eusebius Werke*. Edited by Eduard Schwartz. GCS, 9.1. Leipzig: Hinrichs, 1903.

Evans, Robert. *Reception History, Tradition and Biblical Interpretation: Gadamer and Jauss in Current Practice*. STCPRIB 4. London: Bloomsbury, 2014.

Farkasfalvy, Denis. *Inspiration & Interpretation: A Theological Introduction to Sacred Scripture*. Washington, DC: Catholic University of America Press, 2010.

Ferguson, Everett. *Backgrounds of Early Christianity*. 3rd ed. Grand Rapids: Eerdmans, 2003.

Finlan, Stephen. "Identity in the Didache Community." In *The Didache: A Missing Piece of the Puzzle in Early Christianity*, edited by Jonathan A. Draper and Clayton N. Jefford, 17–32. ECL 14. Atlanta: Society of Biblical Literature, 2015.

Finn, R. *Almsgiving in the Later Roman Empire: Christian Promotion and Practice, 313–450*. Oxford: Oxford University Press, 2006.

Fitzmyer, Joseph A. *A Guide to the Dead Sea Scrolls and Related Literature*. Revised and Expanded. Grand Rapids: Eerdmans, 2008.

Fornberg, Tord. "The Annunciation: A Study in Reception History." In *The New Testament as Reception*, edited by Mogens Müller and Henrik Tronier, 157–80. JSNTSup 230. Sheffield, UK: Sheffield Academic, 2002.

Foster, Paul. "Echoes without Resonance: Critiquing Certain Aspects of Recent Scholarly Trends in the Study of the Jewish Scriptures in the New Testament." *JSNT* 38 (2015) 96–111.

France, R. T. *The Gospel of Matthew*. NICNT. Grand Rapids: Eerdmans, 2007.

Gallagher, Edmon L., and John D. Meade. *The Biblical Canon Lists from Early Christianity: Texts and Analysis*. Oxford: Oxford University Press, 2017.

Garleff, Gunnar. *Urchristliche Identität in Matthäusevangelium Didache und Jakobusbrief*. BVB 9. Münster: Lit Verlag, 2004.

Garrison, Roman. *Redemptive Almsgiving in Early Christianity*. JSNTSup 77. Sheffield, UK: Sheffield Academic, 1993.

Garrow, Alan J. P. "The Didache and Revelation." In *The Didache: A Missing Piece of the Puzzle in Early Christianity*, edited by Jonathan A. Draper and Clayton N. Jefford, 497–514. ECL 14. Atlanta: Society of Biblical Literature, 2015.

———. "The Eschatological Tradition Behind 1 Thessalonians: *Didache* 16." *JSNT* 32 (2009) 191–215.

———. *The Gospel of Matthew's Dependence on the Didache*. LNTS 254. London: T. & T. Clark, 2004.

Gathercole, Simon J. "The Titles of the Gospels in the Earliest New Testament Manuscripts." *ZNW* 104 (2013) 33–76.

Gero, Stephen. "The So-Called Ointment Prayer in the Coptic Version of the Didache: A Re-Evaluation." *HTR* 70 (1977) 67–84.

Giambrone, Anthony. "'According to the Commandment' (*Did.* 1.5): Lexical Reflections on Almsgiving as 'The Commandment.'" *NTS* 60 (2014) 448–65.

Gibbs, Jeffrey A. *Matthew 1:1—11:1*. ConcC. St. Louis, MO: Concordia, 2006.

Giet, Stanislas. *L'enigme de La Didache*. Publications de La Faculté des Lettres de l'Université de Strasbourg. Paris: University of Strasbourg, 1970.

Glover, Richard. "The *Didache*'s Quotations and the Synoptic Gospels." *NTS* 5 (1959) 12–29.

Goff, Matthew. "Wisdom and Apocalypticism." In *The Oxford Handbook of Apocalyptic Literature*, edited by John J. Collins, 52–68. Oxford: Oxford University Press, 2014.

Goodman, Martin. *A History of Judaism*. Princeton, NJ: Princeton University Press, 2018.

Gregory, Andrew. "Reflections on the Didache and Its Community: A Response." In *The Didache: A Missing Piece of the Puzzle in Early Christianity*, edited by Jonathan

A. Draper and Clayton N. Jefford, 123–36. ECL 14. Atlanta: Society of Biblical Literature, 2015.

———. *The Reception of Luke and Acts in the Period before Irenaeus: Looking for Luke in the Second Century*. WUNT 2/169. Tübingen: Mohr Siebeck, 2003.

Gregory, Andrew F., and Christopher M. Tuckett. "Reflections on Method: What Constitutes the Use of the Writings That Later Formed the New Testament in the Apostolic Fathers?" In *The Reception of the New Testament in the Apostolic Fathers*, edited by Andrew F. Gregory and Christopher M. Tuckett, 61–82. NTAF. Oxford: Oxford University Press, 2005.

Gronevald, Michael, ed. *Psalmenkommentar (Tura Papyrus), Teil II: Kommentar zu Eccl. 3–4, 12*. PTA 22. Bonn: Habelt, 1977.

———, ed. *Psalmenkommentar (Tura Papyrus), Teil III: Kommentar zu Psalm 29–34*. PTA 8. Bonn: Habelt, 1969.

Grosvenor, Edwin A. "An Interview with Bishop Bryennios—The Discovery of the Teaching." *Andover Rev* 2 (1884) 515–16.

Grundeken, Mark. *Community Building in the* Shepherd of Hermas: *A Critical Study of Some Key Aspects*. VCSup 131. Leiden: Brill, 2015.

Gupta, Nijay K. *The Lord's Prayer*. SHBC. Macon, GA: Smyth & Helwys, 2018.

Gurtner, Daniel M. *The Torn Veil: Matthew's Exposition of the Death of Jesus*. SNTSMS 139. Cambridge: Cambridge University Press, 2007.

Hagner, Donald A. *Matthew 1–13*. WBC 33A. Dallas: Word, 1993.

Harder, Kenneth J., and Clayton N. Jefford. "A Bibliography of Literature on the Didache." In *The Didache in Context: Essays on Its Text, History, and Transmission*, edited by Clayton N. Jefford, 368–82. NovTSup 77. Leiden: Brill, 1995.

Hare, Douglas R. A. *Matthew*. IBC. Louisville, KY: John Knox, 1993.

Harl, Kenneth W. *Coinage in the Roman Economy, 300 B.C. to A.D. 700*. ASH. Baltimore, MD: Johns Hopkins University Press, 1996.

Harris, J. Rendel. *The Teaching of the Apostles: Newly Edited, with Facsimile Text and a Commentary*. Baltimore, MD: Johns Hopkins University, 1887.

———. *Three Pages of the Bryennios Manuscript*. Baltimore, MD: Johns Hopkins University, 1885.

Hartin, Patrick J. "Ethics in the Letter of James, the Gospel of Matthew, and the Didache: Their Place in Early Christian Literature." In *Matthew, James, and Didache: Three Related Documents in Their Jewish and Christian Settings*, edited by Huub van de Sandt and Jürgen K. Zangenberg, 289–314. SBLSS 45. Atlanta: Society of Biblical Literature, 2008.

Hartman, Av Lars. "Obligatory Baptism—But Why? On Baptism in the Didache and in the Shepherd of Hermas." *SEÅ* 59 (1994) 127–43.

Hays, Richard B. *Echoes of Scripture in the Gospels*. Waco, TX: Baylor University Press, 2016.

———. *Echoes of Scripture in the Letters of Paul*. New Haven, CT: Yale University Press, 1989.

Hellholm, David. *Das Visionenbuch des Hermas als Apokalypse: Formgeschichtliche und texttheoretische Studien zu einer literarischen Gattung. Methodologische Vorüberlegungen und makrostrukturelle Textanalyse*. ConBNT 13.1. Lund: CWK Gleerup, 1980.

Henderson, Ian H. "Didache and Orality in Synoptic Comparison." *JBL* 111 (1992) 283–306.

Hengel, Martin. *The Four Gospels and the One Gospel of Jesus Christ: An Investigation of the Collection and Origin of the Canonical Gospels.* Translated by John Bowden. Harrisburg, PA: Trinity, 2000.

Hildebrand, Stephen M. "The Trinity in the Ante-Nicene Fathers." In *The Oxford Handbook of the Trinity*, 95–108. Oxford: Oxford University Press, 2011.

Hilgenfeld, Adolf. *Evangeliorum secundum Hebraeos, secundum Petrum, secundum Aegyptios, Matthiae traditionum, Petri et Pauli praedicationis et actuum, Petri apocalypseos, Didascaliae apostolorum antiquioris quae supersunt.* 2nd ed. Novum Testamentum extra canonem receptum, Part 4. Leipzig: Weigel, 1884.

Hill, Charles E. *Regnum Caelorum: Patterns of Millennial Thought in Early Christianity.* 2nd ed. Grand Rapids: Eerdmans, 2001.

Hitchcock, Roswell D., and Francis Brown. Διδαχὴ Τῶν Δωδέκα Ἀποστόλων: *Teaching of the Twelve Apostles.* 2nd ed. New York: Scribner's Sons, 1885.

Hogg, Michael A., and Craig McGarty. "Self-Categorization and Social Identity." In *Social Identity Theory: Constructive and Critical Advances*, edited by Dominic Abrams and Michael A. Hogg, 10–27. New York: Springer-Verlag, 1990.

Hollander, H. W., and M. de Jonge. *The Testaments of the Twelve Patriarchs: A Commentary.* SVTP 8. Leiden: Brill, 1985.

Holmes, Michael W., ed. *The Apostolic Fathers: Greek Texts and English Translations.* 3rd ed. Grand Rapids: Baker Academic, 2007.

Horn, Cornelia B., and John W. Martens. *"Let the Little Children Come to Me": Childhood and Children in Early Christianity.* Washington, DC: Catholic University of America Press, 2009.

Horner, G. "A New Papyrus Fragment of the *Didache* in Coptic." *JTS* 25 (1924) 225–31.

———. *The Statutes of the Apostles or Canones Ecclesiastici.* London: Williams & Norgate, 1904.

Horst, P. W. van der. *The Sentences of Pseudo-Phocylides: With Introduction and Commentary.* SVTP 4. Leiden: Brill, 1978.

Hubbard, Thomas K., ed. *Homosexuality in Greece and Rome: A Sourcebook of Basic Documents.* Berkeley: University of California Press, 2003.

Huizenga, Leroy A. "The Old Testament in the New, Intertextuality and Allegory." *JSNT* 38 (2015) 17–35.

Hultin, Jeremy F. *The Ethics of Obscene Speech in Early Christianity and Its Environment.* NovTSup 128. Leiden: Brill, 2008.

Hunt, A. S. *Oxyrhynchus Papyri.* Vol. 15. London: Oxford University Press, 1922.

Hvalvik, Reidar, and Karl Olav Sandnes, eds. *Early Christian Prayer and Identity Formation.* WUNT 336. Tübingen: Mohr Siebeck, 2014.

———. "Early Christian Prayer and Identity Formation: Introducing the Project." In *Early Christian Prayer and Identity Formation*, edited by Hvalvik Reidar and Karl Olav Sandnes, 1–12. WUNT 336. Tübingen: Mohr Siebeck, 2014.

Instone-Brewer, David. "Temple and Priesthood." In *The World of the New Testament: Cultural, Social, and Historical Contexts*, edited by Joel B. Green and Lee Martin McDonald, 197–206. Grand Rapids: Baker Academic, 2013.

Jefford, Clayton N. "An Ancient Witness to the Apostolic Decree of Acts 15?" *PEGLMBS* 10 (1990) 204–13.

———. *The Apostolic Fathers and the New Testament.* Peabody, MA: Hendrickson, 2006.

———. "Authority and Perspective in the Didache." In *The Didache: A Missing Piece of the Puzzle in Early Christianity*, edited by Jonathan A. Draper and Clayton N. Jefford, 33–58. ECL 14. Atlanta: Society of Biblical Literature, 2015.

———. "Conflict at Antioch: Ignatius and the Didache at Odds." StPatr 36 (2001) 262–69.

———. "Did Ignatius of Antioch Know the *Didache*?" In *The Didache in Context: Essays on Its Text, History, and Transmission*, edited by Clayton N. Jefford, 330–51. NovTSup 77. Leiden: Brill, 1995.

———. "Didache." In *Eerdmans Dictionary of the Bible*, edited by David Noel Freedman, 345–46. Grand Rapids: Eerdmans, 2000.

———. "Didache." In *The New Westminster Dictionary of Church History*, edited by Robert Benedetto, 195–96. Louisville, KY: Westminster John Knox, 2008.

———. "Didache." In *Dictionary of Scripture and Ethics*, edited by Joel B. Green, 228–29. Grand Rapids: Baker Academic, 2011.

———. *Didache: The Teaching of the Twelve Apostles*. ECA 5. Salem, OR: Polebridge, 2013.

———. "The Didache and Eucharist: Signs of Community?" In *Early Christian Communities between Ideal and Reality*, edited by Mark Grundeken and Joseph Verheyden, 29–49. WUNT 342. Tübingen: Mohr Siebeck, 2015.

———, ed. *The Didache in Context: Essays on Its Text, History, and Transmission*. NovTSup 77. Leiden: Brill, 1995.

———. "Household Codes and Conflict in the Early Church." StPatr 31 (1997) 121–27.

———. "Introduction: Dynamics, Methodologies, and Progress in Didache Studies." In *The Didache: A Missing Piece of the Puzzle in Early Christianity*, edited by Jonathan A. Draper and Clayton N. Jefford, 1–13. ECL 14. Atlanta: Society of Biblical Literature, 2015.

———. "Locating the *Didache*." Forum 3 (2014) 39–68.

———. "The Milieu of Matthew, the Didache, and Ignatius of Antioch: Agreements and Differences." In *Matthew and the Didache: Two Documents from the Same Jewish-Christian Milieu?* edited by Huub van de Sandt, 35–47. Minneapolis, MN: Fortress, 2005.

———. "Presbyters in the Community of the *Didache*." StPat 21 (1989) 122–28.

———. "Prophecy and Prophetism in the Apostolic Fathers." In *Prophets and Prophecy in Jewish and Early Christian Literature*, edited by Joseph Verheyden, Korinna Zamfir, and Tobias Nicklas, 295–316. WUNT 2/286. Tübingen: Mohr Siebeck, 2010.

———. *Reading the Apostolic Fathers: A Student's Introduction*. 2nd ed. Grand Rapids: Baker Academic, 2012.

———. "Reflections on the Role of Jewish Christianity in Second-Century Antioch." In *Le Judéo-Christianisme dans tous ses États*, edited by Simon C. Mimouni, 147–67. Paris: Les Éditions Du Cerf, 2001.

———. *The Sayings of Jesus in the Teaching of the Twelve Apostles*. VCSup 11. Leiden: Brill, 1989.

———. "Social Locators as a Bridge between the Didache and Matthew." In *Trajectories through the New Testament and the Apostolic Fathers*, edited by Andrew F. Gregory and Christopher M. Tuckett, 245–64. Oxford: Oxford University Press, 2005

———. "Tradition and Witness in Antioch: Acts 15 and Didache 6." PRSt 19 (1992) 409–19.

---. "Tradition and Witness in Antioch: Acts 15 and Didache 6." In *Perspectives on Contemporary New Testament Questions: Essays in Honor of T. C. Smith*, edited by Edgar V. McKnight, 75–89. Lewiston, NY: Mellen, 1992.

---. "The Wisdom of Sirach and the Glue of the Matthew-Didache Tradition." In *Intertextuality in the Second Century*, edited by D. Jeffrey Bingham and Clayton N. Jefford, 8–23. BibAC 11. Leiden: Brill, 2016.

Jefford, Clayton N., and Stephen J. Patterson. "A Note on *Didache* 12.2a (Coptic)." *SecCent* 7 (1989) 65–75.

Johanson, Bruce C. *To All the Brethren: A Text-Linguistic and Rhetorical Approach to 1 Thessalonians*. ConBNT 16. Stockholm: Almqvist & Wiksell International, 1987.

Jones, F. Stanley, and Paul A. Mirecki. "Considerations of the Coptic Papyrus of the *Didache* (British Library Oriental Manuscript 9271)." In *The Didache in Context: Essays on Its Text, History, and Transmission*, edited by Clayton N. Jefford, 37–46. NovTSup 77. Leiden: Brill, 1995.

Jonge, Marinus de. "Christian Influence in the Testaments of the Twelve Patriarchs." *NovT* 4 (1960) 182–235.

---. "Christian Influence in the Testaments of the Twelve Patriarchs." In *Studies on the Testaments of the Twelve Patriarchs: Text and Interpretation*, edited by M. de Jonge, 193–246. SVTP 3. Leiden: Brill, 1975.

---. "Once More: Christian Influence on the Testaments of the Twelve Patriarchs." *NovT* 5 (1962) 311–19.

---. *The Testaments of the Twelve Patriarchs: A Critical Edition of the Greek Text*. PVTG. Leiden: Brill, 1978.

---. "The Testaments of the Twelve Patriarchs and the 'Two Ways.'" In *Biblical Traditions in Transmission: Essays in Honour of Michael A. Knibb*, edited by Charlotte Hempel and Judith M. Lieu, 179–194. JSJSup 111. Leiden: Brill, 2006.

Kahlos, Maijastina. "The Early Church." In *The Cambridge History of Magic and Witchcraft in the West: From Antiquity to the Present*, edited by David Collins S.J., 148–82. Cambridge: Cambridge University Press, 2015.

Kamlah, Ehrhard. *Die Form der katalogischen Paränese im Neuen Testament*. WUNT 7. Tübingen: Mohr Siebeck, 1964.

Kannengiesser, Charles, ed. *Handbook of Patristic Exegesis*. 2 vols. BibAC 2. Atlanta: Society of Biblical Literature, 2006.

Kelhoffer, James A. *Conceptions of "Gospel" and Legitimacy in Early Christianity*. WUNT 324. Tübingen: Mohr Siebeck, 2014.

---. "'How Soon a Book' Revisited: ΕΥΑΓΓΕΛΙΟΝ as a Reference to 'Gospel' Materials in the First Half of the Second Century." *ZNW* 95 (2004) 1–34.

Khomych, Taras. "The Admonition to Assemble Together in *Didache* 16.2 Reappraised." *VC* 61 (2007) 121–41.

---. "Another Gospel: Exploring Early Christian Diversity with Paul and the Didache." In *The Didache: A Missing Piece of the Puzzle in Early Christianity*, edited by Jonathan A. Draper and Clayton N. Jefford, 455–76. ECL 14. Atlanta: Society of Biblical Literature, 2015.

---. "'If Anyone Is Holy . . .': Didache 10:6 Reconsidered." In *Your Sun Shall Never Set Again, and Your Moon Shall Wane No More: Essays in Honor of Fr. Alexander Nadson on the Occasion of His Eightieth Birthday and Fiftieth Anniversary of His Priesthood*, edited by I. Dubianetskaya, A. McMillin, and H. Sahanovic, 517–24. Minsk, Belarus: Technalohija, 2009.

———. "The Motif of Gathering in Didache 14 Reconsidered." StPatr 45 (2010) 297–302.

———. "Perfection in the Didache: Ethical Objective or Eschatological Hope?" StPatr 51 (2011) 3–13.

Kloppenborg, John S. "*Didache* 1.1—6.1, James, Matthew, and the Torah." In *Trajectories through the New Testament and the Apostolic Fathers*, edited by Andrew Gregory and Christopher Tuckett, 193–221. NTAF. Oxford: Oxford University Press, 2005.

———. "Didache 16 6–8 and Special Matthaean Tradition." *ZNW* 70 (1979) 54–67.

———. "Poverty and Piety in Matthew, James, and the Didache." In *Matthew, James, and Didache: Three Related Documents in Their Jewish and Christian Settings*, edited by Huub van de Sandt and Jürgen K. Zangenberg, 201–32. SBLSS 45. Atlanta: Society of Biblical Literature, 2008.

———. "The Sayings of Jesus in the Didache." MA thesis, University of St. Michael's College, 1976.

———. "The Transformation of Moral Exhortation in *Didache* 1–5." In *The Didache in Context: Essays on Its Text, History, and Transmission*, edited by Clayton N. Jefford, 88–109. NovTSup 77. Leiden: Brill, 1995.

———. "The Use of the Synoptics or Q in *Did.* 1:3b—2:1." In *Matthew and the Didache: Two Documents from the Same Jewish-Christian Milieu?* edited by Huub van de Sandt, 105–29. Minneapolis, MN: Fortress, 2005.

Knapp, Henry M. "Melito's Use of Scripture in *Peri Pascha*: Second-Century Typology." *VC* 54 (2000) 343–74.

Knight, Mark. "*Wirkungsgeschichte*, Reception History, Reception Theory." *JSNT* 33 (2010) 137–46.

Knopf, D. Rudolf. *Die Lehre der Zwölf Apostel dei Zwei Clemensbriefe*. AV 1. Tübingen: Mohr Siebeck, 1920.

Koch, Dietrich-Alex. "Die Debatte über den Titel der Didache." *ZNW* 105 (2014) 264–88.

———. "Eucharistic Meal and Eucharistic Prayers in Didache 9 and 10." *ST* 64 (2010) 77–96.

———. "Die Eucharistischen Gebete von Didache 9 und 10 und das Rätsel von Didache 10:6." In *Jesus, Paul, and Early Christianity: Studies in Honour of Henk Jan de Jonge*, edited by Rieuwerd Buitenwerf, Harm Hollander, and Johannes Tromp, 195–211. NovTSup 130. Leiden: Brill, 2008.

Kraft, Robert A. *Barnabas and the Didache*. Edited by R. M. Grant. AF 3. New York: Thomas Nelson & Sons, 1965.

———. "Early Developments of the 'Two-Ways Tradition(s),' in Retrospect." In *For a Later Generation: The Transformation of Tradition in Israel, Early Judaism, and Early Christianity*, edited by Randal A. Argall, Beverly A. Bow, and Rodney A. Werline, 136–43. Harrisburg, PA: Trinity, 2000.

Kruger, Michael J. *Canon Revisited: Establishing the Origins and Authority of the New Testament Books*. Wheaton, IL: Crossway, 2012.

Kurek-Chomycz, Dominika A. "The Sweet Scent of the Gospel in the Didache and in Second Corinthians: Some Comments on Two Recent Interpretations of the *Stinoufi* Prayer in the Coptic Did. 10.8." *VC* 63 (2009) 323–44.

Kvalbein, Hans. "The Lord's Prayer and the Eucharist Prayers in the *Didache*." In *Early Christian Prayer and Identity Formation*, edited by Reidar Hvalvik and Karl Olav Sandnes, 233–66. WUNT 336. Tübingen: Mohr Siebeck, 2014.

Ladd, George Eldon. "The Eschatology of the Didache." PhD diss., Harvard University, 1949.
Lanfer, Peter Thacher. *Remembering Eden: The Reception History of Genesis 3:22-24*. Oxford: Oxford University Press, 2012.
Larsen, Matthew David. "Addressing the Elephant That's Not in the Room: Comparing the Eucharistic Prayers in Didache 9-10 and the Last Supper." *Neot* 45 (2011) 252-74.
Larsen, Matthew, and Michael Svigel. "The First Century Two Ways Catechesis and Hebrews 6:1-6." In *The Didache: A Missing Piece of the Puzzle in Early Christianity*, edited by Jonathan A. Draper and Clayton N. Jefford, 477-96. ECL 14. Atlanta: Society of Biblical Literature, 2015.
Lawrence, Jonathan. *Washing in Water: Trajectories of Ritual Bathing in the Hebrew Bible and Second Temple Literature*. ABib 23. Atlanta: Society of Biblical Literature, 2006.
Layton, Bentley. "The Sources, Dates and Transmission of Didache 1:3b—2:1." *HTR* 61 (1968) 343-83.
Leonhardt-Balzer, Jutta. "Dualism." In *The Eerdmans Dictionary of Early Judaism*, edited by John J. Collins and Daniel C. Harlow, 553-56. Grand Rapids: Eerdmans, 2010.
Levinsohn, Stephen H. *Discourse Features of New Testament Greek: A Coursebook on the Information Structure of New Testament Greek*. 2nd ed. Dallas: SIL International, 2000.
Lieb, Michael, Emma Mason, and Jonathan Roberts, eds. *The Oxford Handbook of the Reception History of the Bible*. Oxford: Oxford University Press, 2011.
Lindemann, Andreas. "Die Endzeitrede in Didache 16 und die Jesus-Apokalypse in Matthäus 24-25." In *Sayings of Jesus: Canonical and Non-Canonical: Essays in Honour of Tjitze Baarda*, edited by William L. Petersen, Johan S. Vos, and Henk J. De Jonge, 155-74. NovTSup 89. Leiden: Brill, 1997.
Lindemann, Andreas, and Henning Paulsen, eds. *Die Apostolischen Väter: Griechisch-deutsche Parallelausgabe*. Tübingen: Mohr, 1992.
Llewelyn, Stephen. "Mt 7:6a: Mistranslation or Interpretation?" *NovT* 31 (1989) 97-103.
Luz, Ulrich. *Matthew 1-7*. Translated by James E. Crouch. Hermeneia. Minneapolis, MN: Fortress, 2007.
———. *Matthew 8-20*. Edited by Helmut Koester. Translated by James E. Crouch. Hermeneia. Minneapolis, MN: Fortress, 2001.
Macaskill, Grant. *Revealed Wisdom and Inaugurated Eschatology in Ancient Judaism and Early Christianity*. JSJSup 115. Leiden: Brill, 2007.
Marcus, Joel. "The *Testaments of the Twelve Patriarchs* and the *Didascalia Apostolorum*: A Common Jewish Christian Milieu?" *JTS* 61 (2010) 596-626.
Massaux, Édouard. *The Influence of the Gospel of Saint Matthew on Christian Literature before Saint Irenaeus: Book 3 The Apologists and the Didache*. Translated by Norman J. Belval and Suzanne Hecht. NGS, 5/3. Macon, GA: Mercer University Press, 1993.
McGowan, Andrew. "Eucharist and Sacrifice: Cultic Tradition and Transformation in Early Christian Ritual Meals." In *Meals and Religious Identity in Early Christianity*, edited by Matthias Klinghardt and Hal Taussig, 191-206. TANZ 56. Tübingen: Francke, 2012.

McKenna, Margaret Mary. "'The Two Ways' in Jewish and Christian Writings of the Greco-Roman Period: A Study of the Form of Repentance Parenesis." PhD diss., University of Pennsylvania, 1981.

Milavec, Aaron. The Birth of Purgatory: Evidence of the Didache." PEGLMBS 12 (1992) 91–104.

———. *The Didache: Faith, Hope, & Life of the Earliest Christian Communities, 50–70 C.E.* New York: Newman, 2003.

———. *The Didache: Text, Translation, Analysis, and Commentary*. Collegeville, MN: Liturgical, 2003.

———. "Distinguishing True and False Prophets: The Protective Wisdom of the Didache." *JECS* 2 (1994) 117–36.

———. "The Economic Safety Net in the Didache Community." *PEGLMBS* 16 (1996) 73–84.

———. "The Pastoral Genius of the Didache: An Analytical Translation and Commentary." In *Religious Writings and Religious Systems: Systemic Analysis of Holy Books in Christianity, Islam, Buddhism, Greco-Roman Religions, Ancient Israel, and Judaism*, edited by Jacob Neusner, Ernest S. Frerichs, and A. J. Levine, 2:89–125. Atlanta: Scholars, 1989.

———. "The Purifying Confession of Failings Required by the *Didache*'s Eucharistic Sacrifice." *BTB* 33 (2003) 64–76.

———. "A Rejoinder." *JECS* 13 (2005) 519–23.

———. "The Saving Efficacy of the Burning Process in *Didache* 16.5." In *The Didache in Context: Essays on Its Text, History, and Transmission*, edited by Clayton N. Jefford, 131–55. NovTSup 77. Leiden: Brill, 1995.

———. "The Social Setting of 'Turning the Other Cheek' and 'Loving One's Enemies' in Light of the *Didache*." *BTB* 25 (1995) 131–43.

———. "Synoptic Tradition in the Didache Revisited." *JECS* 11 (2003) 443–80.

———. "When, Why, and for Whom Was the Didache Created? Insights into the Social and Historical Setting of the Didache Communities." In *Matthew and the Didache: Two Documents from the Same Jewish-Christian Milieu?* edited by Huub van de Sandt, 63–84. Minneapolis, MN: Fortress, 2005.

———. "A Window on Gentile Christianity before the Written Gospel." *FRARL* 18 (June 2005) 7–16.

Mitchell, Margaret. "Concerning ΠΕΡΙ ΔΕ in 1 Corinthians." *NovT* 31 (1989) 229–56.

Mitchell, Nathan. "Baptism in the Didache." In *The Didache in Context: Essays on Its Text, History, and Transmission*, edited by Clayton N. Jefford, 226–55. NovTSup 77. New York: Brill, 1995.

Morris, Leon. *The Gospel according to Matthew*. PNTC. Grand Rapids: Eerdmans, 1992.

Moss, Candida R. *Ancient Christian Martyrdom: Diverse Practices, Theologies, and Traditions*. New Haven, CT: Yale University Press, 2012.

———. "Nailing Down and Tying Up: Lessons in Intertextual Impossibility from the Martyrdom of Polycarp." *VC* 67 (2013) 117–36.

Moyise, Steve. "Intertextuality and the Study of the Old Testament in the New Testament." In *The Old Testament in the New Testament: Essays in Honour of J. L. North*, edited by Steve Moyise, 14–41. JSNTSup 189. Sheffield, UK: Sheffield Academic, 2000.

Myllykoski, Matti. "Without Decree: Pagan Sacrificial Meat and the Early History of the Didache." In *The Didache: A Missing Piece of the Puzzle in Early Christianity*, edited by Jonathan A. Draper and Clayton N. Jefford, 429–53. ECL 14. Atlanta: Society of Biblical Literature Press, 2015.

Nickelsburg, George W. E. "Seeking the Origins of the Two-Ways Tradition in Jewish and Christian Ethical Texts." In *A Multiform Heritage: Studies on Early Judaism and Christianity in Honor of Robert A. Kraft*, edited by Benjamin G. Wright, 95–108. HS 24. Atlanta: Scholars Press, 1999.

Niederwimmer, Kurt. *Die Didache*. KAV 1. Göttingen: Vandenhoeck & Ruprecht, 1989.

———. *The Didache: A Commentary*. Translated by Linda M. Maloney. 2nd ed. Hermeneia. Minneapolis, MN: Augsburg Fortress, 1998.

———. "Der Didachist und seine Quellen." In *The Didache in Context: Essays on Its Text, History, and Transmission*, edited by Clayton N. Jefford, 15–36. NovTSup 77. Leiden: Brill, 1995.

———. "Der Didachist und seine Quellen." In *Quaestiones theologicae: Gesammelte Aufsätze*, edited by Wilhem Pratscher and Markus Öhler, 243–66. BZNW 90. Berlin: de Gruyter, 1998.

———. "Doctrina apostolorum (Cod. Mellic. 597)." In *Quaestiones theologicae: Gesammelte Aufsätze*, edited by Wilhem Pratscher and Markus Öhler, 88–94. BZNW 90. Berlin: de Gruyter, 1998.

———. "Textprobleme der Didache." WS 16 (1982) 114–30.

Nienhuis, David R. *Not by Paul Alone: The Formation of the Catholic Epistle Collection and the Christian Canon*. Waco, TX: Baylor University Press, 2007.

Nikander, Perttu. "The Sectio Evangelica (Didache 1.3b–2.1) and Performance." In *The Didache: A Missing Piece of the Puzzle in Early Christianity*, edited by Jonathan A. Draper and Clayton N. Jefford, 287–310. ECL 14. Atlanta: Society of Biblical Literature, 2015.

Nolland, John. *The Gospel of Matthew: A Commentary on the Greek Text*. NICNT. Grand Rapids: Eerdmans, 2005.

O'Keefe, John J., and Russell R. Reno. *Sanctified Vision: An Introduction to Early Christian Interpretation of the Bible*. Baltimore, MD: John Hopkins University Press, 2005.

O'Loughlin, Thomas. *The Didache: A Window on the Earliest Christians*. Grand Rapids: Baker Academic, 2010.

———. "The Missionary Strategy of the Didache." *Transformation* 28 (2011) 77–92.

Osborne, Grant R. *Matthew*. Vol. 1. ECNT. Grand Rapids: Zondervan, 2010.

Osiek, Carolyn. *Shepherd of Hermas*. Hermeneia. Minneapolis, MN: Fortress, 1999.

Overman, J. Andrew. "Problems with Pluralism in Second Temple Judaism: Matthew, James, and the Didache in Their Jewish-Roman Milieu." In *Matthew, James, and Didache: Three Related Documents in Their Jewish and Christian Settings*, edited by Huub van de Sandt and Jürgen K. Zangenberg, 259–70. SBLSS 45. Atlanta: Society of Biblical Literature, 2008.

Páez, Darío, Christina Martínex-Taboada, Juan José Arróspide, Patricia Insúa, and Sabino Ayestarán. "Constructing Social Identity: The Role of Status, Collective Values, Collective Self-Esteem, Perception and Social Behaviour." In *Social Identity: International Perspectives*, edited by Stephen Worchel, J. Francisco Morales, Darío Páez, and Jean-Claude Deschamps, 211–29. London: Sage, 1998.

Paget, James Carleton. "The Interpretation of the Bible in the Second Century." In *From the Beginnings to 600*, edited by James Carleton Paget and Joachim Schaper, 1:549–83. The New Cambridge History of the Bible. Cambridge: Cambridge University Press, 2013.

Palmer, David Robert. "The Teaching of the Twelve Apostles: A Critical Greek Edition with Footnotes Covering Textual Variants." Accessed December 29 2017. http://www.bibletranslation.ws/trans/didache.pdf.

Pardee, Nancy. "The Curse That Saves (*Didache* 16.5)." In *The Didache in Context: Essays on Its Text, History, and Transmission*, edited by Clayton N. Jefford, 156–76. NovTSup 77. Leiden: Brill, 1995.

———. *The Genre and Development of the Didache*. WUNT 2/339. Tübingen: Mohr Siebeck, 2012.

———. "Visualizing the Christian Community at Antioch: The Window of the Didache." *Forum* 3 (2014) 69–90.

Pardee, Nancy D. "Didache." Edited by Dale C. Allison Jr., Hans-Josef Klauck, Volker Leppin, and Choon-Leong Seow. *Encyclopedia of the Bible and Its Reception*. 6. Berlin: De Gruyter, 2013.

Parris, David Paul. *Reception Theory and Biblical Hermeneutics*. PTMS. Eugene, OR: Pickwick, 2009.

Patterson, Stephen J. "Didache 11–13: The Legacy of Radical Itinerancy in Early Christianity." In *The Didache in Context: Essays on Its Text, History, and Transmission*, edited by Clayton N. Jefford, 313–29. NovTSup 77. Leiden: Brill, 1995.

Pelikan, Jaroslav. *Credo: Historical and Theological Guide to Creeds and Confessions of Faith in the Christian Tradition*. New Haven, CT: Yale University Press, 2003.

Pennington, Jonathan T. *Heaven and Earth in the Gospel of Matthew*. NovTSup 126. Leiden: Brill, 2007.

———. *Reading the Gospels Wisely: A Narrative and Theological Introduction*. Grand Rapids: Baker Academic, 2012.

Pennington, Jonathan T., and Sean M. McDonough, eds. *Cosmology and New Testament Theology*. LNTS 355. London: T. & T. Clark, 2008.

Peradse, Gregor. "Die »Lehre der Zwölf Apostel« in der Georgischen Überlieferung." *ZNW* 31 (1932) 111–16.

Percy, William Armstrong, III. *Pederasty and Pedagogy in Archaic Greece*. Champaign, IL: University of Illinois Press, 1998.

Périclès-Pierre, Joannou, ed. *Fonti: Discipline générale antique (IVe–IXe S.)*. Rome: Grottaferrata, 1963.

Petersen, William L. "Patristic Biblical Quotations and Method: Four Changes to Lightfoot's Edition of *Second Clement*." *VC* 60 (2006) 389–419.

Peterson, David. *Hebrews and Perfection: An Examination of the Concept of Perfection in the "Epistle to the Hebrews."* SNTSMS 47. Cambridge: Cambridge University Press, 1982.

Pitts, Andrew W. "Philosophical and Epistolary Contexts for Pauline Paraenesis." In *Paul and the Ancient Letter Form*, edited by Stanely E. Porter and Sean A. Adams, 6:269–306. PS. Leiden: Brill, 2010.

Prostmeier, Ferdinand R. *Der Barnabasbrief*. KAV 8. Göttingen: Vandenhoeck & Ruprecht, 1999.

Quarles, Charles. *Sermon on the Mount: Restoring Christ's Message to the Modern Church*. Vol. 11. NAC Studies in Bible & Theology. Nashville, TN: B&H, 2011.

Radner, Ephraim. *Time and the Word: Figural Reading of the Christian Scriptures*. Grand Rapids: Eerdmans, 2016.

Reitzenstein, Richard. "Ps.-Cyprian, *De centesima, de sexagesima, de tricesima*: Eine frühchristliche Schrift von den dreierlei Früchten des Lebens." *ZNW* 15 (1914) 60–90.

Rhodes, James N. *The Epistle of Barnabas and the Deuteronomic Tradition: Polemics, Paraenesis, and the Legacy of the Golden-Calf Incident*. WUNT 2/188. Tübingen: Mohr Siebeck, 2004.

———. "The Two Ways Tradition in the *Epistle of Barnabas*: Revisiting an Old Question." *CBQ* 73 (2011) 797–816.

Riggs, John W. "From Gracious Table to Sacramental Elements: The Tradition-History of Didache 9 and 10." *SecCent* 4 (1984) 83–101.

———. "The Sacred Food of *Didache* 9–10 and Second Century Ecclesiologies." In *The Didache in Context: Essays on Its Text, History, and Transmission*, edited by Clayton N. Jefford, 256–83. NovTSup 77. New York: Brill, 1995.

Roberts, Jonathan, and Christopher Rowland. "Introduction." *JSNT* 33 (2010) 131–36.

Robinson, J. Armitage. *Barnabas, Hermas and the Didache*. London: SPCK, 1920.

Rordorf, Willy. "Τὰ ἅγια τοῖς ἁγίοις." *Irén* 72 (1999) 346–64.

———. "Does the Didache Contain Jesus Tradition Independently of the Synoptic Gospels?" In *Jesus and the Oral Gospel Tradition*, edited by Henry Wansbrough, 394–423. JSNTSup 64. Sheffield, UK: Sheffield Academic, 1991.

———. "La *Didachè* en 1999." *StPatr* 36 (2001) 293–99.

———. "Die Mahlgebete in Didache Kap. 9–10: Ein Neuer Status Quaestionis." *VC* 51 (1997) 229–46.

———. "Le problème de la transmission textuelle de Didachè." In *Überlieferungsgeschichtliche Untersuchungen*, edited by F. Paschke, 499–513. TUGAL 125. Berlin: Akademie-Verlag, 1981.

Rordorf, Willy, and André Tuilier. *La Doctrine des Douze Apôtres (Didachè): Introduction, Texte Critique, Traduction, Notes, Appendice, Annexe et Index*. 2nd ed. SC 248. Paris: Cerf, 1978.

Rothschild, Clare K. *New Essays on the Apostolic Fathers*. WUNT 375. Tübingen: Mohr Siebeck, 2017.

Rouwhorst, Gerard. "Didache 9–10: A Litmus Test for the Research on Early Christian Liturgy Eucharist." In *Matthew and the Didache: Two Documents from the Same Jewish-Christian Milieu?* edited by Huub van de Sandt, 143–56. Minneapolis, MN: Fortress, 2005.

Runge, Steven E. *Discourse Grammar of the Greek New Testament: A Practical Introduction for Teaching and Exegesis*. Peabody, MA: Hendrickson, 2010.

Sabatier, Paul. Διδαχὴ τῶν δωδέκα ἀποστόλων: *La Didache ou l'Enseignement des douze apôtres*. Paris: Fischbacher, 1885.

Schaff, Philip. *The Oldest Church Manual Called the* Teaching of the Twelve Apostles. New York: Funk & Wagnalls, 1885.

Schiffman, Lawrence H., and James C. VanderKam. "Preface." In *Encyclopedia of the Dead Sea Scrolls*, edited by Lawrence H. Schiffman and James C. VanderKam, 1:vii–xiv. Oxford: Oxford University Press, 2000.

Schmidt, Carl. "Das koptische Didache-Fragment des British Museum." *ZNW* 23 (1925) 81–99.

Schöllgen, Georg. "The Didache as Church Order: An Examination of the Purpose for the Composition of the Didache and its Consequences for Interpretation." In

*The Didache in Modern Research*, edited by Jonathan A. Draper, 43–71. AGJU 37. Leiden: Brill, 1996.

———. "Die Didache als Kirchenordnung: Zur Frage des Abfassungszweckes und seinen Konsequenzen für die Interpretation." *JAC* 29 (1986) 5–26.

———. "Die Didache—ein frühes Zeugnis für Landgemeinden?" *ZNW* 76 (1985) 140–43.

———. "Didache: Zwölf-Apostel-Lehre." In *Didache. Zwuolf-Apostel-Lehre/Traditio Apostolica. Apostolische Überlieferung*, edited by Georg Schöllgen and W. Geerlings, 1:23–139. Fontes Christiani. Freiburg, CH: Herder, 1991.

———. "Wandernde oder seßhafte Lehrer in der Didache?" *BN* 52 (1990) 19–26.

Schröter, Jens. "Jesus Tradition in Matthew, James, and the Didache: Searching for Characteristic Emphases." In *Matthew, James, and Didache: Three Related Documents in Their Jewish and Christian Settings*, edited by Huub van de Sandt and Jürgen K. Zangenberg, 233–55. SBLSS 45. Atlanta: Society of Biblical Literature, 2008.

Schwiebert, Jonathan. *Knowledge and the Coming Kingdom: The Didache's Meal Ritual and Its Place in Early Christianity*. LNTS 373. London: T. & T. Clark, 2008.

———. "Pray 'In This Way': Formalized Speech in Didache 9–10." In *The Didache: A Missing Piece of the Puzzle in Early Christianity*, edited by Jonathan A. Draper and Clayton N. Jefford, 189–207. ECL 14. Atlanta: Society of Biblical Literature, 2015.

Seeliger, Hans Reinhard. "Considerations on the Background and Purpose of the Apocalyptic Conclusion of the Didache." In *The* Didache *in Modern Research*, edited by Jonathan A. Draper, 373–82. AGJU 37. Leiden: Brill, 1996.

———. "Erwägungen zu Hintergrund und Zweck des apostolischen Schlusskapitels der *Didache*." StPatr 21 (1989) 185–92.

Seitz, Christopher R. *Figured Out: Typology and Providence in Christian Scripture*. Louisville, KY: Westminster John Knox, 2001.

Seitz, Oscar J. F. "Antecedents and Signification of the Term ΔΙΨΥΧΟΣ." *JBL* 66 (1947) 211–19.

Skehan, Patrick. "Didache 1,6 and Sirach 12,1." *Bib* 44 (1963) 533–36.

Skinner, Marilyn B. *Sexuality in Greek and Roman Culture*. Malden, MA: Wiley-Blackwell, 2014.

Slee, Michelle. *The Church in Antioch in the First Century CE: Communion and Conflict*. JSNTSup 244. Sheffield, UK: Sheffield Academic, 2003.

Smith, Julien C. H. "The *Epistle of Barnabas* and the Two Ways of Teaching Authority." *VC* 68 (2014) 465–97.

Smith, Murray J. "The Lord Jesus and His Coming in the Didache." In *The Didache: A Missing Piece of the Puzzle in Early Christianity*, edited by Jonathan A. Draper and Clayton N. Jefford, 363–407. ECL 14. Atlanta: Society of Biblical Literature, 2015.

Smith, Zachary B. "Of Firstfruits and Social Fixtures: How Didache 13 Uses Torah to Reform Roman Patronage." *EC* 8 (2017) 251–68.

Stewart, Alistair C. "The Fragment on the Mountain: A Note on Didache 9.4a." *Neot* 49 (2015) 175–88.

———. *The Original Bishops: Office and Order in the First Christian Communities*. Grand Rapids: Baker Academic, 2014.

Stewart-Sykes, Alistair, ed. *On the Two Ways: Life or Death, Light or Darkness: Foundational Texts in the Tradition*. PPS 41. Yonkers, NY: St. Vladimir's Seminary Press, 2011.

———. "Ἀποκύησις Λόγῳ Ἀληθείας: Paraenesis and Baptism in Matthew, James, and the Didache." In *Matthew, James, and Didache: Three Related Documents in Their Jewish and Christian Settings*, edited by Huub van de Sandt and Jürgen K. Zangenberg, 341–59. SBLSS 45. Atlanta: Society of Biblical Literature, 2008.

Stowers, Stanley K. *Letter Writing in Greco-Roman Antiquity*. LEC. Philadelphia: Westminster, 1986.

Stuckenbruck, Loren T. *The Myth of Rebellious Angels: Studies in Second Temple Judaism and New Testament Texts*. WUNT 335. Tübingen: Mohr Siebeck, 2014.

Suggs, M. Jack. "The Christian Two Ways Tradition: Its Antiquity, Form, and Function." In *Studies in New Testament and Early Christian Literature: Essays in Honor of Allen P. Wikgren*, edited by David Edward Aune, 60–74. NovTSup 33. Leiden: Brill, 1972.

Syreeni, Kari. "The Sermon on the Mount and the Two Ways Teaching of the Didache." In *Matthew and the Didache: Two Documents from the Same Jewish-Christian Milieu?* edited by Huub van de Sandt, 87–103. Minneapolis, MN: Fortress, 2005.

Talbert, Charles H. *Matthew*. PCNT. Grand Rapids: Baker Academic, 2010.

Taylor, Charles. *The Teaching of the Twelve Apostles with Illustrations from the Talmud*. Cambridge: Deighton Bell, 1886.

Theissen, Gerd. *The First Followers of Jesus: A Sociological Analysis of Earliest Christianity*. Translated by J. Bowden. London: SCM, 1978.

Thomas, Samuel I. "Living Water by the Dead Sea: Some Water Metaphors in the Qumran Scrolls." In *Thinking of Water in the Early Second Temple Period*, edited by Ehud Ben Zvi and Christoph Levin, 375–92. BZAW 461. Berlin: De Gruyter, 2014.

Tidwell, Neville L. A. "Didache XIV:1 (ΚΑΤΑ ΚΥΡΙΑΚΗΝ ΔΕ ΚΥΡΙΟΥ) Revisited." *VC* 53 (1999) 197–207.

Tomson, Peter J. "The Didache, Matthew, and Barnabas as Sources for Early Second Century Jewish and Christian History." In *Jews and Christians in the First and Second Centuries: How to Write Their History*, edited by Peter J. Tomson and Joshua Schwartz, 348–82. CRINT 13. Leiden: Brill, 2014.

———. "The Lord's Prayer (Didache 8) at the Faultline of Judaism and Christianity." In *The Didache: A Missing Piece of the Puzzle in Early Christianity*, edited by Jonathan A. Draper and Clayton N. Jefford, 165–87. ECL 14. Atlanta: Society of Biblical Literature, 2015.

Trigg, Joseph. "The Apostolic Fathers and Apologists." In *A History of Biblical Interpretations: The Ancient Period*, edited by Alan J. Hauser and Duane F. Watson, 1:304–33. Grand Rapids: Eerdmans, 2003.

Trobisch, David. *The First Edition of the New Testament*. Oxford: Oxford University Press, 2000.

Tuckett, Christopher M. "The Didache and the Synoptics Once More: A Response to Aaron Milavec." *JECS* 13 (2005) 509–18.

———. "The Didache and the Writings That Later Formed the New Testament." In *The Reception of the New Testament in the Apostolic Fathers*, edited by Andrew F. Gregory and Christopher M. Tuckett, 83–127. Oxford: Oxford University Press, 2005.

———. "Synoptic Tradition in the Didache." In *The New Testament in Early Christianity: La Reception es Éscrits Néotestamentaires Dans Le Christianisme Primitif*, edited by Jean-Marie Sevrin, 197–230. BETL 86. Leuven: Leuven University Press, 1989.

———. "Synoptic Tradition in the Didache." In *The Didache in Modern Research*, edited by Jonathan A. Draper, 92–128. AGJU 37. Leiden: Brill, 1996.

Tuilier, André. "Les charismatique itinérants dans la Didachè et dans l'Évangile de Matthieu." In *Matthew and the Didache: Two Documents from the Same Jewish-Christian-Milieu?* edited by Huub Van de Sandt, 157–72. Minneapolis, MN: Fortress, 2005.

Turner, David L. *Matthew*. BECNT. Grand Rapids: Baker Academic, 2008.

Vagi, David, ed. *Coinage and History of the Roman Empire*. 2 vols. New York: Routledge, 1999.

van de Sandt, Huub. "Baptism and Holiness: Two Requirements Authorizing Participation in the Didache's Eucharist." In *The Didache: A Missing Piece of the Puzzle in Early Christianity*, edited by Jonathan A. Draper and Clayton N. Jefford, 139–64. ECL 14. Atlanta: Society of Biblical Literature, 2015.

———. "'Bearing the Entire Yoke of the Lord': An Explanation of Didache 6:2 in the Light of Matthew 11:28–30." In *The Scriptures of Israel in Jewish and Christian Tradition: Essays in Honour of Maarten J. J. Menken*, edited by Bart J. Koet, Steve Moyise, and Joseph Verheyden, 331–44. NovTSup 148. Leiden: Brill, 2013.

———. "Didache 3,1–6: A Transformation of an Existing Jewish Hortatory Pattern." *JSJ* 23 (1992) 21–41.

———. "The Didache Redefining Its Jewish Identity in View of Gentiles Joining the Community." In Empsychoi Logoi—*Religious Innovations in Antiquity: Studies in Honour of Pieter Willem van der Horst*, edited by Alberdina Houtman, Albert de Jonge, and Magda Misset-van de Weg, 247–65. AJEC 73. Leiden: Brill, 2008.

———. "'Do Not Give What Is Holy to the Dogs' (Did 9:5D and Matt 7:6A): The Eucharistic Food of the Didache in Its Jewish Purity Setting." *VC* 56 (2002) 223–46.

———. "Essentials of Ethics in Matthew and the *Didache*: A Comparison at a Conceptual and Practical Level." In *Early Christian Ethics in Interaction with Jewish and Greco-Roman Contexts*, edited by Jan Willem van Henten and Joseph Verheyden, 243–61. STR 17. Leiden: Brill, 2013.

———. "James 4, 1–4 in the Light of the Jewish Two Ways Tradition 3, 1–6." *Bib* 88 (2007) 38–63.

———. "Law and Ethics in Matthew's Antitheses and James's Letter: A Reorientation of Halakah in Line with the Jewish Two Ways 3:1–6." In *Matthew, James, and Didache: Three Related Documents in Their Jewish and Christian Settings*, edited by Huub van de Sandt and Jürgen K. Zangenberg, 315–38. SBLSS 45. Atlanta: Society of Biblical Literature, 2008.

———. "Matthew and the Didache." In *Matthew and His Christian Contemporaries*, edited by David C. Sim and Boris Repschinski, 123–38. LNTS 333. London: T. & T. Clark, 2008.

———, ed. *Matthew and the Didache: Two Documents from the Same Jewish-Christian Milieu?* Minneapolis, MN: Fortress, 2005.

———. "Two Windows on a Developing Jewish-Christian Reproof Practice: Matt 18:15–17 and *Did.* 15:3." In *Matthew and the Didache: Two Documents from the Same Jewish-Christian Milieu?* edited by Huub van de Sandt, 173–92. Minneapolis, MN: Fortress, 2005.

———. "Why Does the Didache Conceive of the Eucharist as a Holy Meal?" *VC* 65 (2011) 1–20.

van de Sandt, Huub, and David Flusser. *The Didache: Its Jewish Sources and Its Place in Early Judaism and Christianity*. CRINT: Section III Jewish Traditions in Early Christian Literature 5. Minneapolis, MN: Fortress, 2002.

van de Sandt, Huub, and Jürgen K. Zangenberg, eds. *Matthew, James, and Didache: Three Related Documents in Their Jewish and Christian Settings*. SBLSS 45. Atlanta: Society of Biblical Literature, 2008.

van der Horst, P. W. *The Sentences of Pseudo-Phocylides: With Introduction and Commentary*. SVTP 4. Leiden: Brill, 1978.

Vanden Eykel, Eric M. *"But Their Faces Were All Looking Up": Author and Reader in the Protevangelium of James*. RJFTC 1. London: T. & T. Clark, 2016.

Varner, William. "The Didache 'Apocalypse' and Matthew 24." *BSac* 165 (2008) 309–22.

———. "The Didache as a Christian Enchiridion." In *Christian Origins and Greco-Roman Culture: Social and Literary Contexts for the New Testament*, edited by Stanley E. Porter and Andrew W. Pitts, 651–61. ECHC 1. Leiden: Brill, 2013.

———. "The Didache's Use of the Old and New Testaments." *MSJ* 16 (2005) 127–51.

———. "How Did the 'Teaching' Teach? The *Didache* as Catechesis." In *Ancient Education and Early Christianity*, edited by Matthew Ryan Hauge and Andrew W. Pitts, 179–202. LNTS 533. London: T. & T. Clark, 2016.

———. *The Way of the Didache: The First Christian Handbook*. New York: University Press of America, 2007.

Verheyden, Joseph. "Eschatology in the Didache and the Gospel of Matthew." In *Matthew and the Didache: Two Documents from the Same Jewish-Christian Milieu?* edited by Huub van de Sandt, 193–215. Assen: Van Gorcum, 2005.

Vermes, Geza. *The Complete Dead Sea Scrolls in English*. Revised. Penguin Classics. London: Penguin, 2011.

Vogt, Peter. "'One Bread Gathered from Many Pieces' (Did. 9:4): The Career of an Early Christian Allegory." In *Early Christian Voices: In Texts, Traditions, and Symbols Essays in Honor of François Bavon*, edited by David H. Warren, Graham Brock, and David W. Pao, 377–91. BibInt 66. Leiden: Brill, 2003.

Vokes, F. E. *The Riddle of the Didache*. London: SPCK, 1938.

von Harnack, Adolf. *Die Lehre der zwölf Apostel nebst Untersuchungen zur ältesten Geschichte der Kirchenverfassung und des Kirchenrechts*. TUGAL 2 1–2. Leipzig: Hinrichs, 1884.

Vööbus, A. "Regarding the Background of the Liturgical Traditions in the Didache: The Question of Literary Relation between Didache IX,4 and the Fourth Gospel." *VC* 23 (1969) 81–87.

Walker, Joan Hazelden. "Reflections on a New Edition of the Didache." *VC* 35 (1981) 35–42.

Welch, John W. "From the Sermon on the Mount to the Didache." In *The Didache: A Missing Piece of the Puzzle in Early Christianity*, edited by Jonathan A. Draper and Clayton N. Jefford, 335–61. ECL 14. Atlanta: Society of Biblical Literature, 2015.

Wengst, Klaus. *Didache (Apostellehre), Barnabasbrief, Zweiter Klemensbrief, Schrift an Diognet: Eingeleitet, herausgegeben, übertragen und erläutert*. SU 2. München: Kösel-Verlag, 1984.

Weren, Wim J. C. "The Ideal Community According to Matthew, James, and the Didache." In *Matthew, James, and Didache: Three Related Documents in Their Jewish and Christian Settings*, edited by Huub van de Sandt and Jürgen K. Zangenberg, 177–200. SBLSS 45. Atlanta: Society of Biblical Literature, 2008.

Whang, Young Chul. "Paul's Letter Paraenesis." In *Paul and the Ancient Letter Form*, edited by Stanley E. Porter and Sean A. Adams, 6:253–68. PS. Leiden: Brill, 2010.

Wilhite, Shawn J. *"One of Life and One of Death": Apocalypticism and the Didache's Two Ways*. Gogias Studies in Early Christianity and Patristics 70. Piscataway, NJ: Gorgias, 2019.

Williams, Craig A. *Roman Homosexuality*. 2nd ed. Oxford: Oxford University Press, 2010.

Wright, N. T. "The Lord's Prayer as a Paradigm of Christian Prayer." In *Into God's Presence: Prayer in the New Testament*, edited by Richard N. Longenecker, 132–54. Grand Rapids: Eerdmans, 2001.

Yeago, David S. "The New Testament and the Nicene Dogma: A Contribution to the Recovery of Theological Exegesis." *ProEccl* 3 (1994) 152–64.

Young, Frances M. *Biblical Exegesis and the Formation of Christian Culture*. Grand Rapids: Baker Academic, 2002.

———. "Typology." In *Crossing the Boundaries: Essays in Biblical Interpretation in Honour of Michael D. Goulder*, edited by Stanley E. Porter, Paul Joyce, and David E. Orton, 29–48. BibInt 8. Leiden: Brill, 1994.

Ysebaert, Joseph. "The So-Called Coptic Ointment Prayer of Didache 10,8 Once More." *VC* 56 (2002) 1–10.

Zahn, Theodor. *Geschichte des neutestamentlichen Kanons*. 2 vols. Leipzig: Deichert, 1888.

Zangenberg, Jürgen K. "Reconstructing the Social and Religious Milieu of the Didache: Observations and Possible Results." In *Matthew, James, and Didache: Three Related Documents in Their Jewish and Christian Settings*, edited by Huub van de Sandt and Jürgen K. Zangenberg, 43–69. SBLSS 45. Atlanta: Society of Biblical Literature, 2008.

Zetterholm, Magnus. *The Formation of Christianity in Antioch*. London: Routledge, 2003.

Ziegler, Joseph. *Duodecim Prophetae*. VTGAASG 13. Göttingen: Vandenhoeck & Ruprecht, 1984.

———, ed. *Sapientia Iesu Filii Sirach*. VTGAASG 12, 2. Göttingen: Vandenhoeck & Ruprecht, 1980.

# Commentary Index

## Hebrew Bible

### Genesis

| | |
|---|---|
| 3:8 | 100 |
| 5:24 | 100 |
| 6:9 | 100, 159n128 |
| 27:40 | 158 |
| 49:27 | 126 |
| 50:15 | 125 |

### Exodus

| | |
|---|---|
| 12:5 | 159n128 |
| 20 | 75 |
| 20:13–16 | 76 |
| 20:16 | 125 |
| 23:7 | 112 |

### Leviticus

| | |
|---|---|
| 14:5–9 | 169n18 |
| 14:50–53 | 169n18 |
| 19:9–10 | 141 |
| 19:17–18 | 127 |
| 19:18 | 103n14, 125 |
| 21:1–16 | 48n66 |
| 23:22 | 208 |
| 26:13 | 158 |

### Numbers

| | |
|---|---|
| 18:8–32 | 207 |
| 18:12 | 207 |
| 19:17 | 169n18 |

### Deuteronomy

| | |
|---|---|
| 4:2 | 83, 148 |
| 5 | 75 |
| 5:17–20 | 76 |
| 5:20 | 125 |
| 6:5 | 103n14 |
| 6:17–18 | 147 |
| 10:12 | 103n14 |
| 10:19 | 103n14 |
| 12:32 | 83, 148n101 |
| 14:28–29 | 208 |
| 15:4 | 141, 208 |
| 15:7–11 | 114, 208 |
| 15:7–8 | 115, 208 |
| 15:8 | 141 |
| 15:11 | 208 |
| 18:1–8 | 207, 208 |
| 18:3–4 | 207 |
| 18:13 | 159n128 |
| 21:3 | 158 |
| 24:10 | 41 |
| 24:19–22 | 208 |
| 28–30 | 100 |
| 30:19 | 100 |

### Judges

| | |
|---|---|
| 20:26 | 159n128 |
| 21:4 | 159n128 |

### 2 Samuel

| | |
|---|---|
| 22:26 | 159n128 |

## 1 Kings

| | |
|---|---|
| 8:61 | 159n128 |
| 11:4 | 159n128 |
| 15:3 | 159n128 |
| 15:14 | 159n128 |

## 1 Chronicles

| | |
|---|---|
| 24:1–19 | 208 |
| 28:9 | 159n128 |
| 29:11–13 | 43 |

## Nehemiah

| | |
|---|---|
| 10:32–39 | 207 |

## Psalms

| | |
|---|---|
| 1 | 99, 100 |
| 1:1–2 | 100 |
| 37:11 | 88, 133, 134 |
| 44:8 | 195 |
| 55:17 | 68 |
| 61:10 | 158 |
| 73 | 151 |

## Proverbs

| | |
|---|---|
| 1–9 | 167 |
| 1:7 | 144, 146 |
| 1:8 | 129 |
| 3:34 | 135 |
| 24:24 | 125 |
| 27:21 | 229 |

## Ecclesiastes

| | |
|---|---|
| 9:7 | 189 |
| 10:19 | 189 |

## Song of Songs

| | |
|---|---|
| 5:2 | 159n128 |
| 6:9 | 159n128 |

## Isaiah

| | |
|---|---|
| 1:25–26 | 228 |
| 11:12 | 183, 191 |
| 14:5 | 158 |
| 38:3 | 147 |
| 40:15 | 158 |
| 42–54 | 181 |
| 44:9–20 | 165 |
| 46:6 | 158 |
| 48:9–10 | 229 |
| 64:4 | 235 |
| 66:2 | 135 |

## Ezekiel

| | |
|---|---|
| 5:1 | 158 |
| 22:20 | 228 |
| 24:11 | 228 |
| 25:12 | 125 |
| 28:25 | 182 |
| 34 | 226 |
| 37:8–9 | 191 |
| 44:30 | 207 |

## Jeremiah

| | |
|---|---|
| 2:20 | 158 |
| 5:5 | 158 |
| 6:29 | 228 |
| 13:19 | 159n128 |
| 26:2 | 148 |
| 31:10 | 182 |
| 39:10 | 158 |
| 49:36 | 183, 191 |

## Daniel

| | |
|---|---|
| 4:27 | 142 |
| 6:9–12 | 43 |
| 6:10 | 68 |
| 7:13–14 | 54, 227 |
| 725 | 227n31 |
| 9:20 | 149 |
| 11:36–39 | 227n31 |

### Joel

| | |
|---|---|
| 4:4 | 125 |

### Amos

| | |
|---|---|
| 9:11–15 | 180 |

### Zephaniah

| | |
|---|---|
| 3:9 | 158 |

### Zechariah

| | |
|---|---|
| 7:10 | 125 |
| 12:10 | 231 |
| 13:9 | 228 |
| 14:5 | 32, 36, 52–56, 57, 59, 88, 230, 231 |

### Malachi

| | |
|---|---|
| 1:10–12 | 51n75 |
| 1:11 | 32, 36, 49–52, 57, 59, 211 |
| 1:14 | 32, 36, 49–52, 57, 59, 211 |

## Ancient Jewish Texts

### Apocryphal Books

#### 1 Maccabees

| | |
|---|---|
| 12:27 | 223 |
| 15:8 | 41 |

#### 4 Maccabees

| | |
|---|---|
| 1.25 | 127 |
| 2.8 | 132 |

#### Sirach

| | |
|---|---|
| 1.5 | 104n20 |
| 2.4 | 136n85 |
| 3.30 | 142 |
| 12.1 | 116 |
| 23.4–5 | 131n73 |
| 23.23 | 130 |
| 28.25 | 158 |
| 29.9 | 115 |
| 44.17 | 159n128 |

#### Baruch

| | |
|---|---|
| 2.9 | 223 |

#### Tobit

| | |
|---|---|
| 4.5–11 | 114 |
| 4.5 | 154 |
| 4.7–11 | 142 |
| 4.21 | 147 |

### Pseudepigrapha

#### 1 Enoch

| | |
|---|---|
| 1.9 | 54 |
| 61.10 | 139 |
| 91.1 | 220 |
| 94.1–5 | 101 |
| 100.4–5 | 101 |
| 100.5 | 54 |
| 104.10–13 | 148 |

#### 2 Enoch

| | |
|---|---|
| 22.10 | 54 |
| 30.14–15 | 101 |
| 41.1 | 158 |
| 61.8 | 158 |

#### 3 Enoch

| | |
|---|---|
| 26.9 | 191 |

#### 2 Esdras

| | |
|---|---|
| 7.1–140 | 101 |
| 13.5 | 183, 191 |

## 4 Ezra

| | |
|---|---|
| 3.34 | 158 |

## Gr. Apocalypse of Ezra

| | |
|---|---|
| 3.6 | 191 |

## Jubilees

| | |
|---|---|
| 7.20–21 | 103n14 |
| 20.2–10 | 103n14 |

## Ascension of Isaiah

| | |
|---|---|
| 4.14–16 | 54 |

## Apocalypse of Elijah

| | |
|---|---|
| 4.25–27 | 55 |
| 5.2 | 54 |
| 5.20–21 | 54 |

## Epistle of Aristeas

| | |
|---|---|
| 8 | 132 |
| 310–11 | 148 |

## Testament of Asher

| | |
|---|---|
| 1–8 | 99 |
| 1.3 | 101 |
| 1.4–9 | 101 |
| 2 | 126 |
| 2.8 | 114, 130 |
| 3.1 | 126 |

## Testament of Benjamin

| | |
|---|---|
| 6.3 | 131n73 |
| 8.2 | 131n73 |

## Testament of Dan

| | |
|---|---|
| 5.3 | 103n14 |

## Testament of Issachar

| | |
|---|---|
| 5.1–2 | 103n14 |
| 7.2–6 | 103n14 |
| 7.2 | 131n73 |

## Testament of Reuben

| | |
|---|---|
| 1.2 | 129 |

## Testament of Simeon

| | |
|---|---|
| 2.1 | 129 |
| 3.1 | 129 |

## Testament of Levi

| | |
|---|---|
| 10.1 | 129 |
| 17.11 | 132 |

## Testament of Zebulum

| | |
|---|---|
| 6.7 | 115 |
| 7.2 | 115 |

## Testament of Job

| | |
|---|---|
| 43.14–15 | 54 |

## Ps.-Phocylides

| | |
|---|---|
| 3 | 121 |
| 7 | 122 |
| 12 | 122 |
| 16 | 122 |
| 23 | 116 |
| 29–30 | 115 |
| 149 | 131n75 |
| 150 | 121 |
| 184–85 | 124n61 |
| 184 | 121 |
| 185 | 121 |

## Apocalypse of Abraham

| | |
|---|---|
| 31.1 | 55 |

## Dead Sea Scrolls

### 1QH

| | |
|---|---|
| I, 36 | 160n128 |
| XVI, 7 | 160n128 |
| XVI, 17 | 160n128 |

### 1QM

| | |
|---|---|
| XII, 1–7 | 54 |

### 1QS

| | |
|---|---|
| I, 8 | 160n128 |
| II, 2 | 160n128 |
| II, 20 | 160n128 |
| III, 9–11 | 160n128 |
| III, 9 | 160n128, 170 |
| III, 13–IV, 26 | 99, 100 |
| III, 16–18 | 100 |
| IV, 2–4 | 100 |
| V, 13–14 | 48n66 |
| V, 13 | 48n66 |
| IX, 19 | 160n128 |
| XI, 11 | 136n85 |
| XI, 17 | 160n128 |
| XIII, 10 | 160n128 |
| XIII, 20–21 | 160n128 |

### 1QSb

| | |
|---|---|
| I, 2 | 160n128 |
| V, 22 | 160n128 |

### 4QMMT

| | |
|---|---|
| 58–62 | 185 |

## Josephus

### Antiquities

| | |
|---|---|
| 1.17 | 148 |
| 1.42 | 127 |
| 12.194 | 158 |

## Philo

### Sacr.

| | |
|---|---|
| 20–40 | 101 |
| 35–36 | 101 |

| | |
|---|---|
| 37 | 160 |
| 43 | 160 |

### Deus

| | |
|---|---|
| 117 | 160 |
| 118 | 160 |

### Leg.

| | |
|---|---|
| 3.219 | 160 |

### Mut.

| | |
|---|---|
| 202 | 131n74 |

### Cher.

| | |
|---|---|
| 9 | 160 |

### Ebr.

| | |
|---|---|
| 135 | 160 |

### Plant.

| | |
|---|---|
| 37 | 160 |

### Spec. Leg.

| | |
|---|---|
| 3.110–16 | 124n61 |
| 3.114–15 | 124n60 |
| 4.48 | 131n74 |

## New Testament

### Matthew

| | |
|---|---|
| 5–7 | 135 |
| 5:3 | 107 |
| 5:5 | 88, 133, 134, 135 |
| 5:7 | 125, 134, 135 |
| 5:8 | 135 |
| 5:9 | 134, 140 |
| 5:10–12 | 118 |
| 5:16 | 59, 111n30 |
| 5:20 | 172 |
| 5:21–26 | 215 |
| 5:21–22 | 130 |
| 5:23–25 | 50 |
| 5:23–24 | 149, 211 |
| 5:25 | 115 |
| 5:26 | 107 |
| 5:27–30 | 109 |
| 5:27–28 | 130 |
| 5:33 | 125 |

## Matthew (continued)

| | |
|---|---|
| 5:38–42 | 110 |
| 5:39–42 | 161 |
| 5:39 | 106, 110 |
| 5:40 | 106, 110 |
| 5:41 | 107, 110 |
| 5:42 | 107 |
| 5:43–47 | 110 |
| 5:43 | 106 |
| 5:44 | 105, 107, 108 |
| 5:45 | 107, 108, 111n30 |
| 5:46 | 108 |
| 5:47 | 106 |
| 5:48 | 78, 106, 110, 111n30, 118, 134, 161 |
| 6 | 39 |
| 6:1–18 | 134, 175 |
| 6:1 | 111n30, 134, 172 |
| 6:2–4 | 215 |
| 6:3 | 38, 107 |
| 6:4 | 111n30 |
| 6:5–18 | 38 |
| 6:5–13 | 215 |
| 6:5–8 | 174 |
| 6:5–7 | 38 |
| 6:6 | 111n30 |
| 6:8 | 38, 111n30 |
| 6:9–13 | 32, 36–45, 57, 65, 68, 175, 215 |
| 6:9 | 39, 111n30 |
| 6:10 | 39 |
| 6:12 | 41 |
| 6:13 | 183, 190 |
| 6:14–15 | 38, 125 |
| 6:14 | 111n30 |
| 6:15 | 111n30 |
| 6:16–18 | 38, 173 |
| 6:16–17 | 172 |
| 6:18 | 111n30 |
| 6:19–34 | 118 |
| 6:21 | 118 |
| 6:24 | 106, 143 |
| 6:26 | 111n30 |
| 6:32 | 111n30, 189 |
| 7:1–5 | 45, 46 |
| 7:5 | 173 |
| 7:6 | 21n83, 32, 36, 45–48, 57, 58, 65, 71, 97, 184, 185 |
| 7:7–11 | 45, 46 |
| 7:9–13 | 173 |
| 7:10–11 | 107 |
| 7:11 | 107, 111n30 |
| 7:12 | 106 |
| 7:13–14 | 100, 106 |
| 7:13 | 106 |
| 7:14 | 106 |
| 7:15–23 | 202 |
| 7:15–20 | 215 |
| 7:15 | 126, 126, 225, 225 |
| 7:16–17 | 172 |
| 7:16 | 202 |
| 7:20 | 202 |
| 7:21 | 111n30, 202 |
| 7:28 | 106 |
| 10:1–5 | 96 |
| 10:16 | 222 |
| 11:1 | 96 |
| 11:29 | 159 |
| 12:18 | 181 |
| 12:31–32 | 201 |
| 13:12 | 110 |
| 15 | 182 |
| 15:4 | 125 |
| 15:7 | 172 |
| 15:17 | 172 |
| 15:21–28 | 48 |
| 15:26–27 | 185 |
| 18:15–17 | 214 |
| 18:16–17 | 22n83 |
| 18:17–20 | 140 |
| 18:34 | 115 |
| 19:16–22 | 120 |
| 19:18 | 125 |
| 19:19 | 105 |
| 19:21 | 110, 161 |
| 20:3 | 206 |
| 20:6 | 206 |
| 20:17 | 96 |
| 22:18 | 172 |
| 22:20 | 54 |
| 22:37–39 | 103 |
| 22:39 | 105, 127 |
| 23:13–29 | 172 |

## COMMENTARY INDEX

| | | | |
|---|---|---|---|
| 24–25 | 216, 221, 223, 225 | 6:13 | 195 |
| 24:9–11 | 229 | 7:10 | 125 |
| 24:9 | 221 | 8:38 | 54 |
| 24:10–12 | 226 | 10:9 | 200 |
| 24:10 | 221 | 10:17–22 | 120 |
| 24:12 | 221 | 10:19 | 125 |
| 24:13 | 222 | 10:45 | 181 |
| 24:14 | 226 | 12:25 | 54, 231 |
| 24:15 | 222 | 12:30–31 | 103 |
| 24:21–22 | 229 | 12:31 | 105, 127 |
| 24:24 | 221 | 13 | 225 |
| 24:29–31 | 66 | 13:13 | 229 |
| 24:29–30 | 222, 229 | 13:25 | 231 |
| 24:30–31 | 230 | 13:26–27 | 230 |
| 24:30 | 97, 222, 230, 231 | 13:27 | 87, 191 |
| 24:31 | 87, 183, 191, 222, 230 | 13:34 | 223 |
| | | 13:37 | 223 |
| 24:32–35 | 222 | 14:22–25 | 178, 179 |
| 24:42 | 221, 223 | 14:22 | 70 |
| 24:44 | 221 | 14:24 | 70, 183 |
| 25:1–13 | 53, 221, 222, 223 | 14:25 | 70, 180 |
| 25:8 | 223 | 14:38 | 223 |
| 25:13 | 221 | 15:21 | 110 |
| 25:28 | 110 | 16:15 | 228n35 |
| 25:31–46 | 226 | | |
| 25:31–40 | 56 | *Luke* | |
| 25:31 | 53, 54 | | |
| 25:41–46 | 222 | 1:69 | 182 |
| 26:19 | 180 | 6:29–30 | 161 |
| 26:26–29 | 178, 179, 180 | 6:29 | 110 |
| 26:26 | 70, 183 | 6:32 | 108 |
| 26:28 | 70, 183 | 6:34 | 108 |
| 26:29 | 70 | 6:35 | 108 |
| 26:38 | 223 | 9:3 | 200 |
| 26:40 | 223 | 9:26 | 54 |
| 27:4 | 111n31 | 10:4 | 200 |
| 27:32 | 110 | 10:27 | 103 |
| 27:51 | 230 | 11:2–4 | 37, 175 |
| 28 | 170 | 11:4 | 41, 42 |
| 28:18–20 | 98 | 11:22 | 110 |
| 28:18 | 31 | 11:41 | 215 |
| 28:19 | 67 | 12:30 | 189 |
| | | 12:33 | 215 |
| *Mark* | | 12:59 | 115 |
| | | 18:11 | 126 |
| 3:31–35 | 129 | 18:12 | 173 |
| 6:8 | 200 | 18:18–23 | 120 |

## Luke (continued)

| | |
|---|---|
| 18:20 | 125 |
| 21:27 | 231 |
| 21:34 | 53 |
| 22:14–23 | 180 |
| 22:16 | 70 |
| 22:17–20 | 178, 179 |
| 22:18 | 180 |
| 22:19 | 70 |
| 22:20–22 | 70, 183 |
| 22:20 | 70, 183 |
| 23:18 | 110 |
| 24 | 181 |
| 24:30–31 | 181 |

## John

| | |
|---|---|
| 4 | 168 |
| 6:12 | 186n74 |
| 7:37–39 | 168 |
| 11 | 182 |
| 13:35 | 59 |
| 14:20 | 63 |
| 19:15 | 110 |
| 20:1 | 209n23 |
| 20:19 | 209n23 |

## Acts

| | |
|---|---|
| 2:38 | 62n6 |
| 2:42 | 92, 97, 209 |
| 2:44–46 | 143 |
| 2:45 | 115 |
| 3:2–3 | 215 |
| 3:10 | 215 |
| 3:13 | 182 |
| 4:24 | 189 |
| 4:25 | 182 |
| 4:30 | 182 |
| 6:3 | 212 |
| 8:12 | 62n6 |
| 8:16 | 62n6 |
| 9:9–19 | 171 |
| 10:2 | 214 |
| 10:4 | 142, 214 |
| 10:28 | 227 |
| 10:31 | 142, 214 |
| 11:26 | 206 |
| 12:48 | 62n6 |
| 14:23 | 212 |
| 15 | 165 |
| 15:10 | 158, 166 |
| 15:20 | 166 |
| 15:29 | 166 |
| 17:24 | 104 |
| 19:5 | 62n6 |
| 20:31 | 223 |
| 20:35 | 115 |
| 24:17 | 215 |

## Romans

| | |
|---|---|
| 3:14 | 145 |
| 4:4 | 41 |
| 8:28 | 136n85 |
| 12 | 107 |
| 12:14 | 31, 108 |
| 13:8–10 | 103n16, 120 |
| 13:8 | 105 |
| 13:9 | 125 |
| 14:1–23 | 165 |
| 15:27 | 143 |

## 1 Corinthians

| | |
|---|---|
| 2:6 | 160n132 |
| 2:9 | 235 |
| 5:3–5 | 140 |
| 5:11 | 126 |
| 6:2–3 | 54 |
| 6:10 | 126 |
| 8:1–13 | 165 |
| 8:8 | 165 |
| 11:20 | 209 |
| 11:24–25 | 70 |
| 11:24 | 70 |
| 15:40 | 54, 230 |
| 15:42 | 54, 230 |
| 15:44 | 54, 230 |
| 16:2 | 209n23 |

## 2 Corinthians

| | |
|---|---|
| 2:5–11 | 140 |
| 2:14–16 | 195n93 |

## Galatians

| | |
|---|---|
| 3:10 | 151 |
| 3:13 | 55, 229 |
| 5 | 74, 75 |
| 5:1 | 158 |
| 5:14 | 103n16 |
| 5:16–24 | 99 |
| 5:19 | 76 |
| 5:20 | 76 |
| 5:21 | 76, 167 |
| 5:22–23 | 75 |
| 5:22 | 76 |
| 5:23 | 76 |
| 5:26 | 132 |

## Ephesians

| | |
|---|---|
| 1:16 | 137 |
| 1:21 | 139 |
| 4:13 | 161n132 |
| 4:25–28 | 132 |
| 4:28 | 118, 132 |
| 4:31 | 145 |
| 5:4 | 130 |
| 5:12 | 130 |
| 5:21 | 145 |
| 6:5 | 145 |

## Philippians

| | |
|---|---|
| 2:3 | 127 |

## Colossians

| | |
|---|---|
| 1:16 | 139 |
| 1:23 | 228n35 |
| 1:28 | 161n132 |
| 2:6 | 160n132 |
| 2:16 | 164 |
| 3:15 | 213 |
| 3:22 | 145 |
| 4:18 | 137 |

## 1 Thessalonians

| | |
|---|---|
| 1:3 | 137 |
| 3:13 | 53, 54, 56n93, 230 |
| 4:6 | 167 |
| 4:13–17 | 56n93 |
| 4:14 | 56n93 |
| 4:15–17 | 230 |
| 4:16 | 230 |
| 5:6 | 53, 223 |
| 5:13 | 88 |

## 2 Thessalonians

| | |
|---|---|
| 1:7 | 54 |
| 2:3 | 227n31 |
| 2:8 | 227n31 |
| 3:10 | 205 |
| 3:12 | 205 |

## 1 Timothy

| | |
|---|---|
| 1:6 | 214 |
| 2:1 | 151 |
| 3 | 84 |
| 3:1–7 | 212 |
| 3:2–13 | 84 |
| 3:3 | 84, 212 |
| 3:6 | 212 |
| 3:8–13 | 212 |
| 3:8 | 84 |
| 3:10 | 84, 212 |
| 4:14 | 115 |
| 5:13 | 206 |
| 5:18 | 208 |
| 6:21 | 214 |

## 2 Timothy

| | |
|---|---|
| 1:3–4 | 137 |
| 2:18 | 214 |
| 3:1 | 225 |
| 3:2 | 132 |

## Titus

| | |
|---|---|
| 1 | 84 |
| 1:5–9 | 84 |
| 1:5 | 212 |
| 1:6–9 | 212 |
| 1:7 | 84 |
| 2:12 | 109 |

## Philemon

| | |
|---|---|
| 4 | 137 |
| 8 | 145 |

## Hebrews

| | |
|---|---|
| 2:17 | 135 |
| 10:15 | 167 |
| 10:22 | 149 |
| 10:24–25 | 224 |
| 13:7 | 79, 137 |
| 13:15 | 70 |

## James

| | |
|---|---|
| 1:4 | 161 |
| 1:8 | 126 |
| 1:17 | 161 |
| 1:20 | 213 |
| 1:25 | 161 |
| 2:8 | 105, 120 |
| 2:11 | 120 |
| 3:2 | 161 |
| 4:6 | 135 |
| 4:8 | 126 |
| 5:14–15 | 195 |
| 5:16 | 149 |

## 1 Peter

| | |
|---|---|
| 1:6–7 | 228 |
| 2:17 | 145 |
| 2:18 | 189 |
| 4:3 | 227 |
| 4:8 | 142 |
| 4:12–15 | 229 |
| 4:12 | 31, 229 |
| 4:16 | 206 |
| 4:19 | 104 |
| 5:1–4 | 84 |
| 5:1–3 | 212 |
| 5:1–2 | 226 |
| 5:2 | 84, 212 |
| 5:6 | 135 |
| 5:8 | 223 |

## 2 Peter

| | |
|---|---|
| 2:10–12 | 132 |
| 2:10 | 79 |
| 3:3 | 225 |

## 1 John

| | |
|---|---|
| 2 | 129 |
| 3:18 | 126 |
| 3:22 | 147 |
| 4:1–6 | 200 |
| 4:12–13 | 63 |

## 2 John

| | |
|---|---|
| 7 | 227 |

## Jude

| | |
|---|---|
| 8 | 79 |
| 9 | 139 |

## Revelation

| | |
|---|---|
| 1:7 | 231 |
| 1:10 | 209 |
| 3:2–3 | 223 |
| 6:9–11 | 55, 56, 231 |
| 7:1 | 87, 191 |
| 7:13–14 | 56, 231 |
| 12:9 | 227 |
| 13 | 227n31 |
| 13:10 | 229 |
| 14:12 | 229 |
| 15–16 | 56 |
| 19:11–16 | 55 |
| 19:14 | 55, 56, 230, 231 |
| 20:8 | 183, 191 |
| 22:18 | 83 |
| 22:19 | 149 |

# Rabbinic Texts

## m. Ber.

| | |
|---|---|
| 6.1 | 181 |

## m. Meg.

| | |
|---|---|
| 3.6 | 173 |

## m. Ta'an.

| | |
|---|---|
| 1.6 | 173 |
| 2.9 | 173 |

# Early Christian Writings

## Apostolic Fathers

### 1 Clement

| | |
|---|---|
| 2.1 | 115 |
| 7.5 | 189 |
| 18.14 | 190 |
| 20.3 | 145 |
| 21.6 | 83, 137, 145 |
| 30.1 | 130 |
| 35.3 | 146 |
| 36.4 | 189 |
| 37.3 | 145 |
| 45.4 | 153 |
| 46.3–4 | 111, 112 |
| 49.5 | 140, 212 |
| 46.9 | 140 |
| 49.2–6 | 142n95 |
| 59.2–3 | 104n22 |
| 59.2 | 104, 111, 181n53 |
| 59.3 | 135, 181n53 |
| 59.4 | 181n53 |
| 60.1 | 104, 104n22, 135 |
| 60.3 | 190 |
| 61.3 | 189 |
| 62.2 | 105n22 |
| 63.2 | 227 |

### 2 Clement

| | |
|---|---|
| 5.2–4 | 225 |
| 6.4 | 130 |
| 13.4 | 135 |
| 16.1–4 | 142n95 |
| 16.4 | 142, 214 |
| 17.3 | 109 |
| 17.7 | 214 |

## Didache

| | |
|---|---|
| 1–6 | 23, 168, 219, 220 |
| 1–5 | 75, 82, 104, 157 |
| 1–4 | 23, 181 |
| 1 | 57 |
| 1.1—15.4 | 25 |
| 1.1—11.2 | 25 |
| 1.1—10.7 | 197 |
| 1.1—6.3 | 24, 25 |
| 1.1—6.2 | 26, 27, 67, 167 |
| 1.1—5.2 | 26 |
| 1.1–2 | 224 |
| 1.1 | 24, 27, 41, 87, 102, 104, 106, 155 |
| 1.2—6.2 | 103 |
| 1.2—4.14 | 24, 26, 27, 102, 103, 155, 159 |
| 1.2—2.7 | 103 |
| 1.2–6 | 27 |
| 1.2–3 | 226 |
| 1.2 | 41, 63, 82, 103, 104, 106, 108, 118, 119, 127, 128, 147, 150, 155, 156, 189, 226 |
| 1.3–2.1 | 105, 159 |
| 1.3–6 | 103, 118 |
| 1.3–5 | 116, 118 |
| 1.3–4 | 6, 7, 111, 135, 153 |
| 1.3 | 31, 68, 73, 82, 83, 103, 104, 105, 106, 107, 108, 109, 110, 118, 126, 128, 167 |
| 1.4–5 | 214 |
| 1.4 | 73, 78, 88, 106, 108, 110, 111, 161, 224 |
| 1.5–6 | 38, 111, 141 |
| 1.5 | 64, 73, 74, 107, 111, 112, 113, 114, 115, 208, 228 |
| 1.6 | 57, 107, 114, 116, 214 |
| 2 | 57, 132 |
| 2.1–7 | 27, 76, 105 |

## Didache (continued)

| | |
|---|---|
| 2.1 | 82, 83, 104, 105, 119, 126, 127, 167 |
| 2.2–7 | 82, 119 |
| 2.2–3 | 12 |
| 2.2 | 75, 76, 109, 119, 121, 122, 123, 124, 129, 131, 136, 152, 153 |
| 2.3–5 | 125 |
| 2.3 | 75, 120, 122, 125, 152 |
| 2.4 | 75, 120, 122, 126, 126 |
| 2.5 | 75, 120, 122, 126, 152 |
| 2.6 | 75, 119, 120, 122, 126, 147, 152, 172, 174 |
| 2.7—3.2 | 6, 8 |
| 2.7 | 68, 75, 76, 119, 122, 127 |
| 3 | 75 |
| 3.1–6 | 27, 83, 128, 133, 137, 152 |
| 3.1 | 75, 76, 124, 128, 129, 132, 154, 167 |
| 3.2 | 75, 76, 109, 130, 152 |
| 3.3–6 | 124 |
| 3.3 | 76, 129, 130, 152, 154, 167 |
| 3.4 | 76, 129, 131, 152, 154, 167 |
| 3.5 | 11, 129, 132, 152, 154, 167 |
| 3.6 | 129, 132, 136, 143, 154, 167 |
| 3.7–10 | 27 |
| 3.7–8 | 75 |
| 3.7 | 88, 133, 134, 153 |
| 3.8–9 | 135 |
| 3.8 | 76, 134 |
| 3.9 | 134, 143, 147 |
| 3.10 | 13, 63, 135, 228 |
| 4.1–4 | 27, 137 |
| 4.1–2 | 80, 81, 85, 137, 138, 147 |
| 4.1 | 61, 65, 79, 80, 83, 97, 124, 129, 133, 137, 138, 144, 154, 167, 198, 199 |
| 4.2 | 139, 140 |
| 4.3–4 | 81, 140, 153 |
| 4.3 | 42, 140 |
| 4.4 | 76, 140 |
| 4.5–8 | 27, 70, 74, 214 |
| 4.5–7 | 143 |
| 4.5 | 129, 141 |
| 4.6 | 42, 70, 74, 141, 142, 214 |
| 4.7 | 143 |
| 4.8 | 74, 129, 143, 153 |
| 4.9–11 | 28, 71 |
| 4.9 | 38, 85, 124, 129, 144, 146 |
| 4.10 | 63, 66, 71, 129, 145, 146 |
| 4.11 | 61, 65, 97, 146 |
| 4.12–14 | 28, 82, 83, 147, 151, 167 |
| 4.12–13 | 97 |
| 4.12 | 65, 147, 152, 174 |
| 4.13 | 65, 83, 147, 197 |
| 4.14 | 42, 47, 68, 149, 155 |
| 5 | 23, 76, 126 |
| 5.1–2 | 25, 28, 150, 155, 156 |
| 5.1 | 24, 41, 76, 109, 130, 131, 145, 150, 151, 152, 155, 172, 174, 190, 219 |
| 5.2 | 61, 63, 73, 76, 77, 104, 108, 129, 151, 152, 153, 155, 156, 157, 159, 167, 167, 189, 219, 225 |
| 6 | 23 |
| 6.1–3 | 24, 157 |
| 6.1–2 | 26, 28, 41, 155, 156, 157 |
| 6.1 | 41, 77, 82, 85, 159, 167, 197, 201, 219 |

# COMMENTARY INDEX

| | | | |
|---|---|---|---|
| 6.2 | 18, 41, 70, 71, 78, 87, 88, 97, 110, 158, 159, 161, 190, 200, 224, 225, 235 | | 199, 214, 215, 234, 235 |
| | | 8.3 | 37, 39, 43, 45, 57, 175, 177, 214 |
| 6.3—10.7 | 28, 156, 163, 164, 176 | 9–10 | 23, 42, 69, 177, 192, 209, 212, 214, 217 |
| 6.3 | 26, 27, 28, 156, 157, 163, 164, 167, 206 | 9 | 164, 178, 186 |
| | | 9.1—10.7 | 26, 28, 177 |
| | | 9.1-5 | 28, 177 |
| 7–16 | 10 | 9.1-4 | 183, 184 |
| 7–15 | 218 | 9.1-3 | 97 |
| 7–10 | 192 | 9.1 | 157, 163, 164, 184 |
| 7–8 | 23, 38 | 9.2-4 | 26, 62 |
| 7 | 167 | 9.2-3 | 69, 183 |
| 7.1—11.2 | 26 | 9.2 | 43, 61, 62, 63, 64, 69, 157, 163, 164, 176, 179, 180, 181, 184, 185, 186, 187, 189, 234 |
| 7.1—10.8 | 24 | | |
| 7.1—8.3 | 28, 166 | | |
| 7.1—8.2 | 26 | | |
| 7.1-4 | 20, 26, 28, 31, 42, 47, 48, 62, 64, 65, 66, 77, 111, 139, 166, 171, 184, 185, 212 | | |
| | | 9.3-4 | 184 |
| | | 9.3 | 43, 61, 63, 64, 69, 71, 157, 163, 164, 176, 181, 184, 186, 187, 189, 234 |
| 7.1-3 | 97 | | |
| 7.1 | 47, 62, 67, 157, 163, 164, 167, 168, 171, 184, 187, 197 | 9.4-5 | 42 |
| | | 9.4 | 43, 51, 55, 61, 69, 87, 182, 183, 184, 188, 190, 228, 229, 234 |
| 7.2 | 164, 170 | | |
| 7.3 | 47, 67, 164, 170, 171, 187 | 9.5 | 22n83, 26, 38, 45–48, 51, 57, 58, 62, 63, 65, 67, 71, 72, 77, 97, 116, 139, 163, 164, 167, 167, 168, 170, 174, 183, 184, 187, 191, 210, 211, 234, 235 |
| 7.4 | 38, 62, 67, 68, 79, 164, 167, 173 | | |
| 7.5 | 164 | | |
| 8.1-2 | 9, 20, 38, 45, 57, 127 | | |
| 8.1 | 26, 28, 38, 67, 68, 77, 152, 163, 164, 171, 172, 174 | | |
| | | 10 | 178, 186 |
| 8.2-3 | 26, 28, 33, 38, 51, 57, 65, 68, 171, 173, 174, 215 | 10.1-7 | 26, 28, 62, 186 |
| | | 10.1 | 163, 164, 178, 184, 186 |
| 8.2 | 36, 36–45, 62, 64, 65, 68, 77, 97, 152, 163, 164, 171, 174, 175, 176, 187, 190, | 10.2-6 | 186 |
| | | 10.2 | 43, 61, 62, 63, 64, 69, 71, 176, 181, 187, 188, 189, 224, 234 |

## Didache (continued)

| | |
|---|---|
| 10.3—12.2 | 6, 9, 192 |
| 10.3–12 | 192 |
| 10.3–4 | 189 |
| 10.3 | 57, 62, 63, 77, 104, 181, 186, 189, 234 |
| 10.4 | 43, 176, 188, 189 |
| 10.5–6 | 42 |
| 10.5 | 43, 51, 55, 62, 65, 69, 78, 88, 97, 161, 176, 183, 188, 190, 191, 228, 229 |
| 10.6 | 48, 51, 71, 72, 140, 167, 168, 185, 185, 190, 191 |
| 10.7 | 86, 163, 164, 191, 193 |
| 10.8 | 24, 27, 28, 192, 193, 194, 195 |
| 11–15 | 219 |
| 11–13 | 23, 85, 86 |
| 11 | 86, 204, 205 |
| 11.1—15.4 | 28 |
| 11.1—13.17 | 24, 28, 196 |
| 11.1–2 | 23, 26, 28, 85, 196, 212 |
| 11.1 | 24, 65, 166, 197, 198, 213 |
| 11.2 | 38, 65, 77, 82, 85, 97, 137, 196, 197, 198, 199, 200, 201, 205, 213 |
| 11.3—15.3 | 26 |
| 11.3—13.7 | 26, 28, 197 |
| 11.3—12.7 | 212 |
| 11.3–12 | 24, 28, 198, 204 |
| 11.3–7 | 9 |
| 11.3–6 | 23 |
| 11.3 | 26, 86, 98, 157, 174, 198, 200, 215 |
| 11.4—13.7 | 26 |
| 11.4–6 | 24 |
| 11.4 | 38, 65, 86, 199, 200, 205, 213 |
| 11.5 | 9, 199, 201, 207 |
| 11.6 | 85, 86, 199, 200, 201, 213 |
| 11.7–12 | 23, 24 |
| 11.7 | 42, 66, 72, 86, 200, 201, 202, 205 |
| 11.8 | 38, 66, 200, 201, 202 |
| 11.9 | 66, 86, 200, 201 |
| 11.10 | 85, 86, 198, 200, 201 |
| 11.11 | 64, 202, 203, 205 |
| 11.12 | 66, 86, 200, 202, 204 |
| 12 | 204, 205 |
| 12.1–5 | 23, 24, 28, 204 |
| 12.1 | 9, 38, 62, 65, 82, 97, 137, 204, 205, 206 |
| 12.2 | 24, 200, 204, 205 |
| 12.3–5 | 24, 205 |
| 12.3–4 | 86, 207 |
| 12.3 | 205, 207 |
| 12.4 | 205, 206 |
| 12.5 | 77, 206 |
| 13 | 192, 204 |
| 13.1–7 | 23, 24, 28, 200, 207 |
| 13.1 | 85, 201, 207 |
| 13.2 | 85, 198, 207 |
| 13.3–4 | 74 |
| 13.3 | 85, 86, 207 |
| 13.4–7 | 208 |
| 13.4 | 9, 208 |
| 13.5 | 114, 208 |
| 13.6 | 208 |
| 13.7 | 74, 114, 208 |
| 14 | 23, 58, 69, 79, 209n21 |
| 14.1—15.4 | 24, 28, 209 |
| 14.1—15.3 | 27 |
| 14.1–3 | 24, 27, 28, 69, 209 |
| 14.1–2 | 51, 81, 149 |
| 14.1 | 38, 42, 47, 50, 59, 65, 66, 80, 209, 210, 224 |
| 14.2–3 | 66 |
| 14.2 | 17, 50, 81, 210, 211 |

| | | | |
|---|---|---|---|
| 14.3 | 49–52, 59, 62, 65, 97, 187, 211, 235 | 16.7–8 | 228 |
| 15.1–2 | 23, 27, 28 | 16.7 | 52–56, 66, 88, 97, 116, 174, 220, 222, 229, 230, 231, 235 |
| 15.1 | 24, 65, 83, 84, 86, 97, 196, 212, 213 | | |
| 15.2 | 84, 213 | 16.8–12 | 233 |
| 15.3—16.8 | 23 | 16.8 | 29, 38, 54, 66, 88, 97, 174, 217, 222, 225, 231, 232, 234 |
| 15.3–4 | 28, 80, 174, 213 | | |
| 15.3 | 17, 22n83, 24, 27, 199, 213, 214, 215 | | |
| | | 16.9–12 | 27, 29, 88, 192, 232 |
| 15.4 | 27, 69, 74, 97, 114, 199, 213, 214, 215, 218 | 16.9 | 24, 234, 235 |
| | | 16.10 | 234 |
| 16 | 31, 53, 57, 87, 88, 97, 177, 216, 217, 218, 219, 220, 227, 228 | 16.11 | 234, 235 |
| | | 16.12 | 234 |

## Barnabas

| | |
|---|---|
| 16.1–8 | 24, 27, 28, 209 |
| 16.1–2 | 29, 41, 53, 59, 88, 139, 161, 162, 217, 218, 223, 225, 232 |

| | |
|---|---|
| 2.6 | 159 |
| 2.8 | 125 |
| 5.5 | 105n22 |
| 6.1 | 181n53 |
| 6.11 | 105n22 |
| 7.6–12 | 55 |
| 9.2 | 181n53 |
| 15.3–5 | 104, 105n22 |
| 15.9 | 209n23 |
| 16.2 | 105n22 |
| 18–20 | 99 |
| 18.1–2 | 220 |
| 18.1 | 92, 101 |
| 19 | 101, 120, 152n106 |
| 19.2 | 104, 105n22, 120, 122, 147 |
| 19.3 | 122, 135 |
| 19.4 | 120, 121, 122, 125 |
| 19.5 | 120, 121, 122 |
| 19.6 | 13, 120, 122 |
| 19.7 | 66, 120, 122, 145, 146, 147 |
| 19.8 | 122 |
| 19.9–10 | 138, 141, 142 |
| 19.10 | 138, 224 |
| 19.11 | 143 |
| 19.12 | 149n102 |
| 20.1 | 76, 120, 130 |
| 21.1 | 220 |

| | |
|---|---|
| 16.1 | 66, 88, 97, 174, 217, 218, 219, 220, 221, 222, 224, 234 |
| 16.2–8 | 225 |
| 16.2 | 59, 78, 80, 88, 110, 161, 217, 219, 222, 224 |
| 16.3–8 | 29, 53, 59, 88, 216, 217, 218, 223, 232, 235 |
| 16.3–5 | 56 |
| 16.3–4 | 29, 56, 88, 225 |
| 16.3 | 53, 56, 88, 219, 222, 223, 225, 226, 231, 235 |
| 16.4 | 29, 53, 73, 88, 153, 221, 222, 225, 226, 227, 228, 229, 235 |
| 16.5 | 29, 31, 53, 55, 56, 88, 221, 222, 225, 227, 228, 229, 231, 235 |
| 16.6 | 53, 55, 222, 225 |
| 16.6–7 | 29, 229, 230 |

## Ignatius of Antioch

### Letter to Magnesians

| | |
|---|---|
| 6.1 | 146 |
| 8.2—9.2 | 55 |
| 9.1 | 66, 209 |

### Letter to the Trallians

| | |
|---|---|
| 3.1 | 146 |

### Letter to the Ephesians

| | |
|---|---|
| 13.1-2 | 224 |
| 13.1 | 80 |
| 15.2 | 161 |
| 20.2 | 188 |

### Letter to the Philadelphians

| | |
|---|---|
| 1.2 | 161 |
| 4.1 | 187 |
| 10.1 | 84, 212 |

### Letter to the Smyrnaeans

| | |
|---|---|
| 4.2 | 161 |
| 9.1 | 83, 137 |
| 10-11 | 161 |
| 10.2 | 161 |
| 11.1 | 161 |
| 11.2 | 84, 161 |
| 11.3 | 161 |

### Letter to Polycarp

| | |
|---|---|
| 7.2 | 84 |

## Polycarp, *To the Philippians*

| | |
|---|---|
| 2.1 | 104, 105n22 |
| 4.2 | 145 |
| 5.2 | 84 |
| 6.1 | 135 |
| 10.2 | 141, 142 |

## Martyrdom of Polycarp

| | |
|---|---|
| 3.2 | 110 |
| 9.2 | 110 |
| 14.1 | 181n53 |
| 14.3 | 181n53 |
| 19.2 | 189 |
| 20.2 | 181n53 |

## Shepherd of Hermas

### Visions

| | |
|---|---|
| 1.1.6 | 105n22 |
| 2.2.4 | 189 |
| 2.4 | 105n22 |
| 4.3.4 | 229 |

### Mandates

| | |
|---|---|
| 1.1 | 105n22, 151 |
| 2.1 | 135 |
| 2.4-7 | 112, 113 |
| 2.4 | 116, 117 |
| 2.6 | 111 |
| 3.2 | 132 |
| 3.5 | 132 |
| 4.1.5 | 130 |
| 5.1.1-2 | 135 |
| 5.2.3 | 135 |
| 5.2.4 | 145 |
| 6.1-2 | 99, 101 |
| 7.5 | 228n35 |
| 8.3-6 | 120 |
| 8.3 | 130 |
| 9.3 | 105n22, 125 |
| 9.4 | 167 |
| 12.3.1 | 202 |

### Similitudes

| | |
|---|---|
| 1.6 | 189 |
| 2 | 142 |
| 2.2 | 142 |
| 2.5 | 142 |
| 2.9 | 142 |
| 5.4.2 | 132 |
| 5.4.3 | 143 |

| | |
|---|---|
| 5.5.1 | 132 |
| 5.6.1 | 79, 139 |
| 5.6.5 | 105n22 |
| 6.5.5 | 126, 132 |
| 8.6.5 | 127 |
| 9.2.1–3 | 191 |
| 9.10.7 | 191 |
| 9.15.1–6 | 191 |
| 9.18.3 | 127 |
| 9.19.2 | 127 |
| 9.22.1 | 132 |
| 9.26.3 | 224 |

## Diognetus

| | |
|---|---|
| 2.3 | 205 |
| 2.8 | 165 |
| 3.2 | 167 |
| 5 | 133 |
| 5.6 | 124n61 |
| 8.7 | 189 |
| 8.11 | 146 |
| 9.2 | 125, 135 |

# New Testament Apocrypha

## Ps.-Clementine

### Homilies

| | |
|---|---|
| 12 | 103n16 |
| 20.2 | 101 |
| 32.3–4 | 103n16 |

### Recognitions

| | |
|---|---|
| 7.37.1 | 171 |

## Sibylline Oracles

| | |
|---|---|
| 2.79 | 116n45 |
| 2.281–83 | 124n61 |
| 3.37 | 126 |
| 8.221 | 54 |
| 8.227–28 | 54 |

## Gospel of Peter

| | |
|---|---|
| 9.35 | 209 |

## Gospel of Thomas

| | |
|---|---|
| 25 | 103n16 |
| 44 | 201n6 |

## Protoevangelium of James

| | |
|---|---|
| 11.2 | 189 |
| 14.1 | 111n31 |
| 23.3 | 111n31 |

## Acts of John

| | |
|---|---|
| 109 | 188 |

## Acts of Peter

| | |
|---|---|
| 4.8 | 226 |

## Acts of Thomas

| | |
|---|---|
| 79 | 202 |

## Questions of Bartholomew

| | |
|---|---|
| V.4 | 201n6 |

## Apocalypse of Peter

| | |
|---|---|
| 2 | 227, 228 |
| 8 | 124n61 |

# Patristic Figures and Ancient Christian Writings

## De Doctrina

| | |
|---|---|
| 1–6 | 99 |
| 2.2 | 121, 122 |
| 2.3 | 122 |
| 2.4 | 122, 125 |
| 2.5 | 122 |

## De Doctrina (continued)

| | |
|---|---|
| 2.6 | 122 |
| 2.7 | 122 |
| 3.4 | 131n76 |
| 5 | 152n106 |

## Apostolic Canons

| | |
|---|---|
| 69 | 173 |

## Apostolic Constitutions

| | |
|---|---|
| II, 26, 3 | 207 |
| III, 5 | 46n55 |
| VII, 2, 4 | 109n27 |
| VII, 24 | 38 |
| VII, 25 | 46n55 |
| VII, 27, 1–2 | 9, 193 |
| VII, 30, 1 | 209 |
| VII, 32 | 55, 233, 235 |
| VII, 35 | 46n56 |
| VII, 44, 1 | 195 |

## Didascalia

| | |
|---|---|
| 2.3–4 | 142n95 |
| 21 | 173 |

## Epitome of the Apostolic Commands

| | |
|---|---|
| 11 | 149 |

## Canons of the Holy Apostles

| | |
|---|---|
| 14.3 | 149 |

## Epistle of the Apostles

| | |
|---|---|
| 15 | 55 |

## Irenaeus of Lyons

### Adversus haereses

| | |
|---|---|
| 2.31 | 131n77 |
| 3.22 | 173n26 |
| 4.17.5–6 | 52n75, 211n28 |
| 5.35.5 | 30 |

## Justin Martyr

### 1 Apology

| | |
|---|---|
| 15.9 | 108 |
| 27 | 123 |
| 61 | 48n67 |
| 61.2 | 171 |
| 61.3 | 168 |
| 67.3 | 209n23 |

### Dialogue with Trypho

| | |
|---|---|
| 24.1 | 209n23 |
| 28 | 52n75 |
| 28.5 | 211n28 |
| 41 | 51n75 |
| 41.2 | 211n28 |
| 41.4 | 209n23 |
| 53.1 | 159 |
| 88.8 | 159 |
| 110 | 227n31, 228 |
| 116 | 52n75 |
| 116.3 | 211n28 |
| 117 | 51n75 |
| 117.1 | 211n28 |
| 117.1 | 211n28 |
| 138.1 | 209n23 |

## Athenagorus

### Leg.

| | |
|---|---|
| 34 | 123 |

## Clement of Alexandria

### Paedagogus

| | |
|---|---|
| 2.10, 89.1 | 12 |
| 3.3.21 | 123n55 |

### Protrepticus

| | |
|---|---|
| 2.11 | 131n74 |
| 10.108.5 | 12 |

### Quis div.

| | |
|---|---|
| 32 | 142n95 |
| 37 | 142n95 |

### Stromateis

| | |
|---|---|
| 1.20, 100.4 | 11 |
| 3.4, 36.5 | 12 |
| 4.18 | 142n95 |
| 5.14 | 101 |
| 5.14, 136.2–3 | 52n75 |
| 7.12 | 173n26 |

## Origen of Alexandria

### De Principiis

| | |
|---|---|
| 3.2.7 | 13, 136n85 |
| 4.2.1–4 | 30 |

### Homily on Genesis

| | |
|---|---|
| 13.3 | 52n75 |

### Homily on Leviticus

| | |
|---|---|
| 2.4.4–5 | 142n95 |
| 10.2 | 173n26 |

### Commentary on Matthew

| | |
|---|---|
| 2.8 | 46n55 |
| 10.8 | 46n55 |

### Commentary on Romans

| | |
|---|---|
| 3,9 | 103n16 |
| 4,1 | 103n16 |
| 4,6 | 103n16 |
| 4,7 | 103n16 |
| 6,5 | 103n16 |
| 9,15 | 103n16 |
| 9,31 | 103n16 |

## Tertullian

### Adversus Judaeos

| | |
|---|---|
| 5.4 | 52n75, 211n28 |
| 5.7 | 52n75, 211n28 |

### Adversus Marcionem

| | |
|---|---|
| 3.22 | 52n75, 211n28 |
| 4.1 | 52n75, 211n28 |

### Apol.

| | |
|---|---|
| 9.8 | 124n61 |

### De baptisme

| | |
|---|---|
| 4 | 170n18 |
| 4.3 | 170n19 |
| 12 | 48n67 |
| 18 | 46n55 |
| 20.1 | 171 |

### De oratione

| | |
|---|---|
| 1 | 44n46 |
| 23 | 173n26 |
| 25 | 68 |

### De ieiunio

| | |
|---|---|
| 10 | 173n26 |

### Prax.

| | |
|---|---|
| 26.9 | 170 |

## Scorp.

| | |
|---|---|
| 6.10–11 | 142n95 |

## Lactantius

### Divine Institutes

| | |
|---|---|
| 4.11 | 52n75 |

## Cyprian

### De dominica oratione

| | |
|---|---|
| 9.9 | 44n46 |

### To Quirinius: Testimonies against the Jews

| | |
|---|---|
| 1.16 | 52n75 |

## Ps.-Cyprian

### De aleatoribus

| | |
|---|---|
| 4 | 17, 93 |

### De centesima, sexagesimal, tricesima

| | |
|---|---|
| 14 | 18 |

## Eusebius of Caesarea

### Historia Ecclesiastica

| | |
|---|---|
| 3.25.4 | 4n15, 13, 93 |

### Demonstratio evangelica

| | |
|---|---|
| 1.10 | 52n75 |
| 3.2.74 | 52n75 |

## Athanasius of Alexandria

### Apologia secunda

| | |
|---|---|
| 1.11 | 46n55 |

### Festal Letter

| | |
|---|---|
| 39 | 93, 94 |
| 39.20 | 15 |

### Frag. Matt.

| | |
|---|---|
| | 206n17 |

## Ps.-Athanasius

### Synopsis Scripturae Sacrae

| | |
|---|---|
| 76 | 15n61 |

## Didymus the Blind

### Commentary on the Psalms

| | |
|---|---|
| 227.26–27 | 93, 94 |

### Commentary on Ecclesiasties

| | |
|---|---|
| 78.22 | 93, 94 |

### Commentary on Zachariah

| | |
|---|---|
| 8 | 52n75 |
| 14 | 55n87, 231n44 |

## Ambrose

### De paenitentia

| | |
|---|---|
| 2.9.87 | 46n55 |

### Sermones in psalmum

| | |
|---|---|
| 118 8.48 | 173n26 |
| 118 18.28 | 173n26 |

## Basil of Caesarea

### De baptisme

| | |
|---|---|
| 2.8 | 52n75 |

### Ep.

| | |
|---|---|
| 240.3 | 206n17 |

## Generalis Elementaria Introductio

| | |
|---|---|
| 3.29 | 52n75 |

## Gregory of Nyssa

### On Virginity

| | |
|---|---|
| 17 | 46n55 |

## Gregory of Nazianzus

### Or.

| | |
|---|---|
| 21.31 | 206n16 |
| 40.11 | 206n17 |

## Cyril of Jerusalem

### Lecture

| | |
|---|---|
| XX–XXIII | 46n55 |

### Catechesis ad illuminandos

| | |
|---|---|
| 18 | 52n75 |

## Cyril of Alexandria

### Catechesis ad Illuminados

| | |
|---|---|
| 18.25 | 52n75 |

### Commentary on Isaiah

| | |
|---|---|
| 417 | 131n74 |
| 1013 | 131n74 |
| 1016 | 131n74 |

### Commentary on Zachariah

| | |
|---|---|
| 14 | 55n87, 231n44 |

## Jerome

### Letter

| | |
|---|---|
| 60.10 | 33n16 |

## John Chrysostom

### Adversus Judaeos

| | |
|---|---|
| 5 | 52n75 |

### Expositiones in Psalmos

| | |
|---|---|
| 8, 113 | 52n75 |

### Homily

| | |
|---|---|
| 6.1 | 206n16 |

### Homily on Acts of the Apostles

| | |
|---|---|
| 4 | 52n75 |

### Homily on Hebrews

| | |
|---|---|
| 17.5 | 140n92, 185n69 |

### Oppugn.

| | |
|---|---|
| 3 | 123 |

## Hippolytus

### Frag. Ruth

| | |
|---|---|
| | 206n17 |

### De Antichrist

| | |
|---|---|
| 6 | 227n31 |

## John Cassian

### Conference

| | |
|---|---|
| 7.29–30 | 46n55 |

## John of Damascus

### Exposition of the Orthodox Faith

| | |
|---|---|
| 4.13 | 46n55 |

## Augustine of Hippo

*Letters of Augustine*

| | |
|---|---|
| 29.3 | 46n55 |

*Enarrat. Ps.*

| | |
|---|---|
| 103 | 117 |
| 146:17 | 117 |

*Sermones*

| | |
|---|---|
| 3.10 | 117 |
| 27.9 | 46n55 |

## Rufinus

*Expositio symboli*

| | |
|---|---|
| 36 | 15, 93, 94 |

*Historia Ecclesiastica*

| | |
|---|---|
| III.25.4 | 93, 94 |

## St. Boniface

*De Abrenuntiatione in baptismate*

| | |
|---|---|
| | 233 |

## Gregory the Great

*Regula Pastoralis*

| | |
|---|---|
| 3.20 | 1178 |

*Vita Chrodegangi episcopi Mettensium*

| | |
|---|---|
| 11.27 | 118 |

## Graeco-Roman Literature

### Pliny the Elder

*Natural History*

| | |
|---|---|
| 7 | 125n61 |
| 20 | 125n61 |
| 25 | 125n61 |
| 28 | 125n61 |
| 30.1–2 | 123 |

### Pliny the Younger

*Epistulae*

| | |
|---|---|
| II.6.1–6 | 47n58 |
| 10.96–97 | 66 |
| 10.96 | 209n23 |

### Silius

*Pun.*

| | |
|---|---|
| 15.20–23 | 101 |

### Xenophon

*Mem.*

| | |
|---|---|
| 2.21–22 | 101 |

### Plato

*Gorg.*

| | |
|---|---|
| 524 | 101 |

*Tim.*

| | |
|---|---|
| 30d | 160 |
| 41c | 160 |
| 92c | 160 |

*Phileb.*

| | |
|---|---|
| 61a | 160 |

## Leg.

| | |
|---|---|
| 647d | 160 |

## Resp.

| | |
|---|---|
| V.460c–d | 124n61 |

## Hippocrytus

### Nature of Children

| | |
|---|---|
| 7–8 | 125n61 |

## Aristotle

### Eth. Nic.

| | |
|---|---|
| 1129b.30 | 160 |
| 1149a.11 | 160 |
| 1156b.34 | 160 |

### Metaph.

| | |
|---|---|
| V.XVI.1 | 160 |
| V.XVI.4 | 160 |
| V.XVI.5 | 160 |

### Pol.

| | |
|---|---|
| 1335b | 125n61 |

## Homer

### Iliad

| | |
|---|---|
| 5.799 | 158 |
| 24.576 | 158 |

## Philostratus

### Vit. Apoll.

| | |
|---|---|
| VI.40 | 158 |

## Achilles Tatius

### Leuc. Clit.

| | |
|---|---|
| V.6.4 | 158 |

## Arisitaenetus

### Er. Ep.

| | |
|---|---|
| 2.7 | 158 |

## Polybius,

### Historia

| | |
|---|---|
| I.45.9 | 158 |

## Pindar

### Nem.

| | |
|---|---|
| 5.51 | 158 |

## Seneca

### De Beneficiis

| | |
|---|---|
| 7 | 103n15 |
| 30.2 | 103n15 |

### De Otio

| | |
|---|---|
| 1.4 | 103n15 |

### Ep.

| | |
|---|---|
| 107.9 | 136n85 |

## Dionysius of Halicarnassus

### Ant. Rom.

| | |
|---|---|
| 3.70 | 131n74 |
| 3.71 | 131n74 |
| 4.62 | 131n74 |
| 8.38 | 131n74 |

## Euripides

### Suppl

| | |
|---|---|
| 500 | 131n74 |